THE BRITISH ISLES
0
100 Miles
0
200km
M 3
A3
motorways
main through routes
National parks
airport
Mainland
Orkney Islands
Lewis
Outer Hebrides
Skye
Inner Hebrides
Mull
Islay
Wick
Moray Firth
Elgin
Inverness
Drumnadrochit
A82
Loch Ness
A9
Peterhead
Aberdeen
North
Sea
Fort William
Ben Nevis
Grampian Mountains
Scotland
Dundee
Perth
St. Andrews
Firth of Forth
A9
A82
Glasgow
M8
Edinburgh
A1
Firth of Clyde
Ayr
A77
Southern Uplands
A74
Tweed
Northumberland National Park
Gretna Green
Newcastle
Sunderland
Londonderry (Derry)
Northern Ireland
Belfast
Enniskillen
Sligo
Stranraer
A75
Solway Firth
Carlisle
Hadrian's Wall
Middlesbrough
Lake District National Park
North York Moors National Park
Isle of Man
Yorkshire Dales National Park
York
Lancashire
A1
York
Blackpool
Blackburn
Bradford
M62
Hull
Irish Sea
Dublin
Manchester
Kirkby
M62
Leeds
Grimsby
IRELAND
Isle of Anglesey
Holyhead
Liverpool
Llanfair P.G.
M1
Sheffield
Speke
Snowdon
Chester
M6
Peak District NP
Stoke-on-Trent
Derbyshire
England
Snowdonia National Park
A5
Cambrian Mountains
Shrewsbury
Staffordshire
Nottingham
Derby
Leicester
Norfolk
Norwich
Great Yarmouth
Waterford
Rosslare
Wales
Aberystwyth
Birmingham
M6
Peterborough
Coventry
A1
A11
Pembrokeshire Coast National Park
Fishguard
St. George's Channel
M5
Warwick
Northampton
Worcester
Stratford-upon-Avon
Cambridge
A12
Ipswich
Brecon Beacons National Park
M11
Braintree
Luton
M1
Hatfield
Harwich
Gloucester
Essex
Colchester
Pembroke
Swansea
M4
M50
Oxford
London
Newport
M40
Thames
Wembley
M25
Southend on Sea
Swindon
Cardiff
Bristol
Bath
M4
Windsor
Greenwich
M2
Exmoor NP
Stonehenge
Westbury
Surrey
Canterbury
M5
A303
M3
A3
M25
M20
Dover
Salisbury
Tunnel
Calais
Devon
Southampton
Ashford
Sussex
Exeter
A30
Portsmouth
Brighton
Eastbourne
Hastings
Paris
Bournemouth
Dartmoor National Park
Isle of Wight
Cornwall
Plymouth
Strait of Dover
Penzance
English Channel
Land's End
Falmouth/Penryn
Scilly Is.
Lizard Point

Learning English

Swift 3

Lehrwerk für Englisch als 2. Fremdsprache

von

Stephanie Ashford
Noreen O'Donovan
Helmut Reisener
sowie
Wolfgang Funk
Rosemary Hellyer-Jones

Ernst Klett Verlag
Stuttgart Düsseldorf Leipzig

Learning English Swift 3

für Englisch als 2. Fremdsprache

von
Stephanie Ashford, Villingen-Schwenningen; Noreen O'Donovan, Pforzheim;
Dr. Helmut Reisener, Lüneburg
sowie Wolfgang Funk, Bamberg; Rosemary Hellyer-Jones, Ehingen (Donau)

Beratende Mitarbeit
Axel Plitsch, Wülfrath; Klaus-Peter Thieser, Dillingen/Saar; Traute Werner, Heidelberg

Visuelle Gestaltung
Christian Dekelver, Weinstadt

Kassetten und CDs

SB Begleitkassette zum Schülerbuch für zu Hause und für den Unterricht mit Texten, Liedern, Ausspracheübungen (Klettnummer 547038)
Begleit-CDs zum Schülerbuch mit gleichem Inhalt (Klettnummer 547078)

HV Kassette mit den Hörtexten für den Unterricht (Klettnummer 547039)
CDs mit gleichem Inhalt (Klettnummer 547079)

Lernsoftware
Zu diesem Band gibt es ein Vokabel- und ein Grammatikprogramm. Diese Programme bieten abwechslungsreiche Übungsformen, Leistungs- und Lernzielkontrollen und ein Lexikon mit dem Wortschatz des Lehrwerks.

1. Auflage A 1 5 4 3 2 1 | 2005 2004 2003 2002 2001
Alle Drucke dieser Auflage können im Unterricht nebeneinander benutzt werden, sie sind untereinander unverändert. Die letzte Zahl bezeichnet das Jahr des Druckes.

Internetadresse: http://www.klett-verlag.de

Redaktion: Peter Cole, Andrew Hutchins, Monique Kunhar; Susann Edele (Assistenz)

Herstellung: Eckhard Schultze

Umschlaggestaltung: Christian Dekelver, Weinstadt
Reproduktion: maurer media+more, Tübingen
Druck: Druckerei Appl, Wemding
ISBN 3-12-547030-7

Gedruckt auf Papier aus chlorfrei gebleichtem Zellstoff, säurefrei.

Vorwort

Hallo und herzlich willkommen bei *Swift 3!*

Wir ‚heben ab' zur dritten Runde mit **Swift**.

Dieser 3. Band enthält sechs *Units*. Sie sind aber anders gegliedert als in **Swift 1** und **2**: *Check-in* und *Check-out* gibt es nach wie vor, dazwischen kommen nun *Texts, Language* und *Skills*, das sind *Unit*-Teile, in denen du dich auf Textarbeit, auf Grammatik und Wortschatz oder auf bestimmte Fertigkeiten konzentrieren kannst.

In *Texts* findest du gelegentlich Verweisschilder (s. unten). Sie weisen auf Übungen hin, die gut zu den einzelnen Texten passen und direkt im Anschluss an diese gemacht werden können. Sie können auch erst zu einem späteren Zeitpunkt eingesetzt werden.

Im Bereich der grammatischen Strukturen kommen in **Swift 3** natürlich neue Pensen hinzu, aber sie sind gut zu schaffen, wenn du immer wieder in den *Grammar*-Anhang hineinschaust. Auch die Vokabelseiten im Anschluss an die *Units* solltest du sorgfältig durcharbeiten.

Im Anschluss an die sechs *Units* findest du ab Seite 130 in *Extra* interessante Originaltexte als Zusatzlektüre. Sie sind thematisch auf die *Units* abgestimmt. Den Abschluss bildet eine Doppelseite mit Tipps für den Umgang mit Texten. Auf *Extra* folgt das Kapitel *Translation* mit Übersetzungsübungen (Deutsch-Englisch und Englisch-Deutsch) und Dolmetsch-übungen. Auf Seite 162 beginnt die *Grammar* und am Ende von **Swift** findest du das *Dictionary*, das den kompletten Wortschatz von **Swift 1-3** enthält. Du hast auf diese Weise dein **Swift**-Wörterbuch immer zur Hand.

So, nun weißt du bereits alles Wesentliche. Zur raschen Orientierung hier noch einmal die Symbole, die dir in **Swift** begegnen werden. Dann kann es wirklich losgehen.
Viel Spaß!

1 SB — Alle Texte, Lieder, Gedichte und Ausspracheübungen, die auf der Begleitkassette/den Begleit-CDs 1 oder 2 zum Schülerbuch (SB) aufgezeichnet sind, erkennst du an diesem Zeichen. (Die einzelnen Track-Nummern sind durch dieses Symbol gekennzeichnet: •)

1 HV — Übungen mit diesem Symbol verweisen auf die Kassette / CD 1 zum Hörverstehen (HV). Die Hörtexte sind nicht im Schülerbuch abgedruckt.

G 1 — In den Übungen, die mit diesem Symbol gekennzeichnet sind, wird neue Grammatik eingeführt. Du findest die Erklärungen unter dem entsprechenden Punkt im Grammatikanhang.

R — *R* steht für *revision.* Du findest dieses Piktogramm bei Übungen, in denen bereits bekannte grammatische Pensen wiederholt werden.

Language 15, 1 — Neu in **Swift 3** ist dieses Symbol. Das Schild verweist auf passende Übungen in einem anderen *Unit*-Teil (hier z. B. *Language*, Seite 15, Übung 1).

D — Dieses Symbol verweist auf den Gebrauch eines Wörterbuchs.

Inhalt

UNIT 1

Young Americans

1

Study the texts and pictures on these two pages and make notes about American teenagers. Compare them with you and your friends. What is similar/different?

Q My guy spends hours e-mailing this English girl he met online. Am I crazy to be jealous?

A Crazy? No way. But unless the Atlantic Ocean suddenly evaporates, you don't have much to worry about either.
This English babe might attract him because she can't laugh in his face like a real girlfriend can – because she's so far away. Even if he is into her, remember that their relationship is virtual; you're the real deal.

A rap: It's Tough to Be a Teenager (1)

It's tough to be a teenager, no one really knows
What the pressure is like in school, this is how it goes.

I wake up every morning and stare into this face
I wanna be good lookin', but I feel like a disgrace.

My friends they seem to like me if I follow through with their dare
But when I try to be myself, they never seem to care.

My mom, well she keeps saying I gotta make the grade
While both my parents love me, it slowly seems to fade.

It seems like everyone I know is trying to be so cool
And every time I try, I end up just a fool.

I've thought about taking drugs, I really don't want to, you know
But I just don't fit in, and it's really startin' to show.

Maybe if I could make the team, I'll stand out in the crowd
If they could see how hard I try, I know they would be proud.

You see I'm still a virgin, my friends they can't find out
'Cause if they really knew the truth, I know they'd laugh and shout.

Sometimes I really get so low, I want to cash it in
My problems really aren't so bad if I think of how life's been.

Sometimes I'm really lost, and wonder what to do
I wonder where to go, who can I talk to.

It's tough to be a teenager, sometimes life's not fair
I wish I had somewhere to go, and someone to *CARE*.

Tony Overman

find out how to get guys to notice you
'TEEN
what rules...
what's cool...
for back to school
BEST-EVER FASHION
• 50 top trends
• big-style bargains
CHANGE WHAT YOU DON'T LIKE ABOUT YOUR LOOKS
QUIZ
how TOGETHER are you?
AUGUST 1996
celeb guys

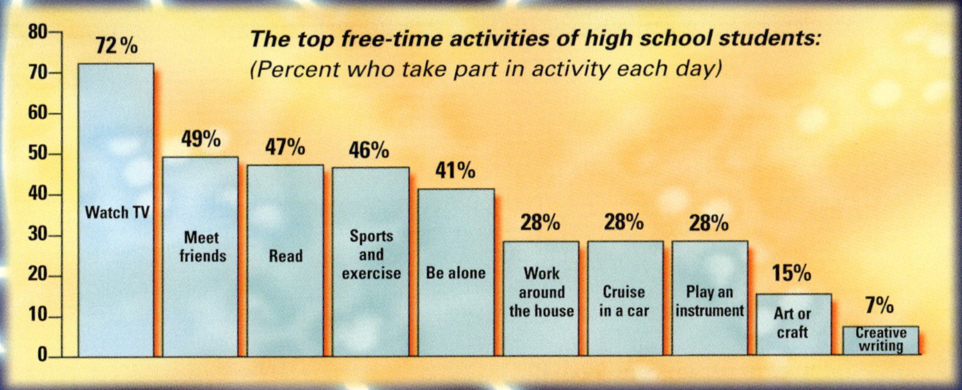
The top free-time activities of high school students:
(Percent who take part in activity each day)
80
70
60
50
40
30
20
10
0
72% Watch TV
49% Meet friends
47% Read
46% Sports and exercise
41% Be alone
28% Work around the house
28% Cruise in a car
28% Play an instrument
15% Art or craft
7% Creative writing

1

A E-mates (2-3)

Benjamin from Manchester, England, and Sarah from Montana, USA, tell how they became friends after meeting in an Internet chatroom.

1 SB

• I'm 15, live in Manchester and lead a normal urban teenage life (TV, phone, friends, music, school) but am really into acting, reading and writing. I love the Internet and spend 30 minutes a day working or e-mailing my friends on my PC.

The second time I went into a chatroom I met Sarah. It was a dark, rainy Saturday night I think. She gave me her address and I e-mailed her straight away.

Her first e-mail was really nice. She used lots of symbols and netspeak which I didn't understand but we agreed on lots of things ... writing, hating cliques of friends, travel. We started e-mailing around twice a week and a friendship began.

I quickly learnt a lot about her: she lives on a huge farm; doesn't go to school (her mum teaches her at home); has no experience of city life; and most of her contact with people is on the Net. The most interesting chats are about our different lives. She loves horses and couldn't believe all I'd ridden was donkeys on the beach. I was amazed when she told me she hasn't got a TV!

We don't talk about our problems but it's only been four months – I think we will in time. The best thing about our friendship, though, is that it's just the two of us. Nobody can feel left out or ignored. Also we were not forced together by school or another group. And neither of us knows each other's friends so we can totally trust each other not to gossip.

It's a great way of getting an insight into another world; it's also easier to make a friendship last when you're not waiting for the postman.

Chatrooms are an easy way to 'meet' people and make e-mail friendships (like Benjamin and Sarah). But because many of them are not monitored they also attract a good number of 'weirdos' so it is important to use a code name and only give your e-mail address when you are sure you can trust the other person. Never give your home address or personal details, or arrange to meet people from a chatroom. On the other hand, e-mail friendships can be fun, cheap (but first ask if you can use the phone line) and a great way to meet someone you may never meet in 'real' life.

Netspeak and symbols for chatting

brb	=	be right back	2	=	to, too, two
b4n	=	bye for now	4	=	for, four
cu	=	see you	10q	=	thank you
imo	=	in my opinion	10u	=	than you
l8r	=	later			
np	=	no problem	;-)	=	happy (face)
oic	=	Oh, I see	:-))	=	very happy
otoh	=	on the other hand	:-(	=	sad
			:-/	=	don't know
r	=	are	:-D	=	laughing
sb	=	somebody	:'-(	=	crying
u	=	you	:-#	=	a kiss
w8	=	wait	@-'-,–	=	a rose

I am 14 and live in Montana in the USA. I like riding horses, reading, writing, e-pals and the great outdoors. I have lessons at home – not school – which I don't like much because there are no friends around.

As I live so far from town the computer is often my only link with people. I spend at least three hours a day on it. I use chatrooms because I like talking to people around the world.

I met a lot of people before chatting to Benjy – including a few weirdos who I avoid. Chatrooms can get really busy and confusing so it's nice to e-mail people direct. Benjy was the first person I liked and trusted enough to give my address to.

I clearly remember when we met. It was a hot Sunday morning in June. I'd arranged to meet a friend in a chatroom but she never came so I started talking to Benjy. He was much funnier and we just decided to write … we didn't arrange a time. It just happened.

I thought it was interesting that he liked coffee (I don't think I know a teen who does) and I was impressed with his school grades. I like his personality and the way he writes real letters not notes.

Our friendship is totally different to the ones I have with friends. We've not exchanged phone numbers (I hate using the phone) but we have talked about meeting up.

The best thing about having an e-pal is it's always interesting to hear about what's going on in a different country. It's also great to just have a friend you know is there for you if you ever need them.

1 Some talking points

1. Compare Benjamin and Sarah. In what ways are they different/similar? What do you think of their 'friendship'?
2. Benjamin says it was Saturday night when he met Sarah. But Sarah says it was Sunday morning. What is wrong here? Think of the time zones.
3. Imagine meeting Benjamin or Sarah in a chatroom. Write a dialogue. Use netspeak if you like.

2 Using the Internet

What are the advantages and disadvantages of communication by e-mail? Work in groups. Use the information on these pages and your own experience to make a list of safety rules for the Internet.

Conjunctions 16 | Vocabulary 15, 1 | Skills 20

1

B Into the great wide open (4)

Eddie waited till he finished high school
He went to Hollywood, got a tattoo
He met a girl out there with a tattoo too
The future was wide open

They moved into a place they both could afford
He found a nightclub, he could work at the door
She had a guitar and she taught him some chords
The sky was the limit

Into the great wide open
Under them skies of blue
Out in the great wide open
A rebel without a clue

The papers said Ed always played from the heart
He got an agent and a roadie named Bart
They made a record and it went in the charts
The sky was the limit

His leather jacket had chains that would jingle
They both met movie stars, partied and mingled
Their A&R man said I don't hear a single
The future was wide open

Into the great wide open ...

Tom Petty & The Heartbreakers

1 Eddie's plans

1. Discuss what the song tells us about Eddie and his plans.
2. What do you think happens to Eddie in the end?
3. Find words and phrases in the song which show that the singer does not take Eddie seriously.

2 A music project

Choose one of these topics.

a) Your favourite song
What is your favourite song in the English language at the moment? Write down the lyrics of the song on a large piece of paper. Add photos, stickers, your own pictures, etc.

b) Music styles
Make a mind map of all the different music styles you can think of. Add photos and short examples.

C The Glory Girl (5-8)

• The Glory family bus rumbled along the highway. The old tires wobbled. The engine missed. The windows and doors rattled. From time to time there was a loud bang as the engine backfired.

Anna Glory was stretched out on one of the back seats of the bus, trying to sleep. She lay on her side with her coat over her like a blanket. Down the aisle the pale-blue outfits of the Glory Gospel Singers waved and swayed on coat-hangers, giving off the faint odor of sweat and Right Guard.

The music her family had sung that night still sounded in Anna's head. The songs had been written that way – to start hands clapping, feet tapping, to make people want to join in on the chorus.

When he calls me, calls me, calls me,
I will answer, answer, answer,
And I'll never, never, never
Answer, 'No.'
Yes, when He calls me, calls me, calls me …

Anna closed her eyes. The music, the lights, the clapping, swaying crowd – it all seemed the way life was meant to be. And she at the back of the auditorium, waiting to sell Glory albums and cassette tapes at intermission – she felt left out, not just from the music and the crowd, but somehow from the rest of the world.

• Anna sighed. She shifted on the hard seat. The Glory bus had once been a school bus, and the seats were worn slick from years of sliding, restless children.

Anna was the only person in the history of the Glory family who could not carry a tune. There had been a brief time, when Anna was seven, when it had been hoped that she could learn to play the drums.

Waiting for the drums to be delivered had been the happiest time of Anna's life. She had imagined how important she would look, beating time on the silver-and-blue Wilson drums, crossing her arms different ways, hitting this drum and that one.

But when the drums came and Anna held the sticks at last, she discovered that she could no more beat time than she could sing. She was clumsy. The drumsticks clattered to the floor. Again and again her father shouted, 'Anna, listen to the music!'

And finally the drums had gone to the twins. They, at age five, took to it like monkeys, and before the week was out they were playing as if they had been doing it all their lives.

'Anyway, darling,' her father had said, 'we need you to sit at the back and sell records.'

'I don't want to sell records,' she'd said, starting to cry.

He'd looked at her. None of the children ever whined or pleaded when their father got that expression on his face. 'You'll get used to it,' he had said and then turned away.

• It had been five years, however, and Anna had not gotten used to it yet.

She looked up the aisle, past her mother's head which was lolling over the edge of the seat, past the twins' legs kicking at each other, past the gold of Angel's hair, to her father. Mr. Glory was driving the bus, holding a Pall Mall cigarette between his teeth. He had to steer with his whole body.

Lately the blue bus had started to take on a will of its own. It went left when it was supposed to go right, swerved into the dirt beside the road for no reason, and Mr. Glory had to be ready for these unexpected moves. Mr. Glory sometimes seemed to be dealing with a team of willful mules instead of a bus.

He trusted the bus, though. 'It gets us there,' he would say when it was criticized for dying down at intersections or for stopping short and causing Mrs. Glory to slide out of her seat. Mr. Glory was proud that the bus had never had a flat, an oil change, or a breakdown in all the years he had been driving it.

Anna's eyes closed. Pall Mall smoke drifted to the back of the bus and hung in the stale, cold air. On wet days Anna felt she could smell old peanut butter sandwiches and sneakers, and if she reached down under the seats she could feel knots of bubble gum so old they were as hard as the metal.

The Glory family's songs seemed to hang in the still, cold air of the bus, too.

Sing with the Glorys,
Yes, come sing with the Glorys,
If you sing with the Glorys
Then you'll never
Sing a-lone

When Anna heard that song, the Glory Gospel Singers' theme song, the last number on the program, she would get up and move to the aisle where everybody could see her. Her father would step closer to the microphone, his guitar shifted out of the way, on his hip.

'Yes, ladies and gentlemen, if you've enjoyed listening to the songs of the Glory Gospel Singers tonight, well, you can have all the songs you've heard on one long-playing album or cassette tape for the low, low price of eight dollars. That's a lot of singing for eight dollars.

'At the back of the auditorium one of the Glory girls, our little Anna – she can't sing, but ain't she pretty? – she'll be waiting to help you with your purchases. Hold up your hand, darling, so they can see where you're at.'

Dutifully Anna would hold up her hand, wave, and then move back out of the light.

'And in the meantime, folks, remember, all the Glory family – Maudine, the twins Joshua and Matthew, our lead singer Angel and yours truly, John Glory – want you to –'

While Mr. Glory was introducing the family, Anna would sit at her table and unlock her cash box. She would straighten the stacks of records and cassette tapes as inside the auditorium the music swelled.

Sing with the Glorys,
Yes, come sing with the Glorys,
If you sing with the Glorys
Then you'll never,
Never,
Never!
Siiiinnnnnng a-lone!

On the back seat of the bus, Anna pulled her coat up around her neck. She closed her eyes. Her body slid on the worn seat as the old bus stubbornly swerved to the left for no reason, and Mr. Glory, with a puff on his Pall Mall, brought it back to the road again.

(from: *The Glory Girl* by Betsy Byars)

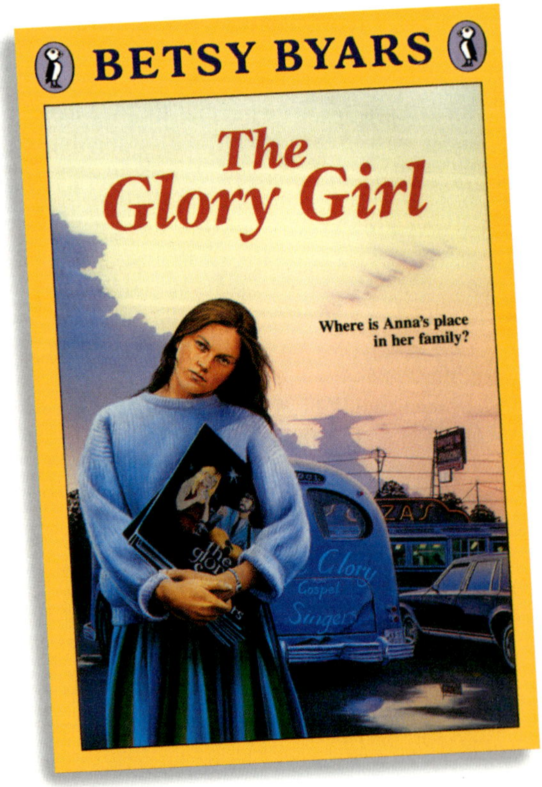

1 Some talking points

1. In the story it says that Anna is clumsy. Do you agree? Why or why not?
2. Discuss whether Anna is the 'black sheep of the family'.
3. Talk about Anna's father. What do you/don't you like about him?
4. Discuss the role Anna's mother plays in the family.
5. Look for clues in the story that tell you how rich the Glorys are.

2 Anna's life

Choose one of these writing tasks.

1. Imagine you are Anna. Do you like the life you are leading? What would you rather do? *(Write about these things in your diary.)*
2. What advice would you give Anna to help her in her situation? *(Write her a letter.)*
3. Continue the story. *(Work in groups or with a partner.)*

Vocabulary 15, 2-4 | Past perfect 17 | Gerunds 18 | Word order 19

A Vocabulary

G 1 — 1 American or British English?

Decide which statement goes with which of these two teenagers. What differences can you find between American English and British English? Make a list.

1. a) My mum and dad were both born here too.
   b) My mom and dad moved here two years ago.
2. a) We live with our three dogs in a small flat.
   b) We live in a nice apartment.
3. a) We even like our neighbors.
   b) We sometimes have trouble with our neighbours.
4. a) I go to the local comprehensive school.
   b) I can't wait to finish high school.
5. a) I'm not a good student. My grades are terrible.
   b) I'm an average pupil. My marks are OK.
6. a) I'm a bit of a weirdo, I guess.
   b) I'm quite normal, I think.
7. a) My favourite colour is green.
   b) My favorite color is gray.
8. a) My dream vacation would be a trip to Mars.
   b) I'd like to go to Italy on holiday.

2 The odd one out

Find the odd one out and explain why it doesn't fit into the group.

1. to e-mail – to chat – to criticize – to monitor
2. sandwich – friendship – personality – difference
3. to drive – to steer – to swerve – to trust
4. lately – in the meantime – totally – a week ago

3 Word stress

Sort the words into the correct groups:

- • -	• - -
confusing	gentlemen
- •	**• -**
appeal	gossip

microphone online
repeated monitor
personal clumsy
impress exchange
relax however
monkey surprising
apartment jealous
disgrace straighten
criticize (to) record
record total teenager
urban replace

G 2 — 4 Word building

"She would **straighten** the **stacks** of **records** and cassette **tapes.**" (The Glory Girl, l. 124)

a) Explain the meaning of the verb *to straighten* and how it is formed.

b) Can you guess the meanings of these verbs? *to soften, to widen, to loosen, to flatten, to toughen.* Write an example sentence for each. Check them in a dictionary.

c) The word *stack* (a noun) can also be used as a verb.
Example: She **stacked** the records on the table.
Choose five of the words on the right and put them in sentences, first as a noun, then as a verb.
Example: I had a horrible dream.
What did you dream?

drink
contact
sound
help
smell
rain
race
record
dream
report
tape

1

G 3

B Conjunctions

1 Two letters

Dear Mom,
$chool $ure i$ cool! Although I'm new here, I have lot$ of friend$ already. A$ $oon a$ I arrived, $ome guy$ $tarted $howing me around. While that wa$ going on, I learned all ort of intere$ting thing$.
A$ I am $tudying hard, I $imply can't think of anything I need, $o ju$t $end me a card $ometime – unle$$ you can think of $omething.
Love,
$i$$y

P. $. Thank$ for $ending the $weater.

Dear Sissy,
Thanks for your NOte. Before you went, we were NOt sure you'd be busy eNOugh at school, but we NOw kNOw you can igNOre all the NOise, so that working NOn-stop to improve your kNOwledge of astroNOmy & techNOlogy will be NO trouble.
Since you ask, I can think of NOthing a NOrmal student might need right NOw. NOr can Dad.
Love,
Mom

P. S. As I write, the first NOvember sNOw is falling.

a) *Find all the conjunctions in the two letters and work out what they mean in the context. Then sort them into these categories:*
- *conjunctions that connect ideas*
- *conjunctions that introduce clauses of time, reason or result*
- *others*

idea + idea	time	reason
and		

b) *Match these sentences.*

1. You can e-mail me straight away
2 I'll give you the CD
3. If I were you, I'd buy this mobile phone
4. Let's try and get into a chatroom
5. You can talk to all sorts of people,
6. You shouldn't give your address to strangers,
7. Soon we were e-mailing each other
8. I would keep away from that guy

nor should you arrange to meet them.
as if we'd been friends for years.
unless I was really sure he was OK.
but you shouldn't give out your personal details.
as soon as I've finished with it.
if I give you my address.
while we're on the Net.
although it isn't as cheap as the other one.

2 A job interview

Study the text carefully and then put in the right conjunctions.

although, and, as, because (2 x), but, if (2 x), or (2 x), so, that, then, unless, until, when (2 x), while

… I left school, I needed a job, … I wrote to lots of companies. However, I heard nothing … one day I was offered an interview with a company in Milwaukee. … I had never heard of them, I decided to go … I was told they were a very modern company. '… they offer me a job, I think I'll take it,' I thought, '… the money's really bad!'

A week later I was at the company's offices. … I was early, a secretary asked me to wait for a few minutes. … I was sitting there, several employees walked by. Each one smiled at the secretary and said, 'Hi, Number 73'. And … they said that, she would answer, 'Hi, Number 26 (… Number 35 … whatever.)' It was very strange, … I didn't say anything.
… I was called in to see a woman and a man. 'We're a totally modern company,' the woman told me. 'So modern … we have numbers here instead of names. … you join us, you'll be Number 94. I am Number 12 … my partner here is Number 157 913 205.'
'Why does he have such a long number?' I asked.
'Oh, … he's Polish,' the woman answered.

G 4

C Past perfect

1 Two texts about Anna Glory

Read these two texts.

A: The family hoped that Anna would become their drummer. But she soon found that she couldn't play the drums – while the twins took to them straight away. So they gave her the tapes and records to sell. One night the family sang their songs again. Afterwards, Anna lay at the back of the bus. The music still sounded in her head. She sighed. She was the only Glory who couldn't sing. She remembered a better time. Now she felt left out.

B: Anna lay at the back of the bus. That night the family had sung their songs again and the music still sounded in her head. She sighed. She was the only Glory who couldn't sing. She remembered a time when the family had hoped that she would become their drummer. But she had soon found that she couldn't play the drums – while the twins had taken to them straight away. So they had given her the tapes and records to sell and now she felt left out.

1. Compare the information in the two texts and the order in which it is given.
2. Find verbs in the simple past in A which are in the past perfect in B, and say why this is.

SAVE

had + *past participle*
Anna **had** never **wanted** to sell tapes.
= past perfect

2 The Glory bus breaks down

Use the past perfect to complete these sentences.

1. One day, after it *(keep going)* for thirty years, the Glory bus broke down.
   Example: One day, after it **had kept going** for thirty years, the Glory bus broke down.
2. When the bus stopped, Mr. Glory wondered if he *(forget)* to fill it up with gas.
3. But no, there was plenty of gas in the tank, something else *(happen)*.
4. Maybe it was because the bus *(never have)* an oil change.
5. Lately the engine *(start)* to backfire a lot.
6. He remembered a time when it *(never do)* that.
7. Once it *(be)* a school bus, but that was a long time ago.
8. In those days the tires *(not wobble)* like they did now.
9. And the doors and windows *(not rattle)* either.
10. … he *(drive)* the old bus for the last time?

3 Eddie goes to Hollywood

Tell Eddie's story. Use the past perfect instead of the simple past where you can.

after …	since …
though …	because …
when …	which/that …

1. left high school/went to Hollywood/always wanted to be a star; 2. got a tattoo/moved in with a girl/met her at a party; 3. hoped for better work/took a cheap job in a night club; 4. during the day/practised guitar chords/girlfriend taught him; 5. became good enough/gave up job/got an agent; 6. first record entered the charts/was seen at the best parties; 7. by the end of the year/things changed; 8. record company dropped him/next two records were failures; 9. girlfriend found a new boyfriend/left Eddie; 10. spent all his money/returned to his hometown in Montana/got a job at the *Hollywood Diner*.

Example:
After he **had left** high school, Eddie went to Hollywood *because* he **had** always **wanted** to be a star.

1

G 5 R

D Gerunds

1 The animal school

One day the animals decided to organize a school. There would be four subjects only – but each animal had to take all four subjects.

Swimming and flying were the duck's favorite subjects. But he needed to practise running, and this was bad for his feet, so in the end he was only average at swimming.

The monkey loved climbing. But he lost interest in flying because the teacher wouldn't let him start from the top of the tree.

The cat enjoyed running and climbing. And she was also interested in flying (after small birds) though no good at it. But she hated swimming.

At the end of the year, a donkey that could run pretty well, and also manage a bit of climbing, swimming and flying, had the highest average and was top of the school.

The dogs stayed out of school because hiding bones was not a subject. Later they started a successful private school.

After George H. Reavis

a) *Looking at the text*
1. What were the four subjects at the animal school?
2. Imagine the subjects the dogs might have in their private school. Use gerunds.
3. Explain what you think the story is trying to say. Do you agree?
4. Note down expressions in which gerunds are used after prepositions.
   Example: to be average *at swimming*.
5. Now describe each animal in the story. Say what they were *good at/interested in/no good at/...* doing.

b) *What about you?*
1. Say what things *you* like/hate doing.
2. Use gerunds to complete these sentences:
   - I'm quite good at ...
   - But I'm not interested in ...
   - I never get tired of ...
   - When I was young, I was afraid of ...
   - People sometimes criticize me for ...

2 I don't like you doing that

After certain verbs you can also use a gerund with a subject of its own.
Example: Anna hated **people** laughing at her.

a) *Does this mean 'Anna hated people who laughed at her' or 'Anna hated it when people laughed at her'?*

b) *Make more sentences like this from the boxes below:*

Anna hated	Anna	breaking down.
Mr. Glory was unhappy about	the bus	not carrying a tune.
The Glorys often worried about	my teacher	selling tapes and records.
Anna's family didn't mind	her	bringing a friend to the party?
I don't like	me	looking at her like that.
Would you mind	her father	giving me too much homework.

E Word order

G 6

1 Some jokes

'Doctor, after the operation on my hands, will I be able to play the piano?'
'Oh, yes. You'll be able to play the piano perfectly.'
'That's absolutely wonderful. I couldn't play at all before.'

'Jimmy, how will you ever get a job if you can't write properly?'
'It's really no problem, miss. I want to be a doctor.'

'Why are you looking so happy today?'
'I've borrowed my neighbor's saxophone.'
'But you can't play the saxophone.'
'Neither can he while I've got it.'

'Do you know, I keep seeing snakes everywhere. This morning I saw six of them in the bathroom.'
'Have you seen a doctor?'
'No, I only see snakes.'

Work with a partner and read the jokes as mini-dialogues. Take turns.
Then look at all the adverbs/adverbial phrases in them and explain the position in the sentence of

- *adverbs of manner (e.g.* slowly*)*
- *adverbs of degree (e.g.* very, really*)*
- *adverbs of indefinite time and frequency (e.g.* always, never*)*
- *adverbs of definite time (e.g.* yesterday*)*

2 Benjamin and Sarah

Put these sentences in the right order.

1. is / Benjamin / into writing. / really
2. a day / spends / on his PC. / usually / 30 minutes / He
3. started / a week. / Sarah / e-mailing / and / each other / He / twice
4. to people. / often / to talk / uses / Sarah / chatrooms
5. both / think / they remember / they met. / when / clearly / They

G 7

3 Agreeing with other people

"So do I, Gary, so do I."

Translate the cartoon (left) and the last line of the third joke (above) into German. Then work out rules for saying 'auch'/'auch nicht' in English. Now react to these statements.

1. I know them quite well. *(Ich auch.)*
2. We don't know her. *(Ich auch nicht.)*
3. I can speak French. *(Wir auch.)*
4. I can't speak Polish. *(Wir auch nicht.)*
5. She likes fish. *(Meine Schwester auch.)*
6. My dad's a brain surgeon. *(Mein Papa auch.)*
7. Yesterday I was late for school. *(Ich auch.)*
8. But you weren't late today. *(Du auch nicht.)*

Avoiding culture shock

People in different countries have different ways of doing things. So, to avoid culture shock, it's important to be prepared before you visit another country.
Here are some notes a group of American exchange students made after their year in Germany. The list is supposed to help future exchange students.

THE GERMAN WAY OF LIFE

Germans close room doors and pull shades.

They aren't friends with their neighbors.

They worry about their health. (There's something wrong with them if they don't.)

They don't necessarily take a shower a day.

Girls often don't shave arms and legs.

They get up early – and go to bed early.

They have small refrigerators. (You shouldn't raid them!)

There is more fresh food, less processed stuff.

Germans eat almost all kinds of food and almost all parts of animals.

Meals are social events (so hold back with your fork until everyone is there!)

If guests want more food, they take it. (Don't wait to be asked or you'll wait forever!)

Germans absolutely love mineral water!

They bring flowers when they visit friends. (Uneven number, no red or white roses unless in love!)

They would never visit other people's homes without an invitation.

They shake hands any time they meet people.

They don't stand in line. (You have to push your way to the front in stores and onto trains.)

Few people use a credit card for shopping.

There are often restroom attendants. (They expect money.)

Weekends (from Saturday afternoon till Sunday evening) are totally dead.

German families go for long walks on Sundays.

Germans don't waste time on polite phrases – they say what they mean.

They don't go overboard on words like 'sorry' and 'please'.

1 Discussing clichés

A lot of the things people say about other countries can be clichés which are not really true, so be careful with them. When you get there and meet the people, things aren't always what you expected.

a) *Discuss the statements on the left. You can say:*

That's nonsense!/I don't believe that at all!
I don't think that's always true. We never ...
I don't think that is typical of ...
I can't comment on that because ...
I have to agree with that. I know lots of people who ...
There's some truth in that.
That's true and there are good reasons for it.

b) *Say what these statements tell you about Americans and their country. Again you should watch out for clichés.*

2 Cultural mistakes (1-4)

People from another culture may think you are rude simply because you use the wrong word, or because you say or do the wrong thing. In the following scenes Daniel, from Ulm, has just arrived to stay with the Scotts, an American family.

a) *Listen to the recording and comment on the cultural mistakes he makes. There are four scenes. You can follow the first two in your book.*

1. *At the front door*

Mother: Well hello, Daniel. Welcome to our home. Did you have a good trip?
Daniel: Yes. – I'm thirsty.
Mother: Oh. Er, yes, well, let's see. Er, right, let's go into the kitchen and get you something to drink, OK?
Daniel: Yes.

2. *In the kitchen*

Mother: Here's the refrigerator. We've got lots of stuff in here. Help yourself any time. Now how about a coke with plenty of ice?
Daniel: No. It's not healthy. Too much sugar. I want mineral water.
Mother: Oh dear. We don't have that, I'm afraid. Sorry. How about a glass of normal water?
Daniel: Normal water? Hm. Can you drink it?

b) *Now try to do better than Daniel. Which of these phrases would you use – and in which situation?*

It was very nice, thank you.
That sounds like a great idea.
Yes, actually, I do. It was a long journey.
Give me a ...
No, thank you. It was lovely, but I couldn't eat any more ...
No way!
Excuse me, but could I please have ...?
Of course I will.
Thanks, but I'd rather have some ..., if you have any.
No, really. I just couldn't, thanks.
Oh yes please. I'd love a ...
I'm sorry. I didn't understand what you meant.

1 A poem puzzle: The dare rap

When you smoke	... you can't think clear.
Smoking turns lungs black	... it's no joke.
If you go ahead and smoke	... your brain will snooze.
If you smoke pot	... you turn into a slug.
When you drink beer	... make the right choice.
When you drink booze	... be a smarty.
If you take a drug	... and causes you to hack.
When you get high	... you are going to croak.
So if you go to a party	... you have a good chance of staying alive.
Listen to my voice	... your brain will rot.
If you never drink and drive	... you might try to fly – and you will die.

1. This rap was written by teenager Shelly Merkes. First match the rhyming pairs and copy the whole poem into your exercise book.
2. Look up any words you don't know in a dictionary.
3. Why do you think Shelly Merkes called it 'The dare rap'?

2 Conjunctions

a) *Find the best conjunction for the context.*

1. My sister's a fantastic piano player (?) she is only ten.
2. You have to practise every day (?) you want to be that good.
3. Tom won't go to discos (?) he hates dancing.
4. (?) I read his e-mail I knew he was a weirdo.
5. The show had already started (?) we arrived at the theatre.
6. 'I don't really like The Bottles.' – '(?) do I.'
7. I won't go to see them (?) you come with me.
8. OK, (?) I think we could find something better to do.

b) *Complete these sentences.*

1. I think of Italy whenever ...
2. She had left the room before ...
3. Since ..., I'll tell you what happened ...
4. I can't do it while ...
5. I haven't seen her since ...
6. He wrote it down so that ...

3 Past perfect

Complete these sentences with the past perfect forms of the verbs:

1. I met Kevin in an Internet chatroom. Before that I (*already have*) a few virtual boyfriends, but some of them (*be*) weirdos.
2. One day, when a friend I (*arrange*) to meet in a chatroom didn't come, I started talking to Kevin instead.
3. He seemed nicer than any of the other guys I (*talk*) to. He mailed me as soon as I (*give*) him my address.
4. After I (*switch*) off my computer that night, I went to bed really happy because at last I (*find*) someone I could trust.
5. We mailed each other several times a week after that, but I knew something (*happen*) when he suddenly stopped writing to me.
6. Maybe he (*meet*) someone else – I never found out.
7. I was angry for weeks because nobody (*ever do*) that to me before.
8. But I was happy that I (*not tell*) any of my friends about him.

4 Gerunds

a) *Complete these statements by filling in the missing gerunds. Then decide whether you agree or disagree with the statements.*

1. (?) to people around the world is often a problem in chatrooms.
2. All Americans love (?) to fast food restaurants.
3. Nobody likes people (?) at them.
4. (?) CDs for a famous pop group would be exciting.
5. Parents don't like their children (?) noisy.
6. The Internet is a good place for (?) your English.
7. Germans enjoy (?) hands with people.
8. The English are not interested in (?) anybody else's language.
9. (?) by credit card is not popular in Germany.
10. I don't say much in English lessons because I'm afraid of (?) mistakes.

be
make
talk
speak
pay
sell
shake
go
laugh
practise

b) *A game: Think of a famous person and use gerunds to write down 10 things about him/her (e.g. what he or she likes/hates/is good at/is bad at/is afraid of/... doing). The others in the class try to guess who it is.*

5 Word order

a) *Decide where to put the adverbs/adverbial phrases.*

1. We don't go camping. (usually, in August)
2. But we took a motorhome. (this year, for two weeks, to Canada)
3. My sister was playing the guitar. (quietly, one night)
4. A strange noise stopped her. (really, suddenly)
5. We opened the door of our motorhome and saw a bear. (slowly, outside)

b) *Put the words in the right order.*

1. tries / at weekends / our family / to get away / always
2. gets back / have / until Dad / usually / to wait / from work / finally / but we
3. in the car / put / today / Mom / all our stuff / already / has
4. in the evening / we / ever / until / 7 o'clock / at least / leave / never
5. on Mondays / back to school / I hate going / does / my sister / so *(two sentences)*
6. do / actually /school is OK / easily / because I can / most subjects / quite.

6 Cartoon fun

1

Auch in *Swift 3* findest du nach jeder *Unit* eine Liste der neuen Vokabeln. Nur die **halbfett** gedruckten Wörter gehören zum obligatorischen Lernwortschatz für alle. Mager gedruckte Wörter gehören entweder zu Übungen und Texten, die nur in bestimmten Bundesländern behandelt werden müssen (in den *Units* mit 〈 〉 gekennzeichnet), oder sie helfen dir beim Verstehen von authentischen Texten, brauchen aber nicht gelernt zu werden. Die folgenden Symbole und Abkürzungen werden verwendet:

Symbole

〈 〉	=	nicht obligatorische Texte und Übungen
*	=	unregelmäßiges Verb (siehe S. 230)
[ˈ]	=	Hauptbetonung
[ˌ]	=	Nebenbetonung
[‿]	=	enge Verbindung zweier Wörter
~	=	Auslassung des zu erklärenden Wortes

Abkürzungen:

BE	=	*British English*
AE	=	*American English*
so.	=	*someone* = jmd(m/n)/jemand(em/en)
sth.	=	*something* = etw/etwas
sg.	=	Singular
pl.	=	Plural
coll.	=	*colloquial* = umgangssprachlich
sl.	=	Slang
old	=	heute so nicht mehr gebräuchlich

CHECK-IN

tough [tʌf]	hart, zäh	Life is really ~ for homeless people.
pressure [ˈpreʃə]	Druck	to press – pressure
I wanna *(coll.)* [aɪ ˈwɒnə]	Ich will	I want to
good lookin' [ˌgʊd ˈlʊkɪn]	gut aussehend	good looking
disgrace [dɪsˈgreɪs]	Schande	
to follow through with sth. [ˌfɒləʊ ˈθruː]	etwas durchziehen	
dare [deə]	Mutprobe	I only stole that CD as a ~.
to **care** [keə]	sich kümmern, Interesse haben	Nobody is interested. = Nobody cares.
I gotta *(coll.)* [aɪ ˈgɑtə]	Ich muss	I've got to
grade *(AE)* [greɪd]	(Schul-)Note	What ~ did you get in the test?
to make* the grade [ˌmeɪk ðə ˈgreɪd]	es zu etwas bringen	to be successful
to **fade** [feɪd]	schwächer werden, ausblenden, ausbleichen	If you leave your swimsuit in the sun, the colours will ~.
like [laɪk]	als ob	
to **end up** [end‿ˈʌp]	enden, landen	If you don't use a map, you may ~ where you didn't want to go.
fool [fuːl]	Narr, Dummkopf	idiot, so. who does silly things
to **fit in** [fɪt‿ˈɪn]	hineinpassen, sich in die Gruppe einfügen	If you are very different from others in a group, you feel you don't ~.
to make* the team [ˌmeɪk ðə ˈtiːm]	ins Team aufgenommen werden	
to **stand* out** [stænd‿ˈaʊt]	herausragen	She stands out (in a crowd). = Everyone notices her.
to **see*** [siː]	*hier:* verstehen	I ~. = I understand.
virgin [ˈvɜːdʒɪn]	Jungfrau	
truth [truːθ]	Wahrheit	true – the truth
low [ləʊ]	niedergeschlagen, niedrig, schwach	You can't enjoy life if you feel ~.
to cash it in [ˌkæʃ‿ɪt‿ˈɪn]	einlösen, *hier:* hinschmeißen, Schluss machen	
guy [gaɪ]	Typ, Kerl	a word for 'man' or 'boy', especially in *AE*
jealous [ˈdʒeləs]	eifersüchtig	Would you feel ~ if you saw your boyfriend with another girl?
unless [ʌnˈles]	wenn nicht, es sei denn	You can't get on the plane ~ you've got a ticket.
to evaporate [ɪˈvæpreɪt]	verdampfen, sich in Luft auflösen	
not … either [nɒt‿ˈaɪðə]	auch nicht	I don't like these jeans, and I don't like this jacket either.

babe *(coll.)* [beɪb]	Baby, Puppe, Mädchen, Kleines	
deal [di:l]	Handel, Abmachung	People often shake hands when they make a ~.
the real deal *(AE)* [ðə 'rɪəl ˌdi:l]	das Echte	
to **get* so. to do sth.** [get]	jmdn dazu bringen, etwas zu tun	to make so. do sth.
teen [ti:n]	Teenager	
to **rule** [ru:l]	herrschen, regieren; entscheiden; angesagt sein	Those who ~ tell all the other people what to do.
bargain ['bɑ:gɪn]	Handel; günstiges Angebot, Schnäppchen	This bike was a ~. It was really cheap.
looks *pl.* [lʊks]	Aussehen	Models have to care about their ~.
celeb [səl'eb]	*Abkürzung für* 'celebrity'	
free-time ['fri:taim]	Freizeit, Freizeit-	Hobbies are ~ activities.
high school *(AE)* ['haisku:l]	Oberschule, Gesamtschule	high school ≠ Hochschule
student *(AE)* ['stju:dnt]	Schüler(in)	*BE*: pupil – *AE*: student
alone [ə'ləʊn]	allein	When nobody's with you, you're ~.
to cruise [kru:z]	mit dem Auto in der Gegend herumfahren	
craft [krɑ:ft]	Handwerk; Kunstgewerbe	

TEXTS

A	to **lead*** [li:d]	führen	
	urban ['ɜ:bən]	städtisch	'Yuppie' stands for 'young ~ professional'.
	teenage ['ti:neɪdʒ]	Jugend-/ Teenager-	
	a (+ day, week, month) [ə]	pro	We meet twice ~ week.
	straight away [ˌstreɪt‿ə'weɪ]	sofort	Don't wait! Do it ~.
	netspeak ['netspi:k]	Internet-Zeichensprache	
	clique [kli:k]	Clique	
	travel ['trævl]	(das) Reisen	
	around [ə'raʊnd]	etwa, ungefähr	about 2 hours = ~ 2 hours
	friendship ['frendʃɪp]	Freundschaft	friend – friendship
	donkey ['dɒŋki]	Esel	an animal similar to a horse, but with bigger ears
	to **amaze** [ə'meɪz]	verblüffen	to surprise very much
	in time [ɪn 'taɪm]	mit der Zeit; rechtzeitig	
	though [ðəʊ]	jedoch, dennoch, trotzdem; obwohl	Ben is a bit crazy. I like him, ~.
	left out [left‿'aʊt]	ausgeschlossen	Stella hasn't invited me to her party. I feel so ~!
	to **force** [fɔ:s]	zwingen	You can't ~ me to do that!
	to **trust** [trʌst]	vertrauen	A friend is so. you can ~.
	to **gossip** ['gɒsɪp]	tratschen	to talk, often about other people behind their backs
	insight ['ɪnsaɪt]	Einblick, Verständnis	
	to **last** [lɑ:st]	dauern, halten	The friendship ended quickly. It didn't ~.
	to **monitor** ['mɒnɪtə]	überwachen	to watch carefully and check
	weirdo ['wɪədəʊ]	verrückter Typ	a crazy person
	on the one hand ... on the other hand [ɒn ðə‿'wʌn hænd ... ɒn ðɪ‿'ʌðə hænd]	einerseits ... andererseits	On the one hand, it sounds fun. But on the other hand, it may be dangerous.
	line [laɪn]	Leitung; Warteschlange	You can only phone when the ~ is free.
	to be* right back [bi: 'raɪt ˌbæk]	gleich zurück sein	I'll be back in a moment. = I'll ~.

	see you ['si: ˌju]	bis bald	another way to say 'goodbye'
	kiss [kɪs]	Kuss	
	pal [pæl]	Kumpel, Freund(in)	
	the great outdoors [greɪt‿ˌaʊt'dɔ:z]	die freie Natur	
	link [lɪŋk]	Verbindung	A ~ between people or things gives them contact.
	to **avoid** [ə'vɔɪd]	meiden, vermeiden	to keep away from so./sth., to prevent sth. from happening
	to **confuse** [kən'fju:z]	verwirren, irritieren, verwechseln	I keep confusing Christine and Christina.
	to **impress** [ɪm'pres]	beeindrucken	Some people buy expensive things just to ~ others.
	personality [ˌpɜ:s'næləti]	Persönlichkeit	person – personal – personality
	to **exchange** [ɪks'tʃeɪndʒ]	aus-/umtauschen	We gave each other our addresses. = We ~d addresses.
2	**advantage** [əd'vɑ:ntɪdʒ]	Vorteil	a positive effect
	disadvantage [ˌdɪsəd'vɑ:ntɪdʒ]	Nachteil	disadvantage ↔ advantage
B	**till** [tɪl]	bis	another word for 'until'
	tattoo [tə'tu:]	Tätowierung	
	to **afford** [ə'fɔ:d]	sich leisten	to have enough money to be able to buy sth.
	chord [kɔ:d]	Akkord	I know how to play a few ~s on the guitar.
	clue [klu:]	Ahnung, Hinweis	If you haven't a ~, you don't know anything at all.
	roadie ['rəʊdi]	Tour-/ Bühnenhelfer(in)	
	named [neɪmd]	namens	
	the charts [tʃɑ:ts]	Hitparade	
	chain [tʃeɪn]	Kette	
	would (= used to) [wʊd]	pflegte, -st, -t, -n zu tun, tat, -est, -et, -en früher	He ~ sing and play the guitar when he was young.
	to jingle ['dʒɪŋgl]	klimpern	
	to party ['pɑ:ti]	feiern	
	to mingle ['mɪŋgl]	sich unter die Leute mischen	
	A&R man [ˌeɪ‿ənd‿'ɑ: mæn] (= Artistes and Repertoire man)	*Mann bei einer Plattenfirma, der die Künstler betreut*	
1	to **take* seriously** [ˌteɪk 'sɪəriəsli]	ernst nehmen	If you take sth. seriously, you don't just laugh about it.
C	to rumble ['rʌmbl]	donnern	
	highway ['haɪweɪ]	Landstraße	*BE*: road – *AE*: highway
	tire *(AE)* ['taɪə]	Reifen	
	to wobble ['wɒbl]	wackeln, schwabbeln	
	to miss [mɪs]	aussetzen	
	to rattle ['rætl]	klappern	
	bang [bæŋ]	Knall	
	to backfire [ˌbæk'faɪə]	fehlzünden	
	to **stretch** [stretʃ]	(sich) strecken, dehnen	I always ~ when I get out of bed.
	aisle [aɪl]	Mittelgang	
	gospel ['gɒspl]	Gospel; Evangelium	
	to **wave** [weɪv]	wehen, winken	People sometimes ~ when they say hello or goodbye.
	to sway [sweɪ]	sich wiegen, schaukeln	
	coat-hanger ['kəʊtˌhæŋə]	Kleiderbügel	Clothes like jackets, coats and shirts can be kept on ~s.
	to give* off [gɪv‿'ɒf]	verströmen	
	odor *(AE)* ['əʊdə]	Geruch	
	Right Guard ['raɪt gɑ:d]	*Name eines Deodorants*	
	sweat [swet]	Schweiß	! ~ rhymes with 'get'.
	to tap [tæp]	klopfen	

to be* meant to be sth. [ment]	etwas sein sollen	the way it is meant to be = the way it should be
auditorium [ˌɔːdɪˈtɔːriəm]	Zuschauerraum	
intermission [ˌɪntəˈmɪʃn]	Pause	
to **sigh** [saɪ]	seufzen	If you're worrying about sth. it's natural to ~.
to shift [ʃift]	(sich) bewegen	
worn [wɔːn]	abgenutzt	
slick [slɪk]	glatt	
to **slide*** [slaɪd]	rutschen	It's fun to ~ on the ice. But don't slip!
restless [ˈrestləs]	rastlos, unruhig	
to carry a tune [ˌkæri‿ə ˈtjuːn]	eine Melodie richtig singen	
brief [briːf]	kurz	
to **deliver** [dɪˈlɪvə]	(aus)liefern, austragen	Letters are ~ed by the postman.
to beat* time [biːt ˈtaɪm]	den Takt schlagen	
at last [ət ˈlɑːst]	endlich	Now the big day is here ~!
clumsy [ˈklʌmzi]	ungeschickt, tollpatschig	~ people often drop things.
to clatter [ˈklætə]	klappern	
again and again [əˌgen‿ənd‿əˈgen]	immer wieder	
twin [twɪn]	Zwilling	a brother or sister who was born on the same day
to **take* to sth./so.** [teɪk]	auf Anhieb mögen, begeistert sein von	to like sth. or so. straight away
monkey [ˈmʌŋki]	Affe	! 'Donkey' doesn't rhyme with 'monkey'.
darling [ˈdɑːlɪŋ]	Liebling	
to plead [pliːd]	bitten	
to **get* used to** [get ˈjuːzd]	sich gewöhnen an	If you do sth. often enough, you ~ it.
however [ˌhaʊˈevə]	jedoch	It was difficult. We managed it, ~.
gotten *(AE)* [ˈgɒtn]	Partizip Perfekt von *'to get'*	*AE*: gotten – *BE*: got
to loll [lɒl]	hängen	
to **steer** [stɪə]	steuern, lenken	to steer a car
lately [ˈleɪtli]	in letzter Zeit	over the last few days or weeks
will [wɪl]	Wille	
of its own [əv‿ɪts‿ˈəʊn]	eigen	
to **be* supposed to do sth.** [səˈpəʊzd]	etw tun sollen	We're supposed to do our homework every day.
to **swerve** [swɜːv]	ausschwenken	to move suddenly to the right or left without warning
dirt [dɜːt]	Schmutz, Dreck	
move [muːv]	Bewegung	
to **deal* with** [ˈdiːl wɪθ]	sich befassen mit, umgehen mit, behandeln, erledigen	If you don't ~ problems, they will only get worse.
team [tiːm]	Gespann	
willful *(AE)* [ˈwɪlfl]	eigenwillig	
mule [mjuːl]	Maultier, Maulesel	
intersection *(AE)* [ɪntəˈsekʃn]	Kreuzung	a place where two or more roads meet or cross
to stop short [stɒp ˈʃɔːt]	plötzlich stehen bleiben	
breakdown [ˈbreɪkdaʊn]	Panne; Zusammenbruch	When a car stops and you can't start it again, you have a ~.
stale [steɪl]	muffig, schal, abgestanden	
peanut [ˈpiːnʌt]	Erdnuss	~ butter tastes good on toast.
sneaker [ˈsniːkə]	Freizeitschuh mit leiser Sohle	
knot [nɒt]	Knoten	
bubble gum [ˈbʌbl gʌm]	Blasenkaugummi	
still [stɪl]	still; reglos	
theme song [ˈθiːm sɒŋ]	Titelsong	
hip [hɪp]	Hüfte	Your leg is fixed to your body at the ~.

	ladies and gentlemen [ˌleɪdiz‿n‿ˈdʒentlmən]	meine Damen und Herren	
	ain't (= isn't) *(coll.)* [eɪnt]	ist nicht	
	purchase [ˈpɜːtʃəs]	Kauf	
	dutiful [ˈdjuːtifl]	pflichtbewusst, gehorsam	
	in the meantime [ɪn ðə ˈmiːntaɪm]	in der Zwischenzeit	during the time between one event and another
	folks [fəʊks]	Leute	
	yours truly [ˌjɔːz ˈtruːli]	ich höchstpersönlich	Talking about yourself, you can say 'yours truly is ...' instead of 'I am ...'.
	to **unlock** [ʌnˈlɒk]	aufschließen, entriegeln	to open with a key
	cash box [ˈkæʃbɒks]	Geldkassette	a metal box to keep money in
	cash [kæʃ]	Bargeld, Kleingeld	Sorry, we don't take ~. Only credit cards.
	to **straighten** [ˈstreɪtn]	gerade richten	to put straight
	stack [stæk]	Stapel	a pile of things like books or papers, one on top of another
	to swell* [swel]	anschwellen	
	puff [pʌf]	Zug an der Zigarette	
	stubborn [ˈstʌbən]	stur, störrisch, hartnäckig	
2	**task** [tɑːsk]	Aufgabe	an exercise or a job that you have to do

LANGUAGE

A1	**neighbor** *(AE)* [ˈneɪbə]	Nachbar(in)	
	comprehensive school *(BE)* [ˌkɒmprɪˈhentsɪv ˌskuːl]	Gesamtschule	*BE*: comprehensive school – *AE*: high school
	mark *(BE)* [mɑːk]	(Schul-)Note	*BE*: mark – *AE*: grade
	gray *(AE)* [greɪ]	grau	
B1	**although** [ɔːlˈðəʊ]	obwohl	I went swimming ~ it was raining.
	as soon as [əzˈsuːn‿əz]	sobald	I had a hot drink ~ I got back home.
	as [æz]	da	I needed it ~ I felt cold.
	sometime [ˈsʌmtaɪm]	irgendwann	something – somehow – ~
	so that [səʊ ˈðæt]	so dass, damit	I'm doing my homework now ~ I can watch TV later.
	since [sɪnts]	da	~ I'm so busy, I won't write a long letter.
	to **connect** [kəˈnekt]	verbinden, zusammenfügen	Links ~ things or people together.
	clause [klɔːz]	(Teil-)Satz	An 'if'-~ is a conditional ~.
	stranger [ˈstreɪndʒə]	Fremde(r)	so. you don't know at all
2	**Polish** [ˈpəʊlɪʃ]	polnisch	
C1	**afterwards** [ˈɑːftəwədz]	nachher, hinterher	Let's have a drink now, then go to the cinema ~.
2	to **break* down** [breɪk ˈdaʊn]	eine Panne haben; zusammenbrechen	to have a breakdown
3	**diner** *(AE)* [ˈdaɪnə]	Esslokal	dinner – dining-room – diner
D1	**duck** [dʌk]	Ente	a bird that likes water
	to **be* good at** *(+ gerund)* [gʊd]	gut können	Monkeys are good at climbing.
E1	**joke** [dʒəʊk]	Witz	It's a good one if it makes you laugh.
	e.g. [ˌiː ˈdʒiː]	(= exempli gratia) zum Beispiel	for example
3	**above** [əˈbʌv]	oben, oben genannt; oberhalb (von)	above ↔ below

SKILLS

	shade [ʃeɪd]	*hier:* Jalousie, Rollo	
	shower ['ʃaʊə]	Dusche; Schauer	Taking a ~ after sport feels great!
	to **shave** [ʃeɪv]	(sich) rasieren	If you don't like hair on your face or legs, you have to ~.
	refrigerator [rɪ'frɪdʒəreɪtə]	Kühlschrank	
	to raid [reɪd]	plündern, überfallen	
	processed food [ˌprəʊsest 'fu:d]	konservierte Nahrung	
	fork [fɔ:k]	Gabel	knife and ~
	uneven [ʌn'i:vn]	ungerade; uneben	1, 3, 5, etc. are ~ numbers.
	to **be* in love** [ɪn 'lʌv]	verliebt sein	to feel love for so.
	to **stand* in line** *(AE)* [ˌstænd‿ɪn 'laɪn]	Schlange stehen	To get on the bus, you often have to ~ until it's your turn.
	front [frʌnt]	vorderer Teil	
	restroom *(AE)* ['restru:m]	öffentliche Toilette	
	restroom attendant ['restru:m‿əˌtendənt]	Toilettenmann/-frau	
	to **waste** [weɪst]	verschwenden	You can ~ time, money, etc.
	to go* overboard on [gəʊ‿'əʊvəbɔ:d]	es übertreiben mit	
2	**rude** [ru:d]	unhöflich	polite ↔ rude
	coke [kəʊk]	Cola	a popular drink

CHECK-OUT

6	to busk [bʌsk]	Straßenmusik machen
	to jog [dʒɒg]	joggen, laufen

COGNATE WORDS

agent ['eɪdʒnt]	Agent(in), Vermittler(in)
apartment *(AE)* [ə'pɑ:tmənt]	Wohnung
to **arrange** [ə'reɪndʒ]	arrangieren, vereinbaren, ordnen, planen
chat [tʃæt]	Unterhaltung, Plauderei (auch im Internet)
to **chat** [tʃæt]	plaudern, chatten
chatroom ['tʃætru:m]	Chatroom (Forum im Internet, wo man sich online unterhalten kann)
cliché ['kli:ʃeɪ]	Klischee
color *(AE)* ['kʌlə]	Farbe
to **comment (on)** ['kɒmənt]	kommentieren, sich äußern
creative [kri'eɪtɪv]	kreativ
to **criticize** ['krɪtɪsaɪz]	kritisieren
cultural ['kʌltʃrəl]	kulturell
to **e-mail** ['i:meɪl]	jmdm eine E-Mail schreiben
fair [feə]	gerecht
to **form** [fɔ:m]	formen, bilden
limit ['lɪmɪt]	Grenze
mineral ['mɪnərəl]	Mineral, Mineral-
online [ˌɒn'laɪn]	online
personal ['pɜ:snəl]	persönlich
private ['praɪvət]	privat
rebel ['rebl]	Rebell(in)
rose [rəʊz]	Rose
sandwich ['sændwɪtʃ]	belegtes Brot
secretary ['sekrətri]	Sekretär(in)
single ['sɪŋgl]	Single; einzeln, einzig
social ['səʊʃl]	sozial; gesellschaftlich
to **sort** [sɔ:t]	sortieren
symbol ['sɪmbl]	Symbol
top [tɒp]	Spitzen-, Spitze
total ['təʊtl]	völlig, ganz
trend [trend]	Trend, Tendenz, Richtung

UNIT 2

New York, New York

So nice, you've got to say it twice? That's what many New Yorkers say. Actually, it's just the correct address: New York City in New York State. But it's one address many people would like to have!

1 New York scenes

a) *Look at the New York scenes on the right.*
Which of the pictures go with the descriptions here?
Example: I think number 1 is a description of scene H.

1. Chinatown, one of Manhattan's many ethnic districts.
2. Times Square, where Broadway crosses Seventh Avenue.
3. The best view is from the 110th floor of the World Trade Center.
4. Relax in Central Park and look up at the skyscrapers.
5. Early immigrants were welcomed by the Statue of Liberty as they sailed past it towards Ellis Island.
6. The United Nations Building overlooks the East River.
7. The Chrysler Building – even prettier than the Empire State!
8. Brokers at the Stock Exchange on Wall Street.

b) *Look at the maps of New York at the back of your book.*
1. Can you find B, C, E and G?
2. Nearly all of these scenes are from the most important part of the city. What is it? What are the others?
3. Work out how long it would take you to walk from Battery Park to the UN. (Yes, walk! Of course you could take a cab, or the subway, but walking is a great way to discover Manhattan!)

1 HV

2 A famous song: New York, New York (5)

There are hundreds of songs about New York, but this one is probably the most famous. It has been sung by many popular singers.

1. You don't need to understand everything. The words and phrases on the right will help you to get the gist. Try to guess what they mean, then look them up to check.
2. Listen to the song and say what New York means to the singer.
3. Would you like to be part of New York? In what way? *(Discuss your ideas in groups.)*

to spread the news
to long to stray
to be up to you
to make it
to melt away
to be (a) part of
doesn't sleep
vagabond shoes
brand new start
the very heart of
top of the heap
little town blues

B
GoldStar
SAMSUNG

C

D
E

CENTRAL PARK PRECINCT
POLICE

G

H
KAMKUO
HONG YING
RICE SHOPPE
WO-HOP

A Among the immigrants

(9-10)

From the 19th century on, New York was the gateway to the USA for most immigrants. At first the "immigrant receiving station" was in a building called Castle Garden, at the south end of Manhattan. It was moved in 1892 to the more famous Ellis island. The following is from an article published in a New York magazine in 1873. At the time, a lot of New Yorkers were getting worried about the growing numbers of immigrants arriving in their city.

1 Talking about the article

1. Pick out the nationalities the writer mentions – and the opinions he/she gives about them. How fair/unfair are these opinions?
2. What do you think the new immigrants were worried about and hoping for? Find where a problem is mentioned or suggested.

2 Find out!

Go and look for facts about immigrants to the USA today.

• In the lower part of Broadway, on our way down to the Battery, we met groups of immigrants, newly landed, walking slowly along the sidewalk, and looking with wonder on everything they saw. Trinity Church and the new Equitable Building seemed to be special objects of attention. I heard a German woman say of that building, "Das muss der Palast sein," an opinion that seemed to be shared by her companions. For a city without a "Palast" of some kind or other is not possible in Germany.

At last we passed through the iron gate into the Battery. Here the groups of immigrants became more frequent, and as we approached the entrance to Castle Garden, we found it almost not possible to make our way through, it was so crowded.

We showed our passports to the officer on duty, and were allowed into the yard, among a crowd of passengers, children, and baggage of all kinds. The steamer Holland, from Liverpool, had just arrived, and the passengers were being landed. Slowly, one by one, the newcomers passed the two officers who register every immigrant's name, birthplace and destination – a job that is often quite difficult. Some do not understand a word of English and can only speak Irish; but these are few, and are nearly always very old people.

On they passed, until a few steps further down they came to the railway counter. By buying a ticket here, a passenger will only pay the fair price, and get the full value for his money, if he pays in foreign money. It is too often the case that passengers buying their tickets in outside offices are shamefully swindled.

• Directly opposite the railway counter are the exchange brokers. A blackboard gives the rates at which foreign coin is exchanged. Whenever a change takes place on Wall Street it is reported to the brokers at the Garden, and the rate on the blackboard is changed. This often seems to confuse our foreign friends.

The German immigrants seem to be those who give the least trouble. They obey instructions, and try to help each other along. The Irish are a little more troublesome, from their many repeated questions. But the most troublesome are the Swedes. They are an excellent class of people, but cause a lot of trouble on arrival. In the first place, they smell of leather, salt fish and onions. Then they talk a language that none but a native Scandinavian can understand. They are also, by nature, rather suspecting.

Opposite the building is the Labor Exchange, with a separate entrance from the Battery. Not only immigrants, but anyone else who wants work, can apply here. Farm hands and mechanics have the best chance. Miners from Wales and other places are always needed. Next come laborers and gardeners. A great number of those looking for work are servant girls, and most of them are Irish.

B Cab cartoons

1 Taxis in New York

a) *Look at the cartoon on the right.*
1. Would you like to take a ride in this cab? Explain why or why not.
2. Imagine you are in the cab and you do something the driver doesn't like. Make up a dialogue.

b) There are lots of funny stories and cartoons about New York cab drivers – maybe because they are such an important part of New York life.
How many possible reasons can you find for this? Which do you think are most important? (short/long journeys? cars? parking problems? public transport? cheap/expensive? safe/dangerous?)

2 Another cab from hell (11-15)

A lot of New York cab drivers are either new immigrants, or students. *Discuss the problems this might cause, then read the comic strip.*

(from *Doonesbury* by Gary Trudeau © UPS)

1. Write out the story of the comic strip in a few sentences. Then compare your "short stories".
2. You know the words below, but they are used a bit differently in the comic strip. Find them there, and explain what they mean in the context.

to save	one way
to head	on me
hide-out	to step
pretty	

⟨3.⟩ Talk in groups/pairs about the passenger and the driver. *(Background/character/how they react, etc.)*

⟨4.⟩ The cartoon appeared in a daily newspaper, with one strip of four frames each day. There is at least one funny point in each strip. Find them.

⟨5.⟩ Write a letter of complaint for the passenger. Decide first who the letter is to. Some of you can write to the cab company, others to a newspaper.

Vocabulary 35,2 | Nouns 38

A Vocabulary

1 City streets – a mind map

This mind map looks like a real city. Copy it out and put in all the city words you can think of.

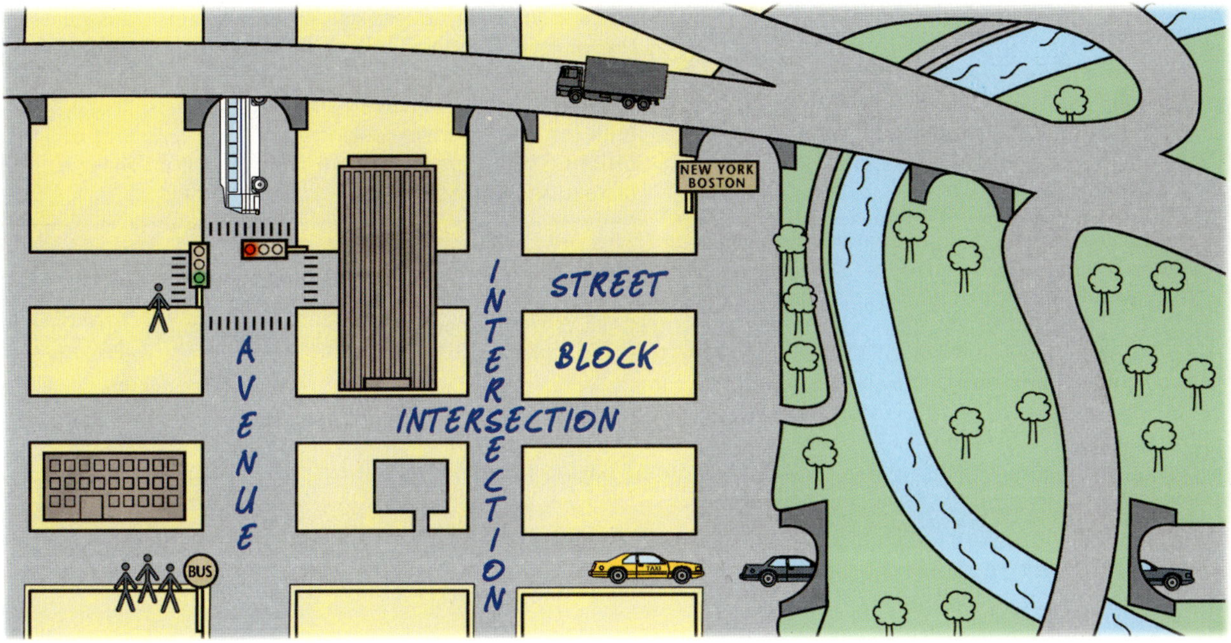

G 8.1

2 Sexist and non-sexist language

a) *Which of these words tell you the person's sex and which don't?*

aborigine; actor; actress; administrator; astronaut; athlete; aunt; author; baby; bandleader; beachgoer; beggar; bloke; bodyguard; boy; boyfriend; brother; businessman; cleaning lady; girl; girlfriend.

D *Make two lists and use your dictionary to complete them.*

b) *Look at lines 26-28 in the text on page 32.* How could the author be sure the passenger was a man? *Correct this first sentence so that it isn't sexist. Use the sentence which follows it* ("It is too often the case ...") *as a model. Then look at page 47 for some suggestions.*

c) *Now correct any of the following sentences which you think are sexist. (Don't use "he/him/his" or "she/her" unless you know the sex of the person.)*

1. The author must have been thinking of the passenger as a man – but how could he be sure?
2. That idiot of a cab driver took me all the way to Pennsylvania – and I only wanted to go to 53rd Street! She should lose her job!
3. The New York cab driver is known for his big mouth. So be prepared to listen politely to your driver's stories and agree with everything he says.
4. Every morning we find some bottles outside the door of our apartment building, left by some drunk, I suppose. He must sleep there every night!
5. If a customer wants to exchange anything, or wants her money back, we do what she wishes.

2

B Participles and infinitives

G 9 — 1 In Carmen's Café (I and II)

Participles (e.g. *broken, breaking*) can be used as adjectives. Such "describing" words are usually placed **before** the noun – but not always!

a) *Look at the adjectives and participles in part I of this story (right) and find rules for their position.*
b) *In part II (below), the marked nouns need describing words. But where do they belong – before or after?*

For a **hungry** man like me, the **little** restaurant on 23rd Street was an **inviting** sight. It looked like a **family-run** place. I could tell by the name **written over the door**: "Carmen's Café". I looked through the window. No sign of Carmen. But I noticed some **handwritten** signs on the window. I went in. All in all, it seemed a **friendly-looking** place. The **nice clean** tables gave a **good** impression – as did the **fresh-smelling** air – fresh, that is, until someone started cooking something **smelling of onions**. There were five or six other customers. I chose a table near the window.

I looked behind the counter to see who was cooking. The person was not Carmen, as I had expected, but a man. This was clear from the name. East European, I supposed. Hadn't been here too long either. When he spoke to the customers as he brought them their food (the thing, whatever it was), I could clearly hear that he had an accent.
The menu was short. The usual things, of course, but also a couple of omelettes, e.g. with chicken or cheese and onion (aha!). But I asked Viktor to make me the breakfast special – with eggs. "Sunny side up or easy over?" he asked. I like eggs, so I asked for "easy over".

working there
called Viktor
written on his shirt
seated at the next table
made with onions
very strong Russian
printed on a blackboard
interesting   fried
fried on both sides

G 10.1 — 2 In Carmen's Café (III)

Write the next part of the story yourselves – with the help of the pictures. For every picture, form a sentence like those in the SAVE box. But try to think of more sentences too, to make it a good story. You can start like this:
For a while, I watched Viktor … my breakfast.

SAVE

I can **feel** my heart **beating**.
He **saw** one of the boys **smiling** at him.
Present participle also possible after the verbs watch, hear, listen to, notice, look at, smell

Once inside, they went straight to the counter …

G 10.2

3 In Carmen's Café (IV)

Here are some phrases with verbs of movement or rest together with participles. Find where they belong in the last part of the story. Be careful to put the verb in the right form.

come asking	go unanswered
come running	sit watching
come marching	stand looking
remain seated	leave confused
remain uncooked	

What to do? I couldn't just ... there ... my breakfast burn up, could I? I went behind the counter and took the pan off the flame. I opened the door leading to a back room and ... there for a moment ... into the darkness. I called out, "Anyone there?" – but my words ... . I put the pan back on the flame, with the potatoes that had ... . While I was doing all this, the other customers had ... ... , just as they had done when the police had ... ... into the cafe and taken Viktor away. But now the two women from the next table ... ... to pay. I checked the prices on the board. Maybe I gave them too much money back – it seemed to ... them a bit ... . But I had no time to think, because just then two new customers ... ... in the door, demanding service. I'm going to have to get some help. I can't run this place on my own.

G 10.1

4 The tourist group: what they did today

a) *Read what these two tourists have to say about their day. Then try to explain the forms they use after verbs of perception.*

SAVE

I heard someone **shout** "Stop!"
I heard some people **shouting**.
The infinitive means you heard it all!

1. I went on a boat trip all round Manhattan. The weather was just right. After all that shopping in the city, it was great to feel the wind *blowing* through my hair. At the end of the trip we were able to watch the sun *go down* behind the skyscrapers.
2. We were on that boat too. Didn't you see us *sitting* near the back, right next to the lifebelts? We saw you *talking* most of the time to an Indian-looking man and *showing* him places on your map. For example, we saw you *point out* the Empire State Building as we passed it.

b) *Decide which form is best: present participle or infinitive? Explain why.*

1. I went on a bus tour through Harlem. Some of the streets looked very poor. We saw a lot of people just (*sit*) on the steps in front of their houses. And I noticed a gang of boys (*look*) a bit angry as we passed. I saw one of them (*try*) to kick our bus! But our guide then took us to a street where we watched a group of young black kids (*clean*) some old people's apartments. They were nice kids.
2. Jim and I went right to the top of the World Trade Center. The ride was so fast, you wouldn't believe it! But all the way up we couldn't even feel it (*move*). And then all of a sudden we were there – we hadn't even felt it (*stop*).
3. We got lost in the Lower East Side. I thought we were still in Little Italy, but we heard people (*speak*) a different language. A man noticed us (*look*) at our map and helped us. We'd wandered into Little Ukraine, he explained.

c) *And what do three more tourists have to say?*

1. take / Staten Island Ferry / great views / cheaper than ... / see / Queen Elizabeth / leave / harbour
2. Susan / want to go shopping / not so boring / see cops / arrest / man / catch / try to steal
3. CDs / New York Philharmonic / want to hear / play / own concert hall / tickets / tonight's concert / hear / perform / Beethoven's Fifth

C All about nouns

G 8.2-3

1 No place for the old?

The three people below all live in New York.

Try to complete what they are saying. The missing words mean either a group of people or a member of the group. (Some of them are in the SAVE box.)

SAVE

an old man/woman – old people – the old
Also: young, poor, rich (person, etc.)

an Irishman/woman – Irish people – the Irish
Also: English, French, etc.

a Korean – (the) Koreans (and others ending in -an)
a Chinese (person) – the Chinese (and others in -ese)

a police officer / a policeman/woman – the police

Clara Blumenfeld (85)

They say Manhattan is no place for … … . Most of my friends have died or moved to Florida. Not many … like me live in this building any more – the new immigrants are mostly from Asia. But it's home to me, and I'm staying. But … … are getting interested in this area and buying up old houses, so … … are being pushed out.

Hea Sukh Lee (20)

Most of the vegetable stores here are run by … like my parents. They came from Korea when I was a kid. They know now they will never be rich, that only … … have a chance to make it. So they are paying college fees for me and my brother. Our people work even harder than … …, though you may think all people from Asia are the same.

Jim Moloney (34)

When my great-great-grandfather came to New York from Ireland in the 1880s, he became … …, because that's what all … … did then. Since then, there's always been a Moloney in … … . I have a son and a daughter, and I hope one of them will become … … … .

R

2 Interesting facts

G 11

a) *Which genitive form is best – with "'s" or with "of"? (Add articles where you need them.)*

1. *Hudson River / name* comes from Henry Hudson, who sailed up there in 1609.
   Start: The name **of** the …
2. *island of Manhattan / original price* was about $24! It was bought from the Indians for *very cheap things / pile* in 1626.
3. A slave market was opened at *Wall Street / east end* in 1711.
4. *R.H. Macy / Department Store* – "the largest store in the world" – was opened in 1858.
5. *Liberty / Statue* was put up in 1886. It was given to the US by France.
6. Many Americans lost all their money in *1929 / famous Wall Street Crash.*
7. From 1931 to 1974, the Empire State Building was *the city / highest building.*
   Now *the World Trade Center / two towers* are highest.

b) *Try to find out more about the city's history!*

D Visiting New York

G 12 1 A snack at the deli

New York delis are famous for their huge, monster sandwiches filled with different kinds of food on many different kinds of bread.

a) *In this "deli dialogue", how is the article "a/an" used – or not used? What is used instead of an article with some nouns? Try to find a rule.*

"Let's go and have a sandwich and some coffee in that deli. It's one of the best in New York. It's such a good place that it was written up in a magazine! It has such good food they voted it number one for something. Pastrami, I think."

"But I haven't got any cash with me, only a credit card – and I don't know if they take them."

"Oh, I'm sure they do. Anyway, I've got quite a lot of cash with me. Oh, come on!"

b) *Now play the roles and continue the dialogue in groups of three. (The third person is the waiter.) What do you use with the nouns for the things you order?*

- the indefinite article (a/an)?
- some/any?
- nothing (if nothing is needed)?

sandwiches: pastrami/chicken/cheese on white/brown/rye bread

to drink: tea/coffee/water
a cup/glass of …

– OK. I'd love …
  – Me too. / I think I'll have … / Let's see …
– Look at that one over there – it's …
  – Wow, it must have …! Looks great /…!
– But I don't think I can …! Would you share …?
  – OK, … . / Oh, no, I want … … …

– Hi, my name's … Have you decided …?
– Would you like …?
– We've got … / The … is …
– On what kind of …?
… …

R G 13 2 Planning their trip

A group of people from Montana are planning a weekend in New York. There are a lot of things they are not sure about, or can't agree on.

"It's cheaper to stay in the Bronx, **isn't it?**" – "But we don't want to stay there, **do we?**"

What else do they say? Use some of these ideas:

said you wanted to …
stay with Aunt Margaret
buy the plane tickets
see a game at Yankee Stadium
be serious
go shopping on Saturday

buy our theater tickets now
go dancing every night
do everything together
go to an all-night music club
stay a bit longer
call it "the city that never sleeps"

…, can we?
…, are you?
…, didn't you?
…, aren't there?
…, hasn't he?
…, don't they?
…, mustn't we?
…, do we?

Creative writing

Not everybody can be a Shakespeare – good at all of the things on the right. But most of you are talented at one or two of them. In group exercises you can find out what you are good at – and get better at it. Or you can try to improve your weak points. But the most important thing is to have fun doing it!

having good ideas
inventing characters
working out a plot
making up dialogues
describing scenes
writing clever or funny lines
finding rhymes and rhythms
playing with words

1 Characters

If you want to write a story or a dialogue, you should first make sure you know your characters. When you know how old they are, where they grew up, what they are afraid of, etc., it's a lot easier to know what they are likely to do in any situation.

a) *Look at the three people in exercise 1 on page 38. They tell you quite a lot about themselves. Imagine them in the following situations:*
1. The owner of the building tells Clara she must buy her apartment or move out. What does she say?
2. Jim's son says the New York police are all corrupt, and his daughter wants to be a pop star. What does he say to them?
3. Hea Sukh wanted one of the few free places at law school. She did better in the exam than the black boy who got the place. (The law school wants 10 % black students.) Write Hea Sukh's letter.

b) *You can also invent some characters of your own. Where do you start? – Anywhere! For example, look at exercise 2 on page 39. You are not told much about the people. Who are they? It's up to you!*

In groups, think about the sentences you made up, and decide what kind of person asks each question:

- Are they a family? – a group of friends? – a school class? – a sports group? …?
- Are all the questions asked by different people?
- What is their relationship?
- Are some of the people disagreeing with each other. Why?

When you have agreed what their sex is, how old they are, what their jobs and interests are, etc., – give them names. This makes them seem real. If you wish, you can invent one or two more members of the group as well.

c) *Now talk about what these people would say or do in these situations in New York:*
1. A famous person is checking into their hotel at the same time as they are.
2. One of them wants to take all the others to some "really wonderful" place.
3. Two of them get "taken for a ride" by a crazy New York taxi driver.

Break into smaller groups. Each writes a short dialogue for one of these situations.

⟨d)⟩ *If one of the dialogues is very funny or interesting in some way, the group may want to turn it into a proper story – with "he said/asked/", "she suggested/shouted", etc. But first look at exercise 2.*

2 Point of view

a) *Practise telling a story in the first person. Take the "Cab from hell" story, pp. 33–34, and write what happened as if you were the driver – or the passenger. That is your point of view. You can't know what the other person is thinking, only what they do and say. But you can guess!*

- I got into this cab the other day on East 46th Street. I only wanted to go to East 53rd Street, but the driver – a young woman – drove west at first. I protested, but she seemed sure ...
- This old guy got into my cab on 46th Street one day. He was making me real nervous from the start with all his questions, so I made a little mistake at ...

b) *Now change your story to the third person: Replace all the first person words ("I", "me", "my", etc.), with "he/him/his" or "she/her", etc. Don't change anything else, so that you keep the same point of view.*

The best way to tell a story in the third person: Choose one point of view, and keep to it!

3 Beginnings ...

How about trying a poem? Topic: climbing all 1,860 steps of the Empire State Building.
Work in pairs.

a) *Make up a first line with the words "climb" and "Empire State" in it. Make sure it has a good rhythm.*
For example: - • - • - • - • *or:* - • - - • - - • - .
Maybe you can make it a rap!

b) *What is the last word? Can you find rhymes for it? (Maybe one will do.) If not, you may wish to change it.*

c) *Now go on from there. You can make it a story about climbing all 1,860 steps, for example. Do you want it to be about one of yourselves or somebody else?*

Tip: You can make lines about the different things that the climber did/felt/saw at "step 79/step 842/...", etc. It's easy to find rhymes for number words!

"I start at the beginning, go to the end, and then stop."
Anthony Burgess

"I always know the ending. That's where I start."
Toni Morrison

"I have never started a poem yet whose end I knew. Writing a poem is discovering."
Robert Frost

"I always write my last line first."
Katherine Anne Porter

4 ... and endings

There are many ways to start a story or a poem. Look at what some famous writers (above right) have said! *Try starting with the ending. Form groups. Each group chooses* ***one*** *of these lines:*

1. ... And Samantha never saw him again.
2. ... But where the little café had been, there was now a video shop.
3. ... Could it really be true, she wondered. Had she finally made it?
4. ... Now the lights of Broadway hurt her eyes.
5. ... Jack hoped none of the others would ever find out what really happened.

The group then works out a story that leads up to that last line.
Think: What characters are in that last line? How many others do you need?
Has something gone wrong, or is it a happy ending?
Where did it all happen? From whose point of view will you tell it?

2

1 What an article!

Why is crime down?

So you think New York is the world capital of crime? Well, a few years ago, you would have been right. But since then, crime has gone down in all big U.S. cities. In New York, there has been such a fall in the number of crimes that even the experts are confused. And we are talking about

[1]*die Rücksichtslosen;* [2]*Mörder;* [3]*geschätzt;* [4]*Mord;* [5]*Täter*

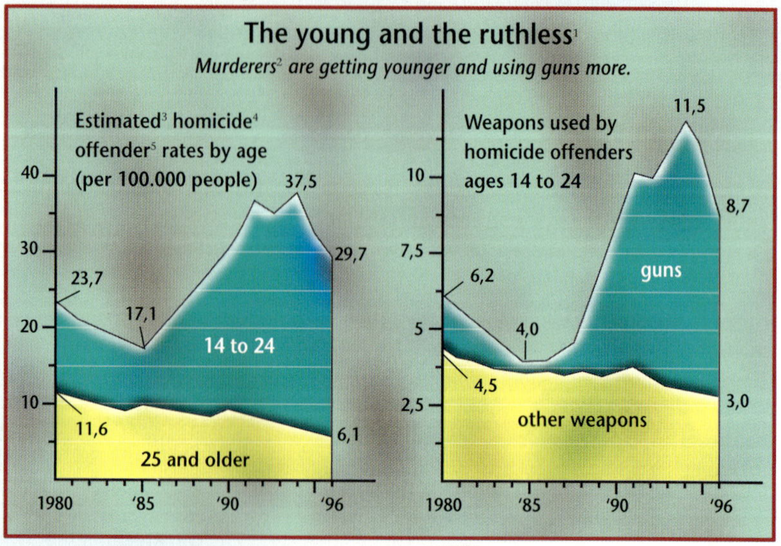

This is the beginning of a magazine article. To understand the rest of it you must first put in the missing articles ("a"/"an" or "the"). But be careful – you don't always need one!

And we are talking about ... crime of all kinds: There are fewer killings, fewer cars are stolen, there are fewer bank robbers in action. But nobody is sure why.

Some say it's because ... police are doing ... better job. This may be ... part of ... story in New York, where every police officer is told to stop even ... small crimes like ... graffiti and ... loud radios. But there has been no change in ... police work in ... other cities.

Others say it's because ... business is better, and more people are working – they have no time for ... crime! But in New York, ... number of people out of work remains at a very high 9 percent.

To understand why ... crime is down, you need to know why it got so high in ... 1980s. We think ... reason was ... crack. This drug is made from ... cocaine, ... favorite drug of ... rich. It is even stronger than ... cocaine, but could be had for ... quite ... low price. Even ... poor could buy it. Even ... school kids could buy it!

So there were ... dealers on every street corner in Harlem and ... Bronx; ... young people were doing ... same thing in ... schools. They needed ... guns, because they were carrying such ... lot of ... money. And ... guns in ... hands of ... young means killing.

But in ... late 1990s, ... kids have turned away from ... crack. Why? We're not sure, but think it's ... "younger brothers" who are behind it. They see ... older brother who is sick, in ... jail, or in ... wheelchair after some shooting. "Today, ... young people have decided that ... crack is not cool," says ... expert. If this is true, it's ... good news.

(from: *U.S. News and World Report*, May 25, 1998, adapted)

2 Understanding the article

a) The author gives many possible reasons for what has happened in New York. *Pick them out, then make a list, like this:*

Reason	right/wrong
police do a better job	

b) *Correct anything wrong in the sentences on the right. Also correct any wrong use of* he/him/his/she/her.

1. The experts cannot explain why there are so many crimes in New York.
2. A New York police officer who ignores a small crime might be in trouble with his boss.
3. The improving business situation means that finding work is no longer a problem in New York.
4. Cocaine is expensive.
5. There were gun dealers on every street corner.
6. A younger brother who sees what crack can do is less likely to spend his money on the drug.
7. The author thinks it is good news that crack has got cheaper, because she uses it herself.

3 Changes

Look at the diagram on page 42.
What information does it give you?
Write at least five sentences.

in 1980 (1996) there were … killings done by …
the number of … went up/down in …
was nearly the same from … to …
got much higher
was going down all the time
began to fall
was highest/lowest in …

4 Who are they?

Give the words or phrases for these persons or groups of people:

1. the group of people whose job it is to stop crime
2. a man or woman who works for them
3. someone who does hard work on the streets or the buildings
4. a worker who looks after the flowers in Central Park
5. someone who buys and sells money etc. on Wall Street
6. a person whose job it is to drive people where they want to go
7. a person from Sweden
8. a person who has come to New York from Sweden or Denmark
9. all the people from Germany
10. a woman from Ireland
11. people who have lots and lots of money
12. one person who has a lot of money
13. someone who is old

5 Voices

a) *Put the participle in the right place – before or after the noun?*

A lot of the bank robbers in the city use cars. And we often find the cars later, just left in the street or pushed into the river. That car was one, I'm sure. And here's another fact: the people are getting younger and younger. Of course some of them are just teenagers.

stolen
used by bank robbers
found in the East River
interesting/stealing cars
having fun

b) *Complete the sentences with verb/participle phrases. Choose the verbs and participles from the box on the left and put the verbs in the right form:*

leave
come
unpunished
unrepaired
running

Yesterday two police officers … … across the park to stop one boy with a loud radio. He had to pay $50! I think they're going too far.

I don't agree. Broken windows … … lead to more broken windows. They show no one cares. Small crimes … … are the same.

c) *Put in the present participle or the infinitive of the verb:*

I noticed a gang … (work) in the subway yesterday. I saw one of them … (pull) something from a woman's back bag and … (give) it to the others. The woman was looking the other way, and didn't seem to feel it … (be) taken! I called the police on my phone, but they heard me … (dial) the number and jumped out at the next station.

6 Back in charge

1. Can you work out what part of New York the picture shows?
2. What do you know about this part of the city?
3. Why do you think the people in the picture look so proud?

Members of the 161st Street block association in Manhattan near a closed-down crack house

2

CHECK-IN

1	**floor** [flɔ:]	Stockwerk, Etage; Boden	From the top ~ you get a good view.
	skyscraper ['skaɪskreɪpə]	Wolkenkratzer	a very tall building
	(exchange) broker [ɪks'tʃeɪndʒ ˌbrəʊkə]	Börsenmakler(in), Devisenhändler(in)	Would you like to work as a(n) ~ on Wall Street?
	to **take** [teɪk]	dauern, (Zeit) brauchen	It ~s me ten minutes to walk to school. The walk ~s ten minutes.
	cab [kæb]	Taxi	another word for a taxi, especially in *AE*
	subway *(AE)* ['sʌbweɪ]	U-Bahn	*BE*: underground – *AE*: subway
2	to make* it ['meɪk‿ɪt]	es schaffen	
	to **melt (away)** [melt]	schmelzen	Snow ~s when the weather gets warm.
	vagabond ['vægəbɒnd]	Vagabund	
	brand new [ˌbrænd 'nju:]	brandneu	
	start [stɑ:t]	Anfang, Start	
	the very heart [ˌveri 'hɑ:t]	Kern	
	top of the heap [ˌtɒp‿əv ðə 'hi:p]	der/die Beste	

TEXTS

A	**century** ['sentʃəri]	Jahrhundert	There are a hundred years in a ~.
	gateway ['geɪtweɪ]	Tor	'the garden gate' – but: 'the ~ to success'
	to **publish** ['pʌblɪʃ]	veröffentlichen, verlegen	public – to publish
	to be **worried** ['wʌrid]	besorgt sein	to worry – to be worried
	sidewalk *(AE)* ['saɪdwɔ:k]	Gehsteig	*BE*: pavement – *AE*: sidewalk
	wonder ['wʌndə]	Verwunderung	
	to **share** [ʃeə]	teilen	Two (or more) people can ~ an opinion, ~ a room, etc.
	for [fɔ:]	denn	'~' is more formal than 'because'.
	entrance ['entrənts]	Eingang	the way in
	passport ['pɑ:spɔ:t]	(Reise-)Pass	If you travel to certain countries you need a ~.
	yard [jɑ:d]	Hof	a place outside, often behind a building, sometimes with walls round it
	steamer ['sti:mə]	Dampfer	
	birthplace ['bɜ:θpleɪs]	Geburtsort	
	destination [destɪ'neɪʃn]	Reiseziel, Bestimmungsort	where you are travelling to
	by *(+ gerund)* [baɪ]	durch, indem	learning ~ doing
	value ['vælju:]	Wert	Different coins have different ~s.
	foreign ['fɒrɪn]	ausländisch	from a country that is not your own
	shameful ['ʃeɪmfl]	schändlich	
	to swindle ['swɪndl]	betrügen, beschummeln	
	rate [reɪt]	Rate, Kurs	The value of foreign money is decided by the ~ of exchange.
	whenever [wen'evə]	jedesmal wenn; wann auch immer	~ you visit a foreign country, you learn sth. new.
	to **obey** [əʊ'beɪ]	gehorchen, befolgen	If you ~ instructions, you do what you are told to do.
	troublesome ['trʌblsəm]	schwierig, lästig	
	Swede [swi:d]	Schwede/Schwedin	so. from Sweden

	onion ['ʌnjən]	Zwiebel	Cutting an ~ can make you cry.
	to suspect [sʌs'pekt]	verdächtigen, misstrauen	
	farm hand ['fɑ:m hænd]	Landarbeiter(in)	so. who helps on a farm
	anyone ['eniwʌn]	jeder (beliebige)	~ can learn a language, it just takes some time.
	to **apply (for)** [ə'plaɪ]	sich bewerben (um/auf/für)	So. who wants work must ~ for a job.
	miner ['maɪnə]	Bergarbeiter(in)	A ~ works under the surface of the earth.
	laborer *(AE)* ['leɪbrə]	ungelernte(r) Arbeiter(in), Hilfsarbeiter(in)	so. who does work which does not need any special skill
	gardener ['gɑ:dnə]	Gärtner(in)	so. who works in gardens and parks
1	to **suggest** [sə'dʒest]	andeuten, suggerieren, vorschlagen	to make a hint at sth., or to offer an idea
B1	**ride** [raɪd]	Fahrt, Ritt	to ride – rider – ride
	U-turn ['ju:tɜ:n]	Kehrtwende	You aren't allowed to make a ~ on the motorway
	turn [tɜ:n]	Abbiegen	'No left ~s' means you aren't allowed to ~ left.
	to **turn** [tɜ:n]	abbiegen	
	package ['pækɪdʒ]	Paket	another word for a parcel
2	to **save** [seɪv]	sparen	If you ~ money, you don't spend so much.
	one way ['wʌnweɪ]	Einbahn-	~ streets can make driving in a big city difficult.
	lane [leɪn]	Spur	Roads are often divided into different ~s.
	damn [dæm]	verdammt	
	to **pick up** [pɪk‿'ʌp]	hochheben, abholen; *hier:* übernehmen	I'll pick you up at seven in front of your house.
	toll [təʊl]	Maut, Gebühr	money you have to pay to drive on certain roads
	to **head to/for** [hed]	zusteuern auf	Where are we going to? = Where are we heading (for)?
	on me [ɒn 'mi:]	auf meine Kosten/Rechnung	
	to **rip so. off** *(sl.)* [rɪp 'ɒf]	ausnehmen, schröpfen	to make so. pay too much money for sth.
	to **misread** [mɪs'ri:d]	falsch lesen	to read – to misread
	hide-out ['haɪdaʊt]	Versteck	
	mid-Atlantic states [mɪdət,læntɪk 'steɪts]	Staaten an der Ostküste der USA	
	brights *(AE)* [braɪts]	Fernlicht	
	to have* no consideration [hæv ,nəʊ kənsɪdə'reɪʃn]	keine Rücksicht nehmen	
	to **step in** [step‿'ɪn]	eintreten, einsteigen	step – to step – to step in
	Philly ['fɪli]	Philadelphia	
	dispatch *(AE)* [dɪ'spætʃ]	Taxizentrale	
	direction [dɪ'rekʃn]	Richtung, *Pl.:* Wegbeschreibung, Anweisungen, Hinweise	If you don't know your way in town, you can ask so. for ~s.
	plaza ['plɑ:zə]	Piazza, Gebäudekomplex	
	fare [feə]	Fahrpreis, Fahrgast	the money you pay for a ride, or: the passenger in a cab.
	meter ['mi:tə]	Zähler, Taxameter	The ~ shows you how much you must pay the cab driver.
	affirmative *(AE)* [ə'fɜ:mətɪv]	*hier:* ja	
	pretty ['prɪti]	ziemlich	~ good = quite good
	sob [sɒb]	schluchz!	
	I can't take (it) any more! [aɪ ,kɑ:nt 'teɪk‿ɪt‿eni mɔ:]	Ich halte das nicht mehr aus!	

to **calm down** [kɑ:m 'daʊn]	sich beruhigen	Before you can relax, you have to ~.
buddy *(AE)* ['bʌdi]	Kumpel	
booth [bu:θ]	Bude, Stand, Kabine, *hier:* Zahlstelle	
background ['bækgraʊnd]	Hintergrund, Herkunft	Questions about your ~: Where are you from? What school did you go to?
daily ['deɪli]	täglich, Tages-	
complaint [kəm'pleɪnt]	Beschwerde, Klage	

LANGUAGE

A2 **sex** [seks]	Geschlecht	The word 'cab driver' doesn't tell you which ~ the person is.
B1 **impression** [ɪm'preʃn]	Eindruck	to press – expression – impression
menu ['menju:]	Speisekarte	! Watch the stress here!
cheese [tʃi:z]	Käse	~ is made from milk.
special ['speʃl]	Sonderangebot, Angebot des Tages	a special meal for a special price
3 **movement** ['mu:vmənt]	Bewegung	to move – movement
to **march** [mɑ:tʃ]	marschieren	to walk like soldiers
to be **seated** ['si:tɪd]	sitzen, sich setzen	They didn't stand up. They remained seated.
pan [pæn]	Pfanne	You can fry an egg in it.
darkness ['dɑ:knəs]	Dunkelheit	dark – darkness
4 **perception** [pə'sepʃn]	Wahrnehmung	verbs of ~: to see, to hear, to watch, etc.
to **blow*** [bləʊ]	wehen, blasen	It can get cold when the wind ~s.
to **point out** [pɔɪnt‿'aʊt]	zeigen auf, hinweisen	to show, often with the help of a finger
C1 **Irishman/woman** ['aɪrɪʃmən/ˌwʊmən]	Ire/Irin	so. from Ireland
Korean [kə'ri:ən]	Koreaner(in)	so. from Korea
college ['kɒlɪdʒ]	Hochschule, Universität; Institut	a kind of university; part of a university
college fees [ˌkɒlɪdʒ 'fi:z]	Studiengebühren	money that has to be paid if you go to college
D1 **deli** *(AE)* ['deli]	Delikatessen-, Feinkostgeschäft	They have great food at the ~.
pastrami [pəs'trɑ:mi]	Pastrami *(eine jüdische Rauchfleischspezialität)*	a kind of smoked beef
rye [raɪ]	Roggen	~ bread is especially popular in Germany.

SKILLS

weak [wi:k]	schwach	strong ↔ weak
plot [plɒt]	Handlung (eines Romans, Theaterstücks)	the main events in a story or play and how they are put together
1 **exam** [ɪg'zæm]	Prüfung	an official test, often taken at school or college
2 **point of view** [ˌpɔɪnt‿əv'vju:]	Standpunkt, Sicht, Perspektive	You can always tell a story from a different ~.

	the other day [ði‿ˌʌðə 'deɪ]	neulich	! the other day ≠ am anderen Tag
3	**ending** ['endɪŋ]	Schluss, Ausgang, Ende	Did the film have a happy ~?

CHECK-OUT

1	**crime** [kraɪm]	Verbrechen	Stealing is just one example of ~.
	gun [gʌn]	Schusswaffe	A ~ can be even more dangerous than a knife.
	jail [dʒeɪl]	Gefängnis	People who get involved in crime often have to go to ~.
5	to **punish** ['pʌnɪʃ]	bestrafen	One way to ~ people is to send them to jail.
6	association [əˌsəʊʃi'eɪʃn]	Verband	

COGNATE WORDS

block [blɒk]	(Häuser-)Block
boss [bɒs]	Chef(in), Boss, Vorgesetzte(r)
clown [klaʊn]	Clown
cocaine [kəʊ'keɪn]	Kokain
control [kən'trəʊl]	Kontrolle
corrupt [kə'rʌpt]	korrupt, verdorben, bestechlich
crack [kræk]	Crack
dealer ['di:lə]	Händler(in), *hier:* Dealer(in), Drogenhändler(in)
diagram ['daɪəgræm]	Diagramm
district ['dɪstrɪkt]	Distrikt, Bezirk, Stadtviertel
ethnic ['eθnɪk]	ethnisch, einer bestimmten Volks-gruppe zugehörig
flame [fleɪm]	Flamme
gang [gæŋ]	Gang, Bande
to **land** [lænd]	landen, von Bord gehen
nervous ['nɜ:vəs]	nervös
newcomer ['nju:kʌmə]	Neuling, Neuankömmling
omelette ['ɒmlet]	Omelett
to **park** [pɑ:k]	parken
professional [prɒ'feʃnl]	professionell
to **protest** [prə'test]	protestieren
Scandinavian [ˌskændɪ'neɪviən]	Skandinavier(in)
sexist ['seksɪst]	sexistisch

Man or woman? – How to avoid sexist language

a) Some nouns clearly tell you the sex of the person in question: e.g. *girl/boy, aunt/uncle, queen/king.* Sometimes different endings are used for the different sexes, e.g. *actor/actress.* You can also change *-man* into *-woman*: e.g. *businessman/businesswoman.* Or just put *'female'* (dt. weiblich) or *'male'* (dt. männlich) in front of the noun.

b) With some nouns, however, you cannot be sure about the person's sex unless the context gives you a clue: e.g. *athlete, guide, shopper.* If you do not know the person's sex and if you cannot tell from the context, you should not just use one sort of pronoun, *'he/him/his'* or *'she/her'*, but both:
"We are going to have a guide in New York." – "I hope he or she will tell us where all the stars live."
If you use pronouns like *everyone/-body, someone/-body, anyone/-body, no-one/-body*, you can also use *'they/their/them'* instead of *'he or she …'*:
"Has everybody got their bags? Then let's go!"
"Could somebody put their clothes on and get some milk, please?"

UNIT 3

Planet Earth

- to save
- oil
- natural resources
- sunlight
- plant and animal life
- water
- national parks
- hurricanes
- environmental groups
- floods

to use up

natural disasters

natural habitat

population control

energy

human beings

the environment

pollution

air

The environment means everything that surrounds us: not just plant and animal life, but also the air, the sunlight and the water we need. Humans have existed for many thousands of years. For a long time they thought that Earth's natural resources would never be used up. Even prehistoric life affected the environment. People killed animals for food and built fires for cooking and to keep themselves warm. And they cut down trees for their fires.

In prehistoric times, human activities had little impact on the environment. In modern times, the world's population has been growing very fast. In 1850 there were around a billion people in the world. Now, with six billion, the things we do can affect the environment dramatically.

1 Organizing the ideas

Try to organize the ideas on this double page into a mind map. What key words would you start with? Add extra information where you can.

2 Listening comprehension: Rock around the clock (6)

A million years is hard to imagine, but think of the Earth's history as a single day. Each minute on this 24-hour clock stands for about three million years.

a) *Listen to the recording. Which of the pictures (below) goes with which number in the box? Work with a partner.*

b) *Talk about what happened in the last second and then write a final part for the recording.*

No.	Years ago	Time
1	4.5 billion	midnight
2	3.96 billion	3:20 a.m.
3	500 million	9:23 p.m.
4	190 million	11:00 p.m.
5	80 million	11:35 p.m.
6	6 million	11:58 p.m.
7	1.8 million	11:59:26 p.m.
8	750,000	11:59:45 p.m.
9	20,000	11:59:59 p.m.

A Here comes Hurricane Irene (16-17)

Before you read the article: Close your eyes and imagine a hurricane coming through your town. What do you feel? What do you hear? What does the place look like afterwards? Write down all the words that come into your head.

Irene tests evacuation-weary residents

By Larry Copeland
USA TODAY
Rocky Mount, N.C.

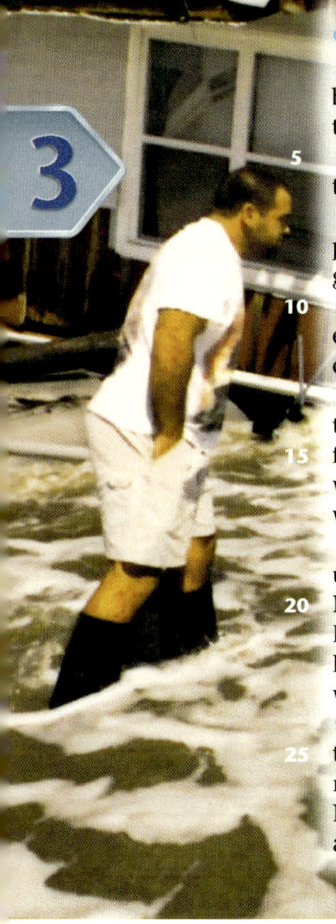

Eva Gray, forced out of her flooded home by Hurricane Floyd a month ago, had just begun to settle into life in a trailer park outside town when the alarm came again last weekend.

Hurricane Irene was headed this way, and it was time to evacuate again.

So she and about 200 other families at the trailer park packed up and headed to shelter on higher ground.

"It's been rough," Gray, 31, said. "It seems like every time you try to get settled, something else comes up."

"You never rest no more," Gray said, sitting on a tiny couch inside the trailer that's been her home for nearly a month. "You've got to constantly watch TV, seeing what the river's going to do, whether a hurricane's coming through."

Gray's trailer and the others will be provided for up to 18 months by the Federal Emergency Management Agency, FEMA spokeswoman Susan Brandt said. But the trailers' risk of toppling in hurricane winds was judged too great over the weekend, so residents were moved to a shelter.

Gray was back in the trailer Monday, after the threat had passed from the third hurricane to menace the area in two months. Storm-weary North Carolinians might find themselves tested again: Tropical Storm Jose formed Monday, and forecasters said it could become a hurricane Wednesday.

"When I heard that, I said some words people probably didn't know I could say," said Gray, who said she hasn't worked since Hurricane Floyd.

Across eastern North Carolina, about 6,000 residents whose homes were damaged by flooding from Floyd are still waiting to return home. And they're still worried about further flooding this week.

Most of the 49 deaths caused by Floyd in North Carolina were the result of flooding.

Edgecombe County got about 6 inches of rain from Hurricane Irene, officials said.

That was more than enough for Kelvin Pell, 43.

He had left his flooded home in Princeville for a shelter, then had left the shelter for the trailer park. As Hurricane Irene approached, Pell had to leave once more, although he intends to return to his home when authorities say Princeville can be lived in again.

"Just when you think you're getting settled, bam, you have to go again," Pell said. "When I left, I didn't know whether to take my stuff or leave my stuff.

So I took some of it and left some of it."

1 True or false?

Check the statements and correct the false ones.

1. When the alarm came again Eva Gray went to shelter in a trailer park.
2. The trailer has been Eva's home for four weeks.
3. She hasn't worked for six weeks.
4. FEMA is short for the Federal Emergency Management Agency.
5. There were three hurricanes in four months.
6. About 6,000 residents intend to return to their damaged homes.
7. Kelvin Pell packed all his stuff when he left.

2 Talking points

1. Why do the people intend to return to their homes? Wouldn't it be better if they left the area forever?
2. Imagine you had to leave your flooded home.
   – Where would you go?
   – What would you do?
   – What would you take with you?
3. What about the area you live in? What kinds of disaster have happened there?

B Protecting our water

a) *Make a list of all the things you use water for. Compare your list with your partner's.*
b) *Now read the following texts. Then explain which one you found most effective and why.*

A waterpoem

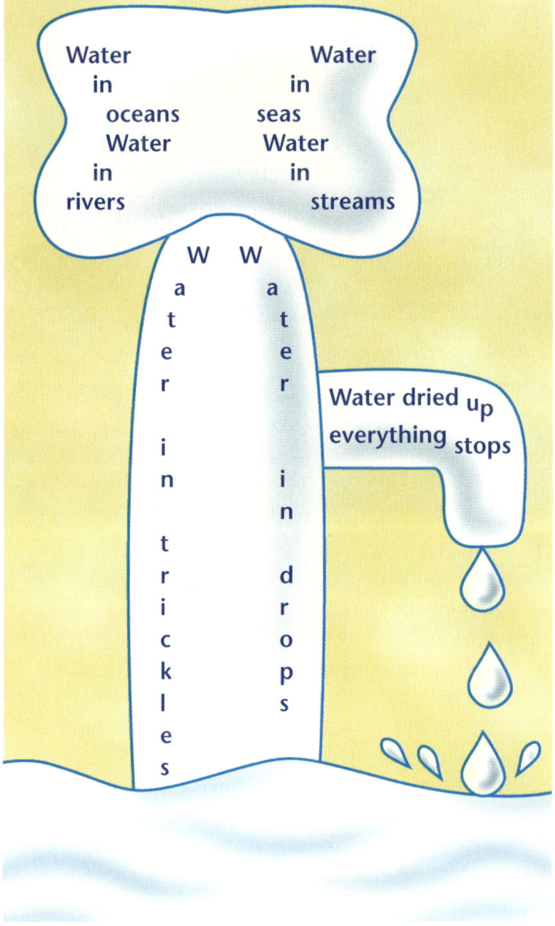

Facts about water

- Over 97 % of the Earth's water is salt water. About 2 % is the ice around the north and south poles. Less than 1 % is fresh water available for human use.
- Humans need to take in about three litres of water a day from eating and drinking.
- The average American uses over 700 litres of water a day for things like cooking, washing, flushing, and watering plants.
- About 74 % of the water used at home is used in the bathroom, about 21 % for laundry and cleaning, and about 5 % is used in the kitchen.

Major threats to our water

Water pollution. Water is polluted when it cannot be used for drinking, swimming, watering crops or providing a habitat. Polluted water can cause disease and kill fish and other animals. Sewage, chemicals from factories and fertilizers on fields are the main causes of water pollution.
To reduce water pollution, some lakes are being cleaned up enough to restore plants and fish to them. Companies continue to look for better ways to dispose of waste, and many farmers are trying to grow crops without using fertilizers or chemicals.
Overuse of water. Another major threat to our water supply is overuse. It is important to save as much water as possible. Some modern toilets and shower heads are designed to use less water. Many people take shorter showers, and they don't let the water run when they brush their teeth.

1 What water is needed for

Use these pictures to explain the importance of water. Add examples of your own.

Example: Water is needed for cooking.

Language 54-55

SB

C Hoover Dam

(18-19)

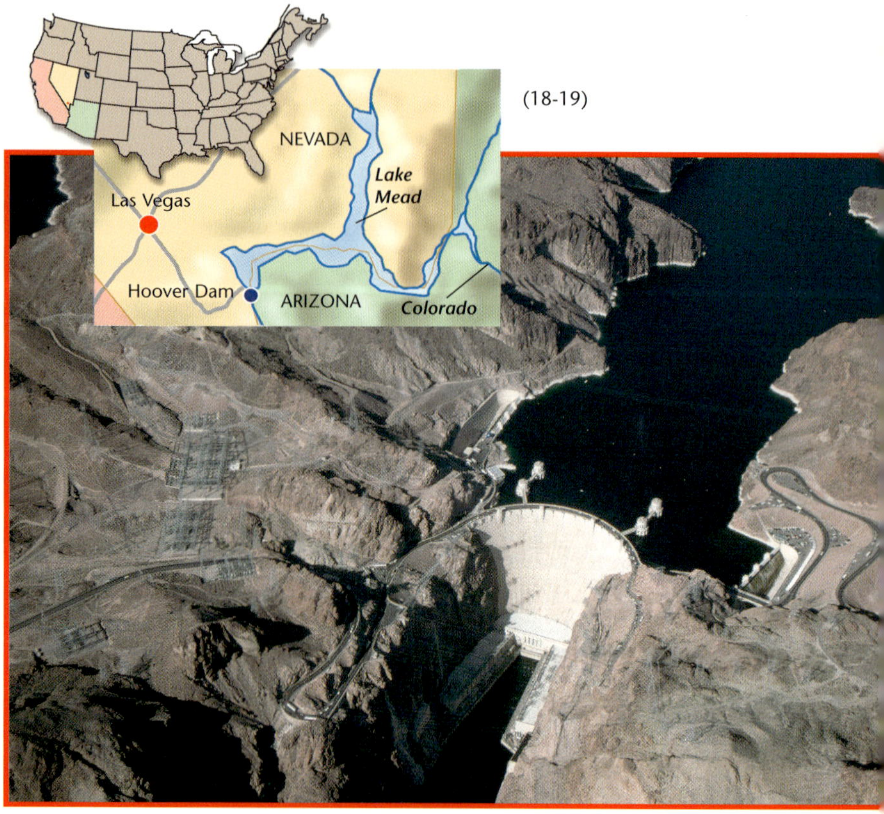

• For millions of years the Colorado River flowed through the dry lands of the American west. In the 1800s and early 1900s the river often flooded low-lying farmland when the snow melted in spring and early summer. But in late summer it often dried to a trickle. To protect the low-lying lands from flooding, and to provide a year-round water supply, the river needed to be controlled. Construction of Hoover Dam (named for Herbert Hoover, the 31st President of the United States) began in 1931 and was completed in 1936.

• With the reservoir (Lake Mead) and river control provided by Hoover Dam, residents of the southwest can use the Colorado waters for many purposes:

Irrigation of a million acres of America's richest crop lands and large areas in Mexico. These lands grow fruit, vegetables and cotton.

Providing water for over 18 million people in Las Vegas, Los Angeles, San Diego, Phoenix, Tucson and other cities in Arizona, Nevada, and California.

Generating cheap hydroelectric power: Hoover Dam generates more than four billion kilowatt-hours a year – enough for 1.3 million people.

Recreation: Lake Mead is one of America's top recreation areas, attracting more than nine million visitors each year for swimming, boating, fishing and other water-related sports.

Wildlife refuges have been developed along the lower river to replace habitat lost with the construction of the dam. Environmental issues were not under discussion when Hoover Dam was planned and built.

Hoover Dam and Lake Mead have also provided a unique setting for film makers and continue to attract television and advertising companies.

1 Explain why

a) *Complete the following sentences and add more information.*

1. The Colorado River needed to be controlled because ...
2. Farmers in the area liked the idea of a dam because ...
3. Residents of the southwestern cities voted for the dam ...
4. Lake Mead is a popular recreation area ...
5. Generating electric power is so important ...
6. Film makers like Hoover Dam ...
7. Environmental issues were not under discussion in the 1930s ...

b) "The text is much too positive." *Do you agree with this opinion?*

2 ⟨Project: The Sun Belt⟩

Choose one of the states in the Sun Belt (California, Arizona etc., south of 37° Latitude). Use the Internet or any other source to find interesting information about it. Then give a report on your state to the class.

population? industry? history?

recreation? agriculture? geography?

D Grand Canyon National Park (20-22)

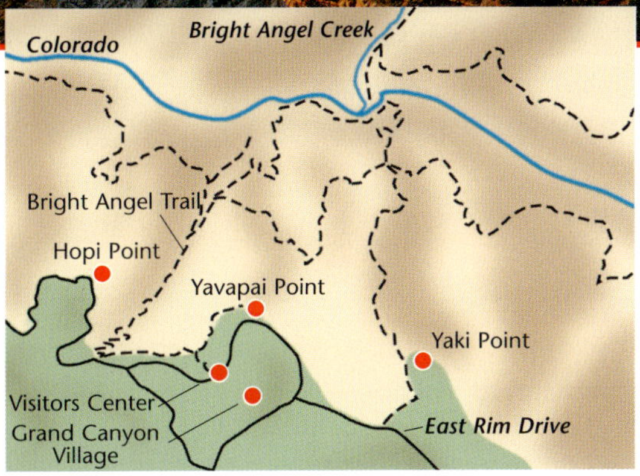

1 The fog parted. It just silently drew back like a set of theater curtains, and suddenly we were on the edge of a sheer, giddying drop of at least a thousand feet. All along the edge you could hear people saying 'Jesus!', like a message being passed down a long line.

And then for many moments all was silence, because out there was the most awesome, most silencing sight that exists on earth.

The scale of the Grand Canyon is almost beyond comprehension. It is ten miles across, a mile deep, 180 miles long. You could set the Empire State Building down in it and still be thousands of feet above it.

2 On Thursday afternoon rangers managed to rescue an injured hiker on the Bright Angel Trail. The man, whom park authorities identified as a 56-year-old German tourist, was found unconscious. He had fallen about 20 or 30 feet, said park spokeswoman Joan Anselmo. The man was taken to the hospital with very serious head injuries.

3

1 Looking at the texts

Compare texts 1, 2 and 3.

1. What kind of text is each one and where would you normally expect to find it?
2. Which text did you find most interesting?

2 … and beyond

1. Imagine you were visiting the Grand Canyon. What things would you do or wouldn't you do?
2. How do you think the accident to the German hiker happened? *(Write a first person report.)*

G 14

A Conditional sentences

1 Thinking about the future

Complete these sentences, then compare your results with your partner's.

1. If there's nothing on TV tonight, I'll ...
2. If my teachers give me too much homework, ...
3. I'll be really pleased if ...
4. If everything goes well this year, ...
5. Nobody will believe me if I ...
6. If *(my favourite team)* win their next match, ...

2 If I could change the world (7)

I saw it on the screen, pollution everywhere
People have no food, I think this is not fair
Never thought about the problems I don't have
All the lucky ones are mostly blind and deaf

Change the world, change the world
Never could stand up for peace
Worry about, worry about
If I could change the world

If I could change the world, no hunger anymore
If I could make a wish, no anger, hate and war
If you could change the world
I wonder what you'd do

Sung by Bed and Breakfast

a) *Listen to the song and make a list of the problems the singer sees in the world.*

b) *What do* ***you*** *think would make the world a better place? The ideas below might help you.*

... (to be) less pollution.
... people (to help) each other more.
... everybody (to have) a home.
... we (think) more about our environment.
... people (to be) not so greedy.
... people (to have) enough food.
... there (to be) not so many disasters.

Example: The world would be a better place if there was less pollution.

3 After Hurricane Floyd

a) *Read the texts and say what we learn about the speakers.*

It's been rough. We aren't even from here, we're from New York. If we had known about these hurricanes, we would never have come down to North Carolina! I wouldn't have gone for that job. In fact I wish I had never seen that ad!

I'd have stayed in Princeville if it hadn't rained so much. But the whole place was flooded. If only I'd had a boat, things would have been easier. Then I could have moved around a bit. Maybe I should have taken more of my stuff.

Example: The first speaker isn't from North Carolina. She's from ... She would never have ...

b) *Match the right parts so that the sentences make sense.*

1. If the weather forecasters had known sooner,
2. If the alarm had come earlier,
3. If FEMA had not provided trailers,
5. If Hurricane Irene hadn't followed Floyd,
6. If the residents had not been moved to shelter,
6. If Kelvin Pell had had a boat,

they could have stayed in the trailer park.
he would have taken more of his stuff.
the alarm would have come earlier.
they would have been in danger in their trailers.
the people would have had more time.
lots of residents would have been homeless.

4 What would you have done?

Would or wouldn't you have done the same as these people? Explain your answer.
Example:
1. If I'd won the prize, I'd have visited the Everglades too. I'd love to see those alligators.

Or:
I wouldn't have chosen the Everglades if I'd won the prize. I'd have preferred Disney World. It sounds a much more exciting place.

5 All three together

a) *Put in the correct verb form.*

1. If I were you, I (go) to sunny California.
2. We (find) another way if you can't manage.
3. If I (have) my life over again, I wouldn't make the same mistakes.
4. If it (rain) again, we'll have to go to a shelter.
5. If she (hear) the warning, she wouldn't have stayed in her home.
6. We'd have frozen to death if they (not save) us.
7. If you send them an e-mail, they (answer) it.
8. If only he had known, he (be) more careful.
9. If I (never see) water again for the rest of my life, I won't be unhappy!
10. I wish I (never move) to North Carolina!
11. Kelvin would have bought a boat if he (have) the money.
12. It (help) if he stopped smoking so much.

b) *Complete these sentences with your own ideas.*

1. If there were no national parks, ...
2. If farmers stopped using fertilizers and chemicals, ...
3. We would save a lot of water if ...
4. A dream would come true if ...
5. My parents wouldn't have been so angry if ...
6. If I'd had a bit more luck, ...

B In Nevada

3

G 15 1 On the road to Las Vegas

a) *Look carefully at the gerunds and infinitives here. Note the verbs that introduce them, and look at the context to discover the differences in meaning. It may sometimes help to translate the sentences.*

b) *Complete these sentences from a letter a teenager from Las Vegas sent to a friend of his. Use the verbs on the right with a gerund or an infinitive.*

1. Great that you're coming to visit me in Las Vegas! Remember ... a good pair of sunglasses with you.
2. Living in Vegas means ... in the Entertainment capital of the world. There are lots of theme parks and other exciting things to do here.
3. You want to see the real Las Vegas? Try ... the famous Strip with its hotels and casinos. Some of them look like castles.
4. If you mean ... to some good music, we could go to the House of Blues. I'll never forget ... George Thorogood play there. He was fantastic!
5. We could go on a cycling tour to Red Rock Canyon. We mustn't forget ... you a good mountain bike.
6. Red Rock Canyon is only 16 miles from Las Vegas. I remember ... an awesome view of it from the Black Velvet Cliffs.

be
get
listen
have
visit
bring
see

R 2 A postcard from Las Vegas

Adjective or adverb? Put in the correct forms.

G 16

Dear Mum and Dad:
We got here (safe) though we (near) took the (wrong) road. We drove (slow) along the Strip with its (flashing) neon signs. (Fortunate) we found a (good) hotel (easy). Yesterday we got up (early) to get tickets for Siegfried & Roy. They did their show (real) (good). And today we went on a (fantastic) cycling tour. It was (terrible) (hard) work getting up the mountain (quick), but then we (sudden) had a (dramatic) view over Red Rock Canyon. I'd (actual) love to stay in Vegas longer, but (sad) we leave for Grand Canyon tomorrow, though that sounds (exciting) too!
See you soon,
Sharon

C Vocabulary

1 Related words – related meanings

a) *Try to find at least one related word to go with each of the following nouns. Write down the word families.*

intention human need head boat water use service
producer name flood generation silence hiker
environment drama friend

Example:
intention (n), to intend (v)

b) *Choose three word families and use all their words in one text that makes sense.*

2 Compound words

a) *Find the words that go together to make nine compounds. Use your dictionary to check whether they are written as one word or two words.*

sun ✓	recreation	head
area	foot	cycling
line	park	alarm
tour	hurricane	air
pollution	box	wear
cash	theme	glasses ✓

Example:
sunglasses

b) *Can you make more compound words that begin or end with these nouns?*

3 The big water mind map

Work in groups and add as many water-related words as you can.
Why not add pictures and make a wall poster for your classroom?

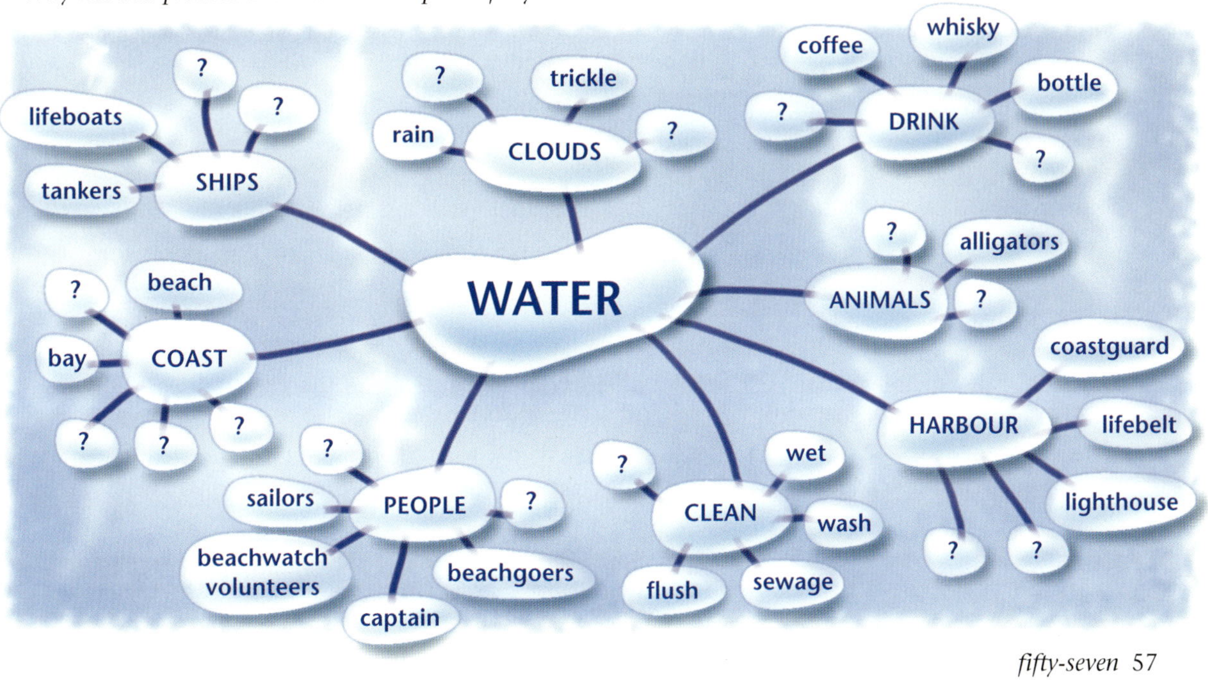

A panel discussion

1 The problem

There are plans to construct a dam across the river Tinto near Canyon City, Arizona. This will create a hydroelectric power station and a huge reservoir, but the little village of San Juan will be lost.

Imagine you are residents of the area. To decide whether the project should go ahead or not, you decide to have a public discussion. A panel of four experts will present different arguments and answer your questions.

2 Organizing the discussion

a) *First choose the four experts and a chairperson.* The rest of you are local people in the audience (either from Canyon City or San Juan).

b) *Prepare the discussion.* This needs to be done by everybody.

1. The **experts** need to prepare their arguments. (Perhaps the teacher can provide role cards with keywords/ideas.)

Expert 1 speaks for the business people and the farmers in the area. They all want the dam.

Expert 2 speaks for the environmentalists in the area. They are against the project.

Expert 3 speaks for a group of people in industry and engineering. They want the dam.

Expert 4 speaks for a group of residents who don't want the dam because they are worried.

2. The **chairperson** has to:
- open the meeting
- ask the panel members to make their statements (or to stop speaking)
- lead the discussion
- give a summary of the arguments
- organize the vote

3. The **audience** have to prepare questions to put to the experts. They should listen carefully while the experts make their statements and then join in the discussion with their questions. They can also bring up new points.

c) *Start the panel discussion (see the tips on page 59).* At the end, when the chairperson has given his/her summary, the audience has to decide whose arguments were best and vote for or against the project.

3 Useful discussion phrases

a) *For the experts who are presenting their case:*

I'd like to begin with …
Next …
Now let's turn to …
Another important thing is …
And finally …
I really believe that you should vote for/against this wonderful/dangerous project because …
Thank you for your attention.

b) *For the chairperson:*

Do we have any questions from the audience?
Yes, sir/madam. What would you like to ask?
Do you have anything to add to that?
I'd like to hear your views on that.
Would anyone like to comment on that?
On the one hand …/on the other hand …

c) *For everyone:*

Expressing your opinion:

I feel strongly that …
The way I/we see it …
In my opinion …
I think …
It's a fact that …

Agreeing and disagreeing:

I (don't) agree that …
I'm for/against the idea of …
I think it's right/wrong to …
I'm sorry, but I disagree there. It's not true that …
You don't really believe that …

Persuading people:

Surely you see that …
Don't forget that …
You might think differently if …
After all, you must agree that …

Interrupting and dealing with interruptions:

If I may just come in here …
I'm sorry, but could I interrupt you there? …
I haven't finished what I was saying …
I'm coming to that …

4 Tips on presenting and discussing

Whatever your role in the discussion is, you have to speak to an audience and you want to persuade people. The following list of tips may help you to do so.

If you are one of the speakers:

✓ Be well prepared. Write down your arguments in note form.
✓ Use your notes but try to speak freely.
✓ Look at your audience as much as you can.
✓ Use pictures, maps, diagrams, etc. if you can.
✓ Don't panic if things go wrong. (Just smile and keep going.)
✓ Don't get angry if some people aren't listening.
✓ Answer people's questions politely.

If you are one of the audience:

✓ Listen carefully to what other people say.
✓ Try not to interrupt.
✓ Take notes while you are listening about points you would like to make.
✓ Wait until the chairperson calls on you before you enter the discussion.
✓ Ask questions politely.

1 Words – words – words

a) *Put these words ending in -y in three lists:*

noun	adjective	adverb
vocabulary	weary	seriously

weary	seriously	vocabulary
angry	deadly	constantly
energy	clumsy	roughly
dramatically	unconsciously	laundry
supply	hungry	personality

b) *Add some more words.*

c) *'Water verbs':* to water, to trickle, to run, …
'Water adjectives': cool, wet, …
'Water nouns': river, drop, …

2 If I had been more careful!

The German hiker who was injured in the Grand Canyon is talking about his experience.
Put in the correct verb forms

1. If I had been more careful, it (not happen) because I (pay) more attention to the warning signs.
2. If I (do) that, I would have known that parts of the Bright Angel Trail were dangerous and I (not try) to climb them.
3. I think I would have been OK if I (have) a helmet on. Then I (not get) these nasty head injuries.
4. It was lucky those people saw me. But they (not find) me if they (not lose) their way!
5. If I (have) a mobile phone, it (not help) because I was unconscious after I fell.
6. Fortunately one of the people had one. Otherwise I (not be taken) to the hospital for hours. Perhaps I (die)!

Start: If I **had been** more careful, it **wouldn't have happened** …

3 Graffiti fun

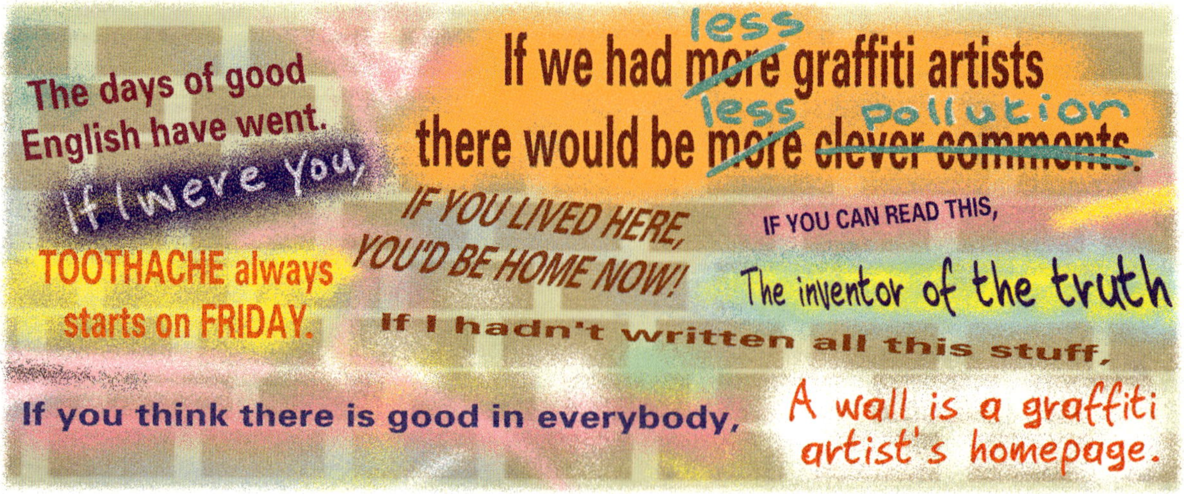

1. Read these graffiti messages. Complete the unfinished ones with their other half *(on the right)*.
2. Add your own graffiti statements and make your own graffiti page. Can you find any graffiti messages on the Internet?

… you haven't met everybody!
… you'd never have seen how clever I am!
… is a liar!!!
… thank a teacher.
… I wouldn't read all this rubbish.

4 From a newspaper article: After the disaster

Complete the following sentences. Use a gerund or infinitive.

1. It's two weeks since the authorities stopped ...	**evacuate** people from their homes.
2. Some residents say they can't remember ...	**have** been in such a disaster.
3. For many of them it means ...	**live** for months in a shelter or a trailer park.
4. The police are warning them not to forget ...	**report** any damage to their insurance companies.
5. A lot of tourists passing through stop ...	**see** the flooding for themselves.
6. Residents get angry at this. "Let them try ...	**live** in a shelter for weeks!" says Kelvin Pell.
7. The evacuation services regret ...	not **have** given out handouts with tips.
8. A spokesperson said, "We'll remember ...	**prepare** handouts for the next hurricane."
9. The weather forecasters said, "We regret ...	**say** that the next hurricane is on its way, folks.
10. But it doesn't look as bad, so we're trying ...	**calm** everybody down this time."

5 Cartoon fun

1. Which of these cartoons do you like best?
2. Try to describe each cartoon as if you are talking to someone who hasn't seen them.

Start like this: "I saw a nice cartoon the other day. The situation was in a library, in the ... section. There were ... "

We've been spending too much time together. I think it's time we started hating other people.

You can't just dump your boyfriend anymore. You have to recycle him.

3

CHECK-IN

	plant [plɑ:nt]	Pflanze; *auch:* Werk, Fabrik	Trees and flowers are ~s.
	environmental [ɪnˌvaɪərn'mentl]	Umwelt-	~ groups want to help to protect the environment.
	to **surround** [sə'raʊnd]	umgeben, umstellen	round – to surround
	human ['hju:mən]	menschlich; Mensch	~ activities = what ~s do
	to use up [ju:z‿'ʌp]	aufbrauchen, verbrauchen	
	to **affect** [ə'fekt]	beeinflussen, sich auswirken auf	Human activities ~ the environment.
	habitat ['hæbɪtæt]	Habitat, Lebensraum	the area in which a certain type of animal or plant lives
	pollution [pə'lu:ʃn]	Verschmutzung	Unfortunately, cars cause a lot of ~.
	to **pollute** [pə'lu:t]	verschmutzen	Cars ~ the environment.
	population [ˌpɒpjə'leɪʃn]	Bevölkerung	the number of people in the world = the world's ~
	to cut* down [kʌt 'daʊn]	fällen	
	impact ['ɪmpækt]	Auswirkung; Aufprall	
2	to stand* for ['stænd fɔ:]	stehen für	'N.Y.C.' stands for 'New York City'.

TEXTS

A	weary ['wɪəri]	müde	
	resident ['rezɪdnt]	Einwohner(in), Anwohner(in), Bewohner(in)	The people who live in a town are its ~s.
	to **flood** [flʌd]	überfluten	If a lot of rain falls, it can ~ the land.
	to **settle into** [ˌsetl‿'ɪntu]	sich einleben	When you have to move to a new home, you first have to ~ it.
	trailer ['treɪlə]	Wohnwagen *(AE)*; Anhänger *(BE)*	a kind of home on wheels
	shelter ['ʃeltə]	Schutz, Obdach, Unterstand	Homeless people have no proper ~.
	ground [graʊnd]	Boden, Grund, Gelände	underground – ground
	rough [rʌf]	rau, schwierig, hart	a ~ time = a difficult time
	to **come* up** [ˌkʌm‿'ʌp]	hochkommen; aufkommen, passieren	If something comes up, it happens (sometimes without warning).
	to **rest** [rest]	rasten, ausruhen	After a long walk you need to ~.
	tiny ['taɪni]	winzig	very, very small
	up to ['ʌp tʊ]	bis zu	
	spokesman/spokeswoman ['spəʊksmən/ˌwʊmən]	Sprecher(in)	a person who speaks for others (e.g. for an organization)
	to topple ['tɒpl]	umfallen, umwerfen	
	to **judge** [dʒʌdʒ]	beurteilen, einschätzen	If you ~ a situation, you decide how bad, difficult, etc. you think it is.
	threat [θret]	Bedrohung	Words like 'I'll kill that dog if it comes on my land!' are a ~.
	to menace ['menəs]	bedrohen	
	North Carolinian [ˌnɔ:θ kærə'lɪnjən]	Bewohner(in) North Carolinas	
	forecaster ['fɔ:kɑ:stə]	Meteorologe, Meteorologin	so. who tells the people what the weather will be like in the near future
	eastern ['i:stən]	östlich	southern – eastern
	inch [ɪntʃ]	Zoll *(Längenmaß, ca. 2,54 cm)*	Six ~es of snow fell in the night.
	official [ə'fɪʃl]	Beamter, Beamtin, Funktionär(in)	office – official – an official

	to **intend** [ɪn'tend]	beabsichtigen	intention – to intend
	bam [bæm]	Bumm!	
B	**salt water** ['sɔ:lt ˌwɔ:tə]	Salzwasser	The water in the sea is ~.
	fresh water ['freʃ ˌwɔ:tə]	Süßwasser	The water in rivers is ~.
	available [ə'veɪləbl]	verfügbar	Sth. that you can get and use is ~.
	use [ju:s]	Gebrauch	to use [z] – the use [s]
	to **flush** [flʌʃ]	spülen, die Wasserspülung betätigen	You ~ the toilet after use.
	to **water** ['wɔ:tə]	gießen, bewässern	Plants soon die if you don't ~ them.
	laundry ['lɔ:ndri]	Wäsche	doing the ~ = washing the dirty clothes, towels, etc.
	stream [stri:m]	Bach, Flüsschen, Strom	stream → RIVER → THE SEA
	trickle ['trɪkl]	Rinnsal, Tröpfeln	A ~ of water is much less than a stream, but much more than a drop.
	drop [drɒp]	Tropfen	rain~s
	to **dry up** [draɪ‿'ʌp]	austrocknen	In summer, the lake dries up.
	crop [krɒp]	Getreide, Feldfrucht, Ernte	The plants that grow in a farmer's fields are his ~s.
	to **provide** [prə'vaɪd]	zur Verfügung stellen, versorgen mit, sorgen für	Hotels ~ meals and rooms for guests.
	fertilizer ['fɜ:tɪlaɪzə]	Dünger	~s are used to make crops grow better.
	cause [kɔ:z]	Ursache, Grund	to cause – cause
	to **restore** [rɪ'stɔ:]	*hier:* zurückgeben	
	overuse [ˌəuvə'ju:s]	übermäßiger Gebrauch	using too much of sth.
	supply [sə'plaɪ]	Versorgung; Vorrat	water ~, electricity ~, food ~
	to **let*** [let]	lassen, jmdm etwas erlauben	Don't ~ the water run all the time while you're brushing your teeth.
	to **brush** [brʌʃ]	bürsten, putzen	
C	**dam** [dæm]	Staudamm	Building a ~ helps to control a river.
	to **flow** [fləʊ]	fließen	If you watch a river, you see the water ~ past.
	to **name after** *(BE)*/**for** *(AE)* ['neɪm‿ɑ:ftə]	benennen nach	Buildings, schools, etc. are often named after famous people.
	irrigation [ˌɪrɪ'geɪʃn]	Bewässerung	~ provides the land with water so that crops will grow.
	acre ['eɪkə]	Morgen *(Flächenmaß, ca. 40,47 Ar)*	A million ~s is a very large area of land.
	hydroelectric power [ˌhaɪdrəʊɪlektrɪk 'paʊə]	Energie aus Wasserkraft	electric – hydroelectric
	recreation [ˌrekri'eɪʃn]	Erholung	A ~ area is a place where people can enjoy sports, etc.
	boating ['bəʊtɪŋ]	Bootfahren	boat – boating
	refuge ['refju:dʒ]	Zuflucht	a place where people (or animals) can find shelter
	to **develop** [dɪ'veləp]	(sich) entwickeln	If a thing ~s, it grows and becomes more complete.
	issue ['ɪʃu:]	Frage, Angelegenheit	sth. that needs to be discussed, a subject or problem
	unique [ju:'ni:k]	einzigartig	There is no other example of a thing that is ~.
⟨2⟩	belt [belt]	Gürtel	
	latitude ['lætɪtju:d]	Breitengrad	
	agriculture ['ægrɪkʌltʃə]	Landwirtschaft	
D	sheer [ʃɪə]	steil, jäh	
	giddying ['gɪdiɪŋ]	schwindelerregend	
	drop [drɒp]	Sturz, Höhenunterschied	
	to **pass** [pɑ:s]	weitergeben	If a message is ~ed, it is given from one person to the next.

silence ['saɪlents]	Stille	silent – silence
awesome ['ɔ:səm]	ehrfurchtgebietend	Visitors all agree that the Grand Canyon is an ~ sight.
to silence ['saɪlents]	zum Schweigen bringen	
scale [skeɪl]	Ausmaß, Maßstab	
beyond [bɪ'ɒnd]	jenseits, über ... hinaus	further than; on the other side of
hiker ['haɪkə]	Wanderer	so. who walks through the countryside (on holiday)
trail [treɪl]	Weg, Pfad, Spur	*BE:* path; *AE:* trail
whom [hu:m]	dem, den, der, die *(Relativpronomen, Objektfall)*	
unconscious [ʌn'kɒntʃəs]	bewusstlos, unbewusst	If you have had a bad accident, you may be ~ for a time.
injury ['ɪndʒəri]	Verletzung	to injure – injury
rim [rɪm]	Rand	
to **permit** [pə'mɪt]	erlauben	to be allowed = to be permitted
to **hike** [haɪk]	wandern	hiker – to hike
clothing ['kləʊðɪŋ]	Kleidung	The clothes you are wearing are your ~.

3

LANGUAGE

A2 **lucky** ['lʌki]	Glücks-	luck – lucky
wish [wɪʃ]	Wunsch	to wish – wish
anger ['æŋgə]	Ärger, Zorn	angry – anger
hate [heɪt]	Hass	love ↔ hate
4 to **prefer** [prɪ'fɜ:]	vorziehen, lieber mögen	Tea or coffee – which do you ~?
forest ['fɒrɪst]	Wald	a large area where a lot of trees grow (~s are larger than woods)
B1 to **introduce** [ˌɪntrə'dju:s]	einleiten	The verb 'mean' can ~ a gerund or an infinitive.
to **mean*** (+ to + *infinitive*) [mi:n]	beabsichtigen, vorhaben	I plan to leave early. = I ~ to leave early.
2 **compound (word)** ['kɒmpaʊnd wɜ:d]	zusammengesetztes Wort	A ~ is made of two or more parts.

SKILLS

1 **panel** ['pænl]	Podium	a group of people who are chosen to discuss or decide sth.
to **create** [kri'eɪt]	schaffen, hervorbringen	to make or produce
power station ['paʊə ˌsteɪʃn]	Kraftwerk	a place where electricity is generated
2 **chairperson** ['tʃeəˌpɜ:sn]	Vorsitzende(r)	the person who is in charge of a meeting or a discussion
environmentalist [ɪnˌvaɪərn'mentlɪst]	Umweltschützer(in)	environment – environmental – environmentalist
engineering [ˌendʒɪ'nɪərɪŋ]	Technik, Maschinenbau, Ingenieurwesen	the work of designing and constructing machines, roads, bridges, etc.
vote [vəʊt]	Abstimmung, Wahl; Stimme	to vote – vote
3 to **express** [ɪk'spres]	ausdrücken	expression – to express
to **persuade** [pə'sweɪd]	überreden, überzeugen	to make so. do sth. they don't want to do by giving them reasons
to **interrupt** [ˌɪntə'rʌpt]	unterbrechen, jmdm ins Wort fallen	to stop sth. for a short time

interruption [ˌintəˈrʌpʃn]	Unterbrechung	to interrupt – interruption

CHECK-OUT

3	**artist** [ˈɑ:tɪst]	Künstler	so. who draws, paints, etc. (as a hobby or a job); so. who is very good at a certain activity
	global warming [ˌgləʊbl ˈwɔ:mɪŋ]	Erderwärmung durch den Treibhauseffekt	

COGNATE WORDS

alarm [əˈlɑ:m]	Alarm
canyon *(AE)* [ˈkænjən]	Schlucht
casino [kəˈsi:nəʊ]	Kasino
constant [ˈkɒntstənt]	konstant, ständig
to **construct** [kənˈstrʌkt]	bauen, konstruieren
construction [kənˈstrʌkʃn]	Bau, Konstruktion
discussion [dɪˈskʌʃn]	Diskussion
dramatic [drəˈmætɪk]	dramatisch
effective [ɪˈfektɪv]	effektiv, wirksam, wirkungsvoll
to **evacuate** [ɪˈvækjueit]	evakuieren, räumen
evacuation [ɪˌvækjuˈeɪʃn]	Evakuierung
to **exist** [ɪgˈzɪst]	existieren, bestehen
to **generate** [ˈdʒenəreɪt]	generieren, erzeugen
handout [ˈhændaʊt]	Handout, ausgeteiltes Papier
hunger [ˈhʌŋgə]	Hunger
to **identify** [aɪˈdentɪfaɪ]	identifizieren
litre *(BE)* [ˈli:tə]	Liter
message [ˈmesɪdʒ]	Mitteilung, Nachricht, Botschaft
neon [ˈni:ɒn]	Neon
ocean [ˈəʊʃn]	Ozean
pole [pəʊl]	Pol
to **present** [prɪˈzent]	präsentieren
president [ˈprezɪdnt]	Präsident/in
ranger *(AE)* [ˈreɪndʒə]	Ranger, Aufseher im Nationalpark
to **recycle** [ˌri:ˈsaɪkl]	recyceln, wiederaufbereiten, wiederverwerten
reservoir [ˈrezəvwɑ:]	Stausee, Reservoir
resources [rɪˈzɔ:sɪz]	Ressourcen, Reserven, Bodenschätze
trick [trɪk]	Trick
tropical [ˈtrɒpɪkl]	tropisch
wind [wɪnd]	Wind

Recycle your vocabulary!

You already know many words which you can also very well use to talk about the environment. Make pairs from the verbs you know on the left and the new words on the right. (There might be more than one possible combination for each verb.)

to discover	to be afraid of
to realize	to prevent
to study	to reduce
to examine	to protect
to care about	to save
to inform about	to ignore
to be responsible for	to damage

POLLUTION
NATURAL HABITATS
(THE RISK OF) NATURAL DISASTERS
THE ENVIRONMENT
ANIMAL AND PLANT LIFE

UNIT 4

Stay tuned

1 Behind the scenes

The pictures on these two pages take you 'behind the scenes' of the media.

a) *Identify the different types of media, and describe what is happening in each picture.*

b) *Which type of media do you think is best at the following? Explain why.*

- entertainment
- news
- education

1

7

6

2 Media words

a) *Check that you know the meaning of the words below and how to say them. Then decide what categories you can put them in.*

actor advertisement article audience to be/go on air broadcast broadsheet cable channel comedy daily director documentary editor game show headline journalist listener local magazine movie national newspaper regional photographer popular reporter presenter producer programme publish reader satellite scandal screen soap opera tabloid thriller video viewer violence weekly western

b) *Can you add any more words to the categories?*

Vocabulary 74, 1

3 A survey

a) *Write questions for a class/school survey of TV viewing habits. Below are some ideas you can use for your questions. Maybe you can think of some more – but limit your questions to about 10.*

- if/when/how often TV is watched
- no. of homes with satellite/cable TV/video recorders
- no. of people with TV in bedroom
- how many watch TV while doing other things (e.g. homework)
- who in your family decides what to watch
- most popular types of programmes
- how people would like TV to change

Useful phrases:
Talking about a survey

- The aim of our survey was to ...
- We (also) wanted to find out ...
- The results show that ...
- As you can see on this diagram ...
- The majority of people said that ...
- More than half/50 per cent/a third/...
- Only a minority ...
- As expected, ...
- One of the most surprising things was ...
- We came to the conclusion that ...

b) *Discuss with your teacher the best way to present your results.*

A Coffee Time, USA (23-26)

a) *Do you ever watch talk shows on TV? What do you like or not like about them? Describe how they are presented and the kind of topics that are discussed.*

b) *The text on the right is the opening scene of a bestselling novel. As you read, make notes about:*
- *the setting*
- *the characters*
- *the theme(s)*

On the morning before it happened, Bruce had been sitting in a television studio opposite two Ken-and-Barbie style presenters.

"His name" (pause) "is Bruce Delamitri," said Ken, using the sincere, deep tone he used for really big guests. "He is probably the biggest celebrity working in the motion-picture industry today. A great writer, a great director. Hollywood's golden boy."

"I heard he makes a great pasta sauce too," said Barbie, to add a little human interest.

"You're watching *Coffee Time USA*. We'll be back after these messages," said the male presenter, whose name was not Ken but Oliver Martin. The studio lights dimmed and the *Coffee Time* logo came up while Oliver and his female colleague, Dale, stacked up their papers in an important manner. There was of course nothing on their papers.

Bruce watched the monitor in front of him as Oliver and Dale disappeared and were replaced on the screen by four babes in bikinis clutching soda bottles and climbing happily out of a sports car.

"A girl, a beach, it's happening, it's real. It's a boost, it's a buzz, it's the way you should feel!"

The studio controller turned down the volume and the bikini babes were left sucking on their bottles in silent delight.

"One and a half minutes on the break," said the floor manager.

This was the signal for the make-up girls to rush in and get to work. Oliver turned to Bruce as they were being made-up.

1 Understanding the text

1. Describe the setting and the characters in one or two sentences.
2. Explain why Bruce is so controversial.
3. Do you think Oliver and Dale are good at their jobs? Give examples.
4. a) Oliver says that his industry is 'not a dream factory' (l. 33). What industry is he talking about?
   b) What do you think the author's own opinion is? Look for examples of irony in which the author gives us his opinion 'between the lines'.

   Example: The presenters stack up their papers in an important manner, even though …

Irony
The contrast between what is said and what is actually meant.

2 Wayne's deal (8-9)

Later, a pair of serial killers called Wayne and Scout break into Bruce Delamitri's Hollywood mansion and threaten to kill him and his family. When the mansion is surrounded by the police, Bruce does a deal with Wayne: If Wayne can prove to the nation that Bruce's violent movies made him shoot people, Wayne should go free. A TV crew is allowed in to broadcast the debate live. The viewer ratings are monitored on a computer by Kerstin, a member of the crew.

"I think what we need to concentrate on is the fact that our industry is not a dream factory. We deal in realism. We show it like it is."

Another layer of make-up was added to Oliver's already heavily made-up face.

"One minute to the break," said the floor manager.

Across the desk, Dale's voice could be heard through a cloud of hairspray. "I mean, surely the big issue, Bruce, has got to be this whole copycat killing, hasn't it? I mean, that's what America is concerned about. Are you concerned about that, Bruce, as an American?"

"America's population is not as young as it was, and soon the number-one issue for most Americans will be adult incontinence."

This was not Bruce. It was the TV. The studio controller had turned up the volume before they went back on air. It was after nine, and the advertisers were switching their focus from workers and schoolkids to a 'coffee time' audience, which meant young mums and old lonelys. Ads with soda-sucking babes were being replaced by nappies for young and old.

"No, I'm not concerned about copycat killings," said Bruce, speaking with difficulty because a young woman was painting some kind of grease on his lips. "I don't believe that people get up from the movie theatre or the TV and do what they just saw. Otherwise the people who watch this show would all have hair like concrete."

Bruce didn't expect Dale to hear his answer. He could see she was the type of interviewer who used her guests' answers as quiet time in which to think about the next question.

"Good, good, you should make that point on air," said Dale, checking her eyeliner.

"Fifteen seconds on the break," said the floor manager. Four, three, two, one, ...

Oliver's face lit up. "We're talking to Bruce Delamitri, the hot – but controversial – tip for tonight's "Best Director" Oscar."

Dale picked up the ball. "Bruce Delamitri's movies are hard, tough, street-wise thrillers, where the life is low and the body count is high. Remind you of something?"

"You tell me, Dale," said Ollie, putting on his serious and thoughtful face.

"How about America's streets?" said Dale. "That's right, the streets of America, hard, tough and dangerous, where the kids grow up fast and dying is a way of life."

"You're saying the movies of Bruce Delamitri reflect the streets of America?"

"Some say reflect, some say influence. America, it's your call. We'll be back after these messages."

The studio lights dimmed again. Oliver and Dale went dark and shuffled their papers. "Do you have sensitive teeth? Does ice-cream make you go *ow*? when you should be going *mmmmm*?"

(from: *Popcorn*, by Ben Elton)

4

3 A talk show

a) *Listen and find out:*
- who Farrah, Velvet, Brooke Daniel and Karl Brezner are.
- the reason(s) Wayne gives for killing people.
- why Kerstin's boss wants to stop showing the scene live and record it instead.
- what Wayne will do if viewers turn off their TV, and what he will do if they don't.

b) *How do you think the viewers will react? What would you do?*

Vocabulary 74, 2

Hold a talk show on the theme 'Is there too much violence on TV?' Decide who will present the show and who will be the controversial star guest. The rest of you are members of the studio audience. Ask questions and express your own opinions.

Asking for opinions
What's your opinion on ...?
I'd like to hear your views on ...
Where do you stand on this issue?
What do you think of ...?

Giving an opinion
I believe/think that ...
It's quite clear that ...
As far as I'm concerned ...
I would say that ...

Playing for time
It depends what you mean by ...
That's a very interesting question.
I'm glad you asked that question.
It's not as simple as that.

B We all have blood on our hands

a) *Work in groups of 3 or 4. Try to imagine what it is like to be world famous (if you aren't already!) and list the pros and cons of a celebrity's life.*

b) *Compare your ideas with the rest of the class. What do you think is the best thing about being a celebrity? What is the worst?*

c) *When Diana, Princess of Wales, was killed in a car crash after being chased by photographers, the singer Madonna decided to speak to "The Times". Read the article quickly for the gist. Look for the message Madonna wants to give the readers.*

When Diana's life hung between the news of the crash and the announcement of her death, Madonna remembered going through the same Paris tunnel, at the same breakneck speed, with the same cameras flashing in her face.

"I was crying out, 'please God, let her live,'" she says, her voice cracking with emotion. "I have been chased through that same tunnel so many times that I have lost count." The fact that the driver had been drinking does not make her any less angry at the paparazzi.

"When I came to Europe to promote *Evita*, I was in Rome and the paparazzi did not even give me time to fasten my baby's seatbelt. We were driving at about 90 miles per hour, and we were being chased. OK, so if there weren't such large offers of money, then these people wouldn't go to such extremes to take the pictures. Then you have to look at the editors and ask who is responsible for this. But even that does not dig deep enough. As much as I want to blame the press, we all have blood on our hands. All of us, even myself. I bought those magazines and I read them. Until we no longer feel that it is right to read about people's private lives, and until we lose our fascination with scandal and sensational news stories, we are never going to act. It is all our faults."

Madonna and Diana met just once, at a charity cocktail party:

"We must have talked for about ten minutes. We made some joke about how the only person who seemed to get more attention than me was her. She said 'I think you handle the press better than I do,' and I said 'You will have to get a skin as thick as an armadillo'."

Madonna says she would love to live in New York, but the press interest in her makes every move unthinkable.

"I can't spend time there because there are kids on electric bikes, with video cameras, and they are holding on to the bumpers of my car. And I think, they don't care if they die. I mean, what have we created?"

She says she loves London, but is too afraid of the media to live there. "You really cannot win. If you ignore them or run away, they think you are being uncooperative. If you cooperate, they say you are being manipulative. They were always doing that with Diana. I find what they are doing now just as unforgivable. They were so awful to her, and now they are putting her on a pedestal and saying she is so wonderful, and yet two weeks ago they were tearing her apart."

The problem, she says, is not limited to America and Europe. When she was in Argentina filming *Evita*, the paparazzi were paying young children to lie under her car and pretend to be run over so that they could get a good picture. She was luckier with her driver than Diana. He spotted the boys and waited until they had gone.

It looks as though Diana was right: Madonna has handled her press relations better than the Princess, and she has a thicker skin. But both have been called icons. Diana achieved stardom through membership of a particular family;

Madonna went the opposite, American way, made famous by the movies.

"Yes, it's true, people have the same obsession with her that they do with me. You are never allowed to make mistakes without being taken apart in the papers."

Is there, then, a need to create people who are too good for us?

"I would say absolutely. We all need people to look up to. The bravest thing about Diana was that she said 'I'm not perfect, I have my problems'. I'm not saying I agree with everything she ever did. But look, what we need is not role models who say 'I'm perfect' but ones who say 'I'm weak, I make mistakes, and I am going to try and change and be a better person'. We need those people more than ever, because everywhere we look, whether it is the movies or TV or even fashion photography, we see the glamorising of death and violence and drug addiction."

She talks about the support she gets from her friends, which helped her to deal with her own fame. "Thank God," she says, "I have my friends, and not a monarchy round my ankles like a ball and chain."

"Freedom of the press, yes, I'm all for it. Write whatever you want to write. But you cannot take pictures of people through their bedroom windows, or chase them through towns at 100 mph. Like I said, we are destroying the things we love."

The Times, 3rd September 1997

1 A closer look

1. a) Describe Madonna's attitude to the media. Do you feel sorry for her?
   b) What examples does she give of the extremes to which the paparazzi go to get photos? What makes them go to such extremes?
2. Madonna says "... we all have blood on our hands". Explain what she means by this.
3. List what Madonna and Diana have in common and what makes them different. Say who you think is the stronger person, and why.
4. a) Sum up what Madonna says about role models, and give your own opinion.
   b) Name some celebrities who fit the type of role model Madonna thinks we need. Do you look up to them? Why, or why not?

2 A call from the editor

That night the telephone rang. It was a friend who edits a weekly magazine. Could I write 2,500 words on Diana by the next evening?

"But I don't know anything about her," I said. "What could I write about?"

"You know – Diana the Icon," he said.

"The Icon? How do you mean?"

"You know – the clothes, the broken marriage, bulimia, landmines, Aids, all those things. What she meant to us all."

"No," I said, "I don't really think I could."

"Look at it another way," he said, "it's worth the price of a new kitchen."

A new kitchen! Even cheap ones, I thought, cost about £6,000. And perhaps my friend was thinking bigger than that. A kitchen for 2,500 words. In such small ways does an event become a phenomenon.

Ian Jack, in *Unbelievable, GRANTA 60*

1. What is Ian Jack asked to do? How does he react at first, and why?
2. What does the editor do to make his offer more attractive?
3. Would you accept it? Why/why not?
4. What sort of journalist do you think Ian Jack is? (Tabloid? Broadsheet?) Explain why.

Tenses 76-77

C The Beatles phenomenon

1 Sgt. Pepper's Lonely Hearts Club Band

Sgt. Pepper's Lonely Hearts Club Band (1967) was voted 'Best Album of the Millennium' in 1999. The cover shows the Beatles (twice) and every influence on their lives they could remember.

1. Talk about what you already know about the Beatles. Perhaps your teacher can help you to identify some of the Beatles' influences.
2. Work in groups. Plan a collage of people or things that have been an influence on your lives up to now, with a picture of yourselves in the middle.

2 A song from the album (27)

a) Most of the Beatles' songs were written by John Lennon and Paul McCartney. *A Day in the Life* is an interesting example of their work because the parts are clearly divided up. The first and last parts were written and sung by John, and the middle part by Paul.
Where do you think Paul's part starts and finishes? Listen to the song for clues!

b) In this song the influence of the media on John Lennon's writing is also clear.
Look at these pieces from newspapers of the time and show how he used them in the song.

The holes in our roads
THERE are 4,000 holes in the road in Blackburn, Lancashire, or one twenty-sixth of a hole per person, says a survey.
If Blackburn is typical there are two million holes in Britain's roads and 300,000 in London.

Tara Brown, 21, son of Lord and L
killed in a car cra
London. He was
member of the Gui
family. Friends of

Odeon Cinema
How I Won The War
starring John Lennon

A day in the life of ... Enid Blyton

c) The BBC banned the song because of its references to drugs.
Identify these references and say whether you agree with the decision or not.
What sort of songs (if any) do you think should be banned in your country today? Give reasons.

A day in the life
(John Lennon/Paul McCartney)

I read the news today oh boy
About a lucky man who made the grade
And though the news was rather sad
Well I just had to laugh
I saw the photograph
He blew his mind out in a car
He didn't notice that the lights had changed
A crowd of people stood and stared
They'd seen his face before
Nobody was really sure
If he was from the House of Lords
I saw a film today oh boy
The English Army had just won the war
A crowd of people turned away
But I just had to look
Having read the book
I'd love to turn you on
Woke up, fell out of bed
Dragged a comb across my head
Found my way downstairs and drank a cup
And looking up I noticed I was late
Found my coat and grabbed my hat
Made the bus in seconds flat
Found my way upstairs and had a smoke
And somebody spoke and I went into a dream
I read the news today oh boy
Four thousand holes in Blackburn, Lancashire
And though the holes were rather small
They had to count them all
Now they know how many holes
It takes to fill The Albert Hall
I'd love to turn you on

3 A revolutionary album

The *Sgt. Pepper* album has been described as revolutionary, even a cultural icon. For the first time on a pop record, it had printed lyrics. The cover also shows the Beatles not as typical pop stars in dark suits, but as old-fashioned brass band players in bright colours. They have all got moustaches, and John Lennon has replaced his contact lenses with glasses.

The music was mixed in a studio on a four-track tape, so it could not be played live on stage. The songs are connected by studio talk, electronic noises and animal sounds, without traditional breaks between them. At the end of the last song, 'A day in the life', an orchestra plays what Lennon described as "a sound building up from nothing to the end of the world". This was recorded beyond a 20,000 hertz frequency so that the final note could only be heard by dogs. There were 40 members of the orchestra, but they sound like 160 because they were recorded on all four tracks of the tape.

For the recording, everyone was asked to wear formal clothing, but they also wore clown's red noses, bald heads, false eyes, fake cigars, and funny hats and glasses. After the orchestra had packed up and gone home, the Beatles and some friends stood around a microphone and recorded a long 'hum' for the end of the track. However, this was never used. Instead, a crashing piano chord was dubbed on twelve days later.

a) *Sum up the ways in which 'Sgt. Pepper's Lonely Hearts Club Band' was revolutionary.*
b) *Discuss what things today's singers or groups have to do to be called 'revolutionary'?*
c) *How important is an album's cover? How might the internet change the role of 'album art'?*
d) *With a partner, discuss the advantages and disadvantages of the following:*
- listening to recordings / going to concerts
- mixing and dubbing / live recordings
- lyrics in English / lyrics in your own language

4 A project on the Beatles (10-14)

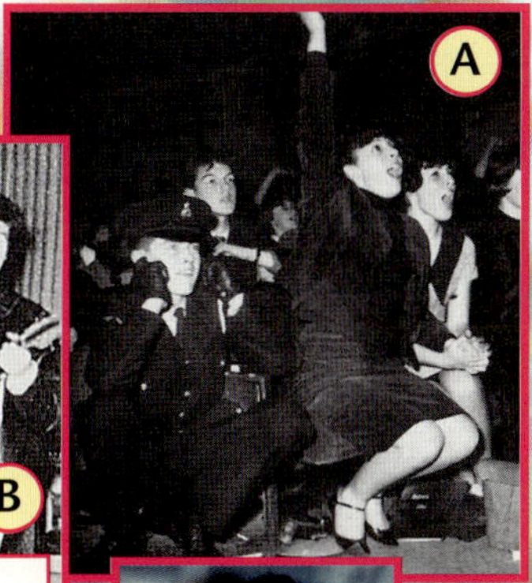

A Beatlemania

B History of the Beatles

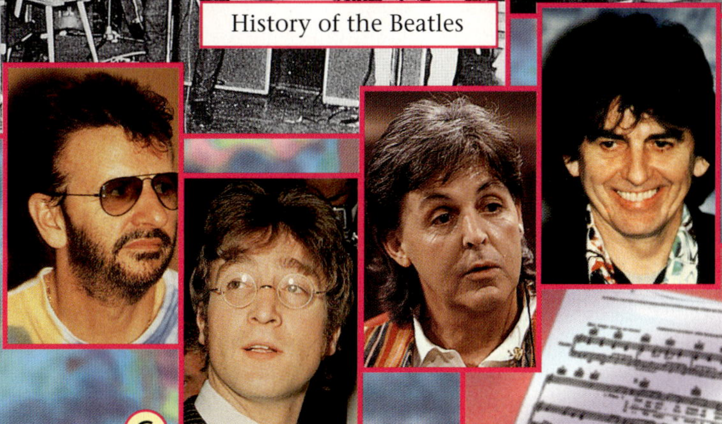

C Profiles of the members

D Music and lyrics

a) *A group of pupils are presenting a project on the Beatles. Listen to the first speaker's part of the presentation, and put the topics in the right order.*

b) *Listen again. Does Matt want people to ask questions during the presentations or afterwards? What exactly does he say? What would you say if you gave a presentation, and why?*

c) *Listen to Kate and take notes. Then compare your notes with a partner. Listen again if necessary. Practise giving mini-presentations using your notes.*

d) *Start your own project on the Beatles or any other pop group. Work in pairs or groups and decide who will deal with which topic.*

A Vocabulary

1 Similar but different

Work with a partner. Take turns, in which one of you explains the link between the words in a pair, and the other explains the difference.

Example: 1. Both are a kind of title. – Yes, but you only say 'headline' for newspaper reports.

1. heading / headline
2. thriller / comedy
3. editor / reporter
4. director / producer
5. broadsheet / tabloid
6. documentary / soap opera
7. viewer / listener
8. movie / film
9. cable / satellite
10. magazine / newspaper
11. publish / broadcast
12. photographers / paparazzi

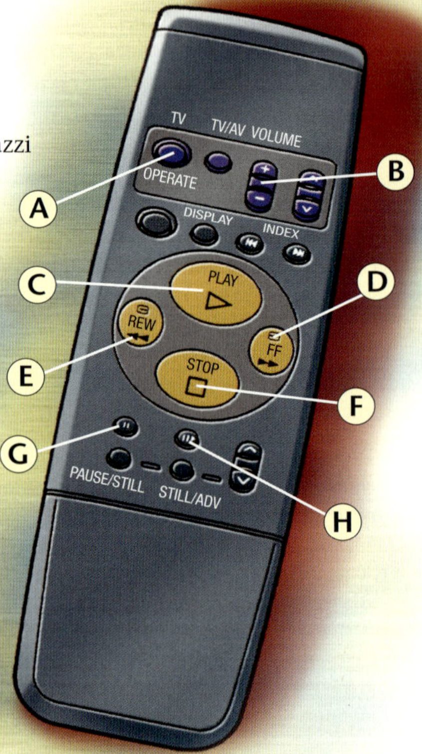

2 How does it work?

a) *Explain what the different buttons are for.*

Example: You press button 'A' to turn on the TV.

SAVE

turn/switch **on**
turn/switch **off**
turn **up/down**
turn/switch **over** (to a different channel)
play/stop
fast forward/rewind

Turn down the volume. (Turn it down.)

b) *You and your friend are watching a video. Your friend has the remote control. What do you say in these situations?*

1. The volume is too low. *You:* Could you turn it ...?
2. Now it's too loud. *(Go on.)*
3. There are some ads on the video. You aren't interested in them.
4. You'd like to see one of the scenes again.
5. You want to go to the toilet, but you don't want to miss any of the film.
6. The film has finished. Maybe there's something good on television.
7. What you're watching is boring. Maybe there's something better on a different channel.
8. You've had enough television.

3 Word rhythm

Put the words in groups to show where the stress falls.

1. First syllable: **cha**nnel, ...
2. Second syllable: a**vail**able, ...
3. Third syllable: unco**op**erative, ...

controversial scandal addiction questionnaire result fascination publish nervous attractive delight absolutely phenomenon sensitive revolutionary pedestal photographer

4 Adjective-noun partners

a) *Find pairs that make likely partners.*

thick – breakneck – seconds – number-one – crashing – bright – a fake – a broken	marriage – cigar – noise – issue – skin – flat – speed – colours

b) *Complete the sentences with the pairs you found in a).*

1. He was wearing a false moustache and smoking ...
2. Madonna isn't too sensitive. In fact, she has a ...
3. The paparazzi were following on motorbikes at ...
4. We rushed out of school and made the bus in ...
5. I never wear black or grey. I prefer ...

TIP
Keep your ears and eyes open for adjective + noun partners. Record these phrases in your vocabulary book.

c) *Write sentences with the other three pairs.*

5 Synonyms

First choose the correct synonym or definition. When you have checked your answers, write sentences to show you know how to use the words.

1. colleague	a) a place of education	b) someone you work with
2. to drag	a) to push something heavy	b) to pull something with difficulty
3. sensitive	a) easily affected	b) sensible
4. I blamed myself.	a) I did something silly.	b) I felt it was my fault.
5. sincere	a) opposite of 'false' or 'fake'	b) serious
6. to dim	a) to get dark slowly	b) to get dark suddenly
7. to dub	a) to record over something	b) to make a copy
8. (to) stack	a) to put in a pile	b) past form of 'stick'

6 Prepositions

Put the parts together to make sentences.

1. The orchestra packed	with	by a photographer.
2. Princess Diana found it difficult to deal	in	a pedestal.
3. A crashing piano chord was put	up	her fame.
4. The media likes to put celebrities	over	at the end of the song.
5. Madonna was nearly run	to	America and Europe.
6. The problem is not only limited	on	and went home.

7 Same verb, two meanings

Some verbs have several meanings. Normally 'have' means 'own', but not in the sentences below. Rewrite them using the synonyms on the right.

giving birth to taking experiencing eating holding undergoing

1. She was **having** a shower when the phone rang.
2. What's all that noise? – My neighbour is **having** a party.
3. You'll have to wait. The group are **having** their breakfast.
4. We're **having** a lot of trouble with the new TV.
5. I stood outside the hospital while Madonna was **having** her baby.
6. Elton John is **having** a hair transplant in a private clinic.

SAVE
She **is having** a baby.
She **has** a child called Liz.
(The child belongs to her.)

4

B Tenses

1 Different form, different meaning

a) *What do you think the people in the pictures are thinking?*
Example: Mona Lisa is probably thinking …

b) *Use the simple present or present progressive.*

1. I *(think)* TV causes violence.
2. Hey, what are you doing? – Be quiet, I *(think)*.
3. Why *(he be)* so silly? He *(usually be)* so sensible!
4. Something's wrong with my eyes! I *(see)* double!
5. Madonna *(see)* red when she hears the word 'paparazzi'.
6. I *(enjoy)* watching TV after I've finished my homework.
7. This is a great holiday. I *(enjoy)* every minute of it.

Mona Lisa *by L. da Vinci*

The Cry *by Edvard Munch*

Simple = permanent states and regular activities
What do you think? (= What is your opinion?)

Progressive = temporary states and activities
What are you thinking? (= What is going through your mind right now?)

2 The forecast for noon (15)

a) *Listen and say which picture goes with the forecast.*

b) *Listen again and note down the verb you hear most often. Try to explain why this future form is used here.*

c) *Write a weather forecast for the other picture.*

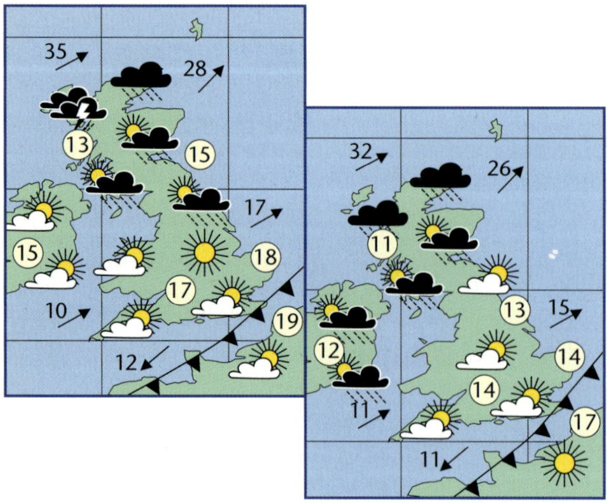

3 Cliffhangers

Episodes of serials often end with 'cliffhangers', exciting or frightening situations where you wonder what is going to happen next. What do you think is going to happen or might happen in the next episodes of these serials?

4 Don't drink and drive

A soft-drink company is working with the police to produce a *Don't Drink and Drive* commercial with actors from the popular soap opera, *Denver Palace*.

1. What does RJ promise his girlfriend Alexis? What future form does he use?
2. What are Mary-Ellen and RJ doing in the second picture?
3. Why does RJ refuse a whisky? What tense does he use in his answer, and why?
4. What is Mary-Ellen's second offer? Does RJ accept it?
5. What tense does he use in his answer? Try to explain why.

Translate the dialogue into German. What tense(s) do you use for the future?

5 Which future form?

a) *Decide which future form is correct or more likely, and say why.*

1. Bruce Delamitri *(goes/will go/is going)* to the Oscar ceremony on Saturday.
2. When *(will/does)* the ceremony start?
3. I'm not sure. I *('ll check/'m going to check)* the programme.
4. Bruce thinks he *(will win/is winning)* an Oscar.
5. He's been nominated, so it *(is quite likely/ is quite likely to)*.
6. On the other hand, he's quite controversial, so he *(may not/is very likely to)* win.
7. Madonna told Diana: "You *(will have to/are having to)* get a skin as thick as an armadillo".
8. Her eyes filled with tears at the news of Diana's death. "I think I *(am going to/will)* cry," she said.
9. If you talk to that News of the World reporter, she *('ll publish/is publishing)* everything you say.
10. The lead singer of Sugar 'n' Spice *(is going to/is having/will have)* a baby!

SAVE

Verb forms for the future
Simple: timetables, official arrangements.
Progressive: personal arrangements
Going to: plans; decisions, talking about future events (that we can see coming)
Will: guesses, expectations, promises, warnings, threats, decisions made at the moment of speaking
be (un)likely (to): (im)probable
may/might (not): (im)possible

b) *Copy the SAVE box and add example sentences from a), or your own, for each category.*

C Forms of the passive

G 19

1 Two word verbs

a) *Work in pairs. Think of pop stars you both like or hate, and say who does what.*

	stare		
The fans ...	talk	about	
The press ...	listen	at	*(name of pop star)*
Some journalists ...	write	to	
I ...	read		
	laugh		

b) *You are one of the pop stars. Say what you hate/love/don't mind.*
Example: I don't mind being written about, as long as I'm not taken apart.

There's only one thing worse than being talked about, and that's not being talked about.
Oscar Wilde

G 20

2 Verbs with two objects

a) *Read the following sentence and then translate it into German. What difference do you notice?*

We were given tickets for the concert.

b) *Now write out the story below with the verbs in the right form, passive or active.*

I *(give)* instructions by the editor to get a photo of Madonna in hospital with her new baby. He *(give)* me some flowers and a Get Well Card and told me to pretend to be a visitor. My colleague Steve, a reporter, *(give)* a paramedic's uniform. He *(teach)* very quickly how to drive an ambulance (not a real one!) and off we went. On the way to the hospital, we stopped to help a woman who *(knock over)* by a truck. Steve *(not teach)* first aid, so I *(give)* it instead. When we arrived at the hospital, Steve *(take)* her to the Accident Department while I looked for Madonna and the baby. When I *(find)* them, I started flashing my camera, but a moment later it *(take)* from me by two nurses. I *(show)* the way out and the police were waiting for me outside. They *(give)* my camera – I never got it back – and I *(ask)* some difficult questions. I *(tell)* them lies, of course. Later I discovered that I *(take)* photos of the wrong baby in the wrong hospital. A false address *(send)* to all the newspapers – one of Madonna's old tricks! Steve and I *(sack)* for this. We *(not pay)* anything for our work, even though we *(promise)* a lot of money. But we *(give)* some good news at last. A thank-you letter *(send)* to the hospital by the woman we *(help)*. Now we *(offer)* jobs by the hospital as paramedics!

c) *Pick out examples of the 'personal passive' (the subject of the passive sentence is the indirect object of the active sentence – see sentence no. 4 in the box).*

d) *Rewrite each of these in two different ways: 1) as a passive sentence starting with a different subject, and 2) as an active sentence. Which of the three do you think sounds best?*

SAVE

Verbs with two objects

Active 1. Madonna sent the editors the wrong address.
2. Madonna sent the wrong address to the editors.
3. Madonna sent it to them.

('wrong address' = direct object; 'the editors' = indirect object)

Passive 4. **The editors were sent** the wrong address.

Listening

1 Me and my big mouth! (16-23)

a) *An American tabloid reporter has secretly recorded a conversation with an English nanny in Los Angeles. Listen to the recording and make notes about the Coopers.*

b) *Before the reporter writes the story, she tells the editor what she found out. What does she say?*

c) *What mistake does one of the speakers make at the end of the recording?*

d) *The nanny's accent is standard southern British English, and the reporter's is standard American English. Listen to the recording again, and identify the differences in how they say these words:*

1. The 'r' in: girl, four, car, York, pairs
2. The vowel sounds in: (a) duty, new (b) ask, fast (c) awful, not, problem, dog, talk
3. The 't' in: write/writer, duty
4. The number of syllables in: secretary

e) *You will hear each sentence twice. Decide whether the first speaker is American or English.*

1. What an awful dog!
2. Talk to the officer on duty in New York.
3. I have four really fast cars.
4. It's not a girl, it's a boy.
5. He's asked his secretary about the problem.
6. I'll write a letter to his father.

f) *Write an article for the Daily Nose about the Coopers. Use the information you heard on the recording, and invent some more colourful details for your readers. Don't forget to give your article a headline.*

2 Song: Let's call the whole thing off! (28)

This song, which is from the 1937 musical 'Shall We Dance?' starring Ginger Rogers and Fred Astaire, makes fun of the difference between British and American pronunciation.

Listen and pick out the words that are compared.

3 Words that stick together

In spoken English, words sometimes 'stick' together, so two or more words can sound like one word. *Match the phrases on the left with their spoken sounds on the right.*

1. He doesn't like it.
2. There isn't any.
3. I'm going to ...
4. You and me
5. What do you mean?
6. What does he want?
7. Where's the boy?
8. What are you doing?
9. Just the same

a) [ˈwɒtsiˌwɒnt]
b) [ˌaɪmˈgəʊɪntə]
c) [ðeərˈɪzəntˌeni]
d) [ˌwɒtjəˈmi:n]
e) [hi:ˈdʌznˌlaɪkɪt]
f) [ˈweəzðəˌbɔɪ]
g) [ˈju:nˌmi:]
h) [ˌdʒesðəˈsəɪm]
i) [ˈwɒtjəˌdu:ɪŋ]

4 Checking understanding

The phrases on the right are useful if you haven't understood something someone said.

a) *What would you say if you wanted the speaker to:*

- explain a word / expression?
- explain an idea more simply?
- repeat a word / expression?
- speak more slowly?
- speak more clearly?
- speak louder?

b) *Ask your teacher to describe his/her favourite film or TV show. If there is something you don't understand, ask your teacher to explain or repeat it.*

c) *Practise the same thing in pairs.*

I'm afraid you're speaking a bit too fast for me.

Excuse me, but could you speak up a bit?

Sorry, but what are 'oysters'?

Did you say 'writer' or 'rider'?

I don't quite follow what you're saying.

What exactly do you mean by that?

I didn't quite catch that last word.

What was that you said?

Listening tips

- Relax.
- Concentrate on main ideas, or what you need to know.
- Don't panic if you don't understand everything. (You've probably understood enough.)
- If you can see who is talking, watch for 'non-verbal clues' (e.g. body language).
- If you can talk to this person, ask questions to check you have understood properly.
- Practise as much as you can. Listen to recordings of people talking. Try to get used to the sound and rhythm of different types of spoken English (regional accents, formal/informal).

1 Word power

Find the odd one out and put it in the right group.

1. smile, suck, eyeliner, cry
2. sexist, sensitive, nanny, uncooperative
3. hip, competitive, ankle, nose
4. laugh, make-up, grease, hairspray
5. model, editor, lip, photographer

2 'Have' for actions

Say what these people are having.

3 *Denver Palace* or *Killer Thriller*?

Choose the best future form for the verbs in brackets.

Wilma: Hey, a new series of *Denver Palace* is on TV tonight!
Fred: What time?
Wilma: It *(start)* at eight-fifteen.
Fred: Oh, I *(not be)* here. I *(meet)* Bernie at the mall.
Wilma: Don't worry. I *(record)* it for you.
Fred: Oh, thanks. Here, I *(give)* you a blank cassette. It's my last one.
Wilma: Thanks. Hey – while you're at the mall, *(you get)* some more?
Fred: OK, if I have time, but I *(not go)* shopping.
Wilma: No? So why *(you go)* to the mall with Bernie?
Fred: We *(watch)* a movie. They have a new movie theater.
Wilma: A movie theater at the mall? That's great.
Fred: Yes, it *(open)* tonight. They *(show)* Bruce Delamitri's new movie, *Killer Thriller*.
Wilma: Well, maybe I *(come)* with you to hold your hand.

4 Opening night at the movie theater

Complete Wilma's story with the verbs on the right.

We (…) to arrive early, but when we got to the movie theater, long lines had already formed outside the ticket office. We (…) to wait half an hour before we (…) our tickets! After that we (…) into the theater and (…) instructions to stand in the back row. All the VIPs (…) the best seats at the front. We left after five minutes and marched back to the ticket office. We (…) free tickets for another evening, but we refused and asked to see the manager. He (…) to us and we explained what had happened. He said it was his colleague's fault, not his, and that he (…) a full report.

were sold
had been promised
was brought
had been told
were shown
were made
were offered
given
had been given

4

CHECK-IN

	to **stay tuned** [ˌsteɪ ˈtjuːnd]	dranbleiben, den Sender beibehalten	If you don't change to a different programme, you ~.
1	**behind the scenes** [bɪˌhaɪnd ðə ˈsiːnz]	hinter den Kulissen	Not everyone knows what happens ~.
	education [ˌedʒʊˈkeɪʃn]	Erziehung, Bildung, Ausbildung	You go to school to get this.
2	**on air** [ɒn‿ˈeə]	auf Sendung	While a programme is on TV or radio, it is ~.
	to **broadcast*** [ˈbrɔːdkɑːst]	senden, ausstrahlen, übertragen	to put on air
	broadsheet [ˈbrɔːdʃiːt]	großformatige Zeitung	A ~ newspaper is printed on large-size paper.
	channel [ˈtʃænl]	Kanal, Programm	On satellite TV, you can get a lot of different ~s.
	daily [ˈdeɪli]	täglich, Tages-	We get a ~ newspaper.
	editor [ˈedɪtə]	Herausgeber(in), Redakteur(in)	so. who is in charge of a newspaper, magazine, etc.
	presenter [prɪˈzentə]	Moderator(in)	the person who introduces a television or radio programme
	tabloid [ˈtæblɔɪd]	kleinformatige, bebilderte Zeitung	A ~ paper is 'easier' to read than a broadsheet.
	viewer [ˈvjuːə]	Fernsehzuschauer(in)	so. who watches TV
	violence [ˈvaɪələnts]	Gewalt	A lot of people think too much ~ is shown on TV.
3	**survey** [ˈsɜːveɪ]	Untersuchung, Umfrage	For a ~, a lot of people have to be asked questions.
	habit [ˈhæbɪt]	Gewohnheit	what you often/regularly do
	aim [eɪm]	Ziel	When you play a game, your ~ is to win it.
	majority [məˈdʒɒrəti]	Mehrheit	more than half
	third [θɜːd]	Drittel; *bis auf* 'half' *und* 'quarter' *entsprechen die Bruchzahlen den Ordinalzahlen*	about 33 percent
	minority [maɪˈnɒrəti]	Minderheit	less than half
	conclusion [kənˈkluːʒn]	Abschluss, Schlussfolgerung, Schluss	You must think about sth. carefully before you can come to a ~.

TEXTS

A	**novel** [ˈnɒvl]	Roman	'Oliver Twist' is a famous ~.
	sincere [sɪnˈsɪə]	aufrichtig	~ people really mean what they say.
	a little [ə ˈlɪtl]	ein wenig, ein bisschen	! a little boy = ein kleiner Junge a little time = ein wenig Zeit
	male [meɪl]	männlich; Mann	Men and boys are ~.
	female [ˈfiːmeɪl]	weiblich; Frau	Women and girls are ~.
	to **stack up** [stæk‿ˈʌp]	aufstapeln	to put together in a pile
	manner [ˈmænə]	Art und Weise	the way in which you do sth.
	to **disappear** [ˌdɪsəˈpɪə]	verschwinden	to appear ↔ to disappear
	babe [beɪb]	Baby, Puppe, Mädchen, Kleines	
	soda *(AE)* [ˈsəʊdə]	Limonade, süßes Erfrischungsgetränk	a sweet drink without alcohol
	boost [buːst]	Auftrieb, Verstärkung	
	buzz [bʌz]	*hier:* euphorisches Hochgefühl	

	controller [kən'trəʊlə]	*hier:* Leiter(in)	
	volume ['vɒlju:m]	Lautstärke	If you want your music louder, you must turn up the ~.
	to **suck** [sʌk]	saugen, lutschen	A sweet lasts longer in your mouth if you don't bite it but ~ it.
	delight [dɪ'laɪt]	Freude, Entzücken	
	floor manager ['flɔ: ˌmænɪdʒə]	Aufnahmeleiter(in)	
	to **rush** [rʌʃ]	eilen, stürzen	to go quickly, to hurry
	to **deal* in** ['di:l‿ɪn]	handeln mit	dealer – to deal with – to deal in
	layer ['leɪə]	Schicht, Lage	In very cold weather it's best to wear several ~s of clothing.
	copycat ['kɒpikæt]	Nachahmungstäter(in)	
	to **be* concerned about** [kən'sɜ:nd]	sich interessieren für, sich Sorgen machen um	to be worried about or care about
	adult ['ædʌlt]	Erwachsene(r), Erwachsenen-	another word for 'grown-up'
	incontinence [ɪn'kɒntɪnents]	Inkontinenz	
	focus ['fəʊkəs]	Brennpunkt, Blickpunkt, Blickrichtung	If the ~ is on sth., it is the centre of attention.
	lonely ['ləʊnli]	einsam; *hier:* einsame Person	An 'old lonely' is an old lonely person.
	nappy *(BE)* ['næpi]	Windel	
	difficulty ['dɪfɪklti]	Schwierigkeit	If you do sth. with ~, you find it difficult to do.
	grease [gri:s]	Fett, Schmiere, Pomade	Actors have to wear ~ on their faces on stage.
	concrete ['kɒŋkri:t]	Beton	a very hard grey material used for building
	to **light* (up)** [laɪt‿'ʌp]	aufleuchten, (sich) erhellen, anzünden	light – to light up – traffic light – lighthouse
	street-wise ['stri:tˌwaɪz]	erfahren im Leben auf der Straße	
	body count ['bɒdi kaʊnt]	Anzahl der Menschen, *hier:* Anzahl der Leichen	
	to **remind so. of sth.** [rɪ'maɪnd]	jmdn an etwas erinnern	! I reminded him of Mum's birthday. – I remembered Mum's birthday.
	thoughtful ['θɔ:tfl]	gedankenvoll, nachdenklich	think – thought – thoughtful
	to **influence** ['ɪnfluents]	beeinflussen	to affect in some way
	to shuffle ['ʃʌfl]	mischen, durchwühlen	
	sensitive ['sentsɪtɪv]	sensibel, empfindlich, einfühlsam	~ people are affected or hurt by things very easily.
	to **go*** [gəʊ]	*hier:* sagen	
1	**irony** ['aɪrəni]	Ironie	~ is a special kind of humour which shows a contrast between the words and the meaning.
2	serial killer [ˌsi:rɪəl 'kɪlə]	Serienkiller, Massenmörder	
	mansion ['mæntʃn]	Herrenhaus, Villa	
	to **prove** [pru:v]	beweisen	to show that sth. is true
	violent ['vaɪələnt]	brutal, gewalttätig, heftig	violent – violence
	to **shoot*** [ʃu:t]	schießen, erschießen	Guns are used for ~ing.
	ratings ['reɪtɪŋz]	Einschaltquoten, Zuschauerzahlen	
3	**on** [ɒn]	*hier:* über, zu	This is a book ~ horses.
	glad [glæd]	froh	If you're ~ about sth., you feel pleased.
	car crash ['kɑ: ˌkræʃ]	Autounfall	crash – to crash – car crash
	breakneck speed [ˌbreɪknek 'spi:d]	halsbrecherische Geschwindigkeit	To travel at ~ is to travel dangerously fast.
	to lose* count [ˌlu:z 'kaʊnt]	die Übersicht verlieren	
	Evita [e'vi:tə]	*Name eines Musicals/Films*	

4

	to **dig*** [dɪg]	graben	Some animals live in holes that they ~ in the ground.
	to **blame** [bleɪm]	beschuldigen, die Schuld zuschreiben	! to blame ≠ blamieren
	only ['əʊnli]	einzig(e)	If you are the ~ person, there's nobody else.
	to **handle** ['hændl]	umgehen mit	to deal with
	skin [skɪn]	Haut	Don't lie in the sun too long if you've got sensitive ~.
	armadillo [ˌɑ:mə'dɪləʊ]	Gürteltier	
	move [mu:v]	Bewegung, Schritt, Zug, Umzug	to move – move – moving
	bumper ['bʌmpə]	Stoßstange	It protects a car against small 'crashes'.
	manipulative [mə'nɪpjələtɪv]	manipulierend	
	unforgivable [ˌʌnfə'gɪvəbl]	unverzeihlich	so bad that even saying 'sorry' isn't enough
	pedestal ['pedɪstl]	Podest, Sockel	
	yet [jet]	doch	The word 'yet' can be used, like 'but', as a link between two sentence parts.
	apart [ə'pɑ:t]	auseinander	to take ~ ↔ to put together
	to **run* over** [rʌn‿'əʊvə]	überfahren	Every year thousands of pets are ~ on the roads.
	as though [əz 'ðəʊ]	als ob	
	to **be* right** [bi: 'raɪt]	Recht haben	
	to **achieve** [ə'tʃi:v]	erreichen, schaffen	If you ~ stardom, you manage to become a star.
	stardom ['stɑ:dəm]	Berühmtheit, Status eines Stars	
	membership ['membəʃɪp]	Mitgliedschaft	member – membership
	particular [pə'tɪkjələ]	besondere(r/s), bestimmte(r/s)	A ~ family is a certain family, or a special one.
	obsession [əb'seʃn]	fixe Idee, Besessenheit	
	to glamorise ['glæməraɪz]	glorifizieren, idealisieren	
	addiction [ə'dɪkʃn]	Sucht	not being able to live without sth., e.g. drugs, alcohol, the Internet, etc.
	support [sə'pɔ:t]	Unterstützung	to support – support – supporting actor
	fame [feɪm]	Ruhm	famous – fame
	ball [bɔ:l]	Kugel	People in jail used to have a ~ and chain round their ankles.
	mph [ˌempi:'eɪtʃ]	Meilen pro Stunde	miles per hour
1	**attitude** ['ætɪtju:d]	Einstellung, Haltung	Your ~ to sth. is your opinion and how you feel on that subject.
	to **sum up** [sʌm‿'ʌp]	zusammenfassen	to express in only a few words, or to give the main points
2	to **edit** ['edɪt]	herausgeben, redigieren	editor – to edit
	marriage ['mærɪdʒ]	Ehe, Heirat	to marry – to be married – marriage
	worth [wɜ:θ]	wert	Jewellery can be ~ a lot of money.
C1	**Sgt., sergeant** ['sɑ:dʒnt]	Feldwebel	
	middle ['mɪdl]	Mitte; mittler(e/r/s)	on the left, in the ~, on the right
2	**per** [pɜ:]	pro	Don't spend more than £10 ~ week!
	BBC [ˌbi:bi:'si:]	British Broadcasting Corporation *(Rundfunkanstalt)*	The ~ is world-famous for its television and radio services.
	to **ban** [bæn]	verbieten, auf den Index setzen	On most flights today, smoking is ~ned.
	reference ['refrnts]	Bezug, Erwähnung; Referenz	to refer to = to make a ~ to; good ~s will help you to get a job more easily
	decision [dɪ'sɪʒn]	Entscheidung	to decide – decision

	to blow* one's mind out *(sl.)* [ˌbləʊ wʌnz 'maɪndˬaʊt]	umwerfen; high machen, sich berauschen	
	House of Lords [ˌhaʊsˬəv 'lɔ:dz]	britisches Oberhaus	
	to **turn so. on** [tɜ:nˬ'ɒn]	jmdn anmachen	That idea doesn't turn me on. = I don't find it attractive.
	to **drag** [dræg]	schleppen, ziehen	to pull, but with difficulty
	comb [kəʊm]	Kamm	You use a ~ for your hair.
	to **make*** [meɪk]	schaffen, erreichen	to manage (to get)
	(time +) **flat** [flæt]	sage und schreibe (nur)	I got to school in ten minutes ~. = I got there in only ten minutes.
	upstairs [ʌp'steəz]	(nach) oben, im/ins obere(n) Stockwerk	upstairs ↔ downstairs
	to have* a smoke [hævˬə 'sməʊk]	(eine) rauchen	
3	**suit** [su:t]	Anzug, Kostüm	a jacket with matching trousers or skirt
	old-fashioned [ˌəʊld'fæʃnd]	altmodisch	modern ↔ old-fashioned
	brass band [ˌbrɑ:s 'bænd]	Blaskapelle	Trumpets and similar instruments play in a ~.
	bright [braɪt]	hell, leuchtend	Yellow is a ~ colour.
	moustache [mə'stɑ:ʃ]	Schnurrbart	hair that grows between a man's nose and mouth
	note [nəʊt]	Note, Ton	! I can't sing the high notes (= die hohen Töne, Noten). I can't read music (= Noten lesen).
	fake [feɪk]	falsch, unecht	~ jewellery can look very much like the real thing.
	hum [hʌm]	Summen	a form of music you make with your lips closed
	to **dub** [dʌb]	synchron aufnehmen, synchronisieren	Usually, English films you see on TV in Germany are ~bed into German.
4	mania ['meɪniə]	Manie	
	profile ['prəʊfaɪl]	Porträt; Profil	a short description of a person's life

LANGUAGE

A2	to **fast forward** [ˌfɑ:st 'fɔ:wəd]	vorspulen	to make the tape move on very quickly
	to **rewind*** [ˌri:'waɪnd]	zurückspulen	to make the tape move back
	remote control [rɪˌməʊt kən'trəʊl]	Fernbedienung	to control – control – remote control
2	**forecast** ['fɔ:kɑ:st]	Vorhersage	The weather ~ tells us what the weather will be like.
4	**soft-drink** [ˌsɒft 'drɪŋk]	alkoholfreies Getränk	a (cold) drink without alcohol
	commercial [kə'mɜ:ʃl]	Werbespot	Ads on TV are usually called ~s.
	soft [sɒft]	weich, zart	soft ↔ hard
5	to **be* likely to** *(+ infinitive)* ['laɪkli]	wahrscheinlich tun	It is likely to rain soon. = It will probably rain soon.
	guess [ges]	Vermutung, Schätzung	to guess – guess

SKILLS

1	**nanny** ['næni]	Kindermädchen	a person who is paid to look after other people's children
	vowel ['vaʊəl]	Vokal	Our ~s are: a, e, i, o, u.

2	to call sth. off [kɔ:l‿'ɒf]	abblasen, absagen	
	to **make* fun of** [meɪk 'fʌn‿əv]	sich lustig machen über	If you laugh at other people, you ~ them.
	pronunciation [prəˌnʌntsi'eɪʃn]	Aussprache	the way words are spoken
4	to **speak* up** [spi:k‿'ʌp]	laut und deutlich sprechen	to speak loudly and clearly

CHECK-OUT

3	**blank** [blæŋk]	leer	A ~ piece of paper has nothing on it yet.
4	**VIP** [ˌvi:ai'pi:]	berühmte Persönlichkeit	short for 'very important person'

COGNATE WORDS

Aids [eɪdz] – Aids
arrangement [ə'reɪndʒmənt] – Arrangement, Vereinbarung, Verabredung, Plan
attractive [ə'træktɪv] – attraktiv, anziehend
bulimia [bʊ'lɪmiə] – Bulimie, Ess-/Brechsucht
cable ['keɪbl] – Kabel
cigar [sɪ'gɑ:] – Zigarre
clinic ['klɪnɪk] – Klinik
cocktail ['kɒkteɪl] – Cocktail
collage [kɒl'ɑ:ʒ] – Collage
colleague ['kɒli:g] – Kollege, Kollegin
contact lens ['kɒntækt ˌlens] – Kontaktlinse
contrast ['kɒntrɑ:st] – Kontrast, Gegensatz
controversial [ˌkɒntrə'vɜ:ʃl] – kontrovers, umstritten
crew [kru:] – Crew, Mannschaft
debate [dɪ'beɪt] – Debatte, Diskussion
definition [ˌdefɪ'nɪʃn] – Definition, Festlegung
to **dim** [dɪm] – dimmen, dämpfen, allmählich verdunkeln
episode ['epɪsəʊd] – Episode, Folge
extreme [ɪk'stri:m] – Extrem, das Äußerste
fascination [ˌfæsɪ'neɪʃn] – Faszination, Reiz
frequency ['fri:kwəntsi] – Frequenz, Häufigkeit
God [gɒd] – Gott
hertz [hɜ:ts] – Hertz *(Maßeinheit der Frequenz)*
icon ['aɪkɒn] – Ikone, Idol
indirect [ˌɪndɪ'rekt] – indirekt, mittelbar
journalist ['dʒɜ:nlɪst] – Journalist(in)
landmine ['lændmaɪn] – Landmine
to **limit** ['lɪmɪt] – limitieren, begrenzen
lip [lɪp] – Lippe
manager ['mænɪdʒə] – Manager(in), Geschäftsführer(in), leitende(r) Angestellte(r), *hier:* Direktor(in)
millennium [mɪ'leniəm] – Jahrtausend
monarchy ['mɒnəki] – Monarchie, Königshaus
monitor ['mɒnɪtə] – Monitor, Kontrollbildschirm
non-verbal [nɒn'vɜ:bl] – nonverbal, ohne Worte
paparazzi [ˌpæpər'ætsi] – Paparazzi, aufdringliche Skandalreporter(innen)
permanent ['pɜ:mənənt] – permanent, ständig
phenomenon [fɪ'nɒmɪnən] – Phänomen
photographer [fə'tɒgrəfə] – Fotograf(in)
photography [fə'tɒgrəfi] – Fotografie (*nicht:* Foto, Bild!); Aufnahmen
presentation [ˌprezn'teɪʃn] – Präsentation, Darbietung, Moderation
princess ['prɪnses] – Prinzessin
to **promote** [prə'məʊt] – fördern, werben für; befördern
realism ['rɪəlɪzm] – Realismus
to **reflect** [rɪ'flekt] – reflektieren, widerspiegeln
regional ['ri:dʒnl] – regional
relation [rɪ'leɪʃn] – Relation, Beziehung, Verhältnis
revolutionary [ˌrevl'u:ʃnri] – revolutionär, nie da gewesen
sauce [sɔ:s] – Sauce (Soße)
scandal ['skændl] – Skandal
sensational [sen'seɪʃnl] – sensationell
soap opera ['səʊp‿ɒprə] – Seifenoper
standard ['stændəd] – Standard, Norm
synonym ['sɪnənɪm] – Synonym
temporary ['tempərəri] – vorübergehend, befristet, temporär
the press [pres] – die Presse
tone [təʊn] – Ton
type [taɪp] – Typ, Art, Sorte
uncooperative [ˌʌnkəu'ɒprətɪv] – wenig entgegenkommend, wenig hilfsbereit

Don't trust false friends!

Many media words are easy to understand because they exist in German too, e.g. *cable, journalist, photographer, monitor.*
But be careful: there are also more difficult words which are similar to German words but have a different meaning. Read the following definitions and find the correct word:

1. It's a jacket and trousers men wear in a bank, for example – not a set of hotel rooms.
2. It's a certain kind of newspaper – you cannot have dinner at it.
3. It's a kind of lemonade as well as something adults put into their drinks.
4. It's quite a long text telling the story of one or several people – not a certain type of short story.
5. It's also a very popular star and not only a picture found in Russian churches.
6. It means saying that someone has done something wrong – not that someone feels embarrassed.
7. It's also a very hard material used for building and not only the opposite of 'abstract'.
8. It means 'not together' and it is not used to describe fashionable clothes.

"I say 'tomato', you say 'zxyzzkzmollnnz' ..."

UNIT 5

Sights and sounds of Ireland

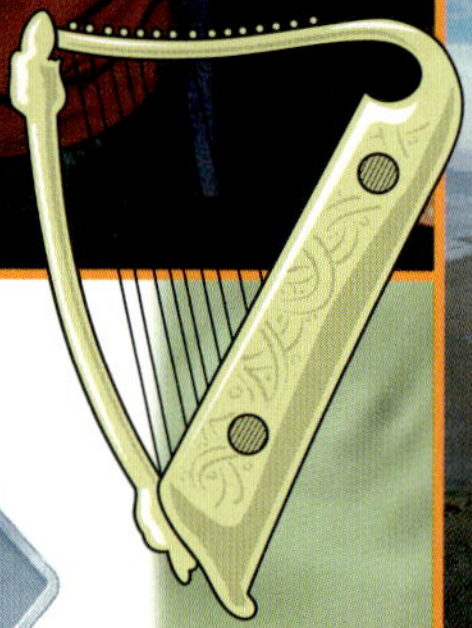

1 Irish music (1-7)

Irish music is known all over the world.

a) *Look at the pictures on this page. Do you know the names of any of these singers, groups, etc.?*
b) *Listen to the radio programme on the recording. Try to match the pieces of music with the pictures.*

Traditional music in a pub

High cross and round tower

Near Banbridge town in the County Down
One morning last July,
From a boreen[1] green came a sweet colleen[2]
And she smiled as she passed me by.
She looked so sweet from her two bare feet
To the sheen[3] of her nut-brown hair,
Such a coaxing elf[4], sure I shook myself
For to see I was really there!

Chorus:
From Bantry Bay up to Derry quay[5],
And from Galway to Dublin town,
No maid[6] I've seen like the brown colleen
That I met in the County Down.

[1](from Gaelic "bothairin") little road; [2](from Gaelic "cailin") girl; [3]*Glanz;* [4]*einschmeichelnde Elfe;* [5]usually: [ki:] *Kai;* [6]*here:* girl

2 A folk song: The star of the County Down

a) *Listen to the last song again and follow the words (see above).*

b) *Now pick out the place-names the singer mentions, and try to find them on the map. Which of them are in the Republic, and which in Northern Ireland?* (There has only been a border since 1921.)

3 The Celtic connection

As you already know, the Celts that came to Scotland were in Ireland first. *What signs of their culture can you find on this page?*

Vocabulary 96, 1

5

Village in West Cork

A Kilkelly (8)

Kilkelly is a small village in County Mayo. It is where songwriter Peter Jones's great-grandfather came from before he emigrated to the USA. When a box of old letters was passed on to him by his father, Peter learned a lot about his family history. The letters also gave him the idea for a song.

Kilkelly, Ireland, 1860, my dear and loving son John,
Your good friend the schoolmaster Pat McNamara's so good as to write these words down.
Your brothers have all gone to find work in England, the house is all empty and sad.
The crop of potatoes is sorely infected, a third to a half of them bad.
And your sister Brigid and Patrick O'Donnell are going to be married in June.
Your mother says not to work on the railroad and be sure to come on home soon.

Kilkelly, Ireland, 1870, my dear and loving son John,
Hallo to your Mrs and to your four children, may they grow healthy and strong.
Michael has got in a wee bit of trouble, I suppose that he never will learn.
And because of the dampness there's no turf to speak of, and now we have nothing to burn.
And Brigid is happy you named the child for her although she's got six of her own.
You say you found work, but you don't say what kind, or when you'll be coming home.

Kilkelly, Ireland, 1880, dear Michael and John, my dear sons,
I'm sorry to give you the very sad news – your mother passed on.
We buried her down at the church in Kilkelly, your brothers and Brigid were there.
You don't have to worry, she died very quickly, remember her in your prayers.
And it's so good to hear that Michael's returning, with money he's sure to buy land.
For the crop has been poor and the people are selling, any price that they can.

Kilkelly, Ireland, 1890, my dear and loving son John,
I suppose I must be close on 80, it's 30 years since you've gone.
Because of all of the money you send me I'm still living out on my own.
Michael has built himself a fine house and Brigid's daughters have grown.
And thank you for sending the family pictures – they're lovely young women and men.
You say you might even come for a visit, what joy to see you again!

Kilkelly, Ireland, 1892, my dear brother John,
I'm sorry I didn't write sooner to tell you your father passed on.
He was living with Brigid, she said he was cheerful and healthy right down to the end.
Ah, you should have seen him playing with the grandchildren of Pat McNamara, your friend.
We buried him down alongside your mother down at the Kilkelly churchyard.
He was a strong and a feisty old man, considering his life was so hard.
And it's funny the way he kept talking about you, he called for you at the end.
Why don't you think about coming to visit, we'd all love to see you again.

1 A closer look at the song

1. Work in groups and collect all the information you can about the *letters*, the *letter-writers*, the *people* and *events* mentioned in the letters, etc.
2. Put all this information together and write a family history.

2 The historical background

Look at these four historical newspaper articles. What possible connections can you find with the people mentioned in the letters?

Tuesday 10th October 1867

ARRESTS IN MANCHESTER

Twenty-nine Irishmen, all believed to be members of the Irish Republican Brotherhood ("Fenians") have been arrested in connection with last month's shooting of a policeman in Manchester when a police van carrying Fenian prisoners was attacked as it

Monday, March 3, 1856

ILLINOIS CENTRAL RAILROAD OPENED

The Illinois Central Railroad has been completed as far as Cairo, Missouri. It is intended in the coming years to extend the line as far as New Orleans.

UNREST IN IRELAND

This year's drop in farm prices continues the trend of the past two years. Since 1876, it has led many Irish farmers to give up farming, and is causing great unrest among those that remain.

Friday 30th August 1860

FEARS GROW OF FAMINE RETURN

Reports are coming in from the West of Ireland of potato blight in the early crop of potatoes. With memories of the catastrophic crop failures of 1845–46 still fresh, it is very much hoped that

3 Imagine …

Imagine you are one of the people mentioned in the letters. Choose one of the following tasks:

1. Write John's answer to any of the first four letters.
2. Write John's answer to the final letter.
3. Write Michael's letter to his father, explaining the "bit of trouble" (l. 9) he got in.
4. Make up a dialogue between Pat McNamara (the schoolmaster) and Brigid.

Infinitives 97

B ⟨The Celtic Tiger⟩

On the west coast

The goal in the immigration game is now Ireland

Population at highest level since 1922

Cottages For Sale

2,000 New Jobs

Golf in Kerry

1 Changes

a) *Look at these pictures, headlines, etc., and say what they suggest about the way Ireland has changed/is changing.*

b) *Talk about whether the changes suggested by the pictures and headlines are good or bad.*

2 Tracking the Celtic tiger (9)

Listen to (or read) the first part of an Australian radio programme to find the answers to these questions:

1. What is meant by the "Celtic tiger"?
2. What signs of it can you see in Dublin?

Nick Rushworth: You may have heard of the so-called "tiger" economies of south-east Asia. Well, Ireland is now the fastest-growing economy in the world. I'm Nick Rushworth, and welcome to Background Briefing. Today, tracking the "Celtic tiger" as Ireland's been dubbed, to see how far it's reached and whether it's endangered.

This is Kildare Street, in Dublin. In fact, it's pretty much any street in Dublin. Because if you look up, the city's skyline is dotted with cranes. Counting cranes is as good an index of growth as any other. So if construction is anything to go by, then Dublin, Ireland, is booming.

As good as the crane index is, maybe a better measure of Ireland's prosperity is simply that the Irish are coming home. Their annual mass exodus is a tradition that goes back to the Great Famine of the 1840s. They've always left Ireland in search of better opportunities abroad – in England, in America, in Australia. Well, last year was the first on record that more people came to live in Ireland than left it. And it's largely due to the tiger.

Dublin skyline

Cottage ruins in Mayo

New industry

3 Radio interviews (24-25)

a) Nick goes to Balbriggan, just at the north edge of Dublin's spreading suburbs, to talk to a farmer, Christy Sweetman.

Listen and try to answer these questions:

1. Why is Christy lucky?
2. How much money did he get for his land?

Christy Sweetman

Mary Harney

b) Later Nick interviews Mary Harney, the Minister for Trade and Employment. First they talk about the situation 12 years before, when Ireland was faced with a weak economy and high unemployment. The government had to do something. Because the standard of education was high, the government was able to use the large number of skilled workers as an argument to get foreign companies to set up factories in Ireland. The government created the lowest taxes in the European Union, and this also helped.

In the rest of the interview you are going to hear what the government has been doing about the problem of emigration. (The words on the right will help you to get the gist.)

Listen and find out:

1. Why was this problem so important to the government?
2. What have they done about it?

to invest
to sustain (schools, ...)
to establish
fund
to encourage
pitch
to research
to launch
reputation
housing
reasonable

Vocabulary 96, 3

C Returning to Dublin (10-16)

Signora got out of her bus and walked up beside the Liffey to O'Connell Bridge. All around her there were young people, tall, confident, laughing, in groups. She remembered reading somewhere about this youthful population, half the country under the age of twenty-four, was it?

She hadn't expected to see such proof of it. And they were dressed brightly, too. Before she had gone away, Dublin had been a grey and drab place. A lot of the buildings had been cleaned, there were smart, expensive cars in the busy traffic lanes. She remembered more bicycles and second-hand cars. The shops were bright and opened up.

For some reason she kept walking down the Liffey after O'Connell Bridge and there she found Temple Bar. It was like the Left Bank in Paris when once she had gone there so many years ago with Mario for a long weekend. Cobbled streets, outdoor cafés, each place full of young people calling to each other and waving at those they knew.

Signora thought it was wonderful. It was a whole new world, she couldn't get enough of it. Eventually, she sat down to have a coffee.

A girl of about eighteen with long red hair, like her own many years ago, served her coffee. She thought Signora was a foreigner.

'What country are you from?' she asked in slow English.

'Sicilia, in Italia,' Signora said.

'Beautiful country, but I tell you I'm not going there until I can speak the language though.'

'And why is that?'

'Well, I'd want to know what the fellows are saying, I mean you wouldn't know what you were letting yourself in for if you didn't know what they were saying.'

'I didn't speak any Italian when I went there, and I sure didn't know what I was letting myself in for,' Signora said. 'But you know it worked out all right ... no, more than all right. It was wonderful.'

'How long did you stay for?'

'A long time. Twenty-six years.'

The girl looked at her in amazement. 'You stayed all that time, you must have loved it.'

'Oh I did, I did.'

'And when did you come back?'

'Today,' Signora said.

The girl was about to move away.

'Excuse me, this seems a very nice part of Dublin. Is this the kind of place I could rent a room, do you think? Just somewhere simple,' Signora said.

She listened glumly as she learned that this was one of the most fashionable parts of town; everyone wanted to live here. There were penthouse apartments, pop stars had bought hotels, business people had invested in townhouses. The place was full of restaurants. It was the last word.

'And please could you tell me where *would* be a place that would be good value to stay, somewhere that hasn't become the last word?'

The girl shook her head of long, dark red hair. It was hard to know. She seemed to be trying to work out whether Signora had any money at all, whether she would have to work to pay her rent, how long she would stay wherever she landed.

Signora decided to help her. 'I have enough money for bed and breakfast for a week, but then I'll have to find a cheap place and maybe somewhere I could do some jobs ... maybe look after children.'

The girl was doubtful. 'They usually want young ones to look after kids.'

'Or maybe over a restaurant and work in it?' Signora asked.

'No, I wouldn't be too hopeful about that, honestly ... They're very hard to get.'

She was nice, the girl. 'Is that your name on your apron? Suzi?'

'Yes, I'm afraid my mother was a Suzi Quatro fan. The singer, you know? She was big years ago, maybe not in Italy.'

'I'm sure she was, it's just that I wasn't listening then. Now, Suzi, I'd love you to tell me what area would be a nice cheap one where I should start looking.'

Suzi listed off the names of places that used to be small areas, suburbs if not exactly villages, well outside the city when Signora was young, but now they were big working-class estates. Half the people there would take someone in to rent a room if their kids had left home maybe. As long as it was cash.

'You're very good to me, Suzi. How do you know all about things like that at your age?'

'Well, that's where I grew up, I know the scene.'

She saw Suzi pause and bite her lip.

'Are you serious about not minding what kind of place it is?'

'Absolutely serious.'

'Listen. I don't get on with my family myself, so I don't live at home any more. And only a week ago they were talking about trying to get somebody to take my room. They could use a few pounds a week – it would have to be cash, you know, and you'd have to say you were a friend if anyone asked ... because of income tax.'

'Do you think I could?' Signora's eyes were shining.

'Listen, now.' Suzi did not want any misunderstandings. 'We're talking about a very ordinary house in an estate of houses that look the same, some a bit better, some a bit worse. They have the telly on all the time, they shout at each other over it and of course my brother's there, Jerry. He's fourteen and awful.'

'I just need a place to stay. I'm sure it would be lovely.'

Suzi wrote down the address and told her which bus to take. 'Why don't you go down the road and ask a few people who I know definitely won't be able to have you and then go by chance, as it were, to my house and ask. Mention the money first and say it won't be for long. They'll like you because you're a bit older, respectable is what they'll say. They'll take you, but don't say you came from me.'

Signora gave her a long look. 'Did they not like your boyfriend?'

'Boyfriends.' Suzi corrected her. 'My father says I'm a slut, but please don't try to deny it when he tells you because it will show you've met me.' Suzi's face looked hard.

Signora wondered if her own face had been hard like that when she left for Sicily all those years ago.

She took the bus and wondered at how the city she had once lived in had grown and spread so wide. In the evening light children played in the streets among the traffic, and then there were small gardens and children cycled round in circles and ran in and out of each other's gardens.

Signora called at the houses that Suzi had suggested. Dublin men and women told her that their houses were full and they needed all the space they had.

'Can you suggest anyone?' she asked.

'Try the Sullivans,' someone suggested.

Now she had her reason. She knocked on the door. Would this be her new home? Was this the roof she would lie under and hope to ease the pain of losing her life in Annunziata?

Jerry opened the door, his mouth full. He had red hair and freckles and he had a sandwich in his hand.

'Yeah?' he said.

(adapted from: *Evening Class* by Maeve Binchy)

5

1 Comparisons and contrasts

The story is full of contrasts – about people, times, and places. *Work in groups to find them.*

- *People:* Signora's past/present; Signora/Suzi and the similarities and differences between them.
- *Times:* The Dublin of 30 years ago/the Dublin of today.
- *Places:* Two very different parts of Dublin.

2 Creative writing

Continue the story with a dialogue between Signora, Jerry, and Mr and/or Mrs Sullivan.

A Vocabulary

1 Words and music

a) *Copy the music lines into your exercise book, and add in all the useful words you know.*

b) *Listen again to the pieces of music you heard at the beginning of this unit – and now try to describe them, using these words.*

c) *Choose your favourite piece of music, and try to describe it to the class.*

technical terms: notes – sound – rhythm –
styles: classical – traditional –
how played: loud – slow –
people: singer – musician –
instruments:

2 City and country

Here is a "mixed bag" of nouns:

animals apartment block bridge bungalow cafe campsite canal capital casino churchyard cottage crop entrance factory farm fence field garden glen hotel industry lake land lane machine market marsh mountain museum nature noise pedestrian penthouse petrol station picnic poverty pub river road scenery sheep shop shopping sportsfield street suburb townhouse traffic trees turf wildlife woods yard

a) *Draw a diagram like this, and put the nouns where you think they belong.*

town/city	both	country

b) *Compare your diagrams. If they are different, try to explain why to each other. For example:*
I put "road" in … because …

3 ⟨Talking about the economy⟩

Put these words in the right places in the sentences on the right.

booming reasonable bargain invest prices skilled opportunities emigration housing taxes establish unemployment encouraged

1. Business people like to … in countries with a lot of … workers.
2. International companies were also … by Ireland's low … to … factories there.
3. When … was a problem, many young people left in search of … in other countries.
4. Now that … has stopped, … is hard to find.
5. When the economy is …, land … often go up.
6. I got this for a … price. – Yes, it was a real …!

4 False friends

Some English words sound just like words you know in German.

a) *These German speakers think they have found a "friend" in their own language. Correct them.*

b) *If the "false friends" actually exist in English, what do they mean? Check them in a dictionary.*

People who complain about jokes are just being a bit too … er, um … — *sensibel?*

You can call me on my … — *Handy?*

Well, at least the film had a happy … — *Happy End?*

No, I can't be at the comedy club at six, but I can make it by seven, er, … — *eventuell?*

The information in this book is completely … — *ganz aktuell?*

B Infinitives

G 21

1 Ireland's national holiday

17th March is St Patrick's Day, a day to look forward to – whether you're Irish or not!

a) *Complete the infinitive phrases.*

1. For a long time, New York was the place to …	wear – but a piece of shamrock used to be enough.
2. Back in Ireland it was just a day to …	be coloured green included the beer and the rivers!
3. But the parades were often too boring to …	be really spectacular.
4. Green was always the colour to …	watch for long.
5. In the USA, on the other hand, the things to …	attend church, go to a pub or watch a parade.
6. The 1989 Parade in Dublin was the first to …	go for a good time on St Patrick's Day.

b) *Look at the SAVE box, and complete the remaining sentences in the same way.*

1. In the 1980s, with more tourists coming to Ireland in the spring, it was time … *(things / change).*
2. Many people thought it was crazy … *(the organizers / colour the Liffey green).* But that's exactly what they did!
3. And it was clever … *(them / find someone really popular / lead the parade)*: Ronan Keating of Boyzone.
4. Since then, Dublin has become the place … *(New Yorkers / get ideas for their own parade).*

SAVE

There are different ways to add a special subject for the infinitive:
… a place **for** my friend **to** stay.
It was nice **of** you **to** come.

c) *Write about a similar parade or event in your own area. Give advice about the things to see and do, etc.*

5

G 22

2 Buskers

One of the joys of Dublin – and of many other big cities – is its buskers. Or is it? Some people feel very differently about them.

a) *Make at least four sentences about the opinions and wishes of the people below.*

Tourists Business people The authorities They	like expect (often) ask prefer order warn want don't want	buskers them the authorities	to play certain popular tunes. to play the same tune over and over again. to play different tunes. to move away. to stop. to ban buskers altogether.

b) *Make up a story about some buskers. Tell the story – in the past tense. You can start:* There were these buskers playing … People were asking them to … But a shop owner didn't want them …

C Reported speech

1 In Dublin's fair city …

G 23.1

a) The Sampsons have flown from the US for a short vacation in Ireland. How are they going to spend their one day in Dublin?

Complete the parts of their dialogue where they report what they have heard or read (see below).

1. *Mom:* Let's go to Trinity College. Our hotel receptionist says …
2. *Lucy:* Yes, our guide book says it …
3. *Dad:* Then we won't have time for the Guinness Brewery! My friend Joe always tells me how …
4. *Mom:* Well, you and Burt can go there, while Lucy and I go to Trinity. And after dinner we'll go to Slattery's Pub. I've heard that …

SAVE

No change in tenses after a reporting verb in the present, present perfect, or future!

5. *Burt:* Nah! Who wants traditional music? I was talking to this guy on a skateboard outside the hotel, and he says we should try Temple Bar …
6. *Lucy:* Yes, Burt's right, it's the hottest place in Dublin. This article here explains that …
7. *Burt:* Huh? Sounds a bore! Forget it!

G 23.2

b) *Read Lucy's diary. Note how the tenses change when you report things in the past tense. Make a list of these changes.*

simple present ➩ simple past
present progressive ➩
present perfect ➩
simple past ➩
…

Can you find a general rule? And what happens to the verbs "would" and "should"?

Our hotel receptionist said we could see the Book of Kells in Trinity College Library. Mom wanted to go there, and I read that the college had been founded in 1591, in what had been an old monastery. But Dad complained that we wouldn't have time for the Guinness Brewery then. His friend Joe always told him how he had enjoyed his visit and thought Dad would enjoy it too. So we agreed that Dad and Burt could go there while Mom and I went to Trinity. And after dinner we would go to Slattery's, where they played the best traditional music in town. But Burt said he'd been talking to a guy who had said we should try Temple Bar. We'd meet the really cool people there. But Burt is funny: When I read out that many of Ireland's arts groups had moved into Temple Bar, he told us to forget it.

2 What they said

a) *Change the following thoughts/words to reported speech. Use a reporting verb in the past tense. (Look for the answers in the story on pp 94-95.)*

Signora: (thinks) It's wonderful! It's a whole new world, I can't get enough of it! (Signora **thought** it ...)

Suzi: Oh, this is one of the most fashionable parts of town. Everyone wants to live here! There are penthouse apartments, pop stars have bought hotels, business people have invested in townhouses. The place is full of restaurants. It's the last word now!

b) *Now change the following to reported speech:*

1. "This seems a very nice part of Dublin." ➪ Signora said that ...
2. "I have just come back from Italy." ➪ She explained ...
3. "They usually want young ones to look after kids." ➪ Suzi thought ...
4. "My mother was a Suzi Quatro fan." ➪ She explained that ...
5. "I don't get on with my family myself, so I don't live at home any more." ➪ She ...
6. "My room's empty, and my parents could use a few pounds a week." ➪ She told ...
7. "It would have to be cash." ➪ She made it clear to Signora that ...

3 Questions, advice, and suggestions

G 24

a) Who asked these questions? (Suzi asked ... if / how / ...)

1. "How long did you stay for?"
2. "Is this the kind of place I could rent a room?"
3. "How do you know all about things like this at your age?"
4. "Is that your name on your apron?"
5. "Are you serious about not minding what kind of a place it is?"

SAVE

She asked her/wanted to know/...
- where she was from.
- whether/if she could speak Italian.

She asked/told/advised/ ... her to ...
not to ...

G 25

b) *Report Suzi's advice,* l. 116: "(Why don't you) go down ... ask ... and then go ... and ask ... Mention ... and say ... but don't say ...! ... but please don't try to deny ...!"
Start: She advised her to ..., ... warned her not to ...

⟨c)⟩ You don't always need to report every word.
Look for other (shorter) ways of reporting questions, suggestions, etc. You'll find some ideas in the box.
Example: She asked her name.

expressed interest in | suggested (doing sth.) | asked (about) | agreed | repeated (the ...) | didn't want to | showed (so. sth.) | refused

5

4 At the Sullivans' (26-29)

1 HV

a) *Listen to the first two dialogues at the Sullivans' door and in their house, and then write a short report. Use different reporting verbs, and say how the people spoke.*

politely? rudely? uncertainly?
in a friendly/unfriendly way?

⟨b)⟩ *Listen to the third dialogue. It is much longer, so you needn't report everything. Look for short ways of telling the story (see ex. 3c) above).*

G 26

5 ⟨No need ...⟩

Sometimes a "time-shift" isn't necessary.
Example: He told me Dublin **is**/was by the sea.
And what about these?

1. "Father was cheerful and healthy right down to the end." – She said he ... *(Check Text A!)*
2. "I was sick last week, but I'm all right now." – He told me ...
3. "Blue and yellow make green." – We learned ...
4. "Ireland is part of Europe." – She stresed ...
5. "Ireland has become a modern country." – They explained that ...

D Pronouns

G 27

1 Kerry jokes

The Irish like to make jokes about about the people of Kerry, a county in the south-west of the country.

Kerrywoman: Ooh, is that a real diamond[1]?
Her boyfriend: I hope so – I paid £2 for it!

– Have you heard the latest Kerry joke?
– I'm warning you. I'm from Kerry, you know!
– That's all right. I'll tell it slowly.

a) *Put the parts together to make more Kerry jokes.*

1. What do you find on the bottom of bottles in Kerry?
2. Have you heard about the Kerryman who got a pair of water skis for Christmas?
3. In a car wash[2], how do you know which one is the Kerryman?

He's the one riding a motorbike.

Open other end.

He's still looking for a lake with a slope[3]!

[1]Diamant; [2]Autowaschanlage; [3]Hang

b) *Complete the first text (left) with pronouns from the box on the left. Then use pronouns from the box on the right to complete the second text.*

myself, yourself, himself, herself, itself, ourselves, yourselves, themselves, each other

1. Neighbouring countries often like to make jokes about ... 2. People should be able to laugh at ...! 3. When the singer Paul Brady complained about the "Irish jokes" you often hear on British radio and TV, he was just another Irishman who couldn't laugh at ... 4. And all this sensitivity from a nation that prided ... on its talent for comedy! 5. But Irish comedians are well able to defend ... by hitting back at the English. 6. Back at home, the Irish amuse ... by telling what the British call "Irish jokes" – but about the people of Kerry! 7. The Germans tell jokes like these about the East Friesians; the French and the Belgians make fun of ... in the same way. 8. So what about your reactions to jokes about your nationality? Are you able to laugh at ...?

some, something, someone/somebody, somewhere, any, anything, anyone/anybody, anywhere, no, nothing, no-one/nobody, nowhere, every, everything, everyone/everybody, everywhere, one, none, both, either, neither

1. The trouble with neighbouring countries is that ... country can take the other quite seriously. 2. It's bad enough when ... countries are the same size. 3. But when ... of them is bigger or stronger, the people of that country seem to think that ... in the other country is a fool, and that ... there can do ... right. 4. If ... there complains, they are told not to be so silly, if they have ... sense of humour at all. 5. When Irish singer Paul Brady complained, ... people said he had absolutely ... sense of humour. 6. The funny thing is that about half the comedians on British radio and TV are Irish – as ... in Britain knows. 7. In the end, there's always ... else you can make fun of for being impossibly stupid. 8. It seems to be the same ... – at least all over Europe.

c) *Rewrite the second sentence so that you don't repeat the information from the first one. Use "so" or "not".*

1. Have you heard this one before? *I hope you haven't heard this one before.* (= I hope **not**.)
2. This is the funniest Kerry joke ever. *At least, I think it's the funniest Kerry joke ever.*
3. Some people think these jokes are insulting. *But I don't think they are insulting.*
4. We all have a sense of humour, don't we? *Well, I hope we all have a sense of humour.*
5. You may think this joke is racist. *If you don't think it's racist, you'll like it.*
6. I can laugh at myself. – *I can laugh at myself, too.*

Using dictionaries

1 A closer look at your dictionary

These tips will help you to find the right words and meanings more easily.

The **head words** are in alphabetical order: e.g. "sensation" comes before "sense" because **a** comes before **e**.

Some words can belong to different **classes** of words, e.g. verb and noun. They are marked **I**, **II**, etc.

Many words have more than one **meaning**. There is a number (1, 2, etc.) for each meaning.

Make sure you know the common **abbreviations**! You can look up the less common ones in the list at the back/front of the dictionary.

These words and abbreviations say if the word is used in a **special way**, or belongs to a special field.

Most dictionaries give you a list of **useful phrases**.

Under one head word you can also find other **related words**, like compounds (e.g. "sense organ" under "sense") and words with different endings (e.g. "sensibly" under "sensible"). But some dictionaries list these words separately. Check both possibilities!

sen.sa.tion [sen'seɪʃn] *s* **1.** Gefühl *nt* Empfindung *f* Sinneseindruck *m* **2.** Sensation *f*, Aufsehen *nt*; **a ~ of falling** das Gefühl zu fallen; **a ~ of hunger** ein Hungergefühl; **cause a ~** Aufsehen erregen; **sen.sa.tional** [sen'seɪʃənl] *adj* sensationell, aufsehenerregend
sense [sens] **I** s **1.** *(physiol)* Sinn *m* **2.** *(fig)* Sinn *m* **3.** **~s** Verstand *m* **4.** Gefühl *nt*; **5.** *(Wort)* Bedeutung *f*; **~ of hearing** Gehörsinn *m*; **~ of sight** Sehvermögen *nt*; **to be out of one's ~s** nicht ganz bei Trost sein; **come to one's ~s** zur Vernunft kommen; **~ of duty** Pflichtbewusstsein *nt*; **common ~** gesunder Menschenverstand; **there is no ~ in doing that** es ist zwecklos, das zu tun; **talk sense** vernünftig sein; **make sense** Sinn ergeben; **in the full ~ of the word** im wahrsten Sinn des Wortes **II** *vt* spüren, empfinden, fühlen **sense.less** ['senslɪs] *adj* **1.** bewusstlos **2.** unvernünftig **3.** *(Diskussion)* sinnlos **sense organ** Sinnesorgan
sen.sible ['sensəbl] *adj* **1.** vernünftig **2.** begreiflich **3.** *(obs)* spürbar, merklich **be ~ of s.th.** sich einer Sache bewusst sein; **be ~ about it** vernünftig sein; **sensibly** ['sensəblɪ] vernünftig, vernünftigerweise
sen.si.tive ['sensətɪv] *adj* **1.** sensibel, empfindsam, empfindlich **2.** *(Verständnis)* einfühlsam **3.** *(Körperteil)* empfindlich **4.** *(phot)* lichtempfindlich **5.** *(fig)* heikel, prekär **be ~ about something** in Bezug auf etw empfindlich sein **~ to cold/heat** kälte-/wärmeempfindlich **sen.si.tiv.ity** ['sensətɪvətɪ] *s* **1.** Sensibilität, Empfindsamkeit *f* **2.** Empfindlichkeit *f* **3.** Einfühlungsvermögen *nt* **4.** Lichtempfindlichkeit *f* **sensitize** ['sensətaɪz] *vt* sensibilisieren

(from: *PONS Schülerwörterbuch. Ab 3. Lernjahr*)

2 Test your dictionary skills!

a) *Now use the information above to help you translate these sentences:*

1. That story doesn't make sense at all!
2. I've got a cold, and my sense of smell is gone.
3. That boy has no sense – he's always in trouble!
4. If you had any sense, you would stay at home.
5. She fell downstairs and was knocked senseless.
6. Mary is a very sensible person.
7. She sensibly took her umbrella with her.
8. Bob is very sensitive to other people's feelings.
9. I think you need to use a more sensitive film.
10. Brushing with Protex makes your teeth really white and reduces their sensitivity to cold.
11. I woke up with a sensation of cold.
12. The book caused a sensation when it came out.

b) If you are trying to think of a word in English, the German-English part of your dictionary can be useful.

sen.sibel [zen'zi:bəl] *adj* sensitive ; **sensi.bi.li.sieren** *vt* sensitize; **Sen.si.bili.tät** *vt* sensitivity

Check what you can find there on the other German words from ex. 4 on p. 96. ("False friends"). If you can't find one (maybe the word is new?) make a guess, and check the English-German part.

It's always best to check both directions to make sure the word you find is right for the context.

5

3 What do you need to look up?

You have found an article about St Patrick on the Internet. But do you understand everything?
Read the article, and make a list of the words you are not sure of. (They don't have to be the marked ones!)

St Patrick

One of the few **undisputed** facts is that Patrick lived in the 5th century A.D. He was born somewhere in Roman-**occupied** Britain – most likely in Wales, though some say Scotland. **According to** his own writings, he was **captured** by pirates from Ireland and spent six years there as a slave, somewhere near the "western sea" i.e. the Atlantic.
Though **baptised** as a **Christian**, he **claims** he was not very religious until his experiences as a slave led him to **pray** to the **Lord**. His prayers were answered in a dream in which a voice told him that a ship was waiting for him on the other side of the country. He ran away, and escaped back to Britain.
But there he had a **vision** of the Irish calling him back. The next bit of his story tells of his education, and how he became a **priest** and later a **bishop**, but it is rather **vague**. He probably studied in France (or Gaul, as it was then). He wanted to be sent on a mission to Ireland, but Palladius got sent there first – which means that Patrick was not the first to bring **Christianity** to the Irish.
But Patrick eventually got his wish. His mission was **chiefly** in the north of the country. He seems to have been very successful in **persuading** the chieftains to **give up** their pagan Celtic **customs** and go over to the new **faith**. All this will have brought him into **conflict** with the Druids, the Celtic priesthood who were still very **powerful**. But he seems to have **prevailed** in the end. He never left Ireland again.
Patrick's mission was so successful that his followers became **missionaries**. While most of Europe lived through the "Dark Ages", Ireland had a "Golden Age" of **scholarship** and religion. Irish **monks** founded monasteries in Scotland, England and all over the continent of Europe.

4 True and false friends

a) You can guess a lot of the marked words
- from the context
- because they are related to English words you do know
- because they are like German words.

But how can you be sure?

b) If you want to talk about the article, it isn't enough to simply guess the meaning. Are you sure how to pronounce these words?

vision – priest – bishop – vague – conflict – scholarship – monk

If not, look them up!

TIP

You need **two** clues, e.g. the context **and** a related word.

"powerful" = power + -ful? (Yes, that fits.)
"vision" = Vision? (Maybe ...)
"Celtic customs" –? (Hmm ... that can't be right!)

G 28

5 Can't find the word?

If you can't find a word in the normal alphabetical order, try looking under a head word. Head words can have many different endings – or prefixes.

Which head word should you look up if you can't find: undisputed, occupied, according, Christianity, chiefly, priesthood, scholarship?

SAVE

Common endings:
-ize, -ify (*verbs*)
-ment, -ence, -ance, -ity, -ship, -hood (*nouns*)
-ful, -al, -ic, -(i)an, -ish (*adjectives*)
-ly (*adverbs*)
Common prefixes:
un-, im-, dis-, re-

1 Word building

a) *Form nouns from these words:*
to react – similar – damp – sensitive

b) *Give the verbs of these nouns:*
thought – colour – servant – rent

c) *Add adjective endings to these words:*
health – danger – tradition – youth – respect

d) *Take one pair from each list (a, b, and c), and make sentences to show the different meanings.*

2 ⟨What is it?⟩

Here are some definitions. What is the word for:

1. the state of business in a country
2. building work
3. a wonderful chance to do something
4. the state of not having a job
5. movement of people out of a country
6. in (or to) another country
7. finding houses for people
8. an apartment at the top of a tall building

3 Reporting dialogues

The dialogues below are from a radio programme. Joanne is being shown a house in Dublin that she might want to buy.

a) *Report what happened, and what the people said.*

greeted[1] said introduced … asked … to invited showed told explained was surprised to hear estimated[2] guessed repeated agreed asked

1. *Woman:* Joanne?
Joanne: Hi, How are you? …
Woman: Claire Allen, from Sherry Fitzgerald – come on in … These are your two main reception rooms[3] here, which you can see are interconnected[4] …

2. *Joanne:* Who lived here?
Woman: It was an old man … who lived here who's gone into a nursing home[5].
Joanne: Ooh, I can see that! … What kind of price are we looking at for this place?
Woman: We're giving a guide price[6] of 345.
Joanne: 345?

[1]*grüßte;* [2]*schätzte;* [3]*Wohnzimmer;* [4]*miteinander verbunden;* [5]*Pflegeheim;* [6]*Richtpreis, Verhandlungsbasis;* [7]*gab zu*

1 HV (30-31) b) You can now listen to two excerpts from the same radio programme. You may have heard them already. Nick is interviewing a farmer, Christy Sweetman. *Listen, then report what was said – in as short a way as you can.*

Here are some more useful verbs:

wanted to know admitted[7] suggested … how much / if / whether …

5

4 Heard at the parade

These people use infinitives to make statements and ask questions.

a) *What do they actually say?*

Angela: St Patrick / bring Christianity / the Irish / really the first …?
Start: Was St Patrick really …?
Liam: Green / colour / wear / Dublin or New York / St Patrick's Day!
Steve: Nobody thinks it's crazy / black Americans / pretend to be Irish / the day!
Eileen: Have you got / some shamrock / Ann / put / her hat?
Tara: It was silly / us / not / find a hotel first. Now / nowhere / stay!
Kevin: Tim / I want / you / keep my place / me.

b) *What did they say? Use reported speech.*

CHECK-IN

	county ['kaʊnti]	Grafschaft, Verwaltungsbezirk	~ Down is one of the six counties of Northern Ireland.
	nut [nʌt]	Nuss	When they are ready for eating, ~s are usually brown.

TEXTS

A	**songwriter** ['sɒŋraɪtə]	Texter(in)/Komponist(in), Liedermacher(in)	so. who writes songs
	dear [dɪə]	lieb, teuer	Letters usually start with 'Dear ...'.
	son [sʌn]	Sohn	Your father is your grandfather's ~.
	schoolmaster ['sku:lˌmɑ:stə]	Schulmeister, Lehrer	an old-fashioned word for a male teacher
	to **be* so good as to** *(+ infinitive)* [səʊ 'gʊd‿əz]	so gut sein zu *(+ Infinitiv)*	
	sorely ['sɔ:li]	schlimm, arg, sehr	'Sorely' means 'very badly'.
	to **infect** [ɪn'fekt]	infizieren, anstecken, verseuchen	The potatoes were ~ed with disease. = They had gone bad in the fields.
	railroad *(AE)* ['reɪlrəʊd]	Eisenbahn	*BE:* railway – *AE:* railroad
	wee *(regional)* [wi:]	winzig, klein	another word for 'very small', especially in Scotland and Ireland
	dampness ['dæmpnəs]	Feuchtigkeit	A lot of rain causes ~.
	turf [tɜ:f]	Torf; Rasen	In Ireland, ~ is traditionally used for burning, e.g. for the heating of people's homes.
	to **pass on** [pɑ:s‿'ɒn]	entschlafen, verscheiden	another way of saying 'to die'
	to **bury** ['beri]	begraben, beerdigen	! 'Bury' rhymes with 'very'.
	prayer ['preə]	Gebet	People make contact with God through ~s.
	daughter ['dɔ:tə]	Tochter	Your sons and ~s are your children.
	visit ['vɪzɪt]	Besuch	to visit – visitor – to come for a visit
	cheerful ['tʃɪəfl]	fröhlich, vergnügt	~ people are optimistic and positive.
	right down to the end [ˌraɪt daʊn tə ðiˌ'end]	bis zum Schluss	until the end
	grandchild ['grændtʃaɪld]	Enkel(in)	grandfather – grandmother – grandchild
	alongside [əˌlɒŋ'saɪd]	neben, entlang	at the side of, next to
	churchyard ['tʃɜ:tʃˌjɑ:d]	Friedhof, Kirchhof	the place, by the church, where people are buried
	feisty ['faɪsti]	lebensfroh	
	to **consider** [kən'sɪdə]	betrachten, überlegen, in Erwägung ziehen	'considering that ...' = 'when you remember that ...'
	hard [hɑ:d]	schwer	a hard life ↔ an easy life
2	**connection** [kə'nekʃn]	Verbindung, Zusammenhang, Anschluss	A link is a ~ between one thing and another.
	fear [fɪə]	Angst, Furcht	a feeling of being afraid
	famine ['fæmɪn]	Hungersnot	When a country has too little food and this causes many deaths, there is ~.
	return [rɪ'tɜ:n]	Rückkehr	to return – return

	potato blight [pə'teɪtəʊ ˌblaɪt]	Kartoffelfäule	a disease that makes potatoes go bad in the fields
	unrest [ʌn'rest]	Unruhen, Unzufriedenheit	rest ↔ unrest
	arrest [ə'rest]	Verhaftung	to arrest – arrest
	brotherhood ['brʌðəhʊd]	Bruderschaft, Bund	brother – brotherhood
	prisoner ['prɪznə]	Gefangene(r), Häftling	a person who is kept in jail
	to **extend** [ɪk'stend]	ausstrecken, ausdehnen, verlängern	If you ~ sth., you make it go further or make it larger.
⟨B⟩	tiger ['taɪgə]	Tiger	
	goal [gəʊl]	Ziel	
	immigration [ˌɪmɪ'greɪʃn]	Immigration, Einwanderung	
⟨2⟩	to track [træk]	aufspüren	
	economy [ɪ'kɒnəmi]	Wirtschaft, Konjunktur	
	to brief [bri:f]	instruieren	
	to endanger [ɪn'deɪndʒə]	gefährden	
	skyline ['skaɪlaɪn]	Skyline, Silhouette	
	to dot [dɒt]	übersäen, verstreuen	
	crane [kreɪn]	Kran	
	index ['ɪndeks]	Index, Hinweis, Anzeichen	
	growth [greʊθ]	Wachstum	
	to boom [bu:m]	boomen, florieren, einen Aufschwung nehmen	
	measure ['meʒə]	Maßstab	
	prosperity [prɒs'perəti]	Wohlstand	
	exodus ['eksədəs]	Auszug, Abwanderung, Völkerwanderung	
	in search of [ɪn 'sɜ:tʃ‿əv]	auf der Suche nach	
	opportunity [ˌɒpə'tju:nəti]	Gelegenheit, Chance, Möglichkeit	
	abroad [ə'brɔ:d]	im/ins Ausland	
	on record [ˌɒn 'rekɔ:d]	schriftlich festgehalten, verzeichnet	
	due to ['dju: tʊ]	auf Grund, wegen	
	ruin ['ru:ɪn]	Ruine	
⟨3⟩	suburb ['sʌbɜ:b]	Vorort	
	trade [treɪd]	Handel	
	employment [ɪm'plɔɪmənt]	Beschäftigung	
	to be* faced with ['feɪst wɪθ]	konfrontiert sein mit	
	unemployment [ˌʌnɪm'plɔɪmənt]	Arbeitslosigkeit	
	skilled worker [ˌskɪld 'wɜ:kə]	Facharbeiter(in)	
	tax [tæks]	Steuer	
	emigration [ˌemɪ'greɪʃn]	Emigration, Auswanderung	
	to invest [ɪn'vest]	investieren	
	to sustain [sə'steɪn]	unterhalten	
	to establish [ɪ'stæblɪʃ]	gründen, einrichten	
	fund [fʌnd]	Fonds, Fördermittel	
	to encourage [ɪn'kʌrɪdʒ]	ermutigen	
	pitch [pɪtʃ]	Anreiz	
	to research [rɪ'sɜ:tʃ]	erforschen	
	to launch [lɔ:ntʃ]	einführen	
	reputation [ˌrepjə'teɪʃn]	Ruf	
	housing ['haʊzɪŋ]	Wohnungsbeschaffung	
	reasonable ['ri:znəbl]	vernünftig, angemessen	
C	**confident** ['kɒnfɪdnt]	zuversichtlich; selbstbewusst, selbstsicher	She's very sure of herself. = She's very ~.
	youthful ['ju:θfl]	jugendlich	So. who is ~, is young and full of life.
	proof [pru:f]	Beweis	to prove – proof
	to **be* dressed** ['drest]	gekleidet sein	to have clothes on
	drab [dræb]	trist, düster, grau	drab ↔ bright, attractive, exciting
	smart [smɑ:t]	schick, flott; schlau	Your new suit looks very ~.
	some [sʌm]	irgend ein	for ~ reason = for a reason she didn't understand
	cobbled ['kɒbld]	mit Kopfsteinpflaster gepflastert	~ streets look attractive, but old-fashioned.

5

outdoor [ˌaut'dɔ:]	Freiluft-, Außen-, (für) draußen, im Freien	~ clothes, ~ shoes, ~ activities, ~ swimming pool, etc.
eventually [ɪ'ventʃuəli]	schließlich, endlich	! eventually ≠ eventuell
to **serve** [sɜ:v]	servieren; (be)dienen	service – servant – to serve
foreigner ['fɒrɪnə]	Ausländer(in)	When you go to another country, you're a ~ there.
fellow ['feləʊ]	Typ, Mann, Kerl	*AE:* 'guy'
to let* oneself in for sth. [ˌlet wʌnself 'ɪn fɔ:]	sich auf etwas einlassen, sich etwas einbrocken	
to **be* about to do sth.** [ˌbi:‿ə'baʊt tə]	im Begriff sein, etwas zu tun, etwas gerade tun wollen	I was about to go when a voice called my name.
to **rent** [rent]	mieten	to pay money for the use of a house, flat, room, etc. that so. else owns
glum [glʌm]	niedergeschlagen, bedrückt	You look a bit ~. = You don't look very happy.
the last word [ðə ˌlɑ:st 'wɜ:d]	der letzte Schrei	the most fashionable thing at the moment
good value [ˌgʊd 'vælju:]	preisgünstig	If a thing is ~, it is not too expensive.
doubtful ['daʊtfl]	zweifelhaft; zweifelnd, skeptisch	unsure about sth. or whether it is likely
hopeful ['həʊpfl]	hoffnungsvoll	to hope – hope – hopeful
honest ['ɒnɪst]	ehrlich, redlich	An ~ person tells the truth.
apron ['eɪprən]	Schürze	It's best to wear an ~ over your clothes when you're cooking.
suburb ['sʌbɜ:b]	Vorort	a small town or a village on the edge of a large city
working-class estate [ˌwɜ:kɪŋ 'klɑ:s‿ɪˌsteɪt]	Arbeitersiedlung	An estate is an area where a lot of houses are built, often similar in style.
to **pause** [pɔ:z]	innehalten, stoppen, stehen bleiben	to stop for a moment
only ['əʊnli]	erst	The baby is ~ two weeks old.
income ['ɪŋkʌm]	Einkommen	the money that you are paid or that comes to you from what you have invested
tax [tæks]	Steuer	money that has to be paid to the government
misunderstanding [ˌmɪsʌndə'stændɪŋ]	Missverständnis	to understand – misunderstanding
ordinary ['ɔ:dnəri]	gewöhnlich, normal	! ordinary ≠ ordinär
definite ['defɪnət]	definitiv, ganz sicher	"Are you coming to the party?" – "Definitely!"
by chance [ˌbaɪ 'tʃɑ:nts]	zufällig	Sth. that happens ~ has not been planned at all.
as it were [æz‿ɪt 'wɜ:]	sozusagen, gleichsam	
respectable [rɪ'spektəbl]	anständig, ehrbar, ansehnlich	Older people often feel they can trust so. who looks '~'.
slut [slʌt]	Schlampe	
to **deny** [dɪ'naɪ]	abstreiten, bestreiten, leugnen	to say that sth. isn't true
to **ease** [i:z]	lindern, erleichtern	If sth. ~s your pain, it makes it better.
freckle ['frekl]	Sommersprosse	Some people get ~s on their skin in the summer.
1 **past** [pɑ:st]	Vergangenheit	time before now
present ['preznt]	Gegenwart	what is happening now
similarity [ˌsɪmɪ'lærəti]	Ähnlichkeit	similar – similarity

LANGUAGE

A2	**mixed bag** [ˌmɪkst ˈbæg]	bunte Mischung, Allerlei	a lot of different things put together
B1	**shamrock** [ˈʃæmrɒk]	Klee(blatt)	Ireland's national 'sign' is the ~.
2	**busker** [ˈbʌskə]	Straßenmusikant(in)	so. who plays music (or sings) in the street, station, etc. and hopes to get money
	to **order** [ˈɔːdə]	befehlen, anordnen; bestellen	A police officer ~ed the buskers to move away.
	tune [tjuːn]	Melodie	"Why don't you sing with us?" – "I don't know the ~."
	over and over again [ˌəʊvə‿ənd‿ˌəʊvə‿əˈgen]	immer wieder, wieder und wieder	A story gets boring if you hear it ~.
	altogether [ˌɔːltəˈgeðə]	insgesamt, *hier:* ganz	! Let's sing all together (alle zusammen). They've banned buskers altogether (ganz).
C1	**fair** *(old)* [feə]	schön	an old-fashioned word for 'beautiful'
	receptionist [rɪˈsepʃnɪst]	Dame/Herr am Empfang	so. who works at a hotel, etc., usually at the desk near the entrance
	brewery [ˈbruːri]	Brauerei	the place where beer is made
	nah *(coll.)* [næː]	nö	
	huh? *(coll.)* [hʌ/hə]	was?	
	bore [bɔː]	Langweiler(in), langweilig(e Sache)	If sth. sounds 'a ~' , it sounds boring.
	to **found** [faʊnd]	gründen	to start (e.g. a school, a college, a business, etc.)
	monastery [ˈmɒnəstri]	Kloster (für Mönche)	
	present [ˈpreznt]	gegenwärtig, jetzig; anwesend	the ~ buildings = the buildings that are standing now
	to **complain** [kəmˈpleɪn]	sich beschweren, sich beklagen, klagen	"Stop ~ing all the time! Can't I do anything right?"
2	**thought** [θɔːt]	Gedanke, Denken	to think – a thought
⟨5⟩	time-shift [ˈtaɪmʃɪft]	Zeitverschiebung	
D1	**neighbouring** [ˈneɪbrɪŋ]	benachbart, angrenzend	neighbour – neighbourhood – neighbouring
	sensitivity [ˌsentsɪˈtɪvəti]	Sensibilität, Einfühlsamkeit, Empfindlichkeit	sensitive – sensitivity
	to **pride oneself on sth.** [ˈpraɪd wʌnself]	sich einer Sache rühmen	If you pride yourself on a thing, it is very important to you.
	either [ˈaɪðə]	eine(r/s) von beiden; beide	Choose ~ of these two songs. ~ of them is nice.
	comedian [kəˈmiːdiən]	Komiker(in)	so. who tells jokes and funny stories
	impossible [ɪmˈpɒsəbl]	unmöglich	possible ↔ impossible
	to **insult** [ɪnˈsʌlt]	beleidigen, beschimpfen	~ing people is worse than making fun of them.
	racist [ˈreɪsɪst]	Rassist(in); rassistisch	

SKILLS

1	**head word** [ˈhed wɜːd]	Stichwort im Wörterbuch	
	abbreviation [əˌbriːviˈeɪʃn]	Abkürzung	'adj' is the ~ for 'adjective'.
2	**cold** [kəʊld]	Kälte	If you have a ~, you are more sensitive to the ~.

CHECK-OUT

3	**excerpt** ['ekss:pt]	Auszug	a part taken from a text

COGNATE WORDS

alphabetical [ˌælfə'betɪkl]	alphabetisch
to **amuse (oneself)** [ə'mju:z]	(sich) amüsieren
beer [bɪə]	Bier
central ['sentrl]	zentral
to **colour** ['kʌlə]	kolorieren, färben
to **emigrate** ['emɪgreɪt]	emigrieren, auswandern
historical [hɪ'stɒrɪkl]	historisch, geschichtlich
penthouse ['penthaʊs]	Penthouse, Dachterrassenwohnung
prefix ['pri:fɪks]	Präfix, Vorsilbe
reaction [ri'ækʃn]	Reaktion
republic [rɪ'pʌblɪk]	Republik
spectacular [spek'tækjələ]	spektakulär
talent ['tælənt]	Talent, Begabung

5

Are you a sensitive person?

Some English adjectives for describing people are easily confused by German speakers.
Note the differences:

- Jenny always notices when I'm sad. She is a very *sensitive* person.
  (dt. sensibel, einfühlsam, empfindlich)
  She showed great *sensitivity* when she visited your mother in hospital.
  (dt. Einfühlungsvermögen, Sensibilität)
- It was a very *sensible* decision to move to a bigger house. The old one was much too small.
  (dt. vernünftig)
  She had invited a *reasonable* number of guests. / £100,000 is a *reasonable* price for this house.
  (dt. vernünftig, angemessen, günstig)

Cartoon fun: Busker's blues

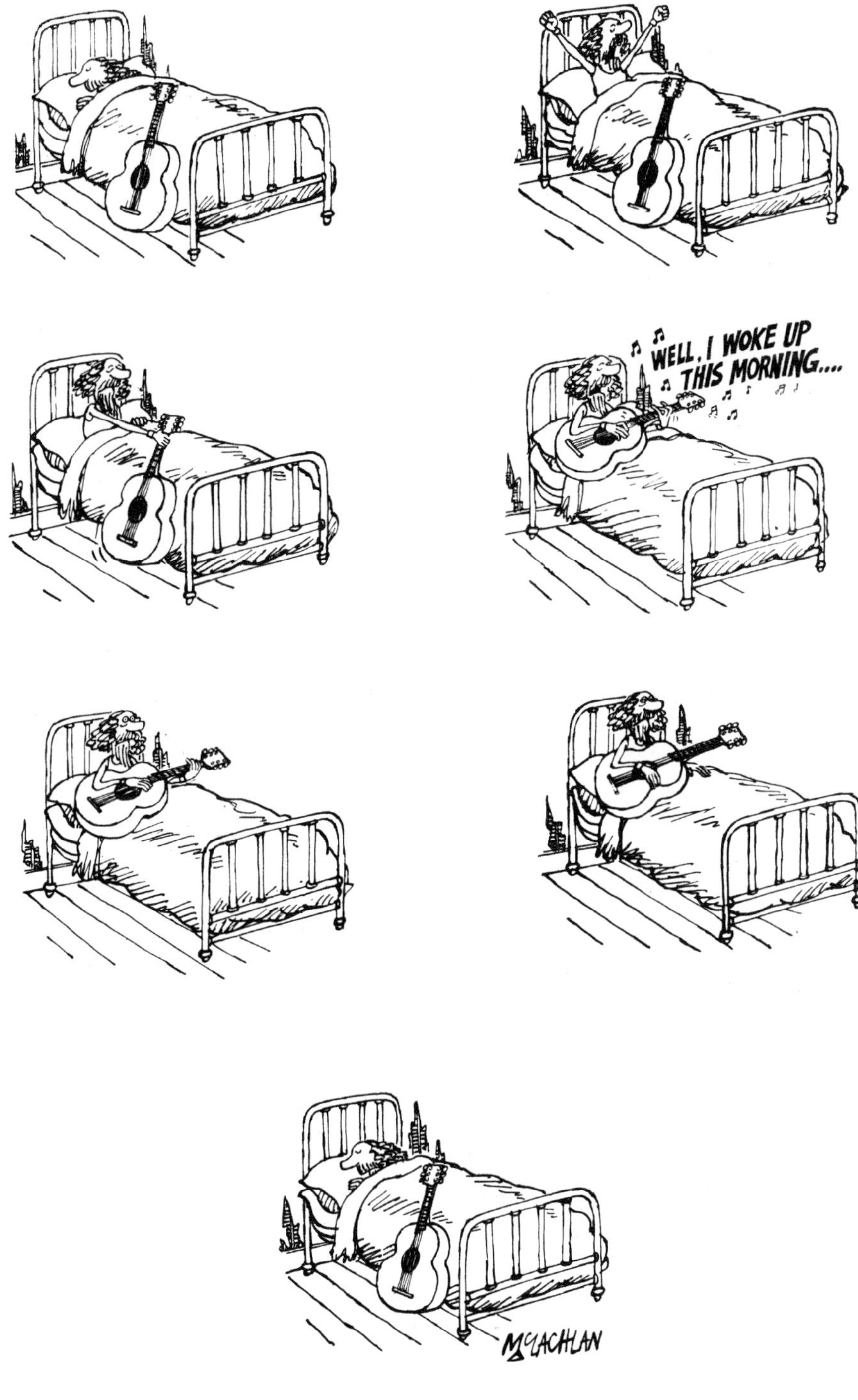

UNIT 6

The world of work

1 Aspects of work

a) *Choose a caption for each photo. Say why you chose it.*

- Looking for work
- Voluntary work
- Housework
- Work and play
- Working for pocket money
- Training for work
- All work and no play?
- Making things work
- Teamwork

b) *Suggest ideas for photos to go with the other two captions.*

c) *Have you ever worked in the holidays, at weekends or after school? Tell the class about it.*

d) *List the pros and cons of 'after school jobs'. Then compare your lists.*

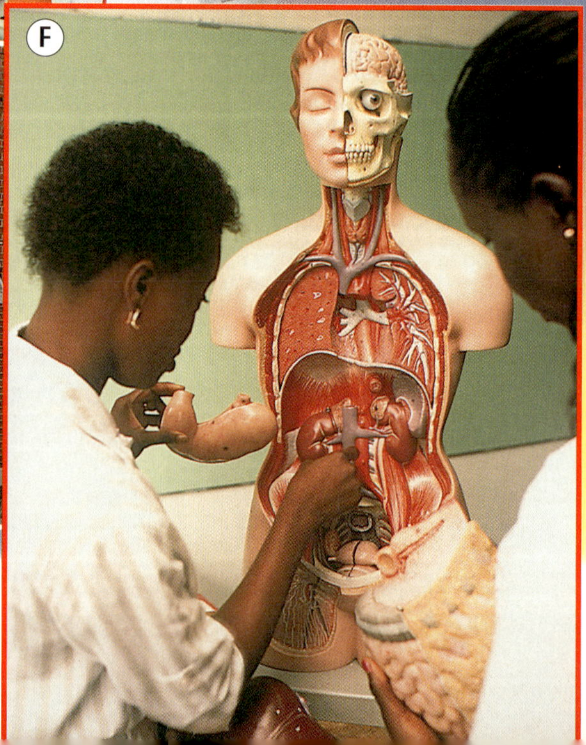

2 Jobs

BABYSITTER

wanted for two evenings a week. Must have experience and good references.
Ring **Hannah Coleman on 0628 602974**

Assistant needed for busy hairdressers (Sats only). No experience necessary. Good tips. Apply within.

Blewitts Heating Systems

We are looking for an experienced, efficient and reliable

HEATING ENGINEER

to join our Service Team in Slough. Attractive salary and conditions. Phone Wendy Craig on 0844 32974 for application details.

PART-TIME CASHIERS

wanted for new

FRESCOS SUPERSTORE

Flexible hours. Double-time pay Sundays. Call Ben Bradley (Staff Manager) on **1234-982304**

Research Assistant

required by nationwide charity to carry out research into child labour in Britain. Must be skilled in current research methods. Salary according to experience and qualifications.
Send curriculum vitae to **Mike Smith, S.O.S. Child Labour, Essex Rd, Islington, NW1 4HP**

Earn while-u-learn! Join our team of

WINDSOR TOUR GUIDES

Ideal for students and unemployed or retired people with an interest in local history. Knowledge of French, German and/or other foreign languages an advantage. Must be willing to take part in two-day training course.
Apply to: **Jeff Smith, Windsor Tourist Promotions, 2b Peascod Street, Windsor, by 15 Feb.**

6

a) *Which jobs might these people apply for? Say why.*

1. Khalid Aziz, 16, wants to learn to drive as soon as he is old enough. He is looking for a part-time job to pay for the lessons.
2. Bridget Wilson, 18, is saving to go on holiday with her friends after her A-level exams. She would prefer to work at weekends than during the week because of school.
3. Gary Norris, 38, has just lost his job at an engineering firm in Yorkshire. A friend tells him the job market in the south-east of England is booming.

b) *What else might their future employers want to know about them? Write one question for each person.*

c) *Suggest other ways of finding a job.*

d) *Ask your teachers to tell you about their work experience (apart from teaching jobs). Find out how they got the job, what they did, what they liked/didn't like, and what they learned from the experience. If you like, you can do a survey and present your results to the class.*

Relative clauses 116, 1

A Child labour (17-20)

Asleep in class? Must be all that illegal work at the supermarket in free periods

CHARLOTTE DAVIS is worried about A-level results. Not her own, but those of her pupils at Wallington High School for Girls, where she is deputy head. Davis believes 60 % of the girls will underachieve in their A-levels and GCSEs because they are working long hours in supermarkets, shoe shops and hairdressers.

Davis accuses the stores of exploiting pupils by encouraging them to work rather than study. One of her pupils was asked by the department store Marks & Spencer to take a one-and-a-half-day training course for a summer job the week before her A-levels. Davis ordered the girl, who was having extra tuition because her revision 'was in a mess', not to do the course and contacted M&S to complain. M&S denied forcing the girl and said it wanted a highly educated workforce.

• Other teachers share Davis's concern. Teachers have told *The Observer* that supermarkets ask pupils for their timetables so they can be called on their mobile phones and asked to work during 'free periods' – the time that is set aside for studying.

'These stores put pressure on the pupils at an age when they are often not strong enough to say No,' said one headteacher in Manchester.

Many employers offer 'double-time' weekend work to schoolchildren rather than adult staff because they are cheaper and more flexible. Some offer pupils four-hour shifts – the maximum they can work before they have to be given a meal break.

The situation has got worse since Sunday shopping and longer opening hours during the week, according to Davis. 'Many of these children work long hours. They fall asleep in class and are unable to prepare properly for the most important exams in their lives.'

• Of the estimated two million children who work, about 80 % do so illegally, according to a book on child labour published by *Save the Children*. Under the present law, child workers have to be over 13 and can work only two hours a day or five on Saturday. They cannot work for more than an hour before school, start before 7am or finish after 7pm, or do any job that is likely to affect their health or education. And they must have a work permit.

According to research by *Save the Children*, the law is broken almost everywhere. Only 1 per cent of child workers in urban Scotland and 7 per cent in North Tyneside had a permit. One third started work before their thirteenth birthday and in Scotland nearly two-thirds 'clocked-on' before 7 am.

• The pressure for children to earn money has increased in recent years, fuelled by the craze for expensive designer clothes and, in poorer areas, by the demands of unemployed parents.

Pay is often poor and at the lower end can be less than 50p an hour – in one case 10p an hour – according to *Save the Children*. The Low Pay Unit found a 15-year-old girl who was paid £30 for a 29 hour week in a café. Most children do delivery work – usually newspapers or milk – babysitting or shop work, but some have been found in sawmills, factories and garages and on fishing boats.

The growth of illegal working has increased concerns about safety. A recent accident involved a 14-year-old boy who was run over by a lorry while delivering newspapers. He had no work permit and the employer's insurance company refused to pay.

'We are not against children working because up to 10 hours a week can benefit them,' said Sarah Roche of the Low Pay Unit. 'But conditions have to be right, and for too many of these children, this is not the case.'

(from: *The Observer*, July 19th, 1998)

6

1 Complete the summary

Charlotte Davis, the (...) of (...), is worried because (...). She accuses employers of (...). Employers sometimes prefer (...) to adults because (...). In order to attract them, they (...). They even ask pupils to give them their (...) in order to (...). Pupils at that age find it difficult to say (...). The situation has been made worse by (...) and (...). There is also growing pressure on children to buy (...). In poorer areas, (...) may even expect their children to earn money. Research by (...) has shown that about (...) children work, of whom (...) work illegally. The research also shows that child labour laws are (...). For example, a lot of children work (...) than they should, in many cases without a (...). The growth of (...) has increased concerns about (...). If a child without a work permit has an (...), the insurance company can refuse to (...). The Low Pay Unit is not against (...), as long as (...) are right.

2 The issue

Mrs Davis is shopping in Frescos on Sunday evening. She is shocked to see Bridget Wilson, the girl who had been told not to do the course at Marks & Spencer, putting cat food on shelves. She marches off to the manager's office, dragging Bridget behind her. *Work in groups of three. Act out the conversation between Charlotte Davis, the store manager and Bridget Wilson.*

Charlotte Davis	Store Manager	Bridget Wilson
The exploitation of your pupils has gone too far! Tell the manager that too much pressure is put on them, and this will affect their exam results. Remind him about Frescos' responsibility to the community as a whole. Profits aren't everything! If he becomes difficult, threaten to take the case to the press.	Young people should be free to work when and where they like – within the law, of course. Teachers have only themselves to blame for poor results! Shoppers love your flexible opening hours, which means having flexible staff. On the other hand, you don't want any bad publicity. Try to make Mrs Davis see your point of view.	This is all very embarrassing. You'd promised to do more revision and you're getting free tuition in the afternoons. On the other hand, you don't like the way your school tries to influence your private life. The money is useful, so you don't want to lose your job!

3 Working in the coal mine

This text is from a report on working conditions in 1841.

a) *Which of the conditions Mary describes would be unusual or illegal in your country today? Give examples.*

b) *Are children still exploited in other ways? If so, what can be done to stop it?*

I have worked down in the pit for five years. My father works in the next pit; I have 12 brothers and sisters – all of them but one live at home; they do weaving and spinning, and one is a counter. Only one of them can read; none of the rest can. They never went to day-school, but three of them go to Sunday-school. I cannot read or write. I work with my brother John. I go down the pit at about seven o'clock, and come out up at six, sometimes seven. I do not like working in the pit, but I have to earn a living. I always work without stockings, or shoes, or trousers. I wear only my chemise. I have to go up to the headings with the men; they are all naked there. I have got used to that now. I was afraid at first and did not like it, but they never behave rudely to me.

Mary Barrett, aged 14, June 15, 1841

B The Industrial Revolution (21-23)

In Britain, the period of technological progress and social change which lasted from about 1750 to 1900 is known as the Industrial Revolution.

The first half of the 18th century saw a growing demand for cheaper cloth and metal goods in Europe and in Britain's colonies. At that time, goods were still made in workshops in or near the workers' homes, so production was limited. However, new machines for spinning and weaving increased output, and by 1750 the factory system was born. These inventions were not just limited to the cotton industry: James Watt, who was one of the greatest engineers of the time, made major improvements to the steam engine and so provided an efficient alternative to water power for all kinds of industries.

Conditions in factories were often very bad, especially for the young. Children who worked in iron and coal mines would begin work at the age of five. Shipyards, gas works, match factories, nail factories, and chimney sweeping businesses also employed children.

The Industrial Revolution was also a social revolution. As the population grew, thousands of people left the land and headed for the towns to work in the factories. This had good and bad sides. Unskilled workers earned more than they had as farm hands or servants, and with mass production, suddenly even the poor could afford things like shoes. For others, work disappeared. New technology destroyed the jobs of many skilled workers, especially handloom weavers.

Canals were built to carry heavy goods such as coal by boat, and steam trains provided a faster means of transport than the traditional horse and carriage.

There are a number of reasons why the Industrial Revolution happened sooner in Britain than in other countries. Britain was politically stable and allowed free trade. Geography helped, too. For example, there were no major forests or mountains to make communication difficult. It was also rich in coal and iron ore, especially in counties such as Staffordshire, Lancashire and Derbyshire. Most importantly, perhaps, there was a huge market for its goods, at home and overseas. Britain received raw materials from the colonies, which then bought the finished products.

1 Understanding the text

a) *Find a heading to go with each paragraph.*
Why Britain? – How it started – Transport – Introduction – Working conditions – Changes in society

b) *Where in the text could you add these sentences?*

1. Britain was a small island with several trading ports such as Hull and Liverpool.
2. For example, India provided Britain with raw cotton, and annual cloth production, which was 50,000 pieces of cloth in 1770, increased to 400,000 in 1800.
3. In 1770 the population was about 8.3 million, by 1821, 14.2 million.
4. The factories were polluted and safety was minimal, which often led to terrible injuries.
5. Many of them did not accept the new machines, and even destroyed them.
6. Before the Industrial Revolution, factories that made cloth used to run on water power, which is why they were called mills.
7. Most died before they reached the age of 25.
8. With increased industry, people had to find a way to get raw materials to the factories cheaply.

An industrial landscape, Glasgow, 1880

2 North and South

a) *Why was most of Britain's wealth from the Industrial Revolution created in the North? Check the text for clues. Look up the places on a map if necessary.*

b) *What do the cartoon and these facts tell us about the North-South divide today and the reasons for it?*

- The fastest growth industries are in financial services and high technology.
- Most biotechnology companies are in and around Surrey and Oxford.
- Financial services are concentrated in London.
- In 2000, houses were about 90 % more expensive in west London than in Yorkshire.
- In 2000, unemployment was three times higher in Glasgow than in London.

'He only works one day a year ... typical northerner.'

c) *Does your country have a North-South or East-West divide? Which are the richest/poorest regions, and why?*

3 Young entrepreneurs (32)

a) Jeff Harrison is dyslexic, yet he has just won the 'Young Entrepreneur of the Year Award'.
Listen and make notes on: • *the opinion his teachers had of him*
• *how his business developed.*

b) *Use your notes to explain why Jeff won the award.*

c) *Do you agree with these statements? Discuss them with a partner.*
1. People who spend too much time with computers lose their friends.
2. You can develop a software company at any age.
3. Young people are better at using computers than adults.
4. You don't need a good education to become a successful entrepreneur.

d) *Which of the statements best expresses the message of the cartoon?*

'Billy can't come out until he finishes developing a software company.'

4 ⟨Simplicity of electricity⟩ (24)

The simplicity
of electricity
is that it never tires
of going down wires.

The invention of plugs
was to stop mugs
who touch wires
becoming electric fires.

The simplicity
of electricity
is that it seems to know
it cannot flow
through plastic.
Fantastic.

by Michael Rosen

Describe in a poem or an advertisement an invention you think is fantastic.

Relative clauses 116-117
Language 118

G 29

A Relative clauses

1 Definitions

a) *Match the sentence parts.*

1. An application 2. A good doctor 3. A heating engineer 4. A retired person 5. A reference 6. A perfect employer 7. A prescription 8. A curriculum vitae 9. A talented cook	is something (that) is someone (who) is (some)one whose	a) describes your life history. b) your employer writes about your character. c) has stopped working because of his/her age. d) meals always taste fantastic. e) you make when you apply for a job. f) staff always do their best. g) installs and repairs heating systems. h) doctors give you to take to the chemist's. i) patients get better quickly.

b) *In which three sentences can you leave the relative pronoun out? How do you know?*
c) *Cover the left column and test your partner.*
Example: What do you call something that describes your life history? – A ...
d) *Use the structure in a) to write definitions of these words.*

1. a timetable	3. a good teacher	5. a salary	7. a librarian
2. a cashier	4. a tour guide	6. a hairdresser	8. a charity

2 Spot the difference

a) The pairs of examples below show two types of relative clause. *Study them carefully, and work out a rule for when to put in commas.*

Windsor Tourist Promotions is looking for a person **who** speaks both French and German.	The job was given to Gina Davis, **who** speaks both French and German.
A book **which** has just been published by Save the Children has some shocking statistics on child labour.	There are some shocking statistics in *Child Labour in Britain*, **which** has just been published by Save the Children.
A boy **who** can hardly read or write has won an award **which** is given to young entrepreneurs.	Jeff Harrison, **who** can hardly read or write, has won the 'Young Entrepreneur of the Year' Award, **which** will help him to develop new software.

b) *Find examples of the second type of relative clause on page 114. Is it more likely in writing or in speaking?*

3 Shortened relative clauses

You can shorten the first type of relative clause by leaving out *that/who/which + the form of 'be'.*
Example: A book **which has just been published** by Save the Children has some shocking statistics.
→ A book **just published** by Save the Children has some shocking statistics.

1. The person who was chosen for the job of heating engineer comes from Yorkshire.
2. The teacher who is giving Bridget extra tuition agrees with Charlotte Davis.
3. The stores that were accused of exploiting pupils said they were not forcing anyone to work.
4. The canals that were built during the Industrial Revolution made it easier to transport coal.
5. Textiles were made from raw materials that had been provided by the colonies.

4 Great inventions

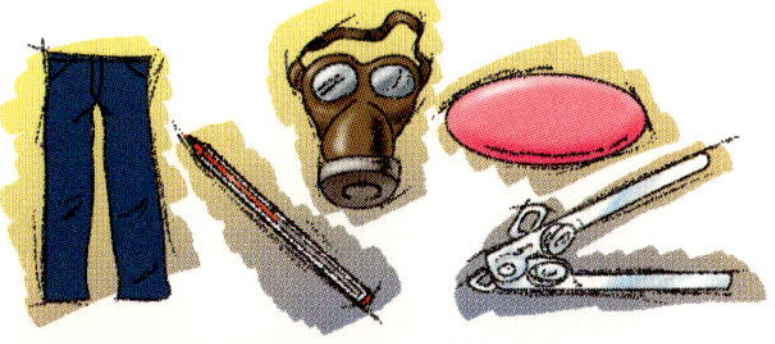

Use 'who', 'which' or 'whose' to add the extra information to the sentences below. (The last sentence has two pieces of information.)
Start: Blue jeans, which were invented by Levi Strauss, were …

1. Blue jeans were designed in the 1850s for men working in the Californian gold mines.
2. The biro was invented by the Hungarian inventor, Laslò Biro.
3. The first can opener was patented in Connecticut in 1858.
4. Garret A. Morgan rescued 30 men in a tunnel while wearing his invention.
5. The frisbee was invented by Walter Frederick.

- He named it after the pie-maker, William Frisbie.
- They were invented by Levi Strauss.
- It is a type of ball-point pen.
- His pie dishes used to be tossed around by college students.
- It appeared 48 years after the invention of the can.
- He invented the gas mask in 1912.

5 Joining sentences

Join the sentences with relative pronouns or contact clauses. Be careful with commas.

1. Last week Sarah started her new job. She loves it.
2. The company is based in the centre of London. It produces software for banks.
3. She heard about it from a friend of hers. The friend works there.
4. The boss is very friendly. His daughter went to the same school as Sarah.
5. She shares an office with a software designer. She gets on really well with him.
6. She's busy in August. That means we won't be able to go on holiday together.
7. The only problem is the salary. It's peanuts.

Use 'which' (not 'that') in extra information clauses.

G 29.8

6 ⟨Emphasising⟩

Emphasise the marked parts. Use 'It was …'/'Was it …?' or 'What …'

1. **Wilhelm Röntgen** discovered X-rays in 1896.
2. Doctors discovered anaesthetics **in the 1700s.**
3. **Christian Barnard** performed the first heart transplant in 1967.
4. James Watt developed his steam engine **at a steel works in England**.
5. Inventors always needed **money for research.**
6. Did **the Celts** build Stonehenge during the Stone Age?
7. Today we are going to talk about **the Industrial Revolution**.

SAVE

It is/was … who

Newcomen invented the steam engine, but **it was** James Watt **who** is remembered for it.

What …

What I need **is** more time.

7 At the supermarket

Finish the sentences using your own ideas.

1. While I was at the supermarket I saw a man who …
2. He was watching a boy from my school, who …
3. Suddenly he went over to the boy and said something which …
4. Then he dragged him off to the store manager's office, which …
5. The store manager wasn't in her office, which …
6. She was talking to a woman whose …
7. The man interrupted their conversation, which …
8. While the man was talking, the boy, who …, suddenly …

B Talking about life

1 Stan Baldwin (33-34)

Stan Baldwin is telling pupils about life in Yorkshire when he was a boy.
a) *Listen and note down what these people used to/didn't use to do, or would/wouldn't do.*
– Stan's father – the Baldwin family – Stan – Stan's mother
b) *Work in pairs. Use your notes to ask and answer questions.*
Example: When did Stan's father use to leave home in the morning? – He used to leave home at …

2 What about you?

G 30

You are 80. Your grandchildren want to know about your childhood.
Write a letter describing:

- where you used to live
- the school you used to go to
- the toys you used to play with
- what you would do in your free time
- where you would spend your holidays
- what you used to eat and drink

SAVE

'Would' and 'used to' can refer to repeated actions and events.
Only 'used to' can refer to past states.
- They would/used to sit around the coal fire in winter.
- Stan's family used to have a coal fire.

3 Strong words

G 31

a) *Put in the words to make the expressions sound stronger.*

1. It's clear that children should not be employed down coal mines. *(quite)*
2. I hope the government will do something about it. *(do)*
3. The mine owners will be angry if the law is changed. *(really)*
4. But think of the poor children working down the mines. *(do)*
5. Mary Barrett can't write her own name. *(even)*
6. In her family there is one child who can read and write. *(only)*

TIP

'Quite' can mean 'very', or 'a bit'.
It depends on how you say it.

6

b) *Say how Bridget disagrees with her parents. Use different forms of the emphatic 'do'.*

1. Bridget, you never told us about your job at Frescos. – But I *did* tell you about it!
2. They shouldn't make their employees work on Sundays. – But they *don't … (Go on.)*
3. Well, why did you work there all last Sunday, then?
4. You really don't need a part-time job.
5. You certainly get enough pocket money.
6. Well, maybe that's because you spend it all on that mobile phone of yours.
7. I know you don't like Mrs Davis.
8. Why don't you ever listen to her, Bridget?
9. She only has your interests at heart.
10. Why didn't you do any revision last night?

C Vocabulary

1 Words for work

a) *Find at least five words for each group.*

- People who work
- Places of work
- Money that is earned/paid
- Adjectives to describe workers

slave – salary – flexible – school – workforce – tip – factory – skilled – employees – pay – coal mine – sawmill – reliable – profit – labour – tax – wages – works – experienced – efficient – office – staff

b) *Write sentences with the words. Try to use one word from each group.*

'... and another thing, stop calling them children, they're kids.'

2 Odd plurals (25)

G 32

Cats have nine lives, and thieves carry knives,
Yet 'roofs' is the plural of roof.
Half a loaf is better than no loaves
Some plurals are odd – here's the proof:
The plural of tooth is teeth, as you know.
And the plural of foot should be feet.
But just add an 's' for the plural of toe,
And put on your boots, not your 'beet'.
The plural of house is houses – that's easy.
But a mouse multiplied makes mice – not so nice.
With more than one louse, you have lice, which is lousy,
But rice is just rice is just rice is just rice.
A goose and a gander have offspring called goslings,
Which gives you a gaggle of geese.
A duck and a drake will be followed by ducklings,
But the babies of moose are called moose, not 'meese'.
The plural of child must be children,
Who may become ladies or heroes.
Change 'a' into 'e' to turn 'man' into 'men'
And remember kilos of potatoes.
In America cents can be pennies, I hear.
In a pound there are one hundred pence.
The penny has dropped, now everything's clear.
Some plurals will never make sense!

a) *Pick out the unusual plural forms in the poem. Can you think of any more examples?*

b) *With the help of your dictionary, write the plural forms of the words below.*

1. tomato
2. shelf
3. photo
4. hoof
5. works
6. tornado
7. bus
8. series

3 Understatement

Show that you agree with the statements, but try to sound less negative. Use adjectives that mean the opposite.

honest ~~exciting~~ reliable flexible tough efficient funny polite

1. That was the most **boring** film I've ever seen. — *You:* I agree. It wasn't exactly **exciting**.
2. He's always late. You really can't depend on him! — *You:* That's true. You can hardly call him ...
3. Those old machines. They're so slow! — *You:* Yes, they're not what I'd call ...
4. That was a *comedy*? Huh! I didn't laugh once! — *You:* I know. It wasn't exactly ...
5. The things that ad promises! One lie after another! — *You:* Yes, ...
6. You could knock him over with a feather! — *You:* True. ...
7. How rude! Did you hear what he said to me? — *You:* I know. ...
8. My boss is so strict. He never bends the rules. — *You:* I agree. ...

Formal/informal language

1 Alan's complaint (26-27)

a) *Read what Alan told a friend and what he wrote. Explain why he wrote the letter and what he wants Mr Blewitt to do.*

It's about that heating system those cowboys put in over the New Year. (...) Well, it's playing up again. Someone came round a couple of days ago to look into the problem, but now the bloody thing's broken down! (...) Yeah, and when I tried to fix it myself I came across an empty beer can. (...) Right, he must've been drinking on the job. Anyway, I keep phoning them but the boss doesn't call back. His secretary said he was on a business trip – then I found out she'd made it all up! (...) No, I don't know how we'll get by without heating – not if it goes on as cold as this. Remember that gas boiler we bought from them? (...) It actually blew up! (...) Yeah, Kate still hasn't got over it. (...) What? (...) Hey, great idea, Barry! I'll write and say I'm not going to put up with the problem any more, so they'll have to come and sort it out straight away. Well, if they can't fix the heating, they'll have to give us money to make up for it. Or else I'll get the lawyers onto them!

21 Green Lane
Slough SL1 8DD

Mr Larry Blewitt (Manager)
Blewitts Heating Systems
Slough Trading Estate
Slough SL2 2ID

18 January 2001

Dear Mr Blewitt,

I refer to the central heating system you installed on 3 January 2001, which is not working properly. Two days ago one of your "engineers" arrived to investigate the matter. However, I regret to inform you that the heating has now ceased to function altogether. And on attempting to repair it myself I found by chance an empty beer can, which leads me to believe that your employee had been consuming alcohol at work.

There has been no response to my repeated phone calls. Furthermore, I discovered that the excuse given by your secretary about your "business trip" was completely invented. My wife and I will not be able to manage without heating if these freezing temperatures continue. The gas boiler which we purchased from your company actually exploded and she has not yet recovered from the shock.

This is a situation which we are no longer willing to tolerate. It must be resolved without delay. If you are unable to repair the heating system, we expect to be compensated financially. Otherwise we shall have no alternative but to take legal steps against you.

I look forward to your prompt response.

Yours sincerely,
Alan Roberts

b) *Fill in what you think Alan's friend said on the telephone.*

6

2 Phrasal verbs

G 33

a) *Here is a list of phrasal verbs Alan uses when he talks to his friend. Read them again in context and match them with the more formal expressions in Alan's letter. Use a dictionary if necessary.*

put in	break down	make up	get over
play up	come across	get by	put up with
come round	call back	go on	sort out
look into	find out	blow up	make up for

b) *What other words/phrases does Alan change when he writes the letter?*

TIP

The phrasal verb 'look up' *(nachschlagen)* is not the same as 'look + up'.

3 A question of style

a) Phrasal verbs are common in informal style. *Look at the list below and decide what is typical of informal or formal style. Give examples by comparing how Alan speaks with how he writes.*

1. being exact
2. short forms
3. defining/non-defining relative clauses
4. passive verb forms
5. 'filler phrases' that give one time to think
6. words with more than two syllables
7. Germanic instead of Romance words
8. using first names
9. slang expressions

Example: Being exact is more typical of formal style. Alan writes "3 January 2001", which is more formal than "over the New Year".

b) *Copy and complete the grid.*

Informal	Formal
…	being exact
…	…

4 Mr Blewitt's response (35)

a) Mr Blewitt has recorded a message for his secretary, Wendy. *Listen and note down the main points.*

b) *Write the letter for Mr Blewitt. Here are some more formal expressions to help you.*

to apologise for
the delay in response was due to
to speak to someone about the matter
to not function properly
unfortunately
to be extremely busy with orders
to deny the accusation
to resolve the situation
to arrange an appointment
without delay
to compensate for the unpleasant experience
to avoid unnecessary legal problems

Start like this: Dear Mr Roberts,
Thank you very much for your letter of 18 January 2001, in which you …

6

5 What's that in plain English?

Where might you see these notices and warnings? Explain what they mean in 'plain English'.

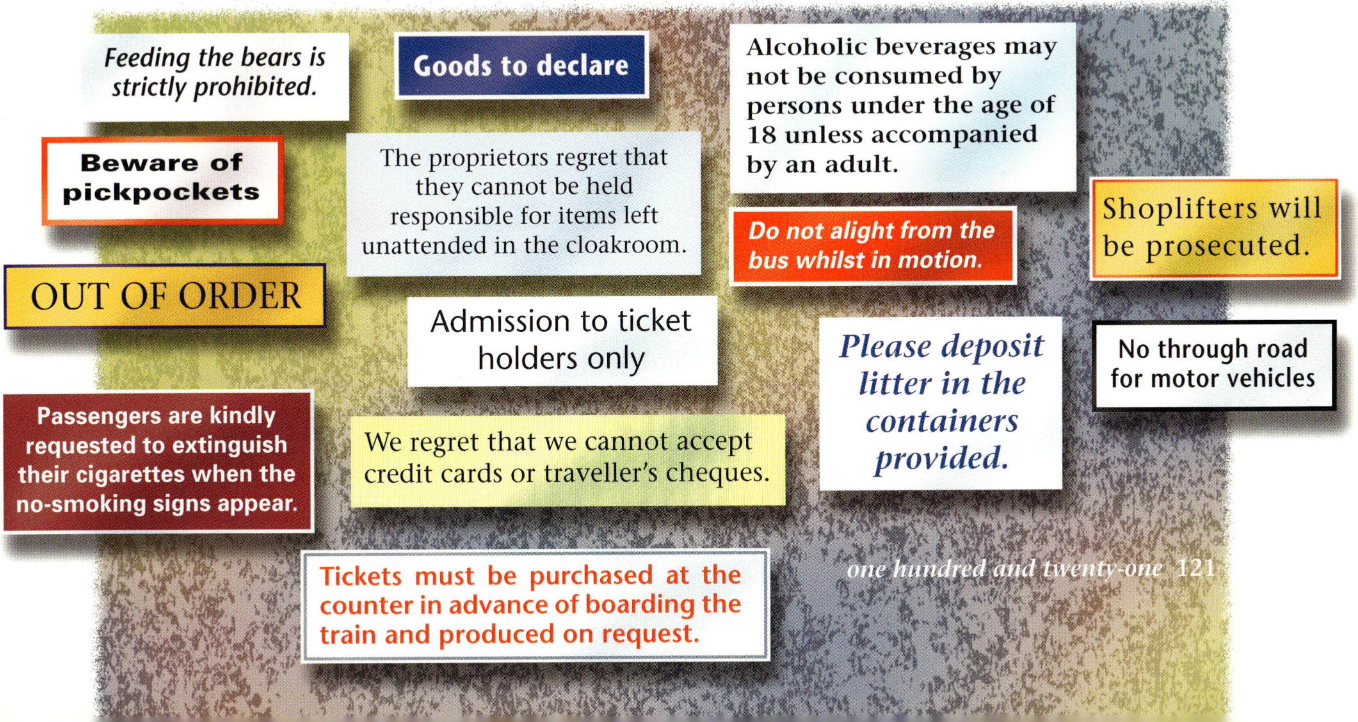

6 Formal or informal?

Some structures have formal and informal versions. Some ways of saying things are more polite than others, for example:

Who is the present for? *(informal)* – For whom is the present? *(very formal)*
Which century did he live in? *(informal)* – In which century did he live? *(formal)*
Tell me the time, please. *(direct)* – Could you tell me the time, please? *(more polite)*

Change the sentences to make them more formal or more polite.

1. Lend me your bike, please.
2. What are you going to pay with?
3. I have no idea who you're talking about.
4. What kind of music are you interested in?
5. I got the job I applied for.
6. Where's the station?

7 Learning to learn: Recording vocabulary

a) *Complete the diagram with 'look'. Use your dictionary to make similar diagrams with the expressions 'take' and 'put'.*

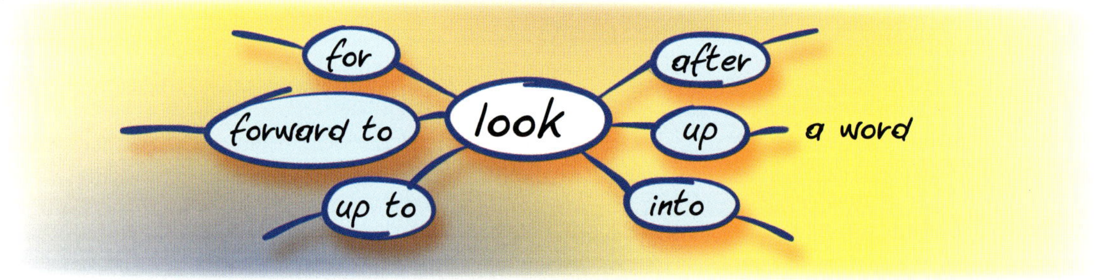

b) *Write answers to these questions, using the phrasal verbs on the right and a dictionary if necessary.*

1. What does a nurse do?
2. How do you feel about your next holiday?
3. Have you got any new hobbies?
4. Which of your parents do you look more like?
5. What technology could you not manage without?
6. How have you decorated your bedroom walls?
7. How much time do you spend on revision?
8. What advice would you give to someone who smokes?

take up	look after
take after	put up
set aside	look forward to
give up	do without

SAVE

Learning phrasal verbs:
- Create diagrams
- Write example sentences
- Make word forks

c) *Copy and complete the word forks with the phrasal verbs.*

	...?
make up	a face
	...?

	...?
put on	an accent
	...?

	...?
get over	a shock
	...?

	...?
pick up	a skill
	...?

an illness a story
a person from the station
a show an excuse
a bad experience clothes
a bad habit

1 Payment for Saturday classes

Rewrite the article with the missing relative clauses (on the left). Put in commas where necessary.

- who are likely to do badly in their GCSE exams
- which is more than the minimum wage for 18-21 year-olds
- which is affecting the standard of education here
- which is trying to improve poor exam results
- who do part-time jobs
- which has some of the worst exam results in the country

Pupils to be paid for Saturday classes

Teenagers in Islington are being offered £3.50 an hour to attend school on Saturday mornings by a local authority (...) The payment (...) will compensate pupils for losing their earnings from Saturday jobs.

Islington (...) set up the scheme to help pupils (...). John Dunford of the Secondary Heads Association said: "We have to accept that there are a lot of pupils (...). A large part of the economy now seems to depend on pupil labour (...)."

2 Used to

How did people live before the Industrial Revolution? Make sentences with 'used to'/'didn't use to'.

1. make all goods by hand
2. cook with microwaves
3. live in blocks of flats
4. heat their homes with wood fires
5. work in factories
6. have lots of children
7. live long and healthy lives
8. send e-mails
9. travel by horse and carriage
10. use anaesthetics in operations

3 Take ..., look ..., put ..., run ...

Complete the phrasal verbs.

1. The plane took ... from Gatwick Airport.
2. When did you take ... badminton?
3. Did you take ... her phone number?
4. I take ... my father. We've got the same eyes.
5. Where's Surrey? – Look it ... in the atlas.
6. Marks & Spencer is famous for looking ... its staff so well.
7. I'm looking ... a part-time job because I need the extra cash.
8. The boiler has broken down again! I'm not willing to put ... this any longer.
9. An environmentalist who was protesting against cars was run ... by a cyclist.

4 Cartoon fun

'Hi! I'm your tutor.'

5 Informal/formal words

a) *Match the informal (Germanic) verbs on the left with the more formal (Romance) ones on the right.*

b) *Write a short text with the formal verbs. Then rewrite it with the informal ones.*

buy – try – stop – need – be sorry – put in – find – look into – make up for – go on

require – compensate – discover – attempt – cease – investigate – install – continue – regret – purchase

CHECK-IN

1	**caption** ['kæpʃn]	Bildunterschrift, -überschrift	title or explanation of a picture
	voluntary ['vɒləntri]	freiwillig	Work for charities is often ~ work.
	training ['treɪnɪŋ]	Ausbildung, Schulung	It prepares you for the job you want to do.
2	**hairdresser** ['heəˌdresə]	Friseur(in)	Your hair is cut at the ~'s.
	tip [tɪp]	Trinkgeld	People usually leave a ~ in a restaurant.
	to **experience** [ɪk'spɪəriənts]	erfahren, erleben, durchmachen	experience – to experience
	reliable [rɪ'laɪəbl]	zuverlässig	He won't be late, don't worry. He's very ~.
	engineer [ˌendʒɪ'nɪə]	Ingenieur(in), Techniker(in)	A heating ~ can repair your heating.
	salary ['sæləri]	Gehalt	the money you are paid each month for your work
	cashier [kæʃ'ɪə]	Kassierer(in)	the person you pay (or who gives you money) in a shop, bank, etc.
	staff [stɑ:f]	Personal	The people who work for an organisation (e.g. teachers at a school, assistants in a shop) are the ~.
	research [rɪ'sɜ:tʃ]	Forschung	So. who does ~ finds out more on a certain subject.
	to **require** [rɪ'kwaɪə]	brauchen, benötigen, erfordern	a formal word for 'to need'
	according to [ə'kɔ:dɪŋ tʊ]	nach, gemäß, laut, zufolge	You'll be paid ~ your experience. = Your salary will depend on your experience.
	curriculum vitae (CV) [kəˌrɪkjələm 'vi:taɪ]	Lebenslauf	A ~ is sometimes called a CV.
	to **earn** [ɜ:n]	verdienen	How much will I ~? = How much will I be paid?
	unemployed [ˌʌnɪm'plɔɪd]	arbeitslos	employee – unemployed
	to **retire** [ri'taɪə]	in den Ruhestand gehen, sich zurückziehen	People over 65 are usually ~d.
	to **be* willing to** *(+ infinitive)* ['wɪlɪŋ tʊ]	bereit sein, gewillt sein zu *(+ Infinitiv)*	I don't mind doing it. = I'm willing to do it.
	A-level ['eɪlevl]	*britischer Schulabschluss, der mit dem Abitur vergleichbar ist*	~ (Advanced level) exams are usually taken in the last year at school.
	future ['fju:tʃə]	zukünftig	Your ~ employer is the person you are going to work for.
	employer [ɪm'plɔɪə]	Arbeitgeber(in)	! employer: gives so. work employee: does work for so.
	apart from [ə'pɑ:t frəm]	außer, abgesehen von	I drink everything, ~ coke.

TEXTS

A	**free period** [ˌfri: 'pɪəriəd]	Hohlstunde, die zum selbstständigen Lernen gedacht ist	'free' time before, between or after lessons (= periods)
	deputy head [ˌdepjəti 'hed]	stellvertretende(r) Schulleiter(in)	head (teacher) – deputy head
	to **underachieve** [ˌʌndərə'tʃi:v]	hinter den Erwartungen zurückbleiben	to achieve – to underachieve
	GCSE [ˌdʒi:si:es'i:]	*britischer Schulabschluss, der mit der mittleren Reife vergleichbar ist*	~ (General Certificate of Secondary Education) exams are usually taken two or three years before A-levels.

	to **accuse** [ə'kju:z]	beschuldigen, anklagen	To ~ so. of doing sth. bad is to say you believe they did it.
	to **exploit** [ɪk'splɔɪt]	ausbeuten, ausnutzen	to use unfairly for your own benefit
	to **encourage** [ɪn'kʌrɪdʒ]	ermutigen, anregen, fördern, *hier:* verleiten	Do TV commercials ~ people to buy things they don't need?
	to **study** ['stʌdi]	*hier:* für die Schule lernen	It doesn't make a difference if you're at college or still at school: You have to ~ at home a lot.
	extra tuition [ˌekstrə tju'ɪʃn]	Nachhilfe-, Förderunterricht	~ can help people to get better results at school.
	revision [rɪ'vɪʒn]	Wiederholung (des Stoffs) zur Prüfungsvorbereitung	If you do your ~ well, you'll feel more confident about the exam.
	to **educate** ['edʒukeɪt]	bilden, ausbilden	education – to educate
	workforce ['wɜ:kfɔ:s]	Arbeiterschaft, Arbeitskräfte	The people who work for a company are its ~.
	concern [kən'sɜ:n]	Besorgnis	caring and worrying about sth. or so.
	to **set* aside** [ˌset‿ə'saɪd]	einplanen, beiseite legen	side – to set aside
	to **estimate** ['estɪmeɪt]	schätzen	It is ~d that two million children work, but nobody knows the exact number.
	work permit ['wɜ:k ˌpɜ:mɪt]	Arbeitserlaubnis	It proves that you are allowed to work.
	to **clock on** [ˌklɒk‿'ɒn]	zu Arbeitsbeginn stempeln oder stechen	Workers ~ before they start work.
	recent ['ri:snt]	kürzlich, jüngste(r/s), neueste(r/s)	a ~ report = a report that was written only a short time ago
	in recent years [ɪn ˌri:snt 'jɪəz]	in den letzten Jahren	in the last few years
	to **fuel** ['fju:əl]	antreiben, anheizen, mit Brennstoff versorgen	If sth. ~s a bad situation, it makes it worse.
	craze [kreɪz]	Fimmel	sth. that is the last word for a while
	demand [dɪ'mɑ:nd]	Forderung, Verlangen, Nachfrage	If a person makes ~s, they tell you what they want and expect to get.
	poor [pɔ:]	schlecht, gering, schwach	good results ↔ poor results
	delivery work [dɪ'lɪvri ˌwɜ:k]	Zustell-, Lieferantentätigkeit	Taking papers round is an example of ~.
	sawmill ['sɔ:mɪl]	Sägemühle, Sägewerk	
	growth [grəʊθ]	Wachstum	to grow – growth
	to **benefit** ['benɪfɪt]	profitieren, gut tun, nützen	If sth. ~s you, it does you good.
1	**in order to** *(+ infinitive)* [ɪn‿'ɔ:də tʊ]	um ... zu ... *(+ Infinitiv)*	They gave a child the job ~ save money.
2	**shelf**, *pl.:* **shelves** [ʃelf, ʃelvz]	Regal, Regalbrett	Most things in supermarkets are on shelves, so you can find them easily.
	exploitation [ˌeksplɔɪ'teɪʃn]	Ausbeutung	to exploit – exploitation
	embarrassing [ɪm'bærəsɪŋ]	peinlich	In ~ situations it can be difficult to know what to say.
3	**coal** [kəʊl]	Kohle	Years ago, ~ was often used for the heating of people's homes.
	mine [maɪn]	Mine, Bergwerk	miner – mine
	pit [pɪt]	Grube, Zeche	another word for 'coal mine'
	but [bʌt]	außer, bis auf, als	We had nothing ~ rain when we were on holiday.
	to **weave** [wi:v]	weben	
	to **spin*** [spɪn]	spinnen	Many years ago, a lot of weaving and spinning was done in people's homes.
	living ['lɪvɪŋ]	Lebensunterhalt	If you earn your own ~, you are independent of others' help.
	stocking ['stɒkɪŋ]	Strumpf	Women usually wear tights today instead of ~s.

	chemise [ʃə'mi:z]	Unterkleid	
	heading ['hedɪŋ]	Schacht	
	naked ['neɪkɪd]	nackt	without any clothes on
	to **behave** [bɪ'heɪv]	sich benehmen, sich verhalten	
B	**technological** [ˌteknə'lɒdʒɪkl]	technologisch, technisch	The Industrial Revolution was a time of great ~ progress and change.
	progress ['prəʊgres]	Fortschritt(e), Verlauf	
	cloth [klɒθ]	Tuch, Stoff	A lot of clothes are made of ~.
	goods [gʊdz]	Güter, Waren	Trucks carry ~.
	output ['aʊtpʊt]	Ertrag, Ausstoß, Produktion, Leistung	the number of things that are produced
	improvement [ɪm'pru:vmənt]	Verbesserung	to improve – improvement
	steam engine ['sti:m‿ˌendʒɪn]	Dampfmaschine	With a ~, steam produces the power.
	shipyard ['ʃɪpjɑ:d]	Werft	a place where ships are built and repaired
	works *(sg. and pl.)* [wɜ:ks]	Werk, Fabrik, Betrieb	A ~ is a place where industrial work is done (e.g. a gas ~, chemical ~, metal ~).
	chimney sweeping ['tʃɪmni ˌswi:pɪŋ]	Schornsteinreinigung	In the days when there were coal fires, the chimneys often had to be cleaned.
	to **employ** [ɪm'plɔɪ]	beschäftigen	employer – employee – to employ
	skilled worker [ˌskɪld 'wɜ:kə]	Facharbeiter(in)	skill – skilled – unskilled
	unskilled worker [ˌʌnskɪld 'wɜ:kə]	Hilfsarbeiter(in), ungelernte(r) Arbeiter(in)	
	handloom ['hændlu:m]	Handwebstuhl	
	weaver ['wi:və]	Weber(in)	to weave – weaver
	carriage ['kærɪdʒ]	Kutsche	! 'Carriage' rhymes with 'marriage'.
	stable ['steɪbl]	stabil	A thing that is ~ is not likely to change or end suddenly.
	to **allow** [ə'laʊ]	erlauben, gestatten	to be allowed to – to allow
	free trade [ˌfri: 'treɪd]	Freihandel	trader – (free) trade
	iron ore [ˌaɪən‿'ɔ:]	Eisenerz	iron – Iron Age – iron ore
	raw material [ˌrɔ: mə'tɪəriəl]	Rohstoff	~s are used to make finished products.
1	**paragraph** ['pærəgrɑ:f]	Absatz, Abschnitt	Texts are usually divided into ~s.
	society [sə'saɪəti]	Gesellschaft	social – society
	trading port ['treɪdɪŋ ˌpɔ:t]	Handelshafen	a port where goods from abroad are received and others sent overseas
	mill [mɪl]	Mühle, Fabrik	mill – sawmill – cotton-mill
2	**wealth** [welθ]	Reichtum	(having a lot of) money
	divide [dɪ'vaɪd]	Kluft, Wasserscheide	to divide – divide
	unemployment [ˌʌnɪm'plɔɪmənt]	Arbeitslosigkeit	unemployed – unemployment
	northerner ['nɔ:ðənə]	Person aus dem Norden	
3	**entrepreneur** [ˌɒntrəprə'nɜ:]	Unternehmer(in)	so. who sets up a business or businesses
	to be* dyslexic [dɪ'sleksɪk]	Legastheniker(in) sein	
⟨4⟩	simplicity [sɪm'plɪsəti]	Einfachheit	
	to tire [taɪə]	ermüden	
	wire [waɪə]	Draht, Leitung	
	plug [plʌg]	Stecker	
	mug [mʌg]	Trottel	

LANGUAGE

3	to **shorten** ['ʃɔ:tn]	verkürzen, kürzen	short – to shorten

4	to patent ['peɪtənt]	patentieren (lassen)	
	pie [paɪ]	Pastete, gedeckter Kuchen	A ~ is made in a ~ dish.
	dish [dɪʃ]	Schale, Schüssel, flache, runde Form	
	mask [mɑ:sk]	Maske	
5	to **be* based in** ['beɪst‿ɪn]	in ... seinen/ihren Sitz haben	A lot of big companies are based in London.
⟨6⟩	to emphasise ['empfəsaɪz]	betonen, hervorheben	to stress
	steel [sti:l]	Stahl	
B2	**childhood** ['tʃaɪldhʊd]	Kindheit	child – childhood
3	emphatic [ɪm'fætɪk]	emphatisch, nachdrücklich, verstärkend	
C2	**odd** [ɒd]	ungewöhnlich, merkwürdig, eigenartig	strange, unexpected
	thief, *pl.:* **thieves** [θi:f, θi:vz]	Dieb	so. who steals
	loaf, *pl.:* **loaves** [ləʊf, ləʊvz]	Laib	You can buy a ~ of bread.
	louse, *pl.:* lice [laʊs, laɪs]	Laus	
	lousy ['laʊzi]	verlaust, lausig	
	goose, *pl.:* **geese** [gu:s, gi:s]	Gans	Old MacDonald had some geese on his farm.
	gander ['gændə]	Ganter, Gänserich	
	offspring *(sg. and pl.)* ['ɒfsprɪŋ]	Sprössling, Nachkommen, Nachwuchs	
	gosling ['gɒzlɪŋ]	junge Gans, Gänschen	
	gaggle ['gægl]	Herde, Schar (Gänse)	
	drake [dreɪk]	Erpel, Enterich	
	duckling ['dʌklɪŋ]	Entenküken, Entlein	
	moose *(sg. and pl.)* [mu:s]	Elch(e)	
	hero ['hɪərəʊ]	Held	so. who has done sth. very brave and is very much loved as a result
	cent [sent]	Cent, *Währungseinheit in den USA*	There are a hundred ~s in a dollar.
	penny *pl.:* pennies *or* pence ['peni]	Penny	! 50 pennies are single coins. 50 pence = 50p (the money or price you pay)
	the penny has dropped [ðə ˌpeni həz 'drɒpt]	Der Groschen ist gefallen.	
	kid [kɪd]	Kitz, Zicklein	
3	**understatement** [ˌʌndə'steɪtmənt]	Untertreibung, Understatement	To say you 'don't like it very much' when you hate sth. is an ~.
	to **depend on** [dɪ'pend]	sich verlassen auf	He's reliable. = You can depend on him.

SKILLS

	informal [ɪn'fɔ:ml]	informell, nicht förmlich	formal ↔ informal
1	**complaint** [kəm'pleɪnt]	Beschwerde, Klage	to complain – complaint
	cowboy ['kaʊbɔɪ]	Cowboy, *hier:* pfuschende Handwerker, Gauner	
	bloody ['blʌdi]	verdammt	

	lawyer ['lɔɪə]	Rechtsanwalt, -anwältin	He or she helps people in legal matters.
	to **refer to** [rɪ'fɜ:]	sich beziehen auf	reference – to refer (to sth.)
	to **investigate** [ɪn'vestɪgeɪt]	untersuchen, nachforschen, ermitteln	to find out more about sth.
	to **regret** [rɪ'gret]	bedauern, bereuen	'I ~ to tell you' is a formal way of saying 'I'm sorry to tell you'.
	to **cease** [si:s]	enden, aufhören	It has ~d to function. = It has stopped working.
	to **attempt** [ə'tempt]	versuchen	a more formal word for 'to try'
	response [rɪ'spɒnts]	Antwort, Erwiderung, Reaktion	a more formal word for 'answer'
	furthermore [ˌfɜ:ðə'mɔ:]	überdies, außerdem	
	to **freeze*** [fri:z]	frieren, gefrieren, einfrieren	When water ~s, you get ice.
	to **purchase** ['pɜ:tʃəs]	kaufen, erwerben	a more formal word for 'to buy'
	to **recover** [rɪ'kʌvə]	sich erholen	After an illness, shock or accident, you need time to ~.
	to **resolve** [rɪ'zɒlv]	lösen (z. B. einen Konflikt)	To ~ a situation is to make it right again.
	delay [dɪ'leɪ]	Verzögerung, Verzug	without ~ = straight away
2	**phrasal verb** [ˌfreɪzl 'vɜ:b]	Verb mit Präposition oder kurzem Adverb	examples of ~s: to play up, to call back
3	Germanic [dʒə'mænɪk]	germanisch	
	Romance [rəʊ'mænts]	romanisch	
4	to **apologise** [ə'pɒlədʒaɪz]	sich entschuldigen	I ~ for being late.
	extreme [ɪk'stri:m]	extrem, äußerste(r,s)	I'm ~ly busy. = I'm very, very busy.
	order ['ɔ:də]	Auftrag, Bestellung	to order – order
	accusation [ˌækjʊ'zeɪʃn]	Anschuldigung, Anklage, Vorwurf	
	appointment [ə'pɔɪntmənt]	Termin, Verabredung	If you want to see a doctor or a lawyer, you'll need to make an ~ before you go.
	(un)pleasant [(ʌn)'pleznt]	(un)angenehm	If an experience is (un)pleasant, you (don't) enjoy it.

COGNATE WORDS

alternative [ɔ:l'tɜ:nətɪv]	Alternative
assistant [ə'sɪstnt]	Assistent(in), Helfer(in)
badminton ['bædmɪntən]	Badminton, Federball
biotechnology [ˌbaɪəʊtek'nɒlədʒi]	Biotechnologie
boiler ['bɔɪlə]	Boiler, Warmwasserbereiter
to **boom** [bu:m]	boomen, florieren, einen Aufschwung nehmen
colony ['kɒləni]	Kolonie
to **compensate** ['kɒmpənseɪt]	kompensieren, entschädigen
to **consume** [kən'sju:m]	konsumieren, zu sich nehmen
efficient [ɪ'fɪʃnt]	effizient, fähig, tüchtig
to **explode** [ɪk'spləʊd]	explodieren
flexible ['fleksɪbl]	flexibel, *hier:* flexible time = Gleitzeit
gas [gæs]	Gas
industrial [ɪn'dʌstriəl]	industriell
kilo ['ki:ləʊ]	Kilo(gramm)
maximum ['mæksɪməm]	Maximum; maximal
to **multiply** ['mʌltɪplaɪ]	multiplizieren, (sich) vervielfachen
period ['pɪəriəd]	Periode, Zeitspanne, Zeitalter; *hier:* Unterrichtsstunde
political [pə'lɪtɪkl]	politisch
prompt [prɒmpt]	prompt, unverzüglich
publicity [pʌb'lɪsɪti]	Publicity, öffentliche Aufmerksamkeit
qualification [ˌkwɒlɪfɪ'keɪʃn]	Qualifikation
revolution [ˌrevl'u:ʃn]	Revolution
to **shock** [ʃɒk]	schockieren
slang [slæŋ]	Slang, Jargon
statistics *(sg. or pl.)* [stə'tɪstɪks]	Statistik
strict [strɪkt]	strikt, streng
textiles *(pl.)* ['tekstaɪlz]	Textilien
to **tolerate** ['tɒləreɪt]	tolerieren, dulden

Phrasal verbs

These are three verbs whose basic meanings you know:

to keep *to touch* *to make*

When they are combined with prepositions or adverbs as phrasal verbs they can have completely different meanings though.

Try to find out what each verb means in the given sentences. Sometimes you only have to add the meanings of the verb and the preposition or adverb to understand the meaning of both together, e.g. with *keep* + *back* = *zurück* + *halten*.
You will find that the meanings of some *phrasal verbs* are totally surprising. Make a list of these difficult verbs and learn their meanings by heart. Use a dictionary if necessary.

to keep	Keep away from my box of chocolates! The Wilsons try to keep up with their rich neighbours. Keep out! This room is private! You should keep in with the director. – He's very important. Keep at it until you've found a solution. You're keeping something back from me. Keep on ringing the bell until someone comes.
to touch	Jenny touched up her make-up before the party. The plane touched down at the airport at 9.30 am. We haven't touched on that topic yet. News of the government's plans touched off a storm of protest.
to make	The children made for the door as quickly as possible. What do you make of this suggestion? The thieves made off with $200,000. They've made the book into a film. I can't make out where our street is on this map.

6

You'll make it!

The English verb 'to make' can mean quite a lot of things, depending on the context and the prepositions that go with it. In the following sentences there are a number of examples. Match them with the correct meanings of 'to make'.

1. What a lovely model house! Who made it?
2. The basketball trainer says I am talented. I hope I'll make the school team.
3. I want to be a musician and my father doesn't like the idea. But I know I'll make it!
4. I don't believe that story! I'm sure you've made it up!
5. If you don't work harder, you won't make the grade.
6. Mrs Winter made me do my homework all over again – only because she couldn't read it!

to get into
to be good enough
to invent
to build
to tell so. to do sth.
to be successful (in one's job)

Diary of a date

(after Unit 1)

5:30 P.M. It's Saturday night – an hour and a half to go before my first date with Suzanne. I'm standing in my room trying to decide on a shirt. Nervous? Yeah. I still can't believe she agreed to go out with me.

5:40 P.M. Still here. Still staring at my clean-shirt options. Enough of this. I go for the blue pullover and jeans and pray she won't notice my scruffy loafers.

7:05 P.M. I ring Suzanne's doorbell. Her mother answers, tells me that Suzanne will be down in a minute, and invites me into the living room to watch TV with The Dad. I try to make conversation.

7:16 P.M. "Hi," Suzanne says as she enters the living room. Wow, does she look great! She's wearing a tight-fitting red shirt. I catch myself staring at her chest and quickly look away. It's definitely not cool to check out a girl's breasts in front of her father.

7:45 P.M. As we're driving to the restaurant, Suzanne suddenly says, "I saw you after school last week, practicing for the play. You were really good." I almost run a red light. She noticed me!

7:55 P.M. We're waiting to be seated at Bob's Burgers, my favorite diner, when suddenly I spot my ex Diane out with some dude. Oh, God. Is this the guy she dropped me to go out with? Maybe she won't see me. Thankfully, the host has a table for us at the back of the restaurant.

8:00 P.M. We both order burgers and fries. Suzanne smiles at me. For about 20 seconds I can't think of anything to say. "Gossip," my friend Tanner had said when he gave me a pep talk that afternoon. "Girls love to gossip." But I can't think of a single thing except that I overslept and nearly missed my history test. Not very exciting. I feel sweat forming on my forehead. Then I remember that Tanner likes Suzanne's friend Jess. I tell her. "Really?" she asks, all interested. Tanner's gonna kill me.

8:10 P.M. The food's here. I'm trying my best not to spill ketchup on my shirt. I find myself carefully dipping my fries into the ketchup one by one instead of my normal stuff-and-chew style.

8:35 P.M. I'm feeling more warmed up now. It's as if we're the only two people in the place. I can't keep my eyes off her. Even the way she eats is adorable. Plus, she laughs at all my jokes. She complimented me in the car. That's two out of three on the Will-She-Kiss Me-Tonight? checklist. All I need her to do is start touching my hand or arm when we're talking or bump into me a few times when we're walking.

9:00 P.M. On the way from the parking lot to the movie theater, Suzanne bumps into me and our hands brush. Just when we get to the ticket window, she bumps into me again and I feel her fingers next to mine. I close my hand around her hand, and she closes hers too. The ticket girl says "Can I help you?" about five times before I hear her. Unfortunately, I have to remove my hand from Suzanne's to pay.

9:35 P.M. I've been moving closer and closer to Suzanne since the movie started. Finally, we're sunk low in our seats, and our shoulders are pushed together. All I can think of is, We're touching! I spend the next 15 minutes wondering whether I should try to hold her hand again or maybe put my hand on her leg. I decide holding hands is probably the safest bet. But after 15 minutes my hand starts to get so sweaty I have to let go to wipe it on my pants. I'm too afraid to go for it again.

10:45 P.M. After the movies, we hit a coffee shop. She pays for the lattes and we sit on the couch in the back. Our legs touch. There have been about three times when the conversation stopped and she's turned her face towards me. I know I can lean forward and kiss her, but I don't. I'm too scared. What if she stops me? What if she doesn't like the way I kiss? I excuse myself to go to the restroom. I don't even need to go.

11:25 P.M. We're at Suzanne's front door talking about the movie's ending, which we've discussed to death already. The Pause comes. It can only be filled by a kiss. She's three steps away. It's a long gap for a guy to cross, but I do, because I can totally tell she wants me to. Finally, I press my lips against hers. It lasts five beautiful seconds. I pull back. We both smile. I kiss her again. Oh, man. Oh, man! I tell her I'll call her, and I drive home.

11:45 P.M. In my room I log in to my PC; I know my friends will be hanging in cyberspace. Messages begin popping up all over my screen. One says, "Did you hook up?" I type, "%*#@ off!" Then Tanner writes, "How'd it go?" I type, "She let me kiss her." I'm feeling pretty proud of myself.

12:30 A.M. I lie in bed and start imagining a different ending for our date. I think of putting my hands around Suzanne's waist and touching my lips to hers like I did less than two hours ago. I wonder when I'll get to kiss her again. Tomorrow is Sunday. I won't even see her or talk to her until Monday at school. Can I call her tomorrow? My friends say you should string girls along or they lose interest. I hate that. Man, I'm never going to get to sleep!

Imagine you are Suzanne.
Write about the date in your own diary.

(adapted from: YM, November 1999)

Going to jump? (28)

(after Unit 1)

Boy	Man
Are you going to jump?	I might.
Can I watch you?	What's your name?
Jonathan.	So is mine.
Does that mean I can watch?	How old are you?
Si … seven.	Do you want to be a fireman?
Yep.	So did I.
Are you a fireman?	No.
Why not?	I changed my mind.
Are you going to jump?	I might.
Have a jelly bean?	No, thanks.
Don't you like them?	I can't remember.
Are you an astronaut?	No.
A traindriver?	No.
Are you going to jump?	I might.
I don't think I will.	Why not?
I can't swim.	Neither can I.
Can you play 'I Spy'?	No.
Something starting with S.	Seagull.
Wrong.	Ship?
No.	Star.
Right. Now it's your turn.	Where do you live, Jonathan?
Over there.	Garden Street?
Yep.	So did I.
Do you like dogs?	I did.
I haven't got a dog.	Neither have I.
I've got a bike.	Do you ride it in the park?
Mummy won't let me on the road.	Neither did mine.
Have you a Mummy?	No.
Are you going to jump?	No.
Why not?	I've changed my mind.
Are you going home?	I don't live here any more.
Where do you live?	A long way away.
I have to go home now.	Goodbye, Jonathan.

Passer-by: Pardon?
Man: I was just saying goodbye to a little boy.
Passer-by: No little boy here, mate. You're imagining things.
(Silence) Thinking of jumping, mate?
Man: I might.

Read the text and explain the situation. Who are the characters? What is going on?

The origins of the USA

(after Unit 2)

a) Did you know?

• The island of Manhattan was bought from the Indians for about $24!
The person who made this great bargain was Peter Minuit. In the early 1600s he was Governor of a small colony on the southern part of the island. The colony needed more land, so in 1626, Peter bought the rest of the island from its Native American owners. They were happy to accept some kettles, knives and cloth for it.

Peter Minuit buys Manhattan from the Indians

• The original name of the city that grew up there was New Amsterdam – not New York!
The colony in question had been set up by Dutch traders a few years earlier. Naturally, they named its main town after the main city of their own country. And the area controlled by the Dutch West India Company (now New York State) was called "New Netherlands".
This situation didn't last, however. There were English colonies north and south of it, and in 1664, the Duke of York came with four warships to take control of the area for the English King.

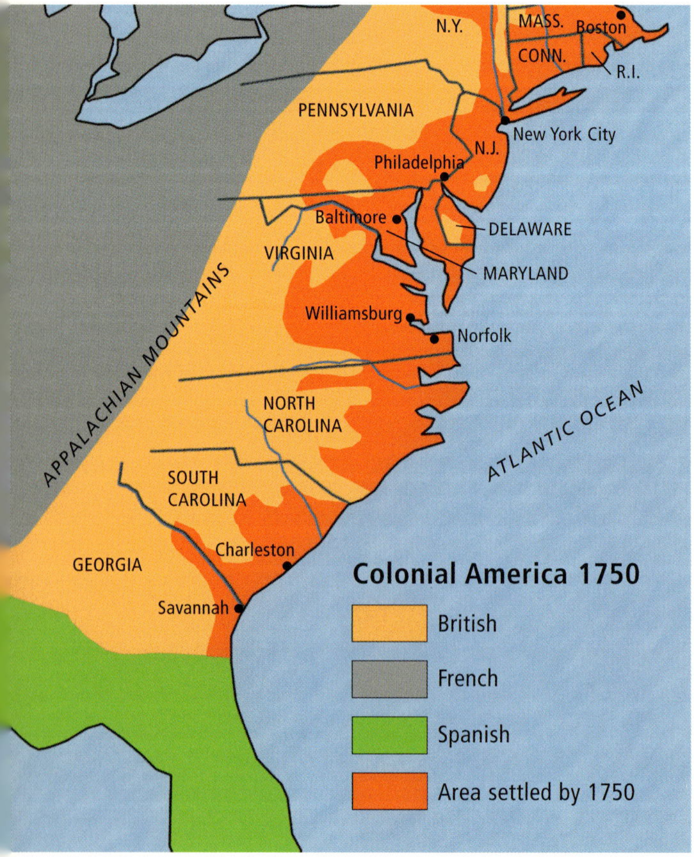

b) The English colonies

Like the Dutch, the English were there for the money. The *New World* was a place for traders to get rich – or to make their country rich. The first permanent English colony was Jamestown, set up by the Virginia Company of London in 1607.
Further north, a new kind of English-speaking settler began to arrive. They were not traders, but people who wanted to practise their religion freely – which was not possible in their home country at the time.
Groups of Puritans set up colonies in the area that became known as "New England". The first and most famous of these was the Plymouth Colony (1620), in what became the state of Massachusetts.
Quakers led by William Penn founded the city of Philadelphia in 1682 – in the state that was named after its founder, Pennsylvania. Maryland was founded in 1634 as a place where Catholics could be free.
All these colonies set up governments. By 1733 there were 13 in all, including some that had broken away from the original colonies.

In groups, prepare a report on one of the early colonies. Here are some keywords for your search:
New Netherlands / Peter Minuit / New York;
Jamestown / Virginia;
Puritans / Mayflower / Plymouth / Massachusetts;
St Mary's colony / Maryland;
William Penn / Philadelphia / Pennsylvania.

No taxation without representation

(after Unit 2)

As time went by, the thirteen colonies became more like each other. People moved from one to the other, so their governments learned to be tolerant of different religions.
At first the colonists were happy to be subject to the British Crown. After all, they were mainly English-speaking people, and they did well trading with the "Mother Country". The British government allowed them to live by their own laws. But there was one point of conflict – taxes.

For Britain, the whole point of colonies was to make money from them. The colonists saw this differently. They were there to make a good life for themselves, and had nothing to do with the London government, in which they were not even represented. Very often they simply ignored tax demands. But in 1766 Britain sent soldiers to enforce the new Stamp Act, which put a tax on all paper used in the colonies. People were put in jail for using unstamped paper. Secret societies called the "Sons of Liberty" were formed in all the major cities to organize protests. In Boston, five people were killed by soldiers after some youths started throwing snowballs at them. This became known as the "Boston Massacre".

The Boston Tea Party

Things got worse when in 1773, the colonists heard of a new Tea Act, which gave the British East India Company a monopoly on the American tea trade. When the first such shipload of tea arrived in Boston harbour, a group of Sons of Liberty dressed up as Indians climbed on board, broke open the boxes of tea and threw them into the sea. This was the famous "Boston Tea Party".

Open war between Britain and the colonies broke out soon after. At first the colonists' slogan was "No taxation without representation!" But for many, this was no longer enough: they wanted independence from Britain. In 1776, the Continental Congress met in Philadelphia and passed the Declaration of Independence, which had been written by Thomas Jefferson. It included the famous words: "We hold these truths to be self-evident, that all men are created equal ..."

IN CONGRESS, JULY 4, 1776.
The unanimous Declaration of the thirteen united States of America,

The statue of Thomas Jefferson in Washington DC

Discuss: The War of Independence continued for seven more years before the British were finally beaten. *So why is this document so important? And why is the Fourth of July the American national holiday?*

We the people ...

(after Unit 2)

George Washington

a) Having become independent, the new country needed to create a new system of government. The individual states already had democratic governments, and they wanted to keep many powers for themselves. But they were willing to give up certain powers (issuing money, running an army, etc.) to the new federal government. To decide the details, a meeting was held under George Washington – the great hero of the War of Independence and later the first US President. Through the summer of 1787, the representatives of the states worked out a Constitution which would not allow any branch of government to get too powerful.

After being accepted by all the states, the Constitution could only be changed if the people of all the states agreed. The first 10 Amendments were added a year later to guarantee such rights as freedom of speech, religion, etc.

b) The pictures below show the most important elements in the American political system.

On election day (a Tuesday in November) Americans vote for local officials, mayors, state parliaments, state governors and for two of the three branches of the federal government.

There is a system of checks and balances between the three branches of government:

The President

A President is elected every four years, and can serve a maximum of two terms.

The Supreme Court

Supreme Court justices are appointed by the President for life.

Congress

Members of the House of Representatives (Congressmen and women) are elected for two years, and Senators (two from each state) for six years.

Republicans

Democrats

c) The Constitution says nothing about political parties. The two main parties developed much later, but today they are very important. The differences between them are not great, and have changed over time. But many people are strong supporters of one or the other, and it is nearly impossible for an independent candidate to get elected to an important office.

To find out more about the way American government works, read the next page!

A visit to Washington D.C.

They say Washington was chosen as the site of the capital of the newly independent United States because it gets so hot there in summer, and cold in winter. That way, they hoped, nobody would want to make politics a full-time job!

It didn't work out that way. But it is true that in the summer, Washington is practically empty of politicians. So if you want to see some politics in action, it's best to go in the spring or the fall.

There are free tours of the Capitol building, and it is possible to watch a session of the House or the Senate. If you are an American citizen, you will need a letter from your Senator or Representative. Foreign tourists just need to show their passports. If you're lucky, some Republicans will be arguing hard to throw out a bill brought in by a Democratic President (or vice-versa).

Of course you will want to visit the White House. You won't be able to look over the President's shoulder as he sits at his desk in the Oval Office – in fact, you won't get in there at all. But you can do a tour of the public rooms on the ground floor and imagine the President meeting important visitors there or trying to persuade politicians of both parties to support him in Congress.

If you want to watch a session of the Supreme Court, get there early: the line of people waiting to get in can be very long, especially if the court is expected to rule whether an important law is constitutional or not. When the court is not in session, there are free tours of the building.

If you want to get away from politics, you have a number of choices. You could visit the famous National Air and Space Museum to see the Wright Brothers' original handmade plane and the Apollo 11 space capsule, for example. Or you could do a boat trip on the river. Or go a few miles out of town to visit George Washington's home. No, that's not about politics! It's a wonderful way to see what life was like in his time – for the famous man himself, for his family, his servants – and his slaves.

The Capitol

The Supreme Court

The Oval Office

Points to discuss

1. *What do you learn here about the way the American political system works? Look at the relationship between the President, Congress and the Supreme Court. Find some examples there for the "checks and balances" that are so important.*
2. *Talk about what you would or wouldn't like to visit in Washington.*

(after Unit 3)

SUNTAN AND SLAUGHTER

While you're enjoying your holiday this year keep your eyes open for animals being harmed to impress tourists

Spain

What to look out for:
Bulls stabbed with darts, with fireworks attached to their horns and their throats cut for the entertainment of the crowd. Bullfighting now receives European Union funding as it's considered a part of Spanish culture. Spanish fiestas also involve live goats and donkeys thrown from buildings, chickens having their throats cut and rabbits being stoned to death.

What you can do:
Don't go to bullfights or buy the souvenirs and complain if your tour operator runs visits from your hotel. Report cruelty to World Society for the Protection of Animals (WSPA – see address above). Write to your Euro MP saying you think it's wrong for the EU to support this.

Canary Islands

What to look out for:
Donkeys forced to work all day in the sun, carrying tourists or baggage with little water or rest. They work to the point of exhaustion and are then tied up at night by the ankles. If they move they fall over, forced to spend the night on their sides.

What you can do:
Keep your eyes open. If you are on the beach all day, check that the animals get regular rest, food and water. Try to explain why you don't want a ride if you suspect the animals are being mistreated.

Africa

What to look out for:
Protected animals illegally poached from wildlife reserves, and used for gifts for the tourist industry. Skins, ivory carvings, tortoiseshell or coral jewellery, multi-coloured feathers and dried starfish and sea horses – many of these products are illegal.

What you can do:
Poachers only kill animals because they know they can make money from tourists. The message is simple – if you don't buy, they don't kill. Go for safe souvenirs made from non-animal products instead.

(adapted from: *Bliss* magazine)

See it, hear it, report it

If you see cruelty in action send photos and details to:

World Society for the Protection of Animals
2 Langley Lane,
London SW8 1TJ

World Wildlife Fund
Panda House, Weyside Park,
Catteshall Lane, Godalming,
Surrey GU7 1XR

Italy

What to look out for:
Circuses which contain endangered animals bought illegally from zoos and taught to perform in ways they never would in the wild. Animals are kept in small cages for up to 16 hours a day and then made to appear in front of a screaming crowd. If they don't perform, they are killed and replaced by other animals smuggled or stolen from zoos.

What you can do:
Only visit animal-free circuses. Report any mistreated or unhappy animals to WSPA.

Turkey

What to look out for:
Young bears, taken from their mothers, are trained to react to music. This is done by making them jump up and down on burning coals so they'll appear to dance to music which they associate with feeling pain. They are pinned to the floor, have a red-hot poker pushed through the nose, and a ring put in. So every time they move, the ring causes great pain.

What you can do:
If you see it, report it to WSPA who ask government officials to rescue the bears and place them in a sanctuary funded by WSPA supporters.

South East Asia

What to look out for:
The sale of tiger bones, sea horses and rhino horn. They are endangered species and therefore this is illegal. Protected species are killed in South East Asia for use in medicines and aphrodisiacs.

What you can do:
Make a note of any products you see containing these items and report them to the WWF. Don't buy the products as this is only encouraging the trade. Call the WWF Eyes & Ears hotline: 01483 426111 for a free info pack.

In many ways I'm a terrible pop star

(after Unit 4)

(adapted from: *The Daily Telegraph*, 25 June 1999)

AT A CORNER table in a café in Battersea, south London, Gary Barlow is having his breakfast. After finishing a stack of buttered white toast, he orders another cappuccino and lights up a cigarette. He is wearing green today "to make up for the vegetables I'm not going to eat".

"I don't really know what I'm wearing," he says, trying not to yawn. "I just pull on whatever is at the end of the bed. I don't even look in the mirror when I get up in the mornings. I really don't care how I look."

With his mud-coloured pudding-bowl hair and his big Fred Flintstone chin, he looks more like a builder on his coffee break than a multi-millionaire pop star. In fact, he looks as if Wilma or Bam Bam has just hit him on the back of the head with a bowling ball. But he can't be as stupid as he looks. At 28 years old, the former member of Take That has a beautiful fiancée and a large personal fortune.

"I don't know to the exact penny, but I think I'm worth about £19m," he says. This does not appear to excite or depress him – it is just another statistic in his amazing life.

It is widely accepted that Barlow was the main talent behind Take That's huge success. They sold more than 15 million albums during the five years together. Although he was teased for being the chubby one nobody fancied, it was Barlow who wrote all the group's songs – hits such as *Back for Good*, *A Million Love Songs* and *Babe*. No wonder that Barlow, who in the end earned six times more than the rest of the group, never minded too much that the "Gary" Take That doll was the least popular.

From the beginning, he always had a problem keeping his weight down so that his body would be a suitable shape for a pop star.

"But tell me, how can anyone eat fish without chips?"

Once a record company executive was sent to meet him at the airport. She took one look at his figure, then opened her mobile phone. "Uh-oh, he's heavy again," she reported back. Didn't he find this hurtful?

"No, not at all," he says, and I almost believe him. Despite his clever way with songs, he seems as emotionally sensitive as a sack of hammers.

"In many ways, I'm a terrible pop star. All those videos and Gucci clothes – I am just not born for that sort of thing," he says, smiling. The band always made jokes about him, but he didn't mind. "It was just a bit of humour."

However, no one was laughing when Take That broke up in February 1996 after Robbie Williams had left the band to start a solo career. Since then, each one has been fighting for the limelight – except for Howard Donald, who amuses himself by playing golf.

Jason Orange has started an acting career. Mark Owen, the cute one who made the girls scream, is singing duets with Boy George.

Although Barlow was expected to have the most successful solo career, events have not gone to plan. He has sacked two managers and was disappointed with his first album, *Open Road*. Although it sold more than two million copies, he now feels that it was over-produced.

"Sometimes I think, whose record is this? It just got watered down so much. Now there are only four songs I can actually bear to listen to. But it was my own fault because I stopped believing in myself and let other people make decisions for me."

He promoted the album with a British tour last year and was pleased when the fans actually listened to the music. "God, I had started to hate all that screaming," he says. "When I sat down at the piano to play my first song at my first gig, I heard the most beautiful noise: silence. I thought, beauty! The fans have grown up at last."

He is much happier with the music on his new album, *Stronger Now!*, and the single, *Stronger*. "It reflects how I feel," and then – oh no! – he starts to recite some of the lyrics.

"*Stronger every day, stronger every night, I'm holding out for peace, but ready now to fight*," he says, holding up a chubby fist. He adds: "I decided that if anyone dared to come near my toes on this new album, they'd be sorry!"

1. *Note down ways in which Gary Barlow can be seen as*
   - *a terrible pop star.*
   - *a successful pop star.*
2. a) *What did Gary learn from his experience with his first album, 'Open Road'?*
   b) *How has he changed since then, and how have his fans changed?*
3. *Is Gary Barlow a good role model? Why, or why not? (Look at what Madonna says on this subject in the interview on page 71.)*
4. *"All you need to be a successful pop star is talent." Do you agree? If not, what else do you think is important?*

Things you learn from the movies

(after Unit 4)

1. In every shopping bag there's at least one stick of French bread.
2. If a large pane of glass is visible, someone will be thrown through it before long.
3. If you decide to start dancing in the street, everyone else will know all the steps.
4. Even when driving down a perfectly straight road, you have to turn the steering wheel from left to right every few moments.
5. Lipstick will never rub off – even while scuba diving.
6. The Eiffel Tower can be seen from any window in Paris.
7. Large, elegant apartments in New York City are well within the price range of most people – whether they are unemployed or not.
8. Police departments give their officers personality tests to make sure they are given a partner who is their total opposite.
9. If you decide to defuse a bomb, don't worry which wire to cut. It will always be the right one.
10. Most laptop computers are powerful enough to destroy the communications systems of any invading extra-terrestrials.
11. When you turn out the lights to go to bed, everything in your room will still be clearly visible, just slightly bluish.
12. If you are blonde and pretty, you can become a world expert on nuclear fission at the age of 22.
13. All beds have special L-shaped sheets that reach the armpit level on a woman but only to waist level on the man lying beside her.
14. It's easy for anybody to land a plane as long as there's someone in the control tower to talk you down.
15. If you need to pretend to be a German or Russian officer, it will not be necessary to speak the language. A German or Russian accent will be enough.
16. A man will show no pain while he is being violently beaten, but will wince if a woman tries to clean his wounds.
17. If staying in a haunted house, women should investigate any strange noises wearing their sexiest underwear.
18. A detective can only solve a case once he is no longer on duty.

(from the Internet, source unknown)

Make your own list of 'Things you learn ...' (... from TV/... from sport/... from teachers/...)

Two Irish poets (29-30)

(after Unit 5)

Ireland is known for its many great writers as well as musicians. Both of the poets on these pages have won the Nobel Prize. *You can choose to read just one of these poems, or both. Or you can form groups for each poem. The pictures will give you an idea what they are about, if you want to choose one.*

The Lake Isle of Innisfree

I will arise and go now, and go to Innisfree,
And a small cabin build there, of clay and wattles made:
Nine bean-rows will I have there, a hive for the honey-bee,
And live alone in the bee-loud glade.

And I shall have some peace there, for peace comes dropping slow,
Dropping from the veils of the morning to where the cricket sings;
There midnight's all-a-glimmer, and noon a purple glow,
And evening full of the linnet's wings.

I will arise and go now, for always night and day
I hear lake water lapping with low sounds by the shore;
While I stand on the roadway, or on the pavement grey,
I hear it in the deep heart's core.

W. B. Yeats

The forge

All I know is a door into the dark,
Outside, old axles and iron hoops rusting;
Inside, the hammered anvil's short-pitched ring,
The unpredictable fantail of sparks
Or hiss when a new shoe toughens in water.
The anvil must be somewhere in the centre,
Horned as a unicorn, at one end square,
Set there immovable: an altar
Where he expends himself in shape and music.
Sometimes, leather-aproned, hairs in his nose,
He leans out on the jamb, recalls a clatter
Of hoofs where traffic is flashing in rows;
Then grunts and goes in, with a slam and a flick,
To beat real iron out, to work the bellows.

Seamus Heaney

a) **The Lake Isle of Innisfree**

1. *What does the speaker intend to do on the island?*
2. *Why does he want to go to there? What is he looking for, or escaping from?*

b) **The forge**

1. *What kind of "shoe" is meant in line 5? How are these shoes made, and who makes them?* (If you don't know the English word, look it up in a German-English dictionary!)
2. *What can be seen looking into the forge – and looking out from it?*

c) **Both poems**

1. *What do the people in the two poems think about the modern world, or feel about their present situation?* (There are two people in poem b), remember!)
2. *What do they (want to) do about it?*
3. *Do you/Would you feel the same way? Why, or why not?*
4. *Pick a line/a few lines/a verse that you like for the sounds. Try to learn that part of the poem off by heart.*

The Border

(after Unit 5)

It's now over 30 years since the latest round of "troubles" broke out in Northern Ireland. "The Troubles" is what the people there call the bombings, shootings, etc. that filled the newspapers and TV for so long. Even after several years of peace, Northern Ireland still spells "trouble" for many people. And in fact, there is still some tension between the two communities there. Ironically, Northern Ireland was created in 1921 to solve a problem. Most of the people of Ireland at that time wanted to be independent of Britain. But some didn't – especially in the north-east, which also had the most industry. They were mainly Protestants who didn't want to be a minority in the new Irish Free State. Instead, a mini-state was created in which the Protestants made up about 60 % of the population. South of the border, a Civil War was fought over this "compromise". And in the North, the 40 % Catholics were unhappy about being cut off from the rest of Ireland. Many felt (and often were) discriminated against.
The present Peace Process is all about finding ways the two communities can feel equally represented in Northern Ireland, and to ensure that any change can only be made by peaceful means.

1 What's in a name?

Look at the place-names in the box. Do you know what they all mean? Say which of the following sentences are correct:

1. Northern Ireland is part of the United Kingdom.
2. Ireland is one of the British Isles.
3. Northern Ireland is not part of Great Britain.
4. The most northern part of Ireland isn't in Northern Ireland.
5. Northern Ireland is often called "Ulster".
6. Part of Ulster is in the Republic of Ireland.

the British Isles	Northern Ireland
Britain	Ulster
Great Britain	United Kingdom
Ireland	the Republic of Ireland

2 Political opinions

a) *What's the word for the people who*
- want to keep the union with Britain?
- are loyal to the British king or queen?
- believe in an Irish nation?
- want to be part of an Irish republic?

loyalist Catholic republican nationalist
Protestant unionist

b) *And which of these opinions and religions go together?*

3 Strong feelings – and long memories

Many people in Ireland still have strong feelings about the historical facts below.
Try to work out what they mean to one or other community, and whether the feelings they have about them are positive or negative.

1169: Normans from England invade Ireland and slowly take over control from the Celtic chieftains.
1609: After a rebellion in Ulster, the rebels' lands are given to Protestant settlers from Scotland. (The Irish had remained Catholic.)
1690: At the Battle of the Boyne, the Catholic King James II loses to William of Orange. Soon after, Catholics lose many rights.
1846: In the Great Famine, millions die in the west and south of Ireland, and the London government does little to help.
1858: The Fenians start to fight for independence (later IRA).
1912: Ulster Volunteers threaten violence in case of "Home Rule".
1969: A Civil Rights Movement to end discrimination against Catholics in Northern Ireland meets with a violent backlash.

Living in Northern Ireland

(after Unit 5)

As everybody knows, the conflict in Northern Ireland is all about religion … Or is it? To find out, let's meet two typical members of the two "communities", Sinead Daly and Rhoda McBride …

Sinead goes to a Catholic school in Derry. (At least, that's what she calls her native city.) At school, she learns all the necessary subjects, but also Irish History and Irish Gaelic. Her best subjects are English and Spanish, and she wants to study languages at university. Her dad wants her to go to Queen's University, Belfast, but she thinks Dublin might be more fun. Both of her parents are teachers. Sinead is quite good at Irish step-dancing, and has won a few prizes at competitions. She hated the classes at first, and only went because her mother insisted, but the *Riverdance* show changed her mind! She isn't interested in sport (dancing is enough exercise, she says), but her two brothers are: Sean is on the school's Gaelic football team. Liam (the eldest) has finished his engineering course at college, but hasn't found a job yet. He says it's because the best jobs are still going to the "other crowd" (i.e. the Protestants). Their mother often talks about the Civil Rights demonstrations she took part in 30 years ago.

Rhoda lives in Londonderry. (At least that's what she calls her native city.) Her father is a policeman in the RUC, her mother runs a small business. Rhoda has one brother, Sam. They both go to a Protestant school. Actually, it's a state school; but all the teachers and school managers and most of the pupils are Protestant – Church of Ireland like herself, or Presbyterian, or Methodist. She can't decide whether to do German or Business Studies at college. Her parents hope she'll get a place at a local college, or perhaps Queen's, in Belfast; but she really wants to get away from home and go to a university in England. She's on the school hockey team. She plays the flute in the school orchestra. She likes to listen to Irish folk music, but didn't learn to play any herself because the classes were in a "dangerous" part of town. Actually, they were in the Catholic area called the Bogside.

1 Comparisons

1. *What have Rhoda and Sinead got in common?*
2. *In what ways are they different?*
3. *How have they and their families been affected by the "Troubles"?*
4. *Now look at these opinions and say who might express them:*

Naah – Catholics will always be discriminated against in Northern Ireland! Sure, wasn't it created to be a "Protestant state for a Protestant people"?

We were right to demonstrate for our civil rights – things would be fine by now if the extremists had kept out of it!

Catholics in the police? No. You can't really trust them to be loyal to the state.

It's funny: Here, I feel British, but when I'm in England I feel Irish! Why should I have to decide?

Keep out of the Bogside – the IRA is still in control there, and they know that you're a policeman's daughter!

Sure, the Protestants are Irish like ourselves, only they don't know it! Take Jimmy Watson, he's one of the best in my dancing class! I can't understand why more don't come!

We get on very well with our Catholic neighbours. But at school, the children must first learn our British traditions.

2 Summing up

1. *Try to say why it is so hard to find a solution that will make everybody happy.*
2. Project: *Find out about the latest developments in the Peace Process. Use newspapers/magazines/the Internet.*

Jon makes a decision

(after Unit 6)

Jon cycled to the canal, threw his bike down and slumped under a tree. God, how he hated being an only child. It was like all his father's hopes and fears and ambitions were focused just on him. It had always been the same – he had to live out all his dreams. Ever since he could remember his parents had wanted him to be the first kid in class to know his six times table, the earliest runner, the fastest reader. Why couldn't they just let him be himself?

He knew his dad had wanted to go to university but couldn't because Grandma was a widow and needed Dad to earn money. To Dad, university had always been the highest thing you could aim for – a sign to the world you were "someone". He knew his father would be upset when Jon didn't go – but he'd just have to get used to it.

He sometimes felt that his mum was secretly on his side. She was really artistic and she seemed bored with the business she ran from the shed – well, studio she called it – in the back garden. She made flower arrangements for weddings and spoke to ladies' lunch clubs and yet somehow she never seemed really excited by what she did. He didn't want to end up like that – doing a job that had no buzz, no excitement to it. His dad went to the office every day and sold houses to people but he never seemed happy.

Jon knew one thing for sure. He'd have to tell them what he really wanted to do. He didn't want to stay at Bellborough Court. He wanted to go to Lee Hill Comprehensive, because there he could do something that really interested him.

And tonight he'd tell them. But after he'd been to the disco.

"So you went to the disco, I see." Jon's father was at the front door when Rob's dad dropped him off. "I trust you will do some revision tomorrow – mock exams are not that far off."

"Dad, I've already done loads," sighed Jon, "And anyway the subject I like best you can't revise for. I'm sick of swotting up about the Civil War and continental shelves and French verbs. I hate all that stuff. I ..."

"Ah, but 'that stuff' as you call it is just what you need on your CV for university," began his father. "They attach a lot of importance to ..."

"I AM NOT GOING TO UNIVERSITY!" shouted Jon.

"Oh, don't let's start that all over again, son," said his father. "With a brain like yours, where else could you go?"

"To art college, actually," said Jon. I've done it, he thought. I've said it.

His father stared at him. He opened his mouth but nothing happened.

"I want to study art and design, Dad," said Jon. "I'm good at it, I enjoy it and I know I can make a living from it. And the best place to learn more is at art college."

"Art college? ART COLLEGE?" Jon's father blustered.

"Yes – I want to be a political cartoonist," said Jon. That's done it, he thought.

A spluttering noise came out of his father's throat. His cheeks turned purple.

"I've never heard such ... it's preposterous ... what are you thinking of, lad?"

"My future," said Jon. And went to bed.

(from: *Just don't make a scene, Mum*, by Rosie Rushton)

1. *Read the text on this page and make notes about Jon, his mum and his dad. Then discuss what you learn of their characters.*
2. *Rewrite the conversation between Jon and his dad (l. 35 to the end) from the father's point of view.*

Two maps of the United Kingdom

(after Unit 6)

*Study the maps of the United Kingdom on this page.
Now draw a map of your country seen from two different points of view.*

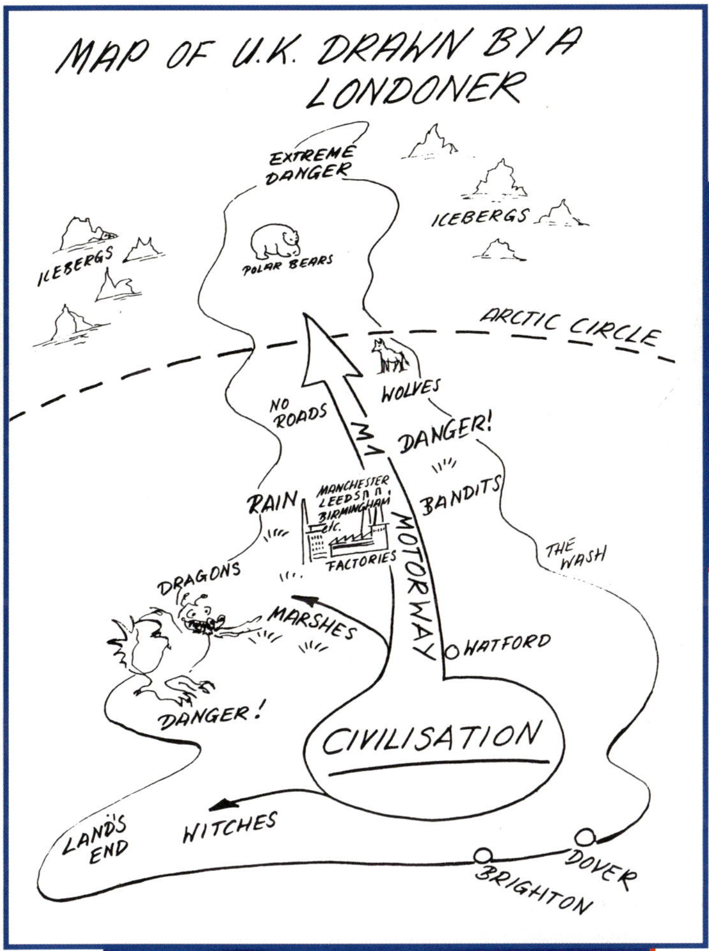

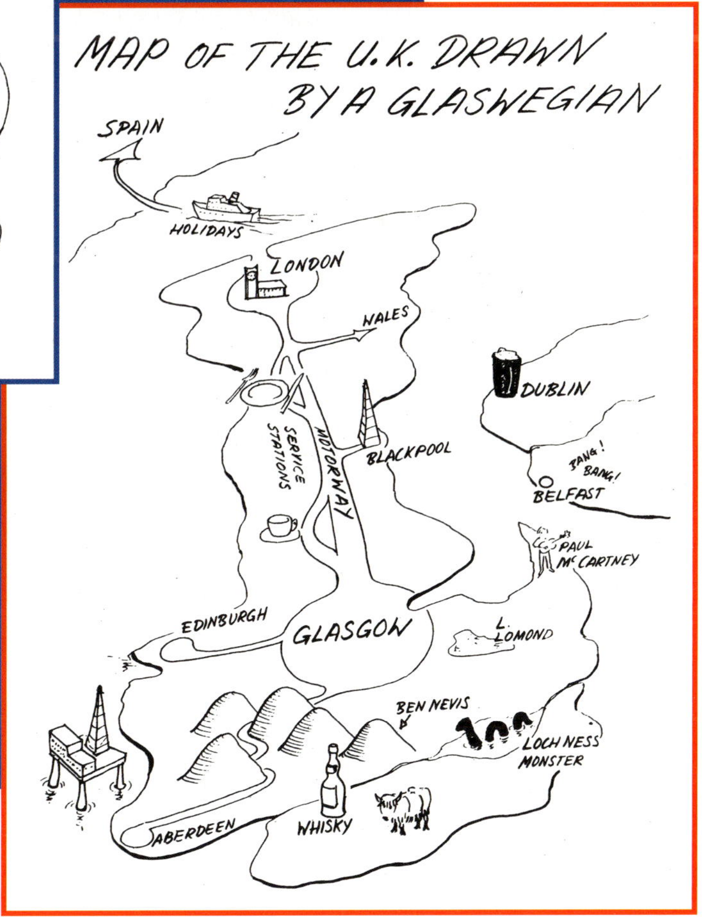

A special project

(after Unit 6)

Britain's government has changed over the centuries, and it is still changing today. Some British pupils have collected some information on this topic, which you can use for your own project.

1. *Copy the mind map. Decide which piece of information goes with which topic, and put in the missing keywords. Add any points you would like to know more about.*
2. *Work in groups. Each group deals with a different topic. Discuss what information you need, where to find it, who will do what, and how to best to present the information. Ask your teacher for help if necessary.*

People talk about "Her majesty's government", but the monarch no longer plays a very big part in deciding how the country is run. The Queen still officially 'opens' Parliament each year and

The word 'parliament' comes from the Norman French word 'parler', which means

In 1215 English barons led their armies against the unpopular King John and forced him to change the way they were ruled. He had to sign a document known as the Magna Carta, which demanded that people could not be punished without a trial and taxes could not be raised without the barons' agreement. These new laws only helped the rich and powerful, so most people's rights stayed the same. However, the Magna Carta is now seen as a symbol of people's rights. The British Constitution developed from the Magna Carta, but it is not written down in one document.

An example of a law passed by the House of Lords was the Factory Act of 1833, which prevented children under nine working in textile mills. Children aged nine to thirteen could not work longer than 12 hours.

Many local matters, such as repairing roads and taking away the rubbish, are organised by local councils. Some of the money comes from central government, and the rest from local taxes.

By 1928, all men and women had the right to vote (universal suffrage).

Elizabeth I (1558-1603) worked with parliament, but the kings following her did not. They believed that as head of the Church they could do as they liked. Charles I ruled for 11 years (1629–1640) without a parliament, raising taxes without their permission. This led to a civil war to find out who would rule the country – the king or Parliament. Landowners and Church leaders were loyal to the king. Most of Parliament's support came from London and many Puritans. Success depended on which side Scotland would take. In 1643 the Scots joined the fight on the side of Parliament.

Green Party
Labour
LIBERAL DEMOCRATS
CONSERVATIVE

The House of Lords, also known as the Upper House, acts as a check on the Government. If a law has to be changed, the House of Lords has to vote on it.

The first parliament met in 1265. The 'Lords' met in one room and the 'commoners' in another. English was now used as well as Norman French.

Talk of 'one man, one vote' and improved conditions for the working class grew in the 19th century into public protest. A group known as the Chartists demanded that all men should have the right to vote and that votes should be secret. They also wanted anyone to be able to become an MP, whatever their background. They were not successful then, but almost all of their demands are part of British law today.

When the Catholic James II also tried to rule without them, the members of Parliament asked James's daughter Mary and her Protestant husband Prince William of Orange to invade Britain. They did so in 1688, and James escaped to France. William and Mary then signed a Declaration of Rights (1689) which made sure that Britain could never be ruled without or against Parliament. This was called the 'Glorious and Bloodless Revolution' because it happened without any fighting.

'You're not splitting from us, we're splitting from you.'

Until November 1999, members of the House of Lords, who are not elected, sat in Parliament because they had either received or inherited a title. Now only the first group can sit and vote in the House of Lords.

In 1903, Emmeline Pankhurst formed the Women's Social and Political Union, whose aim was the right of women to vote. They began by speaking in public, writing letters and signing petitions. When this did not have any results, they became militant. They chained themselves to railings, smashed windows and held protest marches. Many were sent to prison. However, their work during World War I helped them. In June 1918 a Bill was passed giving women aged 30 and over the right to vote.

In 1536 King Henry VIII took away rights from the church and made himself the Head of the Church of England. British Kings and Queens are still Head of the Church of England, at least in name.

The Parliament today consists of the House of Commons, the House of Lords and (officially) the Monarch.

The House of Commons is made up of Members of Parliament (MPs) who have been elected. Most MPs belong to a political party, such as the Conservative or Labour Party. The party with the most MPs forms the Government and the leader becomes the Prime Minister. He or she has a Cabinet of ministers who help decide what the Government will do.

Reading and understanding

1 First impressions: skimming

When you find something new to read, you will want to know
a) if it is interesting enough for you to read, and
b) *how* you want to read it.
To decide this, you **skim** it first.

1. **What kind of text is it?** Look first at what hits your eye:

   the way it is printed on the page   title/heading/headline   slogan   picture/photo/drawing/diagram   paragraph   lines   dialogue   list   frame   speech bubble   name   address   handwriting

   (☞ Check which details go with the kinds of texts on the right!)

2. **What is it about?** If the heading or picture doesn't tell you, skim a bit further: Look for key words. You'll soon know if it's a subject you are interested in! *(☞ Try this out on the text below.)*

3. **What can I get from it?** Maybe you can get information from it?

Kinds of texts

advertisement
article
brochure
cartoon
comic strip
e-mail
dictionary/ encyclopedia entry
instructions
letter
play
poem
postcard
poster
script
story
timetable

2 Looking for information: scanning

If you know exactly what you want to find out, you can save a lot of time. Maybe you needn't read the whole text. You can just **scan** for the information you want.
☞ Practise on the text on the right. It is from an American encyclopedia.
Find out : a) the number of players on a team; b) the difference between a hurling stick and a hockey stick.

How quickly can you find this information? Time yourself! Scan the text for a word that you can expect in the context – such as "players" or "stick". (Look for the shape of the words.) You will probably find the information there.

HURLING is an ancient game quite similar to field hockey. It is played mainly in Ireland, where it originated and where it has become very popular, together with Gaelic football and soccer. It is sometimes played in other countries. In the United States it is sponsored by the Gaelic Athletic Association of New York.
The game is played by two teams of fifteen players each, on a field 140 yards long. Each player has a stick similar to the one used in hockey, except that it is wider and flatter. A player may strike or push the ball with his stick; he may also balance the ball on his stick and run with it or hurl it (thus giving rise to the name). The ball may be caught in the hand, but thrown only with the stick.
The aim of the game is to get the ball and to drive or hurl it into the opponents' goal. The goalposts are H-shaped, and alternatively the ball may be hurled over the bar to score a point (3 points = 1 goal).

3 Structure

Most texts are organized in some way. Newspaper articles, encyclopedia entries, etc. are usually broken up into **paragraphs**. Each paragraph deals with a different aspect of the subject.

☞ Look again at the encyclopedia entry on "Hurling" above.

1. How many paragraphs are there, and what are they about? (Use your dictionary if you need to.) Make up a suitable heading for each paragraph.
2. Make a photocopy of it, and cut out the paragraphs. Then try to arrange them in a different way that also makes sense. Check that they link up properly: You may need to change the way the subject is referred to: "hurling", "the game", or "it" – depending on where it is in the text.

4 Getting the message

If you want to fully understand what you are reading, you must know the answer to the question: *Who is speaking?*

a) In many texts, **the author** is speaking directly to you, the reader. This is true of a letter or an e-mail sent specially **to you**. But it is also true of most **non-fiction**: articles, books, advertisements, etc. The author is trying to speak to as many people as possible – including you.
In this case, the message is clear: The author is trying to give you information, or tell you how to do something, or persuade you that he or she is right about something (even if he/she isn't: "non-fiction" doesn't mean "true"!).

☞ *Check a few of the texts in this book, and say what the author's message or intention is. Maybe you can think of extra intentions too. (To make you laugh? To seem clever? ...)*

b) With **fiction** it's different. **Stories** are about **characters**. What they say isn't necessarily what the author thinks – even when the story is told from one character's **point of view**. You must look for other signals, and "get the message" from what happens in the story (the **plot**), and the way it is told. Above all, look out for **irony**!

☞ *What does the author think of the TV presenters in "Coffee Time, USA" (pp. 68-69)? And what about the cab driver in the comic strip (pp. 33-34)?*

Even when there is a **narrator**, describing what happens in the first person, this "I" is not always speaking for the author. He or she is a character in the story too!

☞ *Look at these two examples from Swift 2. One of them might be about what happened to the author, one definitely isn't. Which is which?*

1. It was just after the North Sea oil wells began to run dry that a man looked over my fence ... His sudden appearance startled me. Still, I thought, he looked harmless. His eyes were bright blue. He was almost bald and his head looked too large for his frail body ... *(Story by Granville Wilson)*
2. The Chowk was the heart of our neighborhood, two hundred yards down the street from where I lived ... *(Story by Farrukh Dhondy)*

The **speaker** in a poem is like the narrator of a story. You can't be sure that what he/she says is the author's opinion – though it might be. You must look for other signals to "get the message".

☞ *Check any of the poems in this book, and say what kind of person the speaker probably is.*

5 Enjoying and remembering

Some authors go to a lot of trouble to make their stories, poems, articles, etc. fun to read and easy to remember. Here are some of the tricks they use. But you will also find such tricks in advertisements, magazine covers, headlines ... After all, the people making them want to get your attention and keep it, so that you will buy their product, go on reading, etc.

☞ *Find at least one example in this book for each of these "tricks".*

Alliteration: repetition of similar sounds, especially at the beginnings of words

Atmosphere: a special feeling that you get from the way things are described

Humour: anything that makes you laugh!

Images: word-pictures that stay in your mind and make you think of certain ideas

Irony: saying one thing and meaning the opposite (sometimes a character says one thing and the story shows it's not true)

Rhyme: similar stressed syllables at line ends

Rhythm: a system of stressed syllables

In dieser chronologischen Wortliste findest du die unbekannten Vokabeln aus den Extras, mit Ausnahme der Cognates und leicht zu erschließender Wörter.

U1 Diary of a date

date [deɪt]	Verabredung
option ['ɒpʃn]	Wahl, Option
to pray [preɪ]	beten
scruffy ['skrʌfi]	vergammelt, verlottert
loafer *(AE)* ['ləʊfə]	Halbschuh, Freizeitschuh
tight [taɪt]	eng
definite ['defɪnət]	bestimmt, eindeutig
breast [brest]	Brust
to run a red light [ˌrʌn‿ə red 'laɪt]	eine rote Ampel überfahren
to seat [si:t]	einen Sitzplatz zuweisen
dude [du:d]	Typ, Kerl
thankful ['θæŋkfl]	dankbar
to order ['ɔ:də]	bestellen
fries [fraɪz]	Pommes frites
pep talk ['pep ˌtɔ:k]	aufmunternde Worte
to oversleep [ˌəʊvə'sli:p]	verschlafen
forehead ['fɒrɪd]	Stirn
style [staɪl]	Stil
adorable [ə'dɔ:rəbl]	bezaubernd, hinreißend
to bump into so. [bʌmp]	jmdn anstoßen
to brush [brʌʃ]	streifen
to remove [rɪ'mu:v]	wegnehmen
sweaty ['sweti]	verschwitzt
to let go [let 'gəʊ]	loslassen
to wipe [waɪp]	abwischen
to hit *(coll.)* [hɪt]	*hier:* reingehen in
latte ['lattə]	Latte *(ital.),* Milchkaffee
to lean forward [ˌli:n 'fɔ:wəd]	sich vorlehnen
to hook up [hʊk‿'ʌp]	einhaken
waist [weɪst]	Taille
to string along [strɪŋ‿ə'lɒŋ]	hinhalten

Going to jump?

to change one's mind [ˌtʃeɪndʒ wʌnz 'maɪnd]	seine Meinung ändern
jelly bean ['dʒeli bi:n]	Geleebonbon
'I Spy' [aɪ 'spaɪ]	Ich sehe was, was du nicht siehst

U2 The origins of the USA

origin ['ɒrɪdʒɪn]	Ursprung
governor ['gʌvnə]	Gouverneur
kettle ['ketl]	Kessel
cloth [klɒθ]	Tuch, Stoff
duke [dju:k]	Herzog
to take control [ˌteɪk kən'trəʊl]	die Herrschaft übernehmen
settler ['setlə]	Siedler(in)
to found [faʊnd]	gründen
founder ['faʊndə]	Gründer
to break away [ˌbreɪk‿ə'weɪ]	sich lossagen

No taxation without representation

taxation [tæk'seɪʃn]	Besteuerung
representation [ˌreprɪzen'teɪʃn]	Vertretung
colonist ['kɒlənɪst]	Kolonist(in), Siedler(in)
to be subject to ['sʌbdʒɪkt]	Untertan(in) sein
tax [tæks]	Steuer
not even [nɒt‿'i:vn]	nicht einmal
demand [dɪ'mɑ:nd]	Forderung
to enforce [ɪn'fɔ:s]	durchsetzen
act [ækt]	Gesetz
jail [dʒeɪl]	Gefängnis
to stamp [stæmp]	stempeln
secret society [ˌsi:krɪt sə'saɪəti]	Geheimbund
son [sʌn]	Sohn
liberty ['lɪbəti]	Freiheit
monopoly [mə'nɒpli]	Monopol
shipload ['ʃɪpləʊd]	Schiffsladung
to dress up [dres‿'ʌp]	sich verkleiden
independence [ˌɪndɪ'pendənts]	Unabhängigkeit
to pass [pɑ:s]	verabschieden
self-evident [ˌself'evɪdnt]	selbstverständlich
to create [kri'eɪt]	(er)schaffen
equal ['i:kwəl]	gleich
unanimous [ju:'nænɪməs]	einstimmig, einmütig

We the people ...

individual [ˌɪndɪ'vɪdʒuəl]	einzeln
to be willing ['wɪlɪŋ]	gewillt sein
to issue money [ˌɪʃu: 'mʌni]	Geld drucken
federal ['fedrəl]	Bundes-, föderal
hero ['hɪərəʊ]	Held
representative [ˌreprɪ'zentətɪv]	Volksvertreter(in)
constitution [kɒntstɪ'tju:ʃn]	Verfassung
to allow [ə'laʊ]	erlauben, gestatten
branch [brɑ:ntʃ]	Zweig, *hier:* Teil
powerful ['paʊəfl]	mächtig
amendment [ə'mendmənt]	Zusatz (zur Verfassung)
speech [spi:tʃ]	Rede

election [ɪ'lekʃn]	Wahl, Abstimmung
official [ə'fɪʃl]	Beamter, Beamtin, Funktionär(in)
checks and balances [ˌtʃeks‿ənd 'bæləntsɪz]	Sicherungssystem gegenseitiger Kontrolle
Supreme Court [su:ˌpri:m 'kɔ:t]	Oberster Gerichtshof
justice ['dʒʌstɪs]	Richter(in); Gerechtigkeit
to appoint [ə'pɔɪnt]	ernennen
term [tɜ:m]	Amtsperiode
Congress ['kɒŋgres]	Kongress *(Parlament in den USA)*
House of Representatives [ˌhaʊs‿əv reprɪ'zentətɪvz]	Repräsentantenhaus *(bildet zusammen mit dem Senat den Kongress)*
party ['pɑ:ti]	Partei
to develop [dɪ'veləp]	(sich) entwickeln
supporter [sə'pɔ:tə]	Anhänger(in)
office ['ɒfɪs]	Amt
Democrat ['deməkræt]	*Angehörige(r) der demokratischen Partei der USA*
Republican [rɪ'pʌblɪkən]	*Angehörige(r) der republikanischen Partei der USA*

A visit to Washington D.C.

politics ['pɒlətɪks]	Politik
to work out [wɜ:k‿'aʊt]	funktionieren, aufgehen
politician [ˌpɒlɪ'tɪʃn]	Politiker(in)
fall *(AE)* [fɔ:l]	Herbst
Capitol ['kæpɪtl]	Kapitol
session ['seʃn]	Sitzung
citizen ['sɪtɪzn]	Staatsbürger(in)
to argue ['ɑ:gju:]	argumentieren, streiten
bill [bɪl]	Gesetzesvorlage
vice versa [ˌvaɪsi 'vɜ:sə]	umgekehrt
Oval Office ['əʊvl‿ɒfɪs]	*Büro des Staatsoberhaupts der Vereinigten Staaten*
ground floor [ˌgraʊnd 'flɔ:]	Erdgeschoss
to persuade [pə'sweɪd]	überreden, überzeugen
constitutional [kɒntstɪ'tju:ʃnl]	verfassungsmäßig
choice [tʃɔɪs]	Wahl, Auswahl
space capsule ['speɪs ˌkæpsju:l]	Raumkapsel

U3 Suntan and slaughter

suntan ['sʌntæn]	Sonnenbräune
slaughter ['slɔ:tə]	Abschlachten, Gemetzel
to harm [hɑ:m]	verletzen
bull [bʊl]	Stier
to stab [stæb]	(er)stechen
dart [dɑ:t]	Pfeil
fireworks ['faɪəwɜ:ks]	Feuerwerk
to attach [ə'tætʃ]	befestigen, anhängen
bullfight ['bʊlfaɪt]	Stierkampf
to fund [fʌnd]	finanziell fördern
to consider [kə'nsɪdə]	betrachten
fiesta [fi'estə]	Fiesta *(span.)*, Fest
goat [gəʊt]	Ziege
rabbit ['ræbɪt]	Kaninchen
to stone [stəʊn]	steinigen
to complain [kɒm'pleɪn]	sich beschweren
tour operator [ˌtʊə‿'ɒpreɪtə]	Reiseveranstalter
cruelty ['kru:əlti]	Grausamkeit
protection [prə'tekʃn]	Schutz
exhaustion [ɪg'zɔ:stʃn]	Erschöpfung
to tie up [taɪ‿'ʌp]	fesseln
to suspect [sə'spekt]	verdächtigen, einen Verdacht hegen
to mistreat [mɪs'tri:t]	misshandeln
to poach [pəʊtʃ]	wildern
reserve [rɪ'zɜ:v]	Reservat
gift [gɪft]	Geschenk
skin [skɪn]	Haut, Fell
ivory carving ['aɪvrɪ ˌkɑ:vɪŋ]	Elfenbeinschnitzerei
tortoiseshell ['tɔ:təʃʃel]	Schildkrötenpanzer
coral ['kɒrəl]	Koralle
starfish ['stɑ:fɪʃ]	Seestern
coal [kəʊl]	Kohle
to associate [ə'səʊʃieɪt]	assoziieren, in Verbindung bringen
to pin [pɪn]	festhalten
red-hot poker [ˌred hɒt 'pəʊkə]	rotglühender Schürhaken
sanctuary ['sæŋktʃʊəri]	Zuflucht, Schutzgebiet
to contain [kən'teɪn]	(ent)halten
to endanger [ɪn'deɪndʒə]	gefährdet
to scream [skri:m]	schreien, brüllen
cage [keɪdʒ]	Käfig
species ['spi:ʃi:z]	Spezies, Art
item ['aɪtəm]	Ding
to encourage [ɪn'kʌrɪdʒ]	ermutigen, fördern

U4 In many ways I'm a terrible pop star

to make up for sth. [ˌmeɪk‿'ʌp]	etwas ausgleichen
to yawn [jɔ:n]	gähnen
mirror ['mɪrə]	Spiegel
pudding-bowl hair [ˌpʊdɪŋ bəʊl 'heə]	Topfschnitt
chin [tʃɪn]	Kinn
builder ['bɪldə]	Bauarbeiter
former ['fɔ:mə]	frühere(r), ehemalige(r)
fiancée [fi'ɑ̃:nseɪ]	Verlobte
to depress [dɪ'pres]	deprimieren
chubby ['tʃʌbɪ]	pummelig
for good [fə 'gʊd]	für immer
to earn [ɜ:n]	verdienen
doll [dɒl]	Puppe
weight [weɪt]	Gewicht
suitable ['su:təbl]	passend, angemessen
executive [ɪg'zekjətɪv]	leitende(r) Angestellte(r)

hurtful ['hɜ:tfl]	verletzend
despite [dɪ'spaɪt]	trotz
to break up [breɪk‿'ʌp]	sich trennen
career [kə'rɪə]	Karriere
limelight ['laɪmlaɪt]	Rampenlicht
cute [kju:t]	süß, niedlich
gig [gɪg]	Gig, Konzert
to recite [rɪ'saɪt]	rezitieren
fist [fɪst]	Faust
to dare [deə]	wagen
to come near so.'s toes	jmdm ins Handwerk pfuschen

Things you learn from the movies

stick of French bread [ˌstɪk‿əv ˌfrentʃ 'bred]	Stange Baguette
pane [peɪn]	Scheibe
visible ['vɪzəbl]	sichtbar
lipstick ['lɪpstɪk]	Lippenstift
to rub off [rʌb‿'ɒf]	(sich) abwischen, *hier:* abgehen
scuba diving ['sku:bə ˌdaɪvɪŋ]	Sporttauchen
price range ['praɪs ˌreɪndʒ]	Preisklasse
unemployed [ˌʌnɪm'plɔɪd]	arbeitslos
to defuse [ˌdi:'fju:z]	entschärfen
wire [waɪə]	Draht, Kabel
powerful ['paʊəfl]	leistungsstark
slightly bluish [ˌslaɪtli 'blu:ɪʃ]	leicht bläulich
nuclear fission [ˌnju:kliə 'fɪʃn]	Kernspaltung
armpit ['ɑ:mpɪt]	Achselhöhle
waist [weɪst]	Taille
to wince [wɪnts]	zusammenzucken
wound [wu:nd]	Wunde
haunted house [ˌhɔ:ntɪd 'haʊs]	Spukhaus
underwear ['ʌndəweə]	Unterwäsche
to solve [sɒlv]	lösen

U5 Two Irish poets

isle [aɪl]	Insel
to arise [ə'raɪz]	aufstehen
cabin ['kæbɪn]	Hütte
clay [kleɪ]	Lehm
wattles ['wɒtlz]	Flechtwerk
bean-row ['bi:n rəʊ]	Bohnenreihe
hive [haɪv]	Bienenkorb
honey-bee [ˌhʌni 'bi:]	Honigbiene
glade [gleɪd]	Lichtung
veil [veɪl]	Schleier
cricket ['krɪkɪt]	Grille
a-glimmer [ə'glɪmə]	schimmernd
purple ['pɜ:pl]	violett
linnet ['lɪnɪt]	Hänfling
wing [wɪŋ]	Flügel
to lap [læp]	plätschern
shore [ʃɔ:]	Ufer, Strand
core [kɔ:]	Kern
forge [fɔ:dʒ]	Schmiede
axle ['æksl]	Achse
hoop [hu:p]	Reifen
to rust [rʌst]	rosten
anvil ['ænvɪl]	Amboss
short-pitched ring [ˌʃɔ:tpɪtʃt 'rɪŋ]	kurzes, helles Klingeln
unpredictable [ˌʌnprɪ'dɪktəbl]	unvorhersehbar
fantail ['fænteɪl]	Pfauenrad
spark [spɑ:k]	Funke
hiss [hɪs]	Zischen
(horse)shoe [ʃu:]	Hufeisen
to toughen ['tʌfn]	härten, aushärten
unicorn ['ju:nɪkɔ:n]	Einhorn
square [skweə]	eckig
immovable [ɪ'mu:vəbl]	unbeweglich
to expend [ɪk'spend]	aufwenden, verbrauchen
leather-aproned [ˌleðə‿'eɪprənd]	lederbeschürzt
jamb [dʒæmb]	Tür- oder Fensterpfosten
to recall [rɪ'kɔ:l]	erinnern
clatter ['klætə]	Geklapper
hoof [hu:f]	Huf
to grunt [grʌnt]	brummen
with a slam and a flick [wɪð‿ə ˌslæm‿ənd‿ə 'flɪk]	mit einer schnellen Handbewegung Tür oder Fenster zuschlagend
bellows ['beləʊz]	Blasebalg

The Border

round [raʊnd]	Runde
tension ['tenʃn]	Spannung
ironically [aɪ'rɒnɪkli]	ironischerweise
to solve [sɒlv]	lösen
civil war [ˌsɪvl 'wɔ:]	Bürgerkrieg
to discriminate against [dɪs'krɪmɪneɪt‿əˌgentst]	diskriminieren, ungleich behandeln
equally ['i:kwəli]	gleichermaßen
to represent [ˌreprɪ'zent]	vertreten
to ensure [ɪn'ʃɔ:]	sicher stellen
1 Ulster ['ʌlstə]	*anderer Name für Nordirland*
2 loyal ['lɔɪəl]	loyal, treu
3 settler ['setlə]	Siedler(in)
battle ['bætl]	Schlacht
Fenian ['fi:niən]	*irischer Freiheitskämpfer*
IRA [ˌaɪɑ:‿'eɪ]	Irish Republican Army
volunteer [ˌvɒlən'tɪə]	Freiwillige(r)
independence [ɪndɪ'pendənts]	Unabhängigkeit
home rule [ˌhəʊm 'ru:l]	Selbstbestimmung
civil rights movement [ˌsɪvl 'raɪts ˌmu:vmənt]	Bürgerrechtsbewegung
to meet with ['mi:t wɪθ]	stoßen auf
backlash ['bæklæʃ]	Gegenschlag

Living in Northern Ireland

native ['neɪtɪv]	Heimat-
to change one's mind [ˌtʃeɪndʒ wʌnz 'maɪnd]	seine Meinung ändern

	eldest ['eldɪst]	der/die Älteste
	RUC [ˌɑ:ju:'si:]	Royal Ulster Constabulary *(nordirische Polizei)*
	Presbyterian [ˌprezbɪ'tɪəriən]	Presbyterianer(in), *Anhänger(in) einer protestantischen Kirche*
	flute [flu:t]	Flöte
1	by now [baɪ 'naʊ]	inzwischen
	to keep out [ki:p'aʊt]	sich heraushalten
	solution [sə'lu:ʃn]	Lösung
	development [dɪ'veləpmənt]	Entwicklung

U6 Jon makes a decision

to slump [slʌmp]	plumpsen
ambition [æm'bɪʃn]	Ehrgeiz
to focus ['fəʊkəs]	sich konzentrieren auf
widow [wɪdəʊ]	Witwe
to aim for [eɪm]	sich zum Ziel setzen
upset [ʌp'set]	bestürzt
artistic [ɑ:'tɪstɪk]	künstlerisch, kunstsinnig
shed [ʃed]	Schuppen
wedding ['wedɪŋ]	Hochzeit
buzz [bʌz]	*hier:* Reiz
for sure [fə 'ʃʊə]	ganz sicher
to drop so. off [drɒp]	absetzen
mock exam [ˌmɒk‿ɪg'zæm]	Probeprüfung unter realistischen Bedingungen
loads [ləʊdz]	jede Menge
to be sick of doing sth. [sɪk]	etwas satt haben
to swot up [swɒt‿'ʌp]	pauken
civil war [ˌsɪvl 'wɔ:]	Bürgerkrieg
continental shelf [ˌkɒntɪnentl 'ʃelf]	Kontinentalsockel
to attach [ə'tætʃ]	beimessen
to bluster ['blʌstə]	toben
to splutter ['splʌtə]	prusten
purple ['pɜ:pl]	lila
preposterous [prɪ'pɒstrəs]	grotesk, absurd
lad [læd]	Junge

Two maps of the United Kingdom

dragon ['drægn]	Drachen
the Wash [wɒʃ]	*Name einer breiten, flachen Bucht im Osten Englands*
Glaswegian [ˌglæz'wi:dʒn]	Bewohner(in) Glasgows

A special project

origin ['ɒrɪdʒɪn]	Ursprung
Magna Carta [ˌmægnə 'kɑ:tə]	Magna Charta
election [ɪ'lekʃn]	Wahl
party ['pɑ:ti]	Partei
Labour ['leɪbə]	*eher links orientierte Partei in Großbritannien*
democracy [dɪ'mɒkrəsi]	Demokratie
devolution [ˌdi:və'lu:ʃn]	Dezentralisierung
majesty ['mædʒəsti]	Majestät
to pass a law [pɑ:s]	ein Gesetz verabschieden
trial [traɪəl]	Gerichtsverfahren
agreement [ə'gri:mənt]	Zustimmung
powerful ['paʊəfl]	mächtig
suffrage ['sʌfrɪdʒ]	Wahlrecht
permission [pə'mɪʃn]	Erlaubnis
civil war [ˌsɪvl 'wɔ:]	Bürgerkrieg
loyal [lɔɪəl]	loyal, treu
Conservative Party [kən'sɜ:vətɪv]	*Konservative Partei in Großbritannien*
Upper House [ˌʌpə 'haʊs]	Oberhaus
check [tʃek]	Kontrolle
to split [splɪt]	(ab)spalten
to consist of [kən'sɪst]	bestehen aus
House of Commons [ˌhaʊs‿əv 'kɒmənz]	*britisches Unterhaus*
Chartists ['tʃɑ:tɪsts]	Chartisten
to elect [ɪ'lekt]	wählen
to inherit [ɪn'herɪt]	erben
prime minister [ˌpraɪm 'mɪnɪstə]	Premierminister
Glorious and Bloodless Revolution [ˌglɔ:rɪəs‿ənd ˌblʌdles rev'lu:ʃn]	*Ereignis, das die Einführung der konstitutionellen Monarchie in GB bewirkte*
Liberal Democrats [ˌlɪbrl 'deməkræts]	*Liberale Partei in GB*
railings ['reɪlɪŋz]	Geländer
prison ['prɪzn]	Gefängnis
bill [bɪl]	Gesetzesvorlage

Reading and understanding

1	encyclopedia [ɪnˌsaɪklə'pi:diə]	Enzyklopädie, Lexikon
2	to scan [skæn]	(einen Text) nach etwas Bestimmtem absuchen
3	suitable ['su:təbl]	passend
	to link up [lɪŋk‿'ʌp]	miteinander verbunden sein
4	fiction ['fɪkʃn]	Fiktion, Erzählliteratur
	non-fiction ['nɒnfɪkʃn]	Sachtexte

Translation

Wie du schon aus **Swift 1** und **2** weißt, kannst du mit diesen Übersetzungsübungen überprüfen, ob der neue Wortschatz und die neue Grammatik sitzen. Wenn du nicht mehr weiter weißt, hilft oft ein Blick in die Texte der jeweiligen Unit oder in die entsprechenden Kapitel im Grammatikanhang. In den Kästchen zwischen den Übersetzungsübungen findest du Tipps, die dir zeigen, worauf du beim Übersetzen besonders achten musst.
Denke daran, dass es nicht so sehr darauf ankommt, Wort für Wort zu übersetzen, sondern die Textaussage so in die andere Sprache zu übertragen, dass ein korrekter und idiomatischer Text entsteht.

1 Rendezvous im Chatroom

Unit 1 Texts

Maike schreibt ihrer E-mate Sandra in Neuseeland. Hilf ihr beim Übersetzen.

Hi Sandra,
stell dir vor, ich habe einen echt coolen neuen E-Mail-Freund. Chuck ist sechzehn und lebt in Wyoming, USA. Er liebt seinen Computer und das Internet, und er liest und schreibt gern, vor allem E-Mails. Ein normales Teenager-Dasein führt er nicht: er hat zu Hause Unterricht. Das findet er ziemlich langweilig, weil er da keine Freunde treffen kann. Weil er so weit von der Stadt entfernt wohnt, muss er seinen Computer benutzen, um sich mit anderen Leuten zu unterhalten.
Erinnerst du dich, dass ich im Bett bleiben musste, weil ich mir das Bein gebrochen hatte? Das war die Zeit, als wir uns das erste Mal im Internet getroffen haben. Chuck hat lustige Sachen über sich geschrieben. Pferde mag er genau wie ich (seine Eltern haben eine eigene Farm), und er liebt es zu reiten. Das Beste an unserer Freundschaft ist, dass keiner von uns beiden die Freunde des anderen kennt, so dass wir völlig darauf vertrauen können, dass keiner über den anderen tratscht.
Mein Freund ist ein bisschen eifersüchtig, weil Chuck mir in seiner letzten E-Mail eine @-'-,- geschickt hat, aber er braucht sich keine Sorgen zu machen, es ist ja nur eine virtuelle Beziehung.
Tschüs, Maike

T Wie du bereits weißt, ist es meistens wenig ratsam, Wort für Wort zu übersetzen. Beachte vor allem folgende Unterschiede zwischen deutschem und englischem Sprachgebrauch:

Verwendung der Zeitformen:
Er hat lustige Sachen über sich geschrieben. Verwendest du hierfür auch im Englischen das Perfekt?

Wortstellung:
Pferde mag er genau wie ich. Kann man im Englischen das Objekt auch an den Satzanfang stellen?

Verwendung von Adjektiven:
Das Beste an unserer Freundschaft … Kannst du „das Beste" Wort für Wort ins Englische übertragen?

Verwendung des Artikels:
Sie hat ein eigenes Haus. (She's got **her** own house/a house of **her** own)
Er hat mir das Herz gebrochen. (He broke **my** heart.)

2 Wie man einen Kulturschock vermeidet — Unit 1 Texts/Skills

Stell dir vor, ihr habt eine Austauschpartnerin (AP) aus den USA bei euch zu Gast. Du fungierst als Dolmetscher im Gespräch mit deinen Eltern.

Vater: Hattest du eine angenehme Reise? *Du: …*
AP: Yes, it was fine, thank you. But it took eight and a half hours. I'm dead tired now. *Du: …*
Mutter: Möchtest du etwas zu trinken? *Du: …*
AP: Oh yes, please, I'm quite thirsty. Can I have some coke, please? *Du: …*
Mutter: Oh je, bei uns gibt es zu Hause kein Cola! Möchtest du ein Glas Mineralwasser? *Du: …*
AP: Oh yes, please, I'd love one. *Du: …*
Mutter: Gut. Sage ihr, dass das Essen fertig ist. Es gibt Leberknödelsuppe[1] und Schweinshaxe mit Sauerkraut[2]. *Du: …*
AP: No, thank you. I had so much food on the plane. I'm not hungry at all. *Du: …*
Mutter: Das gibt's doch gar nicht! Mag sie vielleicht ein Stück Pizza? Ich hab' noch was in der Tiefkühltruhe[3]. *Du: …*
AP: That sounds like a great idea. I love pizza. *Du: …*
Du teilst ihren Geschmack und sagst ihr, dass du Schweinshaxe auch nicht magst. Du: …
Vater: Möchtest du vielleicht deine Eltern anrufen? *Du: …*
AP: Oh that's very kind of you, but an e-mail would be much cheaper. *Du: …*
Vater: Das ist ja eine Superidee! Komm, ich zeig dir meinen neuen Rechner! *Du: …*

T Als Dolmetscher bist du Vermittler(in) zwischen Gesprächspartnern. Das bedeutet, dass du das, was andere Leute sagen und meinen, wiedergibst. Oft geschieht das in der indirekten Rede, z. B.

My father would like to know if …	*My mother says (that) …*
Mein Vater möchte gerne wissen, ob …	*Sie meint, dass …*

3 New York, das Tor zu den Vereinigten Staaten — Unit 2 Texts

Übersetze den folgenden Ausschnitt aus dem Tagebuch eines jungen deutschen Einwanderers ins Englische.

New York, 27. Juni 1873

Endlich sind wir in Amerika! Ich konnte es erst so richtig glauben, als wir an der Freiheitsstatue vorüber fuhren. Unser Schiff legte am späten Nachmittag im Hafen von New York an und wir wurden an Land gebracht. Langsam, einer nach dem anderen, mussten wir Neuankömmlinge an den diensthabenden Beamten der Einwanderungsbehörde vorüber ziehen, die unsere Namen, unseren Geburtsort und unser Reiseziel aufschrieben. Sie waren sehr streng und unfreundlich, weil wir kein Englisch konnten. Danach gingen wir weiter zum Fahrkartenschalter, wo wir Fahrkarten für unsere Weiterreise nach Chicago kaufen wollten. Genau gegenüber befanden sich die Geldwechsler, die die Wechselkurse auf einer Tafel notierten. Wir fanden das sehr verwirrend und kauften unsere Fahrkarten an einem Schalterbüro außerhalb. Der Mann dort bot uns einen sehr fairen Preis und nahm auch unser deutsches Geld.

Neben den deutschen Einwanderern gibt es viele, die aus Irland oder aus Schweden kommen. Ich glaube, viele New Yorker sehen die wachsende Zahl von Einwanderern mit Unbehagen. Sie meinen, wir nehmen ihnen die Arbeitsplätze weg. Dabei bekommen die Einwanderer oft nur schlecht bezahlte Stellen als Hilfsarbeiter, Landarbeiter und Mechaniker. Nur die Berglaute aus Wales und anderswo werden immer gebraucht. Und Mädchen aus Irland finden schnell eine Anstellung als Dienstmädchen.

[1] *liver dumpling soup* [2] *knuckle of pork and sauerkraut* [3] *freezer*

4 Eindrücke von New York City

Unit 2 Language

Peter wird von seiner Englischlehrerin gebeten, im Unterricht von seinem Aufenthalt in New York City zu berichten. Hilf ihm beim Formulieren.

New York City ist die größte Stadt der USA. Mehr als 7 Millionen Menschen leben dort. Die Stadt teilt sich in fünf "boroughs": Queens, Staten Island, Brooklyn, the Bronx und Manhattan. Bei den Touristen ist natürlich Manhattan am beliebtesten.

Am zweiten Tag unseres Urlaubs unternahmen wir eine Busfahrt durch Harlem. Einige Straßen sahen wirklich sehr armselig aus. Wir sahen eine Menge junger Leute Basketball spielen. Wir wollten auch eine Rundfahrt um Manhattan herum mit dem Schiff machen, aber das Wetter war zu schlecht.

Am Tag darauf fuhren wir bis ganz nach oben auf das Empire State Building, das einmal das höchste Gebäude der Welt war. Den ganzen Weg nach oben merkte man nicht, wie der Aufzug[1] sich bewegte, und plötzlich waren wir im 89. Stock! Ich hatte nicht einmal bemerkt, wie er anhielt. Auf der Aussichtsplattform[2] hörte ich Menschen in den verschiedensten Sprachen reden.

Aber wieder hatten wir kein Glück mit dem Wetter: es hörte einfach nicht auf zu regnen, und so konnten wir auch nicht die Sonne hinter den Wolkenkratzern untergehen[3] sehen.

5 Wasser – zeitlos wichtig

Unit 3 Texts

Du möchtest den folgenden Text für eine Informationstafel verwenden. Übersetze ihn ins Deutsche.

In prehistoric times people did not need constructions providing water, but when agricultural villages developed into towns the problem of supplying water became increasingly important. Before 2000 BC the rulers of Babylonia and Egypt constructed systems of dams and canals controlling the Euphrates and Nile rivers and providing a year-round water supply for irrigation. Such irrigation canals also supplied water for the use in houses. The first people to make sure that their water supply was clean were the Romans, who as early as in the 2nd century BC constructed a unique system of aqueducts, settling basins[4] and filters, which brought fresh water from the mountains into the city of Rome.

[1] *elevator (AE)* [2] *observatory* [3] *to go down* [4] *Auffangbecken*

6 Ein Ferienjob im Grand Canyon

Unit 3 Texts

Du möchtest deine Ferien in den USA verbringen. Verfasse einen formellen Brief an die Student Conservation Association, die an Jugendliche aus aller Welt Ferienjobs in Nationalparks vermittelt.

Student Conservation Association
P.O. Box 550,
Charlestown, NH 03603

Dein Brief sollte folgende Punkte beinhalten:
- du stellst dich kurz vor: Alter, Schule, Hobbys
- du sagst, wie lange du schon Englisch lernst
- du erwähnst, dass du von einem Bekannten gehört hast, dass die SCA Ferienjobs vermittelt
- du möchtest dich für ein SCA-Programm bewerben[1]
- du interessierst dich für eine Tätigkeit im Grand Canyon während deiner Sommerferien
- du fragst, ob du ein Zeugnis[2] bekommen könntest
- du nennst abschließend einen (überzeugenden) Grund, weshalb die SCA dich vermitteln sollte (vielleicht bist du Mitglied in einer Umweltgruppe?)
- du bittest sie, dir weitere Informationen zu senden

Vergiss Anrede und Schlussformel nicht.

7 Ein Streit mit Folgen

Unit 3 Language

Der 43-jährige deutsche Tourist Karl May liegt nach einem Sturz im Grand Canyon mit schweren Kopfverletzungen im Krankenhaus. Die Mitglieder seiner Reisegruppe wissen natürlich alles besser ...

Wenn seine Freundin aufgehört hätte, dauernd über Las Vegas zu reden, hätte er nicht mit ihr gestritten.
Wenn er nicht mit seiner Freundin gestritten hätte, wäre er nicht allein zu der Tour aufgebrochen.
Er wäre nicht gestürzt, wenn er das richtige Schuhwerk getragen hätte.
Wenn er daran gedacht hätte, einen Helm zu tragen, hätte er nicht so schlimme Kopfverletzungen davongetragen.
Wenn einer der Touristen kein Handy dabei gehabt hätte, hätte man ihn nicht so schnell ins Krankenhaus bringen können.

8 Freiwild für Paparazzi?

Unit 4 Texts

Übersetze den folgenden Text über Madonna für eine Wandzeitung in eurem Klassenzimmer.

Nach dem Tod von Prinzessin Diana im Jahr 1997 bei einem Autounfall in Paris entschließt sich der amerikanische Popstar Madonna, einer britischen Zeitung ein Interview zu geben, in dem sie sich über die Pressefotografen beschwert[3].

Sie habe, so sagt Madonna in dem Artikel, dieselben Erfahrungen gemacht wie Diana. Als sie nach Europa gekommen sei, um ihr Musical *Evita* vorzustellen, habe man auch sie mit halsbrecherischer Geschwindigkeit durch die Straßen von Rom gejagt, nur weil ein paar profitgierige[4] Journalisten ein Foto von ihrem Baby machen wollten. Der amerikanische Musicalstar betont, dass aber nicht nur die Paparazzi und deren Verleger, sondern auch die, die solche Illustrierten kaufen und lesen, für diese Situation verantwortlich seien.

Lady Di habe sie nur einmal getroffen, und zwar bei einer Wohltätigkeitsveranstaltung. Dort hätten sie über die Frage gescherzt, wer denn nun mehr Aufmerksamkeit auf sich zöge: Diana oder sie selbst. Auf die Frage nach ihrem Lieblingswohnort antwortet die Popdiva New York, sagt aber, dass das riesige Interesse der Medien an ihrer Person dies unmöglich mache. Mit London sei es jedoch dasselbe. Auch hier habe sie zu große Angst vor den Medien. Wie man es mache, mache man es verkehrt: Wenn man sie ignoriere oder ihnen aus dem Weg gehe, gelte man als nicht kooperativ. Wenn sie aber mit ihnen zusammenarbeite, heiße es, sie spanne sie für ihre Zwecke ein.

[1] *to apply for* [2] *reference* [3] *to complain (about)* [4] *profit-hungry*

9 Sir Paul kommt zurück

Übersetze den folgenden Text über Sir Paul McCartneys Auftritt in The Cavern für deine Eltern.

The Daily Telegraph, 15.12.1999

Long and winding road leads Sir Paul back to The Cavern

Sir Paul McCartney made a return journey to his native Liverpool yesterday to play at The Cavern for the first time in 36 years.

In the Sixties, the original backstreet club in a cellar in Matthew Street formed the launch pad[1] for The Beatles. Hundreds of fans crowded outside a replica built next to the site in the hope of catching sight of one of the city's favourite sons.

An audience of just 300, mostly from the media, had tickets for the long-awaited event for which Sir Paul was joined by a band of old rockers, among them being Dave Gilmour, guitarist with Pink Floyd. When plain Paul McCartney and his three fellow Beatles entertained lunchtime audiences in 1961 they were paid £5. The multi-millionaire knight, who has homes in the south of England and the United States, said yesterday: "It's fantastic to be back at The Cavern. This is where it all began for me." 15,000 fans were being catered for[2] in Liverpool's Chavasse Park, while a global audience was able to look in through the Internet.

The Cavern is no longer be found at its original site. The club was destroyed 26 years ago, with the approval[3] of Liverpool city council, to make room for the construction of ventilation shafts[4] for the city's underground. The owners of the new Cavern have done their best to make up for[5] that decision. They have used bricks[6] from the original cellar to build the new club and have kept the original address, 10 Matthew Street.

Paul McCartney back at The Cavern after 36 years

[1] *Startrampe* [2] *hier: untergebracht* [3] *Zustimmung* [4] *Schacht* [5] *etw. wettmachen* [6] *Backstein*

T Wie du schon weißt, ist es meistens nicht empfehlenswert, einen Text Wort für Wort vom Englischen ins Deutsche (und umgekehrt) zu übertragen; oft sind die Satzkonstruktionen recht unterschiedlich. Vergleiche folgende Konstruktionen:

Relativsatz ☞ Infinitivkonstruktion
die schlimmste Hungersnot, die sich ereignete – the worst famine to happen

Nebensatz ☞ Partizipialkonstruktion
Krankheiten, die in Zusammenhang mit der Hungersnot standen – famine-related diseases

Adverb ☞ verbale Konstruktion
sie exportierten weiterhin – they continued to export

Nominale Konstruktion ☞ verbale Konstruktion
interessiert an einer Rückkehr – interested in coming back (see text 11)

10 Hungersnot in Irland

Unit 5 Texts

Du hast zusammen mit einem/einer Partner/in den Auftrag, für eine Ausstellung über Irland Informationen zur Potato Famine zu suchen. Übertragt folgenden Artikel, den ihr in einem deutschen Nachschlagewerk gefunden habt, ins Englische.

potato plant

Als im Jahr 1845 der *Fungus Phytophtora* aus Nordamerika eingeschleppt wurde, war das Wetter in Irland ungewöhnlich kühl und nass. Die Braunfäule, eine Krankheit, die die Kartoffelpflanze völlig zerstört, breitete sich schnell aus. So verfaulte fast die ganze Ernte jenes Jahres auf den Feldern. Weitere Missernten folgten in den Jahren 1846 bis 1849 und das Ergebnis war die schlimmste Hungersnot, die sich im 19. Jahrhundert in Europa ereignete.

Die Hilfe der britischen Regierung, insgesamt etwa 8 Millionen Pfund, reichte nicht aus. Sie gab Darlehen[1], unterstützte Suppenküchen[2] und schuf Arbeitsplätze. Während der Hungersnot verkauften jedoch viele irische Farmen weiterhin hochwertige[3] Nahrungsmittel nach Großbritannien, weil sie für arme irische Bauern zu teuer waren. Maismehl[4] aus den Vereinigten Staaten von Amerika half dann gegen die Hungersnot.

Die Bevölkerung Irlands ging von beinahe 8,5 Millionen im Jahr 1844 auf fast 6,5 Millionen im Jahr 1851 zurück. Etwa 1,1 Millionen Menschen starben an Unterernährung[5] oder Krankheiten, die in Zusammenhang mit der Hungersnot standen. Die Zahl der Iren, die nach Nordamerika und Großbritannien auswanderten, erreichte etwa 1,5 Millionen. In den folgenden Jahren fiel die Zahl der Bevölkerung Irlands auf Grund der Auswanderung nach Übersee und der niedrigeren Geburtenraten[6] weiter zurück. Als Irland im Jahre 1921 politisch unabhängig wurde, war seine Bevölkerung nur noch halb so groß wie in den frühen vierziger Jahren des 19. Jahrhunderts.

[1] *loan* [2] *soup kitchen* [3] *high quality* [4] *cornmeal* [5] *starvation* [6] *birth rate*

11 ⟨Der Erfolg des Celtic Tiger⟩

Unit 5 Texts

Übersetze den folgenden Zeitungsartikel ins Englische.

Die irische Handels- und Arbeitsministerin gab einem australischen Radioreporter ein Interview, in dem sie sich über den Wirtschaftsboom in ihrem Land äußerte.

Alles habe, so die Politikerin[1], in den späten achtziger Jahren des 20. Jahrhunderts begonnen, als die Regierung gezwungen war zu handeln, da die Wirtschaft schwach und die Arbeitslosigkeit hoch war.

Die niedrigsten Steuersätze in der Europäischen Union und der hohe Ausbildungsstand hätten viele ausländische Unternehmen dazu veranlasst, in Irland Betriebe anzusiedeln.

Die Ministerin betonte, dass die Auswanderung eines der wichtigsten politischen Themen gewesen sei: obwohl die Eltern viel in die Zukunft ihrer Kinder investiert hätten, hätten junge Iren in großer Zahl ihr Zuhause verlassen und seien nach Amerika, Großbritannien und andere Teile Europas gegangen. Familien seien so auseinander gerissen worden. Doch jetzt sei die Situation anders: mehr und mehr irische Auswanderer seien an einer Rückkehr interessiert. Die irische Regierung habe überdies Geldmittel bereit gestellt, um hoch qualifizierte[2] Arbeitskräfte aus dem Bereich Technologie zu ermutigen, nach Irland zurückzukehren und hier Unternehmen zu gründen.

Abschließend stellte die Ministerin voller Stolz fest, dass Irland, nach den Vereinigten Staaten von Amerika, weltweit der zweitgrößte Exporteur von Softwareprodukten sei.

12 Echt witzig!?

Unit 5 Language

Stell dir vor, ihr habt eine(n) Austauschpartner(in) (AP) aus Irland bei euch zu Gast. Du bist Dolmetscher(in) im Gespräch mit deinen Eltern.

Vater: Stimmt es eigentlich, dass die Engländer so viele Witze über euch Iren machen?

Du: …

AP: Of course, neighbouring countries often like to make jokes about each other. But isn't it the same in Germany?

Du: …

Vater: Sicher, die Norddeutschen erzählen sich lustige Geschichten über die Ostfriesen; die Süddeutschen und die Österreicher[3] machen sich über einander lustig, nur die Bayern[4] haben überhaupt keinen Humor, die sind so empfindlich.

Du: …

Mutter: Das stimmt überhaupt nicht, die Bayern können sehr wohl über sich selbst lachen. Die Österreicher sind noch viel empfindlicher!

Du: …

AP: That's funny. When they are abroad, the Irish complain that the English make jokes about them, but back at home, the Irish amuse themselves by telling what the British call 'Irish jokes', but about the people of Kerry!

Du: …

Vater: Naja, das Problem mit benachbarten Ländern ist, dass keines das andere so richtig ernst nimmt, z. B. Deutschland und Österreich. Und wenn dann ein Land größer oder stärker ist als das andere, dann kann es schon sein, dass das kleinere Land besonders empfindlich reagiert …

Du:

AP: Oh yes, a couple of years ago, the Irish singer Paul Brady complained about the Irish jokes you could often hear on British radio and TV, but some people said he had absolutely no sense of humour.

Du: …

Mutter: Na, es gibt schon Witze, die sind rassistisch oder sexistisch, z. B. all die Blondinenwitze[5] …

Vater: Ach die sind doch harmlos! Übrigens, kennt ihr schon den neuesten Ostfriesenwitz: Warum gibt es in Ostfriesland[6] so viele Handys?

Du: …

[1]politician [2]highly qualified [3]Austrians [4]Bavarians [5]jokes about blondes [6]East Friesia

13 Eine neue Form der Ausbeutung

Unit 6 Texts

Für deine(n) Austauschpartner(in) fasst du das folgende Gespräch auf Englisch zusammen.
Start like this: Last week, our maths teacher saw Martina …

Martina: Stellt euch vor, letztes Wochenende hat mich der Mathelehrer im Supermarkt gesehen!

Simone: Na und? Was ist das schon Besonderes?

Martina: Naja, ich hab' gerade an der Kasse gearbeitet. Ich arbeite dort jeden Freitag Nachmittag und Samstag Vormittag.

Simone: Und? Hat er was gesagt?

Martina: Er hat gemeint, jetzt wüsste er, warum ich in Mathe so schlecht bin. Aber ich hasse es, wenn sich Lehrer in mein Privatleben einmischen[1]!

Dieter: Ich auch! Typisch Lehrer! Die sagen immer, dass wir im Unterricht einschlafen, weil wir so lang arbeiten! Dabei liegt das an ihrem langweiligen Unterricht! Ich arbeite beim ILDA. Dort räume ich für €5 die Stunde Regale ein. Meine Eltern finden das nicht in Ordnung. Sie werfen den Managern vor, die Schüler auszubeuten. Aber ich brauche das Geld für neue Computerspiele, und von meinen Eltern krieg ich nicht viel, die sind beide arbeitslos.

Nadine: Meine Mutter hat nichts dagegen, wenn Jugendliche arbeiten. Bis zu 12 Stunden die Woche kann es sogar gut für sie sein, meint sie, bloß müssen die Arbeitsbedingungen stimmen.

Simone: Ich hatte schon einen Job bei *H&R Fashion*, aber dann wollten die, dass ich einen Jobkurs während der Schulzeit mitmache. Mein Vater hat sich beschwert, und dann war ich den Job los!

Ralph: Ich darf nur in den Ferien arbeiten. Dann arbeite ich in einer Tankstelle. Das finde ich echt cool, denn dort lerne ich alles über Autos und kriege jede Menge Trinkgelder. Das Geld kann ich gut gebrauchen, denn mein Handy kommt mich teurer als ich dachte.

14 Bedeutende Erfinder

Unit 6 Texts

Übersetze die folgenden Texte über zwei wichtige Persönlichkeiten der Industriellen Revolution ins Deutsche.

James Hargreaves, (1720–1778), English inventor and industrialist, invented a machine with which one worker could spin several threads[2] at once. At the time he constructed the machine, which he named after his daughter Jenny, he was a poor, uneducated spinner and weaver living in Lancashire. It was the spinning jenny which made possible the automatic production of cotton thread. After he began to sell the machines to help support his large family, hand spinners who were afraid of unemployment broke into his house and destroyed a number of jennies, causing Hargreaves to move to Nottingham in 1768. There he founded a spinning mill and was quite successful as a yarn[3] manufacturer[4] in competition with other users of the jenny. Although many handworkers were strongly against it, spinning became a factory industry and an important part of the factory system in England.

James Watt

James Watt, (1736–1819), Scottish inventor and engineer, was able to improve the steam engine, which had been invented by Thomas Savery and Thomas Newcomen at the beginning of the 18th century. It was used at the time to pump water from mines. Watt was given a first patent in 1769 for designing a separate condensing chamber[5] and other improvements on Newcomen's engine. At this time, Watt was the partner of the inventor John Roebuck, who had given him money for his research. Some years later Watt began the production of steam engines together with Matthew Boulton, a Birmingham factory owner. Watt continued his research and patented several other important inventions. When he retired from the firm in 1800 he concentrated on research work.

[1]*to interfere (in)* [2]*Faden* [3]*Garn* [4]*Hersteller* [5]*Kondensationskammer*

Grammar

Es geht wieder weiter mit den Grammatikregeln. Gar so viel Neues kommt in diesem Jahr nicht mehr dazu. Wir können auf immer mehr Bekanntes aus den beiden vorhergehenden Jahren zurückgreifen und damit alles noch besser verankern und vernetzen. Schau bitte einfach weiterhin genau nach, wenn du

- dir Überblicke verschaffen willst
- etwas genauer geklärt haben möchtest
- mal etwas vergessen hast
- dich auf einen Test oder eine Klassenarbeit vorbereitest.

Zu Orientierung stellen wir auch wieder die bewährten (unten aufgeführten) „Wegweiser" auf.

S = Sehen: Die Übersichten zeigen, was zusammengehört.

M = Merken: Die Merkhilfen unterstützen das Gedächtnis.

W = Wissen: Die Zusammenhänge und Hintergründe erleichtern das Verstehen und Behalten.

R = Revision: Die Wiederholung hilft beim Einordnen und Vernetzen.

A = Anwenden: In den Übungen kannst du die Regeln gleich anwenden (Lösungen auf Seite 199).

Also dann, viel Spaß und Erfolg weiterhin!

UNIT 1

1 Britisches und amerikanisches Englisch – British and American English

Bei einer ganzen Reihe von Wörtern hast du schon Unterschiede zwischen dem *British English* (BE) und dem *American English* (AE) bemerkt. Das kann sich auf die Wortbedeutung oder auf die Schreibung beziehen.

1 **Wortbedeutung** *(meaning)*: Hier geht es um eine Sache mit jeweils zwei Wörtern.

W

Wohnung	flat (BE) apartment (AE)
Schüler	pupil (BE) student (AE)

2 **Schreibung** *(spelling)*: Hier geht es um dasselbe Wort (und um dieselbe Sache), aber um unterschiedliche Schreibweisen.

W

Farbe	colour (BE) color (AE)
Zentrum	centre (BE) center (AE)

Durch diese unterschiedlichen Schreibungen können manchmal ganze Sätze total anders aussehen:

W

BE: Our neighbour's favourite colour is grey.

AE: Our neighbor's favorite color is gray.

Könntest du weitere Beispiele zusammentragen?

R

a)	BE:	holiday	petrol	...
	AE:	vacation	gas	...
b)	BE:	travelling	...	
	AE:	traveling	...	

W

Du solltest aber auch in Betracht ziehen:

Die unterschiedlichen Versionen sind meist überall bekannt, wo Englisch gesprochen wird. Medien, Telekommunikation und internationale Kontakte sorgen für ein immer schnelleres Nebeneinanderbestehen bzw. für eine immer größer werdende Vermischung der unterschiedlichen Varianten. Englisch wird eben immer mehr zur internationalen Verständigungssprache.
Beim Schreiben solltest du aber immer darauf achten, dass du in einem Text durchgehend entweder AE oder BE benutzt und die beiden Sprachvarianten nicht mischst.

2 Wortbildung – Word building

Bei diesem Punkt soll es darum gehen, wie man weitere Verben gewinnen kann.

1 Adjektiv – Verb

This text is not **short** enough. Can you **shorten** it ?

Den Bestand der Verben, die du bereits gelernt hast, kannst du noch wesentlich erhöhen, wenn du bestimmte Adjektive mit der Nachsilbe **-en** versiehst:

S

Adjektiv	Verb	Adjektiv	Verb
sweet	to sweeten	fat	to fatten
sharp	to sharpen	light	to lighten
short	to shorten	sick	to sicken
soft	to soften	loose	to loosen
hard	to harden	worse	to worsen
dark	to darken	thick	to thicken

Die so entstandenen Verben sind alle regelmäßig. Sie lassen sich in jeder Hinsicht als ganz normale Verben behandeln.

My tea wasn't **sweet** enough.
I've **sweetened** it a bit more.

2 Substantiv – Verb

When will this **rain** stop ? It **has been raining** for hours now.

Den Schatz deiner Verben kannst du gleich noch einmal erhöhen, denn zahlreiche Substantive können in eine Verbfunktion übertreten.

Substantiv	Verb	Substantiv	Verb
bridge	to bridge	crash	to crash
butter	to butter	end	to end
excuse [ɪk'skjuːs]	to excuse [ɪk'skjuːz]	escape	to escape
care	to care	help	to help
change	to change	hope	to hope
check	to check	look	to look
contact	to contact	walk	to walk
head	to head	start	to start
cover	to cover	fight	to fight

Auch hier werden die Verben ganz normal verwendet:

Asterix often needed **help** and Obelix always **helped** him.

Aber Achtung!
Eine Reihe von Verben sind natürlich unregelmäßig und dir als solche ja auch bekannt: *the fight – to fight / fought / fought*

3 Konjunktionen – Conjunctions

Du kennst schon die Konjunktionen *and, but, or* und *neither … nor*. Sie verbinden zwei Sätze oder Ideen. Auch eine Reihe von Konjunktionen, die einen Nebensatz einleiten, sind dir schon lange bekannt: *if, when, because* und so weiter. Hier soll es darum gehen, etwas Ordnung und Übersicht bei diesen Konjunktionen zu schaffen. Man kann sie nämlich in bestimmte Bedeutungsgruppen einteilen, die sich danach richten, um welche Nebensätze es geht.

1 Nebensätze der Zeit – Clauses of time

My uncle often falls asleep **while** he's watching TV.

while (während);
as (während); *as soon as* (sobald); *before* (bevor);
until / till (bis); *not … until* (erst … wenn);
when (als / wenn); *whenever* (immer wenn / wann auch immer)

2 Nebensätze des Ortes und der Richtung – Clauses of place and direction

Anna would get up and move to the aisle **where** everyone could see her.

where (wo / wohin);
wherever (wo / wohin auch immer)

3 Nebensätze des Grundes – Clauses of reason

She was unhappy **because** she felt left out.

because (weil); *as / since* (da)

W

Nebensätze mit *because* stehen in der Regel hinter dem Hauptsatz. Dagegen werden Nebensätze mit *as* und *since* (im Sinne von „weil" oder „da") meist vorangestellt.
Beispiel: *As we couldn't get any tickets for the cinema, we stayed at home and watched TV.*

Since hat zwei Bedeutungen:
In der Bedeutung „seit" leitet es Nebensätze der Zeit ein. (Tipp: seit Zeit)
In der Bedeutung „da" leitet es Nebensätze des Grundes ein.

4 Nebensätze der Einräumung und der Gegenüberstellung – Clauses of concession and contrast

She sent him a long e-mail **although** they had talked on the phone for hours.

although / though / even though (obwohl);
whereas (während / wohingegen)

5 Nebensätze der Bedingung – Clauses of condition

I'll hand this book back **unless** you want to read it.

We can go on holiday **even if** we don't win the prize.

if (wenn / falls); *even if* (selbst wenn); *unless* (sofern nicht / außer wenn / es sei denn);
Nebensätze mit *unless* stehen in der Regel im *simple present* (niemals im *will-future*!), der zugeordnete Hauptsatz dagegen meist im *will-future*.

6 Nebensätze des Vergleichs – Clauses of comparison

It looks **as if** it might rain.

as if / as though (als ob)

7 Nebensätze des Zwecks und der Folge – Clauses of purpose and result

The songs were written **in such a way that** people wanted to join in.

so that (damit / so dass);
so/such … (so / solch …, dass)
in such a way that (so dass)

A Verbinde die Satzteile so, dass sich ein Sinn ergibt:

1. My mum always reads the newspaper
2. My grandad usually watches TV
3. Wherever we go on holiday,
4. My mum writes lots of e-mails,
5. It looks
6. The jokes in that book are so funny
7. My dad is angry

a) as if the rain will stop.
b) because his car broke down.
c) while she is having breakfast.
d) until the last programme is over.
e) it must be somewhere in the south.
f) whereas her sister sends messages by fax.
g) that you just have to laugh.

4 Die Vorvergangenheit – The past perfect

Wenn du über Ereignisse und Aktivitäten in der Vergangenheit (*simple past*) berichten willst, so kann es auch um solche gehen, die in der Vergangenheit zeitlich noch weiter zurückliegen. Dazu brauchst du das *past perfect.*
Das *simple past* drückt aus, was sich früher (damals) ereignete und was abgeschlossen ist.
Das *past perfect* drückt aus, was in der Vergangenheit, auf die wir uns beziehen, schon vorbei war.

She remember**ed** a time when she **had** not **felt** left out.
The music her family **had sung** that night still sound**ed** in Anna's head.

Sätze im *past perfect* stehen also immer in der Nähe von Sätzen im *simple past.* Die Bildung des *past perfect* ist einfach: Sie geschieht durch das Zusammengehen von *had* mit dem *past participle.*

S

In der Vergangenheit schon vorbei	Inzwischen auch vorbei
▽	▽
The bus **had** never **stopped** before.	But one day it **broke** down.
Their first two records **had been** failures.	But the third record **brought** a change.
After the girl **had found** a new boyfriend,	she **left** my poor brother.

A Wie kannst du diese Sätze ins Englische übertragen?

1. Nachdem er die CD gekauft hatte, hörte er sie sich zu Hause an.
2. Wir hatten das Lied noch nie gehört, aber wir mochten es sofort.
3. Das Mädchen erzählte seiner Freundin nicht, dass es seine Hausaufgaben vergessen hatte.
4. Die Lehrerin wusste nicht, dass einige Schüler die Geschichte schon gelesen hatten.
5. Sie waren sehr ärgerlich, weil sie nicht an ihre Mobiltelefone gedacht hatten.

5 Das Gerund – The gerund

Du erinnerst dich sicher gut daran: Die *ing*-Form eines Verbs lässt sich wie ein Substantiv behandeln.

a) **Hiding** bones was not a subject.
b) He practised **running.**
c) She was bad at **climbing.**
d) They had always dreamed of **starting** a private school.

1. Dabei kann diese Form *(gerund)* **Subjekt** eines Satzes sein. (wer? / was?):
   Swimming was his favourite subject. – (Das) Schwimmen war sein Lieblingsfach.
   (Vgl. auch a) im obigen Kasten.)

2. Diese Form kann aber auch **Objekt** eines Satzes sein (wen? / was?):
   The cat hated **swimming.** – Die Katze hasste (das) Schwimmen.
   (Vgl. auch b) im obigen Kasten.)

3. Einer Reihe von Adjektiven sind bestimmte Präpositionen fest zugeordnet, so z.B.: *good at; famous for; crazy about.* Beziehen sich diese Adjektive auf eine Tätigkeit, so wird diese Tätigkeit mit einem Gerund angegeben:
   The monkey was **good at climbing.**
   Der Affe war gut im Klettern. (Vgl. auch c) im obigen Kasten.)

M **Achtung! Kleine Hürde!**
Bei *good at* heißt es in der Verneinung *no good at* bzw. *not any good at.*
I'm **no good at** drawing.
Oder: I'm **bad at** drawing.

4. Die feste Zuordnung von Präpositionen tritt auch bei bestimmten Verben auf:
   He was **criticized for starting** from the top of the tree. (Vgl. auch d) im obigen Kasten.)

A Du willst ausdrücken, dass …

1. du das Rauchen hasst. 2. dir das Schwimmen gefällt. 3. dein Bruder es genießt, Klavier zu spielen. 4. deine Schwester stolz auf das Erfinden von Computerspielen ist. 5. das Internet-Surfen ein Problem für deine Tante ist. 6. dein kleiner Bruder Angst davor hat, alleine einkaufen zu gehen.

5. Nach Verben wie *like, hate, don't mind* kann vor dem Gerund ein Nomen oder Pronomen eingeschoben werden, das als Sinnsubjekt der Gerund-Konstruktion betrachtet werden kann.

I don't like **them** laughing at me.
(… wie **sie** sich über mich lustig machen.)

I hate **people** doing that.
(… wenn **die Leute** das tun.)

6 Wortstellung in Sätzen mit Adverbien oder adverbialen Bestimmungen – Word order in sentences with adverbs or adverbial phrases

Wie oder auf welche Weise geschieht etwas? Wenn du diese Frage beantworten willst, benötigst du ein Adverb, das meist in Verbindung mit einem Verb auftritt. (Daher auch der Name „**Ad**verb".) Dazu gehören die auf *-ly* endenden Adverbien, außerdem einige endungslose Adverbien wie *fast* und *well.*

Die Adverbien der Art und Weise *(adverbs of manner)* haben im Satz meist End- oder Binnenstellung.

1 Adverbien in Endstellung – Adverbs in final position

		Verb	Adverb
a)	The doctor	talked	quietly.
b)	She	listened	carefully.

Hier gibt es kein Objekt. Das Adverb der Art und Weise steht meist **direkt nach Verben** ohne Objekt.

		Verb	Objekt	Adverb
c)	He	plays	the piano	perfectly.
d)	We	see	the doctor	regularly.

Hat das Verb ein direktes Objekt, so steht das Adverb meist erst **nach** diesem **Objekt.**

2 Adverbien in Binnenstellung – Adverbs in middle position

a) He **easily** learned to play the saxophone.
b) They **slowly** came in with their present.

Adverbien der Art und Weise können **vor** dem Vollverb stehen, und zwar wenn keine besondere Betonung auf dem Adverb steht.

3 Gradadverbien – Adverbs of degree

Gradadverbien dienen dazu, andere Wörter zu verstärken oder aber abzuschwächen. Zu ihnen gehören *-ly*-Adverbien wie *awfully* und *completely,* aber auch nicht abgeleitete Adverbien wie *quite, rather* und *very*. Die Gradadverbien werden fast immer attributiv gebraucht. Ansonsten nehmen sie Endposition im Satz ein.

Attributiv: I **wholly** agree with you.
Endposition: The scene had changed **completely**.

This is very good. – Well, it's not good **enough**.

Das Gradadverb *enough* steht immer am Satzende.

The taxi came **very** early.

Das Gradadverb *very* verstärkt Adjektive und andere Adverbien.

The band was **absolutely** fantastic!

She speaks English **awfully** well.

Bestimmte Gradadverbien können dazu dienen, schon ausdrucksvolle Adjektive noch weiter zu verstärken.

M

Merke dir, dass Gradadverbien wie *absolutely, completely* etc. neben ‚normalen' Adjektiven wie *good* oder *nice* nicht stehen können. Zudem lassen sich viele ‚starke' Adjektive nicht mit *very* oder *rather* verstärken.

4 Adverbien der unbestimmten Zeit und Häufigkeit – Adverbs of indefinite time and frequency

I **often** use my brother's computer. But he **never** gives me his CD-ROMs.

Zu diesen Adverbien gehören *soon, often, always, sometimes, usually, mostly, always, never, ever, …*

Sometimes they get into trouble.
Soon he was reading her e-mail.

Die Adverbien der unbestimmten Zeit und Häufigkeit haben meist Binnenstellung. (Vgl. 6.2) Einige von ihnen wie z.B. *soon* und *sometimes* können allerdings auch am Satzanfang stehen.

She has **often** talked to her neighbours.
You can **always** phone me.

In Sätzen mit Hilfsverben oder Modalverben steht ein Ein-Wort-Adverb der unbestimmten Zeit und Häufigkeit stets direkt nach dem Hilfsverb oder Modalverb.

5 Adverbien der bestimmten Zeit und Häufigkeit – Adverbs of definite time and frequency

a) **Yesterday** I saw the doctor for a check-up.
b) He examined me **twice**.
c) I called him **a week ago**.

- Zu den Adverbien der bestimmten Zeit gehören präzisere Zeitangaben wie *today, yesterday, tonight* usw. Sie können am Anfang oder Ende eines Satzes stehen. (Vgl. a) im Kasten.)
- Zu den Adverbien der bestimmten Häufigkeit gehören solche wie *daily, weekly, once, twice* usw. Diese findest du **nur am Satzende**. (Vgl. b) im Kasten.)
  Beide Gruppen, also die Adverbien der bestimmten Häufigkeit wie auch die der bestimmten Zeit, haben **niemals Binnenstellung**!
- Wortgruppen wie *last night, next weekend, a month ago, …* sind zusammengesetzte adverbiale Bestimmungen. Sie werden genau wie einzelne Adverbien behandelt. Sie stehen ebenfalls am Anfang oder Ende eines Satzes und haben keine Binnenstellung (Vgl. c) im Kasten.)

7 Kurzsätze und Kurzantworten mit *so, nor, neither* – Short additions to statements and short answers with *so, nor, neither*

Wenn du einen vorhergehenden Aussagesatz kommentieren oder ihm etwas hinzufügen willst, dann benutzt du Kurzsätze mit *so, nor, neither*. Sie entsprechen den deutschen Kurzsätzen mit auch / auch nicht.

1 *So* nach bejahtem Satz – So after a positive statement

I **enjoy** swimming. – And so **does** my brother.

My sister **was** late. – So **was** my friend.

I **can** hear their music. – So **can** I. / I **can** too.

Dem Vollverb des Aussagesatzes wird mit *do* bzw. *does* entsprochen. Gibt es im Aussagesatz ein Hilfs- oder Modalverb, so wird dieses im Kurzsatz wieder aufgenommen.
Kurzsätze mit *so* können umgangssprachlich auch durch Sätze mit *too* ersetzt werden.

2 ***Neither / nor* nach verneinten Aussagen – *Neither / nor* after negative sentences**

I **don't like** that new song.
– Nor **do** we.
My parents **weren't** on holiday.
– Neither **were** our neighbours.
My sister **can't** speak Spanish.
– Nor **can** my parents.
– My parents **can't** either.

Grundsätzlich werden die verneinten Formen der Hilfs- und Modalverben des Ausgangssatzes in den Kurzsätzen **bejaht** wieder aufgenommen.

Kurzsätze mit *neither / nor* werden häufig durch Kurzsätze bestehend aus Subjekt, verneintem Hilfsverb + *either* ersetzt.

Grundsätzlich ist hier abschließend anzumerken, dass Kurzsätze mit *so / nor / neither* in Unterhaltungen wegen des Eingehens auf das zuvor Gesagte ein wichtiges kommunikatives Element darstellen.

UNIT 2

8 Personenbezeichnungen – Talking about people

1 Wenn man über andere Personen spricht, dann spielt bei deren Benennung oft der Beruf, das Hobby oder eine häufige oder regelmäßige Tätigkeit eine Rolle. Bei vielen Bezeichnungen sind es die Endungen, die das ausdrücken:

A

-er: teacher, driver, passenger, beachgoer, ...
-or: doctor, actor, inventor, ...
-ian: electrician, musician, ...
-ist: chemist, cyclist, ...
-ess: actress, authoress, ...
-man / **-woman**: businessman, policewoman, ...

◀ Kannst du die Listen weiterführen?

Im Hinblick auf männliche oder weibliche Bezeichnungen heißt es aber aufpassen. Bei den Endungen *-ess/-man/-woman* wird eine klare Auskunft darüber gegeben, ob es sich um eine weibliche oder männliche Person (oder mehrere Personen) handelt. Bei den anderen Endungen kann es sich sowohl um männliche als auch um weibliche Personen handeln. Meist sagen erst die folgenden Sätze, um wen es sich handelt.

1. Our new [teacher] is great. [She] teaches in a very interesting way.
2. The [taxidriver] wanted to talk to [his] passenger. But [she] didn't understand him.

Zu 1: Erst im zweiten Satz erfahren wir durch das **she**, dass es sich um eine Lehrer**in** handelt.
Zu 2: Im ersten Satz erfahren wir durch das **his**, dass der Taxifahrer männlich ist. Und erst der zweite Satz sagt uns, dass der Fahrgast eine Frau oder ein Mädchen ist.

2 Auch die Herkunft und die Nationalität spielt bei Personenbenennungen oft eine Rolle:

S

COUNTRY	ADJECTIVE	INDIVIDUALS	THE PEOPLE	THE LANGUAGE
Ireland	an Irish writer	an Irishman/ -woman	the Irish	English/Irish
Britain	a British ship	a Briton	the British	English
China	Chinese food	a Chinese	the Chinese	Chinese
France	French wine	a Frenchman/ -woman	the French	French
The Nether-lands	Dutch cheese	a Dutchman/ -woman	the Dutch	Dutch
Korea	a Korean car	a Korean	the Koreans	Korean
Sweden	a Swedish pop group	a Swede	the Swedes	Swedish
Canada	a Canadian author	a Canadian	the Canadians	English/ French

W

Bitte beachten:

a) Adjektive auf **-ian** oder **-an** kann man wie normale Nomen (mit Plural *-s*) gebrauchen:
Asian / Asians
American / Americans

b) Nationalitätenbezeichnungen auf **-ese** dagegen haben **nie** ein Plural *-s*:
the Chinese
the Japanese

c) Adjektive auf **-ch** oder **-ish** bezeichnen immer das ganze Volk, und zwar stets mit Artikel, jedoch ohne Plural *-s*:
the French
the Dutch

Bei der Angabe der Nationalität bei Einzelpersonen erfolgt die Zusammensetzung mit **-man / -woman**
a Scotsman
an Englishwoman

3 Und natürlich können auch gemeinsame Eigenschaften oder das, was Personengruppen verbindet, wichtig sein, wenn man über Leute spricht.

W

A lot of rich people live in Manhattan. → Manhattan is the home of the rich.
This is a club for young people. → The young like coming here.
Each town has a home for poor people. → The poor can go there to live for a while.
The numer of old people is increasing. → The old will need lots of help from the young.

the blind = alle Blinden / die Blinden ganz allgemein.

Die als Nomen gebrauchten Adjektive beziehen sich stets auf die Gesamtheit einer Gruppe.

Even **the very young** are interested in computer games.

Es wird die Pluralform verwendet, obwohl kein Plural *-s* auftritt.

Gesamtgruppe:	A lot has been done for **the sick**. *(… für die Kranken)*
Einzelne Personen:	Two more **sick people** came to the doctor. *(Zwei weitere Kranke …)*

Bezieht man sich auf einzelne Personen aus diesen Gruppen, so muss man zusätzliche Nomen wie z.B. *man / woman, boy / girl, person, people,* … hinzufügen.

9 Funktionen des Partizips – Functions of the participle

That looks like an **inviting** menu.
I asked for **scrambled** eggs.

Hier haben das *present participle (inviting)* und das *past participle (scrambled)* die Funktion von **Adjektiven.** Sie beschreiben die Substantive genauer und sind deshalb **attributiv** gebraucht, stehen also **vor** ihren Substantiven.

A woman **eating** an omelette spoke to us.
The name **printed** on the door was Russian.

Hier sind die beiden *participles (eating / printed)* als **adverbiale Bestimmungen** gebraucht und entsprechen Nebensätzen. (Vgl. auch Punkt 29.5) Sie stehen folglich **hinter den Substantiven**, auf die sie sich beziehen.

W

Wichtig sind noch die folgenden beiden Aspekte:

- das *present participle* (*-ing*) hat aktivische Bedeutung:
  … the **man working** in the shop …
  … the **girl speaking** with a strong accent …
- das *past participle* dagegen hat passivische Bedeutung:
  … a **boy called** Ronny …
  … the **eggs fried** on both sides.

A Übertrage ins Englische; verwende *present participles* und *past participles*:

1. New York ist eine aufregende Stadt.
2. Besucher, die zum ersten Mal nach New York kommen, sind gewöhnlich aufgeregt.
3. Wegen des U-Bahnsystems sind sie meist verwirrt.
4. Es kann sehr verwirrend sein, in Madison Square Gardens den richtigen U-Bahnzug zu finden.
5. Die ersten Einwanderer aus Schweden wurden als misstrauisch angesehen.
6. Ihre Sprache wurde nicht verstanden.
7. Aber Leute, die arbeiten wollten, wurden gebraucht.

10 Partizip und Infinitiv – Participles and infinitives

1 Nach Verben der Sinneswahrnehmung – After verbs of perception

present participle

Can you **see** the girl **eating** an ice-cream?
I **noticed** our neighbour **feeding** his dogs.

Hier steht die Wahrnehmung des **Ablaufs** im Vordergrund.
Meist wird **nur ein Teil** des ablaufenden Geschehens wahrgenommen und beschrieben.
(Das *present participle* entspricht der *progressive form* im einfachen Satz.)

infinitive

We **watched** the waiter **bring** the food and then **talk** to the customers.
She **heard** the phone **ring** but when she went to answer it was dead.

Hier ist das Gesamtgeschehen (vom Anfang bis zum Ende) von Interesse.
Es kann zwar von kurzer Dauer sein, aber es werden auch die Folgen und Folgehandlungen wahrgenommen.
(Der Infinitiv entspricht hier eher der *simple form* im einfachen Satz.

A Übertrage ins Englische; verwende *present participles* und *past participles*:

1. Sie beobachteten, wie er das Essen zurückbrachte und es dann auf den Tisch stellte.
2. Ich sah, dass unsere Katze ihr Futter fraß.
3. Wir hörten den Hund unserer Nachbarn bellen und schlossen das Fenster.
4. Ich konnte wahrnehmen, dass deine Schwester an ihrem Computer arbeitete.
5. Hast du unsere Großmutter im Garten arbeiten gesehen?

2 Nach Verben der Bewegung und Ruhe – After verbs of motion and rest

The children **came running** when they saw their parents returning.

She **sat reading** her letter by the window.

Nach den Verben *come, go, sit* und *stand* können *present participles* stehen, um auszudrücken, auf welche Weise eine Person sitzt, steht, kommt, usw. Der Partizip hat hier eine aktivische Bedeutung.

I wrote to her several times, but all my letters **went unanswered**.
When the children had left, he **remained seated** and picked up his book.

Nach den Verben *go* und *remain* können *past participles* stehen, mit denen du den Zustand ausdrückst, in dem eine Sache ist, wenn sie verlassen oder gelassen wird. Mit *remain* + *past participle* drückst du aus, dass der Zustand einer Person oder einer Sache sich nicht ändert. Der Partizip hat hier eine passivische Bedeutung.

11 Der *s*-Genitiv und der *of*-Genitiv – The s-genitive and the of-genitive

In den vorhergehenden Bänden war von den beiden Genitivformen schon oft die Rede. Hier sollen zur Veranschaulichung noch einmal die wichtigsten Punkte als Übersicht präsentiert werden.

1 Gebrauch des Genitivs – Using the genitive

Wenn du sagen willst, dass etwas oder jemand zu einer bestimmten Person gehört, dann brauchst du den *s*-Genitiv.

Auch bei Ländern, Städten usw. kannst du das *s*-Genitiv gebrauchen, wenn du sie beim Namen nennst.

Auch Zeitangaben können mit dem *s*-Genitiv gemacht werden.

- My mother**'s** father**'s** ... er ... my grandfather**'s** name is Victor.
- Some thieves have stolen the girls**'** bikes.
- Are these the children**'s** balls?
- What about Liz**'s** homework?
- The world**'s** highest building will soon be found in Hong Kong.
- There is a new programme to help America**'s** poor.
- We will be with you in three days**'** time.

Beim *of*-Genitiv steht unabhängig von den Personen der **Sachbezug** im Vordergrund. Dies gilt auch im Hinblick auf Themen- und Zeitbezüge.

Bestimmte feste Verbindungen mit Ortsnamen weisen ebenfalls das *of*-Genitiv auf.

- The price **of** this ticket is one pound fifty.
- What's the name **of** the oldest building in your town?
- *Oh, that cello* is the title **of** a piece **of** music written by Charlie Chaplin.
- Oscar Wilde wrote his comedies during the second half **of** the 19th century.
- They have got a flat in the centre **of** London.

2 Schreibung und Aussprache des *s*-Genitivs – Spelling and pronunciation of the s-genitive

Im Singular wird ein Apostroph und ein *s* an das Substantiv angefügt. Hier gibt es wie beim Plural-*s* Ausspracheregeln zu beachten.

Bei Pluralformen auf *s* wird nur ein Apostroph angefügt. Bei anderen Pluralformen wird ein Apostroph + ein *s* angefügt, genau wie beim Singular. Auch die Aussprache funktioniert hier genau wie beim Singular.

Achtung bei Familiennamen:
Bei Namen auf -*s* (Wilkins/Burns) kann entweder ein Apostroph + *s* oder nur ein Apostroph angefügt werden.

S

[s] nach stimmlosem Laut:
p, t, k, usw.

[z] nach stimmhaftem Laut:
Vokale, b, d, g, l, usw.

[ɪz] nach Zischlaut:
s, z, ts, S, usw.

The Wilkins**'s** car / The Burns**'** children

12 Unbestimmter und bestimmter Artikel; *some* und *any* – The indefinite and the definite article; *some* and *any*

Dass die englischen Artikel von der Form her etwas einfacher sind als im Deutschen, weißt du ja bereits. Im Gebrauch gibt es jedoch einige Abweichungen, weshalb wir hier noch einmal eine Übersicht der wichtigsten Fälle zeigen.

1 Der unbestimmte Artikel – The indefinite article

He's **a** taxi driver.
She's **a** Korean.
She married **an** American.

I was travelling at ten miles **an** hour.
The apples cost £1 **a** kilo.

a lot of people – **a** couple of minutes
a few pounds

Bei der Angabe des Berufs oder der Nationalität eines Einzelnen steht im Englischen immer der unbestimmte Artikel. (Beachte aber die Informationen unter Grammatik-Punkt 8!)
Bei Maß- und Zeitangaben mit der Bedeutung ‚pro' verwendest du ebenfalls den unbestimmten Artikel.
Bestimmte Mengenangaben verwenden den unbestimmten Artikel.

A bike isn't useful. (We need a car.)
One bike isn't useful. (We need two.)

1m = **a/one** metre – 100 = **a/one** hundred

Das andere kleine Wort *one* wird nur dann benutzt, wenn du betonen willst, dass es dir um eine(n) einzige(n) geht. Ansonsten sind **a(n)** und **one** bei Zahlenangaben austauschbar.

What a wonderful view!
Such a nice place!
It was **quite a** surprise. (eine ziemliche ...)
It only took **half an** hour.

Merke:
Der unbestimmte Artikel steht hinter *what, such, quite* (= ziemlich) und *half*.

2 Der bestimmte Artikel – The definite article

Beispiele:

the United States, **the** Netherlands
the Thames, **the** Pacific Ocean
in **the** north
The horse is a useful animal.

Regel: Es steht immer ein bestimmter Artikel bei:

- Ländernamen im Plural
- Flüssen, Seen, Ozeanen
- Himmelsrichtungen
- Tieren als Gattungsbezeichnung

Denmark, England
Broadway, Times Square
Have you had breakfast? – March is in spring. – Today is Friday.
The people smelled of leather.
They were full of hope.
He spent five years in prison.
I was never good at science.
She hated washing the dog.

Kein bestimmter Artikel bei:

- Ländernamen im Singular
- Straßen, Plätzen
- Mahlzeiten, Ferienzeiten (allgemein), Wochentagen, Monaten, Jahreszeiten
- Substanzen, die allgemein gebraucht werden
- abstrakten Begriffen
- Gebäuden als Institutionen
- Schulfächern
- Gerundien (allgemein)

The breakfast in the hotel wasn't very interesting.
The ambition he showed was incredible.
I could smell **the** leather of her handbag.
The prison in town was near **the** school.
New York? Oh, I don't like all **the** running around!

Beim Gebrauch mancher dieser Begriffe muss aber in Ausnahmen der bestimmter Artikel verwendet werden, und zwar dann, wenn die Sache genau definiert werden soll.

3 *Some* und *any*

Some und *any* dienen zum Ausdruck von unbestimmten Mengenangaben – sowohl bei zählbaren als auch bei unzählbaren Nomen –, und zwar:

Let's buy **some** fruit.
Have you got **some** apples?

some bei bejahten Sätzen oder bei Fragen, auf die hin ein *Yes* erwartet wird.

Do you need **any** help?
I can't see **any** birds in the garden.
Haven't you got **any** money?

any bei sonstigen Fragen und bei Verneinungen.

We bought **a couple of** sandwiches.
They asked us **several** times.
I only have **very little** money.

Für Angaben, bei denen man einen groben Eindruck der vorhandenen Menge bekommt, stehen dir andere Wörter zur Verfügung.

Für das englische Wort *some* gibt es im Deutschen meist keine Entsprechung, d.h. die deutsche Sprache kommt ganz ohne ein Wort aus. Vergleiche:
Can you give me **some money**? – Kannst du mir **Geld** geben?
There are **some trees** over there. – Da drüben gibt es **Bäume**.

4 Die Zusammensetzungen von *some* und *any* – Compounds with some and any

Wie du bereits weißt, sind *something, somebody, anywhere* usw. Zusammensetzungen von *some* und *any*. Diese Zusammensetzungen werden nach genau denselben Regeln verwendet wie die Grundformen auch.

bejahte Aussagen	Fragen	verneinte Aussagen
I want to buy **something** for her birthday.	Can you think of **anything**?	No, sorry. I can't think of **anything**.
My boot must be **somewhere**!	Have you seen it **anywhere**?	No, sorry. I can't find it **anywhere**.

13 Bestätigungsfragen – Questions tags

Wie beim Schlüssel den Anhänger, so gibt es auch in der gesprochenen Sprache so genannte Frageanhängsel (*question tags*), mit denen man Bestätigung oder Zustimmung erlangen möchte. Sie entsprechen solchen Äußerungen wie ... nicht wahr? ... oder? ... gell?

Im Englischen hängt man eine Bestätigungsfrage an den Aussagesatz an:

Bejahter Aussagesatz	verneinte Bestätigungsfrage	Verneinter Aussagesatz	bejahte Bestätigungsfrage
You are 15,	aren't you?	You aren't sick,	are you?
She is older,	isn't she?	Grandpa's in the house,	isn't he?
You have finished,	haven't you?	They haven't seen it,	have they?
He's got a computer,	hasn't he?	She hasn't got my comic,	has she?
This looks good,	doesn't it?	It doesn't hurt,	does it?
They will enjoy this,	won't they?	They won't say no,	will they?
You can understand,	can't you?	She can't speak German,	can she?
We must go now,	mustn't we?	They mustn't find out,	must they?

Es ist eigentlich nur immer der folgende ‚Mechanismus' zu beachten: Die Besätigungsfrage greift das Hilfsverb und das Subjekt des Aussagesatzes wieder auf, wobei das Subjekt dann immer als Personalpronomen erscheint. Gibt es im Aussagesatz **kein** Hilfsverb, so erscheint in der Bestätigungsfrage einfach eine Form von *to do, does, did* oder *don't, doesn't, didn't*.

W

Übrigens … Bestätigungsfragen sprichst du mit steigender Satzmelodie (Intonation), wenn du nicht sicher bist, ob deine Aussage richtig oder falsch ist: She is with you, isn't she?

Bist du deiner Sache sicher und erwartest du eigentlich gar keine Antwort, so gehst du mit der Stimme nach unten: Nice weather today, isn't it?

UNIT 3

14 Bedingungssätze (Typ III) – Conditional clauses (Type III)

Nachdem du im letzten Jahr schon die Bedingungssätze der Typen I und II kennen gelernt hast, ist der Typ III jetzt kein Problem mehr und wir können danach alle drei Typen auf einen Blick zusammenstellen.

If we **had known** about these hurricanes, we **would** never **have come**.

Bei Typ III der Bedingungssätze geht es um irreale, also um nicht erfüllbare Bedingungen. (Die angesprochenen Möglichkeit und Bedingung beziehen sich auf die Vergangenheit und können demnach jetzt nicht mehr erfüllt werden.) Auch das *past perfect* hat hier im *if*-Satz nicht seine übliche Bedeutung (… gewusst hatten …), sondern die Möglichkeit wird angesprochen: (… gewusst hätten …).

Und hier nun alle drei *if*-Satztypen auf einen Blick:

S

Typ	Bedingung	*if*-Satz	Hauptsatz
I	erfüllbar	If it's cold,	we won't go to the lake.
II	möglich/offen	If I could make a wish,	nobody would be homeless.
III	nicht erfüllbar (nicht mehr zu ändern)	If the alarm had come earlier,	things would have been easier.

Merksätze:

Typ I: In diesem Bedingungssatz drückt die *if-clause* die Bedingung aus und der Hauptsatz sagt, was passiert, falls diese Bedingung erfüllt wird. – In der *if-clause* steht immer das Präsens, während der Hauptsatz mit dem *will-future* gebildet wird. Bedingungssätze können entweder mit der *if-clause* oder mit dem Hauptsatz beginnen.

M

Achtung!
In der *if-clause* steht nie ein *will*.
Vor *if* steht nie ein Komma.

Typ II: Mit dem *conditional II* drückst du eine Bedingung aus, über die du nachdenkst, die aber ganz offen ist. Sie kann möglicherweise eintreten, vielleicht aber auch nicht. Die *if-clause* steht immer im Präteritum. Aber gemeint ist nicht die Vergangenheit, sondern die **gedachte Möglichkeit.** Im Hauptsatz steht immer *would* oder *wouldn't.* Du kannst wieder mit der *if-clause* oder mit dem Hauptsatz beginnen.

Typ III: s.o.: Und damit haben wir diesen Bereich auch komplett beieinander!

A Wie kannst du diese Sätze ins Deutsche übertragen?

1. Wenn mein Bruder mir sein Moped gäbe, würde ich viel Zeit sparen.
2. Aber wenn es regnet, gibt mein Bruder mir sein Moped nicht.
3. Wenn ich so alt bin wie mein Bruder, dann habe ich auch ein Moped.
4. Hätte ich von einem Unfall gehört, dann hätte ich euch davon erzählt.
5. Wäret ihr gekommen, wenn ich angerufen hätte?
6. Wenn ich mein Geld nicht vergessen hätte, dann hätte ich die CD gekauft.
7. Wenn ich auch Computerspiele erfinden könnte, dann würde ich viel Geld verdienen.

15 Gerundium oder Infinitiv? – Gerund or infinitive?

☹ My sister **hates working** in the garden.
☺ But my mother **loves to** work here.

Nach den Verben *begin, start, continue, like, love, hate, intend* und *prefer* hast du die freie Wahl zwischen Gerundium oder Infinitiv, ohne dass es zu Bedeutungsverschiebungen kommt.

We'd **like to meet** you in Las Vegas.

Allerdings!
Nach *would like / should like* oder *love* und deren Zusammenziehungen (*I'd like … / They'd love …*) **ist nur der Infinitiv möglich.**

Doch nun zu den Bedeutungsunterschieden:

1 Da ist zunächst das Verb 

wichtig:

We **stopped working** at five o'clock.

Bei *stop + gerund* wird ausgedrückt, dass eine Handlung beendet wird, also nicht länger andauert.
Der Satz bis zu *stop* hat hier keine eigenständige Bedeutung; ohne den Zusatz mit Partizip ergibt sich kein Sinn (vgl. rechts).

My friends **stopped to go** for a swim.

Bei *stop + infinitive* geht es inhaltlich darum, dass eine neue Handlung beginnen soll. Es gibt sozusagen einen STOPP zwecks Beginn einer neuen (anderen) Aktivität.
Der Satz bis zu *stop* kann auch alleine stehen und ergibt einen Sinn, denn aus dem Kontext wissen wir, dass jemand gerade fährt, redet, läuft usw.

2 Und nun zu den Verben **forget – remember – regret**

She didn't **remember flying** to Las Vegas.
I don't **regret telling** her about the party.

Mit dem *gerund* ist ausgedrückt: Eine Handlung, ein Ereignis ist vorbei. Man vergisst, erinnert sich oder bedauert es, dabei gewesen zu sein oder es/etwas nicht getan zu haben.

We mustn't **forget to send** them an e-mail.
I **regret to say** that we won't be able to come.

Mit dem *infinitive* ist ausgedrückt, dass das Ereignis, die Handlung noch nicht statt gefunden hat. Das soll noch erfolgen oder erfolgt gerade.

3 Und nun zum Verb **mean**

Flying in the morning **means getting up** early.

Mean + gerund drückt aus, dass eine Handlung bestimmte Resultate, Folgen, Konsequenzen hat.

Well, I **mean to fly** to Las Vegas early on Friday.

Mean + infinitive drückt aus, dass jemand etwas fest vorhat.

4 Und schließlich noch das Verb **try**

Are you feeling unwell? Why don't you **try eating** less before you fly?

Beim Gerund geht es um andere Alternativen oder Methoden.

I **tried to listen** to the pilot, but the engine was too loud.

Beim Infinitiv geht es um (vergebliche) Versuche oder Bemühungen, etwas zu tun.

M Ein bekannter Scherz (auf Kosten der amerikanischen Fluggesellschaft TWA) hieß immer:

Try Walking Across.

A Verbinde die Satzteile, so dass sich ein Sinn ergibt:

1. At 11 o'clock my grandfather usually stops
2. My sister would love
3. But flying to New York means
4. My aunt told me she had tried
5. And it worked! After five hours, two stewardesses were trying
6. My aunt will never forget
7. She said that when in New York I mustn't forget

a) sleeping on board the plane.
b) watching TV.
c) seeing New York for the first time.
d) to send her a postcard.
e) travelling through six time zones.
f) to wake her up.
g) to go to New York like my aunt.

16 Adjektiv oder Adverb? – Adjective or adverb?

Wir erinnern noch einmal:

That was a **nice** meeting.	Adjektive beschreiben Beschaffenheit, Eigenschaften und Zustände.
She talked to me **nicely**.	Adverben beschreiben, auf welche Weise etwas getan wird.
care**ful** / care**fully** terri**ble** / terri**bly** happ**y** / happ**ily**	Bei den abgeleiteten Adverben gibt es ein paar Schreib-Besonderheiten zu beachten.
good / well hard / hard fast / fast late / late	Und dann gibt es ja noch die paar nicht abgeleiteten Adverben, die man sich merken muss.
I like walking in the country but I **hardly** get the opportunity. (kaum) Have you seen any good films **lately**? (neulich)	Wichtig hier sind auch die besonderen abgeleiteten Formen, die von der Bedeutung her sich sehr von dem entsprechenden Adjektiv und Adverb unterscheiden.
We took an ear**ly** flight and so we had to get up **early**.	Manche formgleiche Adjektive sind schon mit dem *-ly* bestückt. Das kann verwirren.
That looks **good**! – This smells **fresh**! – That sounds **fine**! Oh, is that your new dress? You **look** very **good** in it. Isn't is lovely? It makes me **feel good** too! Shall we go home? You don't **look** very **well**. Yes, okay – I don't **feel well** at all.	Und schließlich noch die festen Verbindungen mit den Verben der Sinneswahrnehmung. Wichtig in diesem Zusammenhang ist der kleine aber feine Bedeutungsunterschied bei *good / well* nach den Verben *look* und *feel*: bei *good* geht es um eine objektive Betrachtung, bei *well* geht es um körperliche Verfassung bzw. Wohlbefinden.

UNIT 4

17 *Present progressive* und *simple present*

Beide Formen verwendest du bereits seit deinem ersten Englisch-Lernjahr. Hier geht es noch einmal um eine Kontrastierung, denn mit ihnen bringst du bestimmte Aspekte deiner Redeabsichten zum Ausdruck.

S

present progessive

1. It'**s raining** again.
2. It's real! It'**s happening**.
3. You'**re watching** Coffee Time, USA.
4. I watch Dale while she **is checking** her eyeliner.

present simple

1. I **see** what you **mean**.
2. I **think** it's OK.
3. I **don't believe** that.
4. America **is** concerned about that.
5. He **makes** a great pasta sauce.
6. They usually **dim** the studio lights.
7. He **checks** the time, then **stacks** up his papers, then **looks** at the monitor, then ...

1 Mit dem *present progressive* drückst du gegenwärtige Zustände und gerade ablaufende Handlungen aus (Beispiele 1-3).
Es kann aber auch der Aspekt der Gleichzeitigkeit und parallel ablaufender Handlungen hinzukommen (Beispiel 4).

Beim *present simple* geht es um länger währende Zustände (Beispiele 1-4). Dazu kommen Aktivitäten, die häufig regelmäßig, manchmal (oder auch nie) vollzogen werden (Beispiele 5 u. 6). Es kann aber auch noch der Aspekt hinzukommen, dass eine Kette oder Abfolge von Einzelhandlungen geschildert werden soll.

W

Bei der Entscheidung, ob *present progressive* oder *simple present* zu wählen ist, spielt insgesamt meist der Zeitfaktor, d.h. die Frage nach der Dauer und nach dem (absehbaren) Ende eine Rolle.

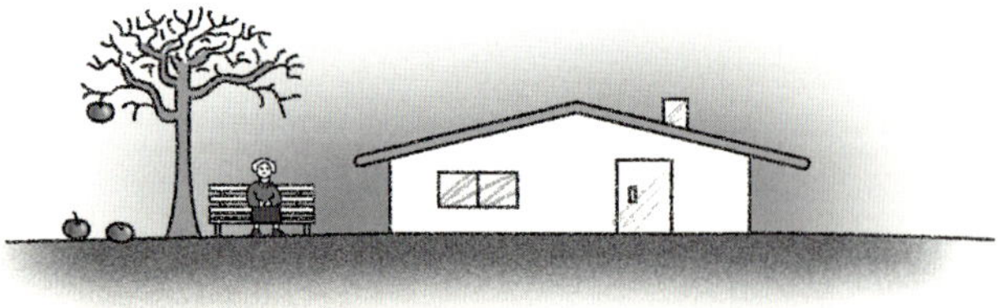

The tree **stands** near the house.

Der Baum steht neben dem Haus im Garten, und das wohl schon seit vielen Jahren und wohl auch noch viele Jahre weiterhin.

One apple **is** still **hanging** in the tree.

Im Apfelbaum hängt noch ein Apfel. Alle anderen sind schon gefallen. Es ist abzusehen, dass dieser Apfel auch bald herunterfallen wird.

The bench **stands** under the tree.

Die Bank steht unter dem Baum. Du willst ausdrücken, dass sie immer dort steht, jahrein, jahraus, im Winter und im Sommer.

The bench **is standing** under the tree.

Oder du willst ausdrücken, dass sie gelegentlich auch mal anderswo steht.

Grandma **is sitting** on the bench.

Großmutter sitzt (gerade) auf der Bank, aber vermutlich nicht gar so lange.

2

S

1. (dis)like, hate, love, prefer, want, wish
2. believe, guess, imagine, know, mean, realize, recognize, remember, suppose, think (= have an opinion), understand
3. hear, see, taste *(tastes good)*, smell *(smells good)*, sound, weigh (= have weight)
4. belong to, depend on, fit, include, involve, need, own
5. appear, seem

Eine Reihe von Verben findest du nicht in der Verlaufsform bzw. nur in ganz bestimmten Bedeutungen. Diese so genannten *stative verbs* musst du dir gut merken – es werden auch weitere hinzukommen!

What **is** he **thinking** about?	I **think** he's angry.
Why **are** you **smelling** the milk?	It **smells** funny.
The man **is tasting** the wine.	What **does** it **taste** like?
He **was weighing** the letter when I came in.	It **weighs** 90g.
She**'s seeing** the doctor.	I **don't see** why!

Vergleiche den Gebrauch bestimmter Verben in der Verlaufsform und in der einfachen Form. Es treten Bedeutungsunterschiede auf.

I **can hear** a train coming.
I **can see** someone in the garden.

Um mit den Verben *hear* und *see* eine andauernde Aktion zu vermitteln, benutzt du das modale Hilfsverb *can*.

18 Formen des Futurs – Future forms

Das Thema „Wetterbericht" ist ein guter Anlass, die Formen des Futurs noch einmal übersichtlich zusammenzustellen.

S

future form	examples
1. *going to* + Verb (Infinitiv)	We**'re going to visit** the studio. He's **going to fall** down!
2. *will* + Verb (Infinitiv)	It **will rain** tomorrow. Dad**'ll help** us.
3. *ing*-Form + Zeitangabe	I**'m watching** this new video tonight.
4. *simple present*	The train **leaves** at five o'clock.

1 going to-future:

I'm **going to talk** to the studio people.
The make-up girls are waiting for their signal. They'**re going to get** to work quickly.

Mit dem *going to*-future kannst du sagen, was du vorhast oder zu tun beabsichtigst.
Das *going to*-future verwendest du auch, wenn ein Ereignis mit großer Wahrscheinlichkeit zu erwarten ist. Es handelt sich dann um eine logische Schlußfolgerung.

2 will-future

The studio controller **will** dim the light before the break.

Das *will-future* verwendest du, wenn ein fester Entschluss oder eine feste Verabredung vorliegt.

I'**ll go** and get your umbrella.

Wenn du spontan zu etwas bereit bist, ohne es vorher geplant zu haben, benutzt du ebenfalls das *will-future*.

It'**ll rain** later in the evening.

Das *will-future* benutzt du auch, wenn ein Ereignis von äußeren Umständen (z.B. vom Wetter) abhängt.

The recording **will start** earlier today.

Außerdem brauchst du das *will-future*, wenn du ausdrücken willst, dass etwas voraussichtlich passieren wird.

3 present progressive

I'**m working** as a make-up girl next year.

Du kannst zukünftige Ereignisse auch mit der Verlaufsform des Verbs im Präsens ausdrücken, wenn du eine Zeitangabe der Zukunft hinzufügst. Du drückst damit aus, dass du etwas fest vorhast.

4 simple present

The recording **begins** at nine o'clock.

Wenn etwas genau zeitlich geregelt und festgelegt ist, kannst du Zukünftiges auch mit dem *simple present* ausdrücken. Das gilt für Fahrpläne, Stundenpläne und sonstige feste Arbeitsabläufe.

A

Wie kannst du bei diesen Äußerungen ausdrücken, dass es sich um Zukünftiges handelt?

1. Es wird morgen nicht sehr kalt sein.
2. Wir werden früh losfahren.
3. Warte mal, ich helfe dir.
4. Am Abend um 9 Uhr sehen wir das Match.
5. Wir werden viel Spaß haben morgen.
6. Werden unsere Freunde alle da sein?
7. Heute Abend gehen wir ins Kino.
8. Aber mein Bruder wird den Film wieder nicht mögen.

19 Präpositionen in Endstellung – Prepositions in final position

Viele Verben, Adjektive und Partizipien gehen ja mit bestimmten Präpositionen feste Verbindungen ein, wie z.B.

laugh at / be angry with / look forward to

In zahlreichen Äußerungen und Fragen kann die Präposition aber an das Ende rücken. Zum Beispiel:

Everyone needs something to look forward **to.** – in *infinitive constructions*

That's the boy the teacher was angry **with.** – in *relative clauses*

Some people are always being laughed **at.** – in *passive constructions*

A Wie kannst du diesen (bösen) Ausspruch des irischen Autors Oscar Wilde von Seite 78 ins Deutsche übertragen?

There's only one thing worse than being talked about, and that's **not** being talked about.

20 Verben mit zwei Objekten: Aktiv und Passiv – Verbs with two objects: active and passive

1 Wenn Menschen miteinander in Beziehung treten, sich helfen und austauschen, dann geht es dabei meist um Verben mit zwei Objekten.

Zu diesen Verben gehören solche wie

bring / take / give / offer / ask / send / show / teach / promise / explain / tell / …

1. They gave my friend **the uniform.** *Hier haben wir ein indirektes und ein direktes Objekt.*
2. They give the uniform **to my friend.** *Hier haben wir ein direktes Objekt und ein indirektes Objekt mit Präposition.*

Hier geht es um die Uniform, die man dem Freund oder der Freundin gibt. Deshalb steht sie zwecks Betonung am Ende.

Jetzt geht es darum, dass man die Uniform dem Freund gibt, nicht anderen Personen.

W

Beim direkten Objekt (1) geht es meist um einen **Sachbezug.**
Beim indirekten Objekt (2) geht es meist um eine **Personenbezeichnung.**
Über die Stellung der Objekte entscheidet deren Länge, bzw. das, was du stärker betonen willst. Was nämlich **betont** werden soll, steht am Ende des Satzes.

2 Nun lassen sich die beiden obigen Sätze, und eben alle Sätze mit Verben mit zwei Objekten auch passivisch ausdrücken:

1. My friend was given the uniform. (not a T-shirt)

Man nennt diese Form auch das persönliche Passiv, da es hier meist um Personen und persönliche Bezüge geht. Diese Form ist die häufigere Form und gängigere.

2. The uniform was given to my friend.

Diese Form wird benutzt, wenn der Personenbezug ganz besonders betont werden soll.

Sowohl das direkte als auch das indirekte Objekt kann Subjekt des Passivsatzes werden. Wird das indirekte Objekt des Aktivsatzes als Subjekt des Passivsatz durch ein Personalpronom ausgedrückt, so steht dieses anders als im Deutschen in der Subjektform. Beispiel:

We were offered an ice-cream. → Man bot **uns** …

Übrigens!: Das Wörtchen „man" leistet beim Übertragen ins Deutsche meist ganz gute Dienste.

A

Schreibe die Sätze um, um die Tabelle zu vervollständigen:

Was? (Aktiv)	**Wem?**	**Was? (Passiv)**
They gave him a book.	They gave a book to him.	He was given a book.
Someone sent John a letter.	?	?
?	They taught a new song to Ann.	?
?	The police showed a photo to her.	?
They offered no-one help.	?	?

UNIT 5

21 Ergänzungen durch Infinitive – Adding information with infinitives

Neben Relativsätzen bieten sich auch Infinitivkonstruktionen an, um mehr Information über eine Person, eine Sache oder eine Idee zu geben. So lassen sich elegant auch zwei Ideen verbinden:

S

I've got a shirt. (I can wear it).	→	I've got a shirt to wear.
London is a city. (It's nice if you visit it.)	→	London is a nice city to visit.
Paul rang me. (It was a kind thing to do.)	→	It was kind of Paul to ring me.
John wrote a letter. (It was a difficult letter.)	→	It was difficult for him to write the letter.

1 Infinitives without their own subject

Come here – I've got something **to say.**
I want a book **to read** on holiday.
Poor Mary can't find anyone **to talk to.**
They brought me something **to look at.**

In diesen Fällen ersetzt die Infinitivkonstruktion einen zweiten Satz oder einen Relativsatz. Das Subjekt des Hauptverbs ist gleichzeitig Subjekt des Infinitivs.

Dublin is the place **to be** on St Patrick's Day.
(**Everyone** should be there.)
Making mistakes is easy **to do.**
(**Anyone** can make them)
The best colour **to wear** is green.
(It should be worn by **everyone.**)

In diesen „unpersönlichen" Sätzen hat der Infinitiv kein ausgewiesenes Subjekt. Es lässt sich aber aus dem Zusammenhang ermitteln und schließt oft die Allgemeinheit ein. Der Infinitiv hat oft eine passivische Bedeutung.

The parades were **too boring to** watch.
It's **too cold to** go out today.
He's not **old enough to** drink beer.

Nach *too* + Adjektiv oder Adjektiv + *enough* folgen ebenfalls Infinitive. Die Sätze können „unpersönlich" sein, können aber auch ein Subjekt beinhalten.

She was **the last to** arrive at the party and **the first to** leave it.
Was I **the only** one **to** notice?

Infinitive folgen auch nach *the first, the last* und *the only one/person* etc.

2 Infinitives with their own special subject

I've brought a book **for her** to read.
Make sure that there's some work **for them** to do.
I hope that there is enough time **for them** to watch the parade.

Hier wird auch ein Satz oder Nebensatz „eingespart". Im Gegensatz zu den Sätzen oben wird für den Infinitiv jedoch ein eigenes – vom Hauptverb abweichendes – Sinnsubjekt mit *for* eingeführt.

It's hard **for us** to imagine life in Ireland in 1846.
It was easy **for them** to get to Dublin.

Die Ergänzung mit dem Infinitiv kann auch die Beschreibung des Verbs durch ein Adjektiv begründen. Das Subjekt wird mit *for* eingeleitet.

It was nice **of you** to visit us.
It was crazy **of the organisers** to colour the Liffey green.
How typical **of the New Yorkers** to have a huge party!

Bezieht sich das Adjektiv auf das Subjekt, wird das Subjekt durch *of* eingeleitet.

22 Infinitive nach Verben des Wünschens und Veranlassens – Infinitives after requesting verbs

I **want to listen** to the buskers.
Tourists **prefer to walk** around the city.
They **expect to spend** a lot of money.
She **likes to visit** her parents often.

Du weißt bereits, dass auf eine Reihe von Verben, die einen Wunsch, einen Befehl oder eine Vorliebe ausdrücken, eine Infinitivkonstruktion folgen kann.

I **want you** to give them some money.
She **warned them** to look after their money.
No-one **expected him** to arrive so late.

Nach vielen solchen Verben ist ebenfalls eine Kombination aus direktem Objekt und Infinitiv möglich: *like, expect, order, prefer, want, warn, …*

M Im Deutschen werden solche Sätze oft mit „dass" und einem Nebensatz ausgedrückt.

23 Die indirekte Rede – Reported speech

Das Thema *reported speech* war schon ein wichtiges Anliegen im zweiten Lernjahr. Wir fassen noch einmal zusammen, es ist aber auch das Eine oder Andere dazugekommen.

Du brauchst die indirekte Rede, wenn du weitergeben möchtest oder sollst, was Andere dir mitgeteilt haben. Deine Aussage besteht in der Regel aus einem Einleitungssatz mit einem Verb des Mitteilens (wie *tell, say, mention, …*) und einem Folgesatz, der meist mit *that* eingeleitet wird. Die Konjunktion *that* kann aber auch entfallen.

1 Die indirekte Rede <u>ohne</u> Zeitverschiebung

Entscheidend ist nun, **wann** du die Nachricht oder Äußerung weitergibst. Geschieht das sofort, so wählst du für den Einleitungssatz das **simple present.**)*

*) Diese Form der Wiedergabe kannst du natürlich auch benutzen, wenn du einem englischsprachigen Bekannten berichten willst, was jemand gerade auf Deutsch sagt oder gesagt hat – wenn du dolmetschst, also. Gibst du die Äußerung erst später wieder, aber ohne dich auf den genauen Zeitpunkt zu beziehen, dann kannst du auch das *present perfect* gebrauchen. In beiden Fällen bleibt die Zeit im (wiedergegebenen) Folgesatz unverändert:

S

direct speech	reported speech
"This guy **comes** from Dublin."	She **says** (that) this guy **comes** from Dublin.
"They **are going** to open a new department store."	*(Later)*: **I've heard** that they **are going** to open a new department store.

W

Beachte aber, dass es in den Folgesätzen oftmals kleine (logische) Veränderungen geben kann. Diese hängen aber ganz stark vom Zusammenhang ab, und können nicht pauschal festgelegt werden. Hier ein paar Beispiele:

John: I love **her.** (May)	→	*Tom:* He says he loves **her.** *May:* He says he loves **me.**
May: **We**'re going to Rome this year.	→	*John:* May says **we**'re going to Rome this year. *Tom:* May says **they**'re going to Rome this year.

2 Die indirekte Rede <u>mit</u> Zeitverschiebung

Diese Form der indirekten Rede brauchst du, wenn du eine Mitteilung oder Äußerung **erst später**, also zeitlich versetzt an andere weitergibst, und wenn der Zeitpunkt, zu dem die Äußerung gemacht wurde, genannt wird oder abgeleitet werden kann. In diesen Fällen leitest du ja den Einleitungssatz mit einem Verb der Mitteilung (*say, tell, explain, fax, ...*) im *past tense* ein. Dadurch kommt es im Folgesatz zu einer Zeitverschiebung nach folgendem Muster:

S

simple present	→	simple past
present progressive	→	past progressive
present perfect	→	past perfect
present perfect progressive	→	past perfect progressive
simple past	→	past perfect
going to-future	→	was/were going to + infinitive
will-future	→	would + infinitive

M: Bei *would, should, could* und *might* in der direkten Rede gibt es keine Zeitverschiebung:
"You **should** visit the city museum." → She said we **should** visit the city museum.

Hier zur Veranschaulichung noch ein paar Beispiele:

S:

direct speech	reported speech
"I **can't** remember your name."	She said (that) she **couldn't** remember my name.
"I**'ve heard** about it."	He mentioned (that) he **had heard** about it.
"She **booked** the room."	They told us (that) she **had booked** the room.
"The weather **won't be** better tomorrow."	They complained (that) the weather **wouldn't be** better the following day.

Damit du dich in deinen Mitteilungen nicht ständig wiederholen musst, solltest du möglichst viele **Verben des Mitteilens** zur Einleitung der indirekten Rede parat haben: *say, tell, shout, explain, mention, complain, agree, answer, write, e-mail, fax, repeat, refuse, suggest, …* *)

*) Bei der indirekten Rede mit der Zeitverschiebung kommen – neben den kleineren logischen Änderungen unter 1 – weitere Anpassungen hinzu; Zeit- und Ortsangaben müssen meist ebenfalls „verschoben“ werden:

W:

today	→	that day
yesterday	→	the day before
tomorrow	→	the next / following day
tonight	→	that night
this week	→	that week
last Monday	→	the Monday before
here	→	there
etc.		

24 Fragen in der indirekten Rede – Reported questions

Bei der Wiedergabe von Fragen in der indirekten Rede musst du darauf achten, ob es in der direkten Rede ein Fragewort gibt oder nicht.

S:

direct speech	reported speech
"Is the bathroom over there?"	She asked me **whether** the bathroom was in that direction.
"**What** have you heard about the famine?"	She wanted to know **what** they had heard about the famine.

Bei Fragen ohne Fragewort leitest du den Nebensatz mit *if* oder *whether* ein. Gibt es ein Fragewort, so stellst du Hilfsverb und Verb an das Satzende. Beachte, dass es auch bei den Fragen die logischen Veränderungen gibt, wie sie in Grammatikpunkt 23, 1 und 2 zusammengestellt sind.

25 Wiedergabe von Aufforderungen, Warnungen und Ratschläge – Reporting requests, warnings and advice.

He **told** us **to** come later.

I **advise** you **to** book that room early enough.

She **warned** the children **not to** go alone.

Aufforderungssätze in der indirekten Rede gibst du mit dem Infinitiv nach Verben wie *tell, ask, advise, warn, ...* + Objekt wieder.

W

Von der Struktur her sind solche Sätze mit denen unter Grammatikpunkt 22 identisch (Infinitive nach Verben des Wünschens und Veranlassens.) Vergleiche:

He told us to go ...
They want us to come ...

She warned us to look ...
We advised them not to be ...

26 Indirekte Rede bei unabänderlichen Tatsachen, Naturgesetzen und Eigenschaften – Reported speech with unchanging facts, laws of nature and characteristics.

Bei der indirekten Rede gibt es meist **keine zeitliche Rückverschiebung**, wenn es um Gewohnheiten, Eigenschaften oder Naturgesetze oder unabänderliche Tatsachen geht. Bei Sätzen mit *could* und *might* ist keine Rückverschiebung möglich.

S

direct speech	reported speech
"Dublin is a wonderful city."	She stressed that Dublin **is** a wonderful city.
"He always goes to his mother's at the weekend."	We were told that he always **spends** the weekend with his mother.

A

Übertrage die folgenden Äußerungen in direkter Rede in solche in der indirekten Rede.

1. "I can't make it." ⟶ He said ...
2. "It may be a problem for me." ⟶ She told us ...
3. "I'm in the team." ⟶ She mentioned ...
4. "I've seen so many bad films." ⟶ He told me ...
5. "She never spoke of herself." ⟶ They said she ...
6. "I could come earlier." ⟶ Dad is on the phone. He says he ...
7. "Can we see you tomorrow?" ⟶ They wanted to know ...
8. "I've been waiting for two weeks." ⟶ He informed us ...
9. "I'm not going to do that again." ⟶ He said he ...
10. "Is the film over now?" ⟶ She wanted to know ...
11. "Green and yellow make blue." ⟶ We learned that ...
12. "More accidents like this could happen." ⟶ He told us ...

27 Pronouns and pro-forms – Pronomen und Proformen

1 Das Reflexivpronomen *-self/-selves* und *each other* – The reflexive pronoun *-self/-selves* and *each other*

S

singular				*plural*			
I	–	**myself**	(mir/mich) selbst	we	–	**ourselves**	(uns) selbst
you	–	**yourself**	(dir/dich) selbst	you	–	**yourselves**	(euch) selbst
he	–	**himself**		they	–	**themselves**	(sich) selbst
she	–	**herself**	(sich) selbst				
it	–	**itself**					

What a lovely cake! Did you make it **yourself**?
I got **myself** some ice cream. Do you want some too?
Leo di Caprio ***himself*** looked at me!

Die Pronomen mit *-self/-selves* verwendest du, um auszudrücken, dass jemand etwas selbst (oder für sich selbst) tut.
Sie können auch zur Betonung dienen.

In the morning he **washes** and **shaves** before he eats his breakfast.

Aber merke: Verben, die im Deutschen mit ‚sich' gebildet werden, werden nicht automatisch im Englischen von den Reflexivpronomen *-self/-selves* begleitet.

The Irish and the English make jokes about **each other.** *(jeder über den anderen)*
But they should also be able to laugh about **themselves.** *(über sich selbst)*

M

Pronomen mit *-self/-selves* und *each other* haben verschiedene Bedeutungen. Bei *each other* tun zwei oder mehrere Personen oder Lebewesen etwas gegenseitig.

2 *Some* und *any* und ihre Zusammensetzungen – *Some* and *any* and their compounds

S

some	**any**
somebody	anybody
someone	anyone
something	anything
somewhere	anywhere

Die unbestimmten Begleiter *some* und *any* sind dir schon bekannt. Sie kommen aber nicht nur allein, sondern auch in Zusammensetzungen vor. Für den Gebrauch gilt auch hier:
somebody/one/… in bejahten Sätzen,
anybody/one/… in Fragen und verneinten Sätzen.

Could I have **something** to drink, please?
Can **somebody** help me, please?

Aber merke:
Wenn du davon ausgehen kannst, dass die Antwort auf eine Frage ‚ja' sein wird, verwendest du *some* und seine Zusammensetzungen.

3 The pro-forms *so* and *not* – die Proformen *so* und *not*

Are you all right? – I think **so**. / I hope **so**.
If **not**, I'll drive you home.
I hope it's nothing serious. – **So** do I!

Mit *so* und *not* kannst du zu einem vorangehenden Satz Stellung nehmen, ohne den Inhalt zu wiederholen. (Siehe auch Grammatikpunkt 7.1.)

28 Vor- und Nachsilben – Prefixes and suffixes

1 Vorsilben

Mit Vorsilben kannst du deinen Wortschatz wesentlich erweitern. Die Kenntnis der Vorsilben hilft dir auch beim Nachschlagen in Wörterbüchern, da dort die Vorsilben oft nicht aufgeführt sind. Es gibt positive und negative Vorsilben. Zu den positiven Vorsilben gehören *re-*, *pre-* und *post-*.

He **re**tested the TV. (He tested it again.)
She opened her **pre**packed lunch. (Her father had packed it the night before.)
Lots of things happened in America after Columbus landed there. These are called **post**-Columbian events.

– Die Vorsilbe *re-* bedeutet noch einmal.

– Die Vorsilbe *pre-* bedeutet davor und hat zeitlichen Bezug.

– Die Vorsilbe *post-* ist ebenfalls zeitbezogen und bedeutet danach.

Zu den negativen Vorsilben gehören *un-*, *in-*, *mis-*, *dis-*, und *non-*. Sie bezeichnen meist negative Gegensätze.

happy – **un**happy (unglücklich)
complete – **in**complete (unvollständig)

M

Beachte:

in- + l	= ill-: legal – illegal
in- + p	= imp-: possible – impossible
in- + m	= imm-: moral – immoral
in- + r	= irr-: regular – irregular

healthy – **un**healthy (nicht gesund [genug])
British – **un**-British (not what Britons do.)

un- bedeutet nicht genug von oder das Gegenteil von etwas.

smoker – **non**-smoker (keine Beziehung zum Rauchen)
British – **non**-British (nicht mit GB oder den Briten verbunden)

Mit *non-* drückst du eine fehlende Beziehung aus.

He used to like it, but now he **dis**likes it.
What a mess! Did I **mis**read the instructions?

Du verwendest *mis-* und *dis-*, wenn sich eine Situation ins völlige Gegenteil verkehrt hat.

2 Nachsilben

Mit Nachsilben kannst du aus einem Basiswort neue Wörter schaffen oder die Bedeutung von Wörtern ändern. Hier ein paar Beispiele:

Nouns: teach**er**, act**or**, steward**ess**, waitr**ess**
move**ment**, arriv**al**, impress**ion**, friend**ship**

-er, *-or* für Berufstätige (*-ess*: weibliche Form)
-ment, *-al*, *-ion*, *-ship* etc. für Dinge

Adjectives: hope**ful**, care**ful**; use**less**, cloud**less**; cloud**y**, sunn**y**; green**ish**; eat**able**, read**able**

Vgl. die entsprechenden deutschen Nachsilben: *-ful* (= -voll); *-less* (= -los); *-y* (= -ig); *-ish* (= -lich); *-able* (= -bar)

Welche Gegensätze kannst du anfügen?

hopeless – ? friendly – ? drinkable – ? happy – ? agree – ? manned – ? manage (well) – ? fair – ? regular – ? careful – ? readable – ? believable – ?

UNIT 6

29 Relativsätze – Relative clauses

1 Zunächst Einiges zur Wiederholung: Du erinnerst dich?

Our doctor, **who** lives in our street, has got a new computer.

My old computer, **which** I had been using for two years, broke down last week.

Spricht man von Personen oder Personengruppen oder Institutionen, so brauchen wir *who*.
Bei Dingen und Tieren setzen wir *which* ein.

Who und *which* sind also nicht nur Fragewörter sondern auch noch Relativpronomen. Sie gelten beide für **Einzahl** und **Mehrzahl.**
Die obigen Beispiele enthalten **nicht-notwendige** Relativsätze, also solche mit zusätzlichen, erläuternden oder ausschmückenden Informationen. Der übergeordnete Satz wäre auch ohne Relativsatz verständlich: *Our doctor has got a new computer.*

2 **Notwendige Relativsätze *(defining relative clauses)***

A good teacher is a person **who** takes an interest in all his pupils.

A dictionary is a book **which (that)** you need for language learning.

Im notwendigen Relativsatz wird festgelegt, wer oder was gemeint ist. Sie sind für das Verständnis des übergeordneten Satzes unentbehrlich.*)

*) (Der Satz *A good teacher is a person* ist zwar grammatikalisch richtig, bringt uns aber nicht sonderlich weit ...!)

3 ***Who, which*** **und *that* im notwendigen Relativsatz**

The man **who** owns the computer shop speaks good English.	←→	The man **that** owns the computer shop speaks good English.
A salary is the money **which** you get for your work.	←→	A salary is the money **that** you get for your work.

Der Relativsatz ist notwendig. Man wüsste ohne ihn nicht, um wen oder was es geht.

Während sich *who* streng nur auf Personen und *which* nur auf Dinge und Tiere bezieht, kann im notwendigen Relativsatz *that* beide ersetzen. Damit kann man es sich einfacher machen. Auch *that* bezieht sich auf Singular und Plural.

4 **Verkürzte Relativsätze *(contact clauses)***

The tour guide (which/that) **we had in Ireland** was very a friendly guy.
The software (which/that) **you have bought** will be useful.

Who, which oder *that* sind hier entfallen, denn bei diesen Sätzen geht es im Relativsatz um den Akkusativ (= wen/was). Das erlaubt die Verkürzung.

Verkürzte Relativsätze nennen wir *contact clauses*. Und Verkürzung ist bekanntlich immer gut.

5 Weiter verkürzte Relativsätze

Neben den in Punkt 4 aufgeführten Möglichkeiten der verkürzten Relativsätze *(contact clauses)* gibt es bei den Relativsätzen noch weitere Verkürzungsmöglichkeiten dahingehend, dass sowohl *who / which / that* als auch die Formen von *to be* entfallen können. Somit schließt sich das Partizip (Präsens oder Perfekt) direkt an das Subjekt des Relativsatzes. Die ursprüngliche Interpunktion bleibt erhalten. In der Kürze liegt bekanntlich die Würze!

S

Ausführlicher Relativsatz	Verkürzung
Lords, the film **which had been nominated** for several Oscars, was a huge success.	*Lords*, the film **nominated** for several Oscars, was a huge success.
Some *Harry Potter* fans **who are waiting** for the next book have written letters to the author.	Some *Harry Potter* fans **waiting** for the next book have written letters to the author.
The *Harry Potter* books, **which were written** in English, have now been translated into many languages.	The *Harry Potter* books, **written** in English, have now been translated into many languages.

6 Relativsätze mit *whose*

Lord Sandwich, **whose** butler invented the sandwich, was crazy about playing cards.

Our neighbours' bird, **whose** cage was open, has flown away.

Bei Relativsätzen mit *whose* sind stets Lebewesen, Dinge oder Erscheinungen im Spiel, denen etwas **zugeordnet** wird. Die deutsche Entsprechung für *whose* ist **deren/dessen.**

7 *Which* in Satzgefügen

Our dog sometimes barks at night, which makes our neighbours angry.

There's a new bus stop near our house, which saves us a lot of time.

Which kann sich nicht nur auf ein einzelnes Substantiv beziehen, sondern auch auf die gesamte vorausgehende Aussage. Es verbindet somit Haupt- und Nebensatz. Der mit *which* eingeleitete Nebensatz erläutert den gesamten Hauptsatz und liefert Zusatzinformation.

M

Dem englischen *which* entspricht meist das deutsche „was".

We told her to see the doctor, which she did.
… was sie (dann, auch, schließlich) tat.

8 Betonung durch Spaltsätze mit *it* oder *what*

Zu den Relativsätzen gehören auch die sogenannten Spaltsätze (*cleft sentences*). In den folgenden zwei Beispielen kann der Ausgangssatz *James Watt developed the steam engine* jeweils in zwei Teile aufgespalten werden:

1. It was James Watt // who developed the steam engine.
2. What James Watt developed // was the steam engine.

Hier einige weitere Beispiele:

Was it our history teacher **who** taught us that?
It's the idea **that** counts.
Was it your parents **who** asked you about it?

Mit *it is/it was* oder deren Umkehrung (bei Fragen) + Relativsatz betont man meistens wer etwas gemacht hat. Verbindungen mit *were*, also für den Plural, gibt es allerdings nicht.

What you need **is** a really good idea.
What he did **was** absolutely brilliant.
What I mean **is** (that) it was a great invention.

Spaltsätze mit *what* betonen eine Sache. Man kann den gleichen Sachverhalt einfacher ausdrücken, z.B. *You need a really good idea*, aber ohne die starke Betonung.

9 Kommasetzung bei den Relativsätzen

Die nicht-notwendigen Relativsätze werden von den Hauptsätzen durch Kommas (und beim Sprechen durch Pausen) abgetrennt.
Bei den notwendigen Relativsätzen gibt es keine Kommas.
Vor dem zusammenfassenden *which* in Satzgefügen steht stets ein Komma.

A

Bilde aus den folgenden Sätzen (jeweils zwei zusammengehörige) ein Satzgefüge mit Hauptsatz und Relativ-Nebensatz. (Die fett gedruckten Teile sollen Relativsatz werden.)

1. The boy **has a blue bike.** He is my brother.
2. Our neighbours have two dogs. **They bark all night.**
3. He has lost his keys. **It makes things difficult for him.**
4. Our friends are on holiday. **We have to feed their cat.**
5. **We met** the girl. She is my cousin.
6. I asked her to **stop that nonsense. She refused to do it.**
7. Who is the man? **You talked to him yesterday.**

30 *Would* und *used to*

Would und *used to* werden gebraucht, um über frühere Gewohnheiten, Aktivitäten aber auch Zustände und Haltungen zu sprechen.

When we were children, we **would** ride around on our old bikes.

In diesem Fall bezieht sich *would* allein auf Vergangenes, und zwar auf (wiederholt) ausgeübte Tätigkeiten und Vorgänge. Dabei kommen entsprechende Verben zum Tragen, die Tätigkeiten und Aktivitäten – nicht Zustände! – beschreiben.

An old tree **used to** stand near our garage. But it is gone now.

Anders als bei *would* kann sich *used to* auch auf frühere Zustände und Haltungen beziehen und ist deshalb bei allen Verbarten passend. Mit *used to* wird oft das Frühere gegen das Heutige abgegrenzt oder kontrastiert.

We never **used to** go sailing when we were young.
There **didn't used to** be a house there.
We **wouldn't** often travel by bus.

Sowohl mit *would* als auch mit *used to* kannst du auch sagen, was damals *nicht* der Fall war.

W

Auf *would* und *used to* folgt immer der Infinitiv. Die Formen sind für alle Personen gleich. *Would* und *used to* gibt es nur in einer Zeitform. Fragen mit *would* (in dieser Bedeutung) sind eher rar.

S

positive	negative	question
I **would** go sailing at the weekend.	We **wouldn't** often watch TV.	**Would** girls play with toy cars when you were young?
We **used to** ride our bikes every day.	She **didn't use(d) to** live here. He **never used to** smoke.	**Did** you **use(d) to** have a coal fire?

31 Betonung und Verstärkung – Stress and emphasis

1 ... durch Gradadverbien

Punkt 6.3 machte deutlich, dass man mit bestimmten Gradadverbien Verstärkung (Emphase) und Betonung ausdrücken kann. Dazu gehören Gradadverbien wie *very, quite, fully, totally, really* etc.

We **fully** accepted his advice.
Wir nahmen seinen Rat voll an.
I **quite** agree with you.
Ich stimme dir voll und ganz zu.
They **really** like you.
Sie mögen dich (aber) wirklich.

W

Vorsicht mit *quite*! Je nach Intonation und Zusammenhang kann es zwei unterschiedliche Bedeutungen haben. Vergleiche:

He's quite clever. (... *ziemlich schlau*)
He's quite mad. (... *komplett verrückt*)

2 ... durch das emphatische *do* / *did* und andere betonte Hilfsverben

Mit dem emphatischen *do* / *did* kannst du unterschiedliche Aspekte des Betonens oder Verstärkens zum Ausdruck bringen.

"Why didn't you ring me?"
"I **did** ring, but you didn't answer the phone."

Mit dem betonten *do* kannst du Aussagen korrigieren, die deiner Meinung nach falsch sind. Damit kannst du auch eigene Aussagen relativieren, z. B. "I don't like sports, but I do like watching tennis on TV."

I **did** enjoy that film. The special effects were great.

Das emphatische *do* und andere (beim Sprechen) betonte Hilfsverben dienen dazu, starke, spontane, emotionsgeladene Reaktionen oder Einstellungen zu äußern.

Do come in. You **will** stay for dinner, I hope?
(Kommen Sie doch bitte ...)

Das emphatische *do* usw. dient auch zur Verstärkung einer Aufforderung. Es kann besonders höflich klingen, aber manchmal auch ungeduldig.

A

Übertrage diese Äußerungen mit Verstärkung, Betonung, Hervorhebung ins Englische.

1. Ich stimme euch voll zu.
2. Sie mögen ihre neue Lehrerin wirklich sehr.
3. Ich höre diese Musik wirklich gern. Sie ist wunderbar.
4. Dieser Baum ist schon sehr alt.
5. Ich mag (zwar) kein italienisches Essen, aber chinesisches Essen mag ich sehr.

32 Singular und Plural

Hier nun noch eine klärende Übersicht über die unregelmäßigen Plurale. Man unterscheidet ja zwischen zählbaren und nicht-zählbaren Pluralen.

- Bei den **nicht-zählbaren** Pluralen geht es um zwei Bereiche:
  1. Stoffnamen wie z. B. *coffee, popcorn, food, butter, …*
  2. Abstrakte Begriffe wie z. B. *peace, freedom, work, love, …*

  Alle diese Substantive werden sozusagen als Ganzes betrachtet.
  Es gibt für sie keine Pluralform.
- Bei den **zählbaren** Pluralen gibt es ja keine Probleme: Es wird eben ein -s an das Substantiv angehängt oder auch ein -es. Merken musst du dir allerdings die unregelmäßigen Formen wie *mouse – mice, child – children.* Auch die Schreibveränderungen beim Endbuchstaben (nach Konsonanten) musst du im Auge behalten. *(bully – bullies)*
- Nun bleibt noch eine Gruppe von Substantiven zu beachten, die ein -s am Ende aufweisen, aber eigentlich **nicht** zählbar (und deshalb singular) sind:
  1. manche Unterrichtsfächer: *Mathematics, Physics, …*
  2. einige Sportarten: *athletics, aerobics, …*
  3. einige Spiele: *cards, darts, …*
- Und noch eine Gruppe gibt es, nämlich Substantive, die nur die Pluralform haben: *jeans, glasses, pants, …*

33 Phrasal verbs

Von einem *phrasal verb* reden wir dann, wenn ein Verb mit einer Präposition (*at, on, to,* usw.) oder mit einem kurzen Adverb (*off, up, away,* usw.) eine feste Verbindung eingeht.

What are you **looking for**?
One of us must **look after** the dog.
This word is new, I must **look** it **up**.

I'm sure he made	**up**	that joke.	
I'm sure he made		that joke	**up.**
I'm sure he made		it	**up.**

Mit jeder neuen Verbindung entsteht ein neuer Begriff mit einer neuen Bedeutung.
To look after sth. (aufpassen) ist etwas ganz Anderes als *to look sth. up* (nachschlagen).

Bei einem *phrasal verb* mit Adverb + Objekt gibt es verschiedene Stellungsmöglichkeiten:
- Ist das Objekt ein Substantiv, so kann das Adverb vor oder nach diesem Objekt stehen.
- Ist das Objekt jedoch ein Personalpronomen, so steht das Adverb immer dahinter.

Grammar exercises (Solutions)

3 (Seite 166)
1c), 2d), 3e), 4f), 5a), 6g), 7b)

4 (Seite 166)
1. After he had bought the CD, he listened to it at home. 2. We had never heard the song, but we liked it straight away. 3. The girl didn't tell her friend that she had forgotten her homework. 4. The teacher didn't know that some pupils had already read the story. 5. They were very angry because they hadn't thought of (using) their mobile phones.

5 (Seite 167)
1. I hate smoking. 2. Swimming is fun. 3. My brother enjoys playing the piano. 4. My sister is proud of inventing (having invented) some computer games.
5. Surfing the Internet is a problem for my aunt.
6. My little brother is afraid of going shopping alone.

9 (Seite 173)
1. New York is an exciting city. 2. Visitors coming to New York for the first time are usually excited. 3. They mostly get confused because of the subway system.
4. Finding the right subway train in Madison Square Gardens can be very confusing. 5. The first immigrants were thought of as rather suspecting. 6. Their language was not understood. 7. But people wanting to work were needed.

10 (Seite 173)
1. They watched him bring back the food and put it on the table. 2. I saw our cat eat its food. 3. We heard our neighbours' dog barking und shut the window. 4. I could hear your sister working at her computer. 5. Did you see our grandmother working in the garden?

14 (Seite 179)
1. If my brother gave me his moped, I would save a lot of time. 2. But if it rains, my brother won't give me his moped. 3. When I'm as old as my brother, I'll have a moped too. 4. If I had heard about an accident, I would have told you about it. 5. Would you have come if I had called? 6. If I hadn't forgotten my money, I would have bought the CD. 7. If I could invent computer games too, I would make/earn a lot of money.

15 (Seite 180)
1b), 2g), 3e), 4a), 5f), 6c), 7d)

18 (Seite 184)
1. It won't be very cold tomorrow. 2. We are going to leave early. 3. Wait, I'll help you. 4. We're watching (going to watch) the match at 9 o'clock in the evening. 5. We're going to have a lot of fun tomorrow. 6. Will all our friends be there? 7. This evening we're going to the cinema. 8. But my brother won't like the film again.

19 (Seite 185)
Schlimm ist es, wenn über einen geredet wird; noch schlimmer freilich, wenn nicht über einen geredet wird.

20 (Seite 186)
Someone sent a letter to John. / John was sent a letter. / They taught Anne a new song. / Anne was taught a new song. / The police showed her a photo. / She was shown a photo (by the police). / They offered help to no-one. / No-one was offered help.

26 (Seite 191)
1. ... he couldn't make it. 2. ... it might be a problem for her. 3. ... that she was in the team. 4. ... he had seen so many bad films. 5. ... had never spoken of herself. 6. ... could come earlier. 7. ... if they could see us the next day. 8. ... that he'd been waiting for two weeks. 9. ... wasn't going to do it again. 10. ... whether the film was over. 11. ... green and yellow make blue. 12. ... more accidents like that could happen.

28 (Seite 193)
hopeful, unfriendly, eatable, unhappy, disagree, unmanned, mismanage, unfair, irregular, careless, unreadable, unbelievable

29 (Seite 196)
1. The boy who has a blue bike is my brother. 2. Our neighbours have two dogs(,) which bark all night. 3. He has lost his keys, which makes things difficult for him.
4. Our friends, whose cat we have to feed, are on holiday. 5. The girl we met is my cousin. 6. I asked her to stop that nonsense, which she refused to do. 7. Who is the man you talked to yesterday?

31 (Seite 198)
1. I completely agree with you. 2. They really (do) like their new teacher. 3. I really (do) like this music. It's absolutely wonderful. 4. This tree really is very old.
5. I don't like Italian food, but I do like Chinese food.

Grammar list

German / Latin	English	Example	Number
Adjektive als Substantive	adjectives as nouns	Manhattan is the home of the **rich**.	8.3
– Adjektiv oder Adverb?	adjective or adverb?	It was a **good** meeting. It went **well**.	16
Adverbien			6
– der Art und Weise	– adverbs of manner	She answered **quickly**.	
– der Zeit und des Ortes	– adverbs of time and place	We **often** miss the bus.	
– Gradadverbien	– adverbs of degree	The band was **really** great.	
– der Zeit und Häufigkeit	– of time and frequency	We **sometimes** go there.	
Artikel	article		
– Gebrauch des bestimmten Artikels	– use of the definite article	**the** United States, **the** west	12.2
– Gebrauch des unbestimmten Artikels	– use of the indefinite article	She works as **a** teacher. The apples are one pound **a** kilo. That's **quite a** good price!	12.1
Bedingungssätze	conditional sentences		14
– Typ I	– type I	**If** it rains, he**'ll** practise indoors.	
– Typ II	– type II	**If** I lived in Florida, I **would** do watersports.	
– Typ III	– type III	**If** I **had been** there, I **would** have seen her.	14
Bestätigungsfragen	question tags	She is with you, **isn't she?**	13
Betonung und Verstärkung	stress and emphasis	I **fully** agree. I **did** enjoy that film.	31
Brit. / Amerik. Englisch	British / American English	flat, colour *(BE)*; apartment, color *(AE)*	1
Formen des Futurs	forms of the future		18
– *will*-Futur	– will-future	It **will** rain later in the afternoon.	
– *going to*-Futur	– going to-future	He's **going to** take part in the race.	
– Verlaufsform im Präsens	– present progressive	She's **running** in the Marathon in May.	
– Präsens (einfache Form)	– simple present	The train **arrives** at half past twelve.	
Gerund / Gerundium	gerund	**Sailing** is fun. I'm good at **swimming**.	5
– Gerund oder Infinitiv?	– gerund or infinitive?	to stop **doing** sth. / to stop **to do** sth.	15
Indirekte Rede	reported speech		23
– ohne Zeitverschiebung	– without timeshift	He **says** he's missed the bus.	
– mit Zeitverschiebung	– with timeshift	She **said** she couldn't make it.	
– indirekte Fragen	– reported questions	She **asked** me **where** we had been.	24
– Aufforderungen	– requests, commands etc.	He **told** us **to** come later.	25
– bei unabänderlichen Tatsachen	– reporting unchanging facts	She **said** that she always **goes** there in the summer.	26
Infinitiv	infinitive		
– nach Verben des Wünschens etc.	– after requesting verbs	They **expect her to** join them. She **warned them not to** go there.	22
– Infinitiv oder Gerund?	– infinitive or gerund?	to stop **doing** sth. / to stop **to do** sth.	15
– Ergänzungen durch Infinitive	– adding information with infinitives	I want a book **to read** on holiday.	21
Konjunktionen	conjunctions	while, when, although, unless, as if	3
Kurzsätze / -antworten mit *so, neither, nor*	short statements / answers with *so, neither, nor*	I don't like it. – **Neither** do I.	7
Mengenangaben mit *some / any*	amounts with *some / any*	I'd like **some** bread. Have you got **any** butter?	12.3
Nebensätze	(subordinate) clauses	He stayed **because he wanted to**.	3

German / Latin	English	Example	Number
of-Genitiv	*of*-genitive	I enjoyed the last part **of** the story.	11
Partizip – Partizip und Infinitiv	participle – participle and infinitive	an **inviting** meal of **scrambled** egg I saw him **fall.** I heard him **crying**.	9 10
Passiv – mit *by-agent* – bei Verben mit 2 Objekten	passive voice – with by-agent – of verbs with 2 objects	The batteries **are checked** every week. The postman was bitten **by** our dog. We **were given** a warm welcome.	 20
Past perfect/Vorvergangenheit	past perfect	When I saw what he **had done** ...	4
Perfekt – mit *since* und *for*	present perfect – with *since* and *for*	**Have you seen** the film yet? I haven't seen her **since** last week.	
Phrasal verbs	phrasal verbs	to **look after** sth. / to **look** sth. **up**	33
Präposition in Endstellung	preposition in final position	something to look forward **to**	19
Präsens/Gegenwart	present	It often **rains**. It's **raining** again.	17
Präteritum (einfache Form)	simple past	It **was** nice. He **worked**. She **slept**.	
Proform	pro-form	I hope **so**. If **not** ...	27.3
Pronomen – *-self, -selves* (Reflexiv-pronomen) – *each other* (reziprokes Pronomen)	pronoun – *-self, -selves* (reflexive pronoun) – *each other* (reciprocal pronoun)	 He cut **himself.** You must help **yourselves.** We were a better team when we helped **each other**.	 27 27
Relativsätze – notwendige Relativsätze – nicht-notwendige Relativsätze – *which* in Satzgefügen	relative clauses – defining relative clauses – non-defining relative clauses – *which* referring to a whole sentence	 I've lost the CD **(which) you lent me**. Our doctor, **who lives in our street**, has got a new computer. I missed my bus, **which was a great way to start the day**.	29
s-Genitiv	*s*-genitive	What about Liz**'s** homework?	11
Singular und Plural unregelmäßige Plurale	singular and plural irregular plurals	butter, jeans bull**ies** / kni**ves** / child**ren** / **mice**	32 32
some und *any*	*some* and *any*	somebody, anything	27.2
Spaltsätze	cleft sentences	It was **the gardener** // who **did it**.	29.8
Verben mit zwei Objekten	verbs with two objects	She showed **her friend the new CD**.	20
Vergangenheit	past tenses	He **has gone. She arrived** yesterday.	
Verlaufsform	progressive form	I am (I was .../I have been ...) singing	17
Vor- und Nachsilben/Präfixe und Suffixe	prefixes and suffixes	re-, pre-, post-, un-, non-; -less, -ful	28
Wortbildung	word building	care/to care; to act/actor; to retest	2, 8, 28
Wortstellung in Sätzen mit Adverbien	word order in sentences with adverbs	**Yesterday** I saw her walking **slowly** down the road.	6
Would und *used to* bei früheren Gewohnheiten	*would* and *used to* for regular past activities	We **used to** have a boat. We **would** go sailing in it nearly every weekend.	30

Dictionary

In dieser alphabetischen Liste ist das gesamte Vokabular von **Swift 1–3** enthalten. Namen werden in gesonderten Listen am Ende dieses *Dictionary* aufgeführt. Mit ° versehene Wörter sind rezeptiv, Einträge in ⟨ ⟩ fakultativ. Ein ⁺ vor dem Eintrag bedeutet, dass das Wort zum Wortschatz in *Track* 2 in den Bänden 1 und 2 gehört. Die Belegstelle nach den Einträgen bezieht sich auf das erstmalige Vorkommen der Wörter:

to **afford** [ə'fɔ:d] sich leisten **III 1**, 12 = **Swift** 3, *Unit* 1, Seite 12

A

A-level ['eɪlevl] *britischer Schulabschluss, der mit dem Abitur vergleichbar ist* **III 6**, 111
⟨**a-glimmer**⟩ [ə'glɪmə] schimmernd **III E**, 140
a (+ *day, week, month*) [ə] pro **III 1**, 10
a, an [ə, ən] ein/eine **I**
  a bit [ə 'bɪt] ein wenig, ein bisschen **I**
  a couple (*of*) ['kʌpl‿əv] ein paar **II**
  (*a*) few [fju:] wenige, ein paar **I**
  a lot [ə 'lɒt] viel, eine Menge **I**
abbreviation [əˌbri:vi'eɪʃn] Abkürzung **III 5**, 101
⁺**ability** [ə'bɪləti] Fähigkeit **II**
to be **able to** ['eɪbl tə] fähig sein, in der Lage sein **II**
Australian **aborigine** [ɒs'treɪliən ˌæbə'rɪdʒni] australische(r) Ureinwohner(in) **II**
to be **about to do sth.** [ˌbi:‿ə'baʊt tə] im Begriff sein, etwas zu tun, etwas gerade tun wollen **III 5**, 94
about [ə'baʊt] über (etw), von (etw) **I**; ungefähr, etwa **I**
  to be about [ə'baʊt] sich handeln um **II**
  to talk (*about*) ['tɔ:k‿əˌbaʊt] sprechen, reden (über) **I**
  What about ...? [ˌwɒt‿ə'baʊt] Was ist mit ...? **I**
above [ə'bʌv] oben, oben genannt; oberhalb (von) **III 1**, 19
⟨**abroad**⟩ [ə'brɔ:d] im/ins Ausland **III 5**, 92
absolute [ˌæbsə'lu:t] völlig, absolut **II**
academy [ə'kædəmi] Akademie **II**
accent ['æksnt] Akzent **II**
to **accept** [ək'sept] annehmen, akzeptieren **II**
accident ['æksɪdnt] Unfall **I**
accommodation [əˌkɒmə'deɪʃn] Unterkunft, Hotelzimmer, Übernachtung **I**
according to [ə'kɔ:dɪŋ tʊ] nach, gemäß, laut, zufolge **III 6**, 111
accordion [ə'kɔ:diən] Akkordeon **II**
⟨**accusation**⟩ [ˌækjʊ'zeɪʃn] Anschuldigung, Anklage, Vorwurf **III 6**, 121
to **accuse** [ə'kju:z] beschuldigen, anklagen **III 6**, 112
stomach **ache** ['stʌmək‿eɪk] Magenschmerzen **II**
to **achieve** [ə'tʃi:v] erreichen, schaffen **III 4**, 70
achievement [ə'tʃi:vmənt] Leistung, Errungenschaft **II**
acre ['eɪkə] Morgen *(Flächenmaß, ca. 40,47 Ar)* **III 3**, 52
across [ə'krɒs] über, durch, darüber **I**
°**acrostic** [ə'krɒstɪk] Akrostichon *(nacheinander zu lesende Buchstaben, die ein Wort ergeben)* **I**
act [ækt] Akt, Aufzug **I**; ⟨Gesetz⟩ **III E**, 133
to **act** [ækt] darstellen, vorführen **I**
action ['ækʃn] Aktion, Handlung **I**
activity [æk'tɪvəti] Aktivität, Tätigkeit **I**
actor ['æktə] Schauspieler **I**
  supporting actor [səˌpɔ:tɪŋ‿'æktə] Schauspieler in einer Nebenrolle **II**
actress ['æktrəs] Schauspielerin **II**
actually ['æktʃuəli] tatsächlich, wirklich **II**
AD (= **Anno Domini**) [ˌeɪ'di:] nach Christus **II**
to **add** [æd] hinzufügen, addieren **I**
addiction [ə'dɪkʃn] Sucht **III 4**, 71
address [ə'dres] Adresse **I**
administrator [əd'mɪnɪstreɪtə] Verwalter(in), Leiter(in) **II**
⟨**adorable**⟩ [ə'dɔ:rəbl] bezaubernd, hinreißend **III E**, 130
⁺to **adore** [ə'dɔ:] anbeten, sehr gern haben **I**
adult ['ædʌlt] Erwachsene(r), Erwachsenen- **III 4**, 69
advantage [əd'vɑ:ntɪdʒ] Vorteil **III 1**, 11
adventure [əd'ventʃə] Abenteuer **I**
to **advertise** ['ædvətaɪz] werben, ankündigen **II**
ad (**advertisement**) [æd (əd'vɜ:tɪsmənt)] Anzeige **I**
advertising ['ædvətaɪzɪŋ] Werbung, Reklame **II**
advice [əd'vaɪs] Rat(schlag), Empfehlung **II**
aerobics [eə'rəʊbɪks] Aerobic, rhythmische Gymnastik **II**
to **affect** [ə'fekt] beeinflussen, sich auswirken auf **III 3**, 49
⟨**affirmative** *(AE)*⟩ [ə'fɜ:mətɪv] ja **III 2**, 34
to **afford** [ə'fɔ:d] sich leisten **III 1**, 12
to be **afraid** [ə'freɪd] sich fürchten, Angst haben **I**
African ['æfrɪkən] afrikanisch, Afrikanisch **II**
after ['ɑ:ftə] nach **I**
  after all [ˌɑ:ftə‿'ɔ:l] schließlich, letztendlich **I**
  to look after [ˌlʊk‿'ɑ:ftə] schauen nach, sorgen für **I**
afternoon [ˌɑ:ftə'nu:n] Nachmittag **I**
afterwards ['ɑ:ftəwədz] nachher, hinterher **III 1**, 17
again [ə'gen] wieder **I**
  again and again [əˌgen‿ənd‿ə'gen] immer wieder **III 1**, 13
  over and over again [ˌəʊvə‿ənd‿ˌəʊvə‿ə'gen] immer wieder, wieder und wieder **III 5**, 97
against [ə'gentst] gegen **I**
age [eɪdʒ] Alter **I**
  iron age ['aɪən‿ˌeɪdʒ] Eisenzeit **II**
agency ['eɪdʒntsi] Geschäftsstelle, Büro, Agentur **II**
agent ['eɪdʒnt] Agent(in), Vermittler(in) **III 1**, 12
  travel agent ['trævl ˌeɪdʒnt] Reisebüroangestellte(r) **II**
aggressive [ə'gresɪv] aggressiv, feindselig **II**
ago [ə'gəʊ] vor *(zeitlich)* **II**
  how long ago? [ˌhaʊ lɒŋ‿ə'gəʊ] wie lange her? **II**
to **agree** [ə'gri:] zustimmen **I**
⟨**agreement**⟩ [ə'gri:mənt] Zustimmung **III E**, 146
⟨**agriculture**⟩ ['ægrɪkʌltʃə] Landwirtschaft **III 3**, 52
ahead [ə'hed] voran, voraus **II**
  ahead of time [ə'hed‿əv 'taɪm] im Voraus **II**
first **aid** [ˌfɜ:st‿'eɪd] Erste Hilfe **II**
Aids [eɪdz] Aids **III 4**, 71
aim [eɪm] Ziel **III 4**, 67
⟨to **aim for**⟩ [eɪm] sich zum Ziel setzen **III E**, 144
⟨ain't (= **isn't**) (*coll.*)⟩ [eɪnt] ist nicht **III 1**, 14
air [eə] Luft **II**
  on air [ɒn‿'eə] auf Sendung **III 4**, 66
airmail ['eəmeɪl] Luftpost **II**
airport ['eəpɔ:t] Flughafen **I**
⟨**aisle**⟩ [aɪl] Mittelgang **III 1**, 13
alarm [ə'lɑ:m] Alarm **III 3**, 50
alcohol ['ælkəhɒl] Alkohol **I**
⁺**alien** ['eɪliən] Ausländer(in), Fremde(r) **I**
all [ɔ:l] alle(s) **I**
  after all [ˌɑ:ftə‿'ɔ:l] schließlich, letztendlich **I**
  all over ['ɔ:l‿əʊvə] überall (in) **II**
  all right [ɔ:l 'raɪt] in Ordnung **I**
  all the time [ˌɔ:l ðə 'taɪm] die ganze Zeit **II**
  all the year round [raʊnd] das ganze Jahr über **II**
  all-round fitness [ˌɔ:lraʊnd 'fɪtnəs] Rund-um-Fitness **II**
  (*not*) after all [ˌɑ:ftə‿'ɔ:l] doch (nicht) **I**
  not ... at all [ˌnɒt‿ə'tɔ:l] überhaupt nicht **I**
⁺**alleged** [ə'ledʒd] angeblich **II**
alligator ['ælɪgeɪtə] Alligator **II**
to **allow** [ə'laʊ] erlauben, gestatten **III 6**, 114
to be **allowed to** [ə'laʊd tʊ] dürfen **II**
almost ['ɔ:lməʊst] fast, beinahe **II**
alone [ə'ləʊn] allein **III 1**, 9
along [ə'lɒŋ] entlang, längs **I**
  Come along! ['kʌm‿əˌlɒŋ] Komm schon! **II**
  ⟨to string along⟩ [strɪŋ‿ə'lɒŋ] hinhalten **III E**, 130
alongside [əˌlɒŋ'saɪd] neben, entlang **III 5**, 90
aloud [ə'laʊd] laut **I**
alphabet ['ælfəbet] Alphabet **I**
alphabetical [ˌælfə'betɪkl] alphabetisch **III 5**, 101
already [ɔ:l'redi] schon, bereits **I**
also ['ɔ:lsəʊ] auch, ebenfalls **I**
alternative [ɔ:l'tɜ:nətɪv] Alternative **III 6**, 114
although [ɔ:l'ðəʊ] obwohl **III 1**, 16
altogether [ˌɔ:ltə'geðə] insgesamt, ganz **III 5**, 97
always ['ɔ:lweɪz] immer **I**
am [æm] bin **I**
  I'm (*I am*) [aɪm] ich bin **I**
to **amaze** [ə'meɪz] verblüffen **III 1**, 10
amazement [ə'meɪzmənt] Erstaunen, Verblüffung **II**
⟨**ambition**⟩ [æm'bɪʃn] Ehrgeiz **III E**, 144
ambitious [æm'bɪʃəs] ehrgeizig **II**
⟨**amendment**⟩ [ə'mendmənt] Zusatz (zur Verfassung) **III E**, 134
⁺**American** [ə'merɪkən] amerikanisch, Amerikaner(in) **I**
Native **American** [ˌneɪtɪv‿ə'merɪkən] amerikanische(r) Ureinwohner(in) **II**
among [ə'mʌŋ] zwischen, unter **I**
°**amplifier** ['æmplɪfaɪə] Verstärker **I**
amputation [ˌæmpjə'teɪʃn] Amputation **II**

to **amuse** (*oneself*) [əˈmjuːz] (sich) amüsieren **III 5**, 100
anaesthetic [ˌænəsˈθetɪk] Betäubungsmittel, Narkose **II**
and [ænd/ənd] und **I**
anger [ˈæŋgə] Ärger, Zorn **III 3**, 54
Angles [ˈæŋglz] (die) Angeln **II**
angry [ˈæŋgri] wütend, ärgerlich **I**
animal [ˈænɪml] Tier **I**
ankle [ˈæŋkl] Knöchel, Fußgelenk **II**
AD (= **Anno Domini**) [ˌeɪˈdiː] nach Christus **II**
announcement [əˈnaʊntsmənt] Ankündigung, Ansage **II**
annual [ˈænjuəl] jährlich, Jahres- **I**
anorexic [ˌænərˈeksɪk] magersüchtig **II**
another [əˈnʌðə] ein(e) andere(r/s) **I**; +ein(e) weitere(r/s) **I**
answer [ˈɑːntsə] Antwort **I**
to **answer** [ˈɑːntsə] antworten **I**
antibiotic [ˌæntɪbaɪˈɒtɪk] Antibiotikum **II**
antique [ænˈtiːk] Antik-, Antiquitäten **I**
°**antonym** [ˈæntənɪm] Antonym **II**
⟨**anvil**⟩ [ˈænvɪl] Amboss **III E**, 141
any [ˈeni] irgendeine(r/s), etwas **I**
  any time [ˌeni ˈtaɪm] jederzeit **I**
  not ... any more [ˌnɒt ... ˌeni ˈmɔː] (überhaupt) nicht mehr, keine ... mehr **II**
anybody [ˈenibɒdi] irgendjemand **I**
anyone [ˈeniwʌn] irgendjemand **I**
anyone [ˈeniwʌn] jeder (beliebige) **III 2**, 32
anything [ˈeniθɪŋ] etwas **I**
anyway [ˈeniweɪ] ohnehin, sowieso **I**
anywhere [ˈeniweə] irgendwohin **I**
apart [əˈpɑːt] auseinander **III 4**, 70
  apart from [əˈpɑːt frəm] außer, abgesehen von **III 6**, 111
apartment (*AE*) [əˈpɑːtmənt] Wohnung **III 1**, 15
to **apologise** [əˈpɒlədʒaɪz] sich entschuldigen **III 6**, 121
to **appear** [əˈpɪə] erscheinen, auftauchen **II**
appearance [əˈpɪərnts] Erscheinen, Auftauchen **II**
apple [ˈæpl] Apfel **II**
application [ˌæplɪˈkeɪʃn] Bewerbungsschreiben **II**
to **apply** (*to*) [əˈplaɪ] (sich) wenden (an) **I**
  to apply (*for*) [əˈplaɪ] sich bewerben (um/auf/für) **III 2**, 32
⟨to **appoint**⟩ [əˈpɔɪnt] ernennen **III E**, 134
appointment [əˈpɔɪntmənt] Termin, Verabredung **III 6**, 121
to **approach** [əˈprəʊtʃ] sich (an)nähern (an) **II**
April [ˈeɪprl] April **I**
apron [ˈeɪprən] Schürze **III 5**, 94
aquarium [əˈkweəriəm] Aquarium **I**
⟨**A&R man**⟩ [ˌeɪ‿ənd‿ˈɑː mæn] (= Artistes and Repertoire man) *Mann bei einer Plattenfirma, der die Künstler betreut* **III 1**, 12
are [ɑː] sind **I**
  aren't (*are not*) [ɑːnt] sind nicht **I**
area [ˈeəriə] Gebiet, Region, Areal **I**
⟨to **argue**⟩ [ˈɑːgjuː] argumentieren, streiten **III E**, 135
argument [ˈɑːgjəmənt] Argument; Streit, Auseinandersetzung **II**
⟨to **arise***⟩ [əˈraɪz] aufstehen **III E**, 140
arm [ɑːm] Arm **I**
⟨**armadillo**⟩ [ˌɑːməˈdɪləʊ] Gürteltier **III 4**, 70
⟨**armpit**⟩ [ˈɑːmpɪt] Achselhöhle **III E**, 139
army [ˈɑːmi] Armee, Heer **II**
around [əˈraʊnd] etwa, ungefähr **III 1**, 10; um ... herum **I**; umher **I**
to **arrange** [əˈreɪndʒ] arrangieren, vereinbaren, ordnen, planen **III 1**, 10
arrangement [əˈreɪndʒmənt] Arrangement, Vereinbarung, Verabredung, Plan **III 4**, 77
arrest [əˈrest] Verhaftung **III 5**, 91
to **arrest** [əˈrest] festnehmen, verhaften **II**
+to get **arrested** [ˌget‿əˈrestɪd] festgenommen werden, verhaftet werden **II**
arrival [əˈraɪvl] Ankunft **I**
to **arrive** [əˈraɪv] ankommen **II**
art [ɑːt] Kunst **II**
Art [ɑːt] °Kunst (*Fach*) **I**
article [ˈɑːtɪkl] (Zeitungs-)Artikel **I**
artist [ˈɑːtɪst] Künstler(in) **III 3**, 60
⟨**artistic**⟩ [ɑːˈtɪstɪk] künstlerisch, kunstsinnig **III E**, 144
as [æz/əz] als, während **II**; da **III 1**, 16; wie **II**
  as it were [æz‿ɪt ˈwɜː] sozusagen, gleichsam **III 5**, 95
  as soon as [əzˈsuːn‿əz] sobald **III 1**, 16
  as though [əz ˈðəʊ] als ob **III 4**, 70
  as well as [əz ˈwel‿əz] sowie, sowohl als auch **II**
  as ... as [æz/əz] (eben)so ... wie **I**
  such as [ˈsʌtʃ‿əz] wie zum Beispiel **II**
to set **aside** [ˌset‿əˈsaɪd] einplanen, beiseite legen **III 6**, 112
to **ask** [ɑːsk] fragen **I**
  to ask so. to do sth. [ɑːsk] jmdn bitten, etw zu tun **II**
to be **asleep** [əˈsliːp] schlafen **II**
  to fall asleep [ˌfɔːl‿əˈsliːp] einschlafen **II**
aspect [ˈæspekt] Gesichtspunkt, Aspekt **II**
assembly [əˈsembli] (Schul-)Versammlung **I**
  assembly hall [əˈsembli ˌhɔːl] Aula, Versammlungssaal **I**
assistant [əˈsɪstnt] Assistent(in), Mitarbeiter(in) **III 6**, 111
⟨to **associate**⟩ [əˈsəʊʃieɪt] assoziieren, in Verbindung bringen **III E**, 137
⟨**association**⟩ [əˌsəʊʃiˈeɪʃn] Verband **III 2**, 43
astronaut [ˈæstrənɔːt] Astronaut(in) **II**
astronomer [əˈstrɒnəmə] Astronom(in) **II**
astronomy [əˈstrɒnəmi] Astronomie **I**
at last [ət ˈlɑːst] endlich **III 1**, 13
at [æt/ət] an/am, in/im, bei **I**
  at home [ət‿ˈhəʊm] zu Hause, daheim **I**
  +at last [ət ˈlɑːst] endlich **II**
  at least [ət ˈliːst] zumindest **II**
  at the moment [ˈməʊmənt] im Moment, zur Zeit **I**
  to go at so. [ˈgəʊ ˌət] auf jmdn losgehen **II**
athlete [ˈæθliːt] Leichtathlet(in), Sportler(in) **II**
athletics [æθˈletɪks] Leichtathletik **II**
atmosphere [ˈætməsfɪə] Atmosphäre **I**
to **attach** [əˈtætʃ] ⟨befestigen, anhängen⟩ **III E**, 136; ⟨beimessen⟩ **III E**, 144
attack [əˈtæk] Angriff **II**
  heart attack [ˈhɑːt‿əˌtæk] Herzinfarkt **I**
to **attack** [əˈtæk] angreifen **II**
to **attempt** [əˈtempt] versuchen **III 6**, 120
to **attend** [əˈtend] beiwohnen, besuchen **II**
⟨restroom **attendant**⟩ [ˈrestruːm‿əˌtendənt] Toilettenmann/-frau **III 1**, 20
+to pay **attention** [ˌpeɪ‿əˈtentʃn] aufmerksam sein, achtsam sein **I**
  to draw attention to [ˌdrɔː‿əˈtentʃn] Aufmerksamkeit ziehen auf **II**
+**attic** [ˈætɪk] Dachboden **I**
attitude [ˈætɪtjuːd] Einstellung, Haltung **III 4**, 71
to **attract** [əˈtrækt] anziehen, anlocken **II**
attraction [əˈtrækʃn] Besonderheit, Attraktion **I**
attractive [əˈtræktɪv] attraktiv, anziehend **III 4**, 71
audience [ˈɔːdiənts] Publikum, Zuhörer **II**
⟨**auditorium**⟩ [ˌɔːdɪˈtɔːriəm] Zuschauerraum **III 1**, 13
August [ˈɔːgəst] August **I**
aunt [ɑːnt] Tante **I**
Australian aborigine [ɒsˈtreɪliən ˌæbəˈrɪdʒni] australische(r) Ureinwohner(in) **II**
author [ˈɔːθə] Autor(in) **II**
authority [ɔːˈθɒrəti] Amt, Behörde **II**
+**autumn** (*BE*) [ˈɔːtəm] Herbst **I**
available [əˈveɪləbl] verfügbar **III 3**, 51
+**avenue** [ˈævənjuː] Allee, (breite) Straße **I**
average [ˈævrɪdʒ] Durchschnitt **I**
to **avoid** [əˈvɔɪd] meiden, vermeiden **III 1**, 11
to **awaken** [əˈweɪkn] aufwecken, aufwachen **II**
award [əˈwɔːd] Preis, Auszeichnung **II**
away [əˈweɪ] weg, fort **I**
  right away [ˌraɪt‿əˈweɪ] sofort **II**
  straight away [ˌstreɪt‿əˈweɪ] sofort **III 1**, 10
awesome [ˈɔːsəm] ehrfurchtgebietend **III 3**, 53
awful [ˈɔːfl] scheußlich, fürchterlich **I**
⟨**axle**⟩ [ˈæksl] Achse **III E**, 141

B

⟨**babe** (*coll.*)⟩ [beɪb] Baby, Puppe, Mädchen, Kleines **III 4**, 68
baby [ˈbeɪbi] Baby **I**
  baby sister [ˌbeɪbi ˈsɪstə] (ganz) kleine Schwester **I**
back [bæk] Rücken **II**
  at the back [bæk] hinten **II**
⟨to be right **back**⟩ [biː ˈraɪt ˌbæk] gleich zurück sein **III 1**, 10
back [bæk] zurück, Hinter- **I**
  to drop back [drɒp ˈbæk] zurückfallen **II**
  to get back [get ˈbæk] zurückkommen, ankommen **II**
  to report back [rɪˌpɔːt ˈbæk] sich zurückmelden **II**
⟨to **backfire**⟩ [ˌbækˈfaɪə] fehlzünden **III 1**, 13
backgammon [ˈbækgæmən] *Name eines Brettspiels* **I**
background [ˈbækgraʊnd] Hintergrund, Herkunft **III 2**, 34
⟨**backlash**⟩ [ˈbæklæʃ] Gegenschlag **III E**, 142
bacon [ˈbeɪkn] Speck **I**
bad [bæd] böse, schlecht **I**
  in a bad way [ˌbæd ˈweɪ] in einem schlechten Zustand **II**
badminton [ˈbædmɪntən] Badminton, Federball **III 6**, 123
bag [bæg] Tüte, Tasche **I**
  mixed bag [ˌmɪkst ˈbæg] bunte Mischung, Allerlei **III 5**, 96
  sleeping bag [ˈsliːpɪŋ ˌbæg] Schlafsack **I**
baggage [ˈbægɪdʒ] Gepäck **I**
bagpipes [ˈbægpaɪps] Dudelsack **II**
bakery [ˈbeɪkri] Bäckerei **II**
⟨checks and **balances**⟩ [ˌtʃeks‿ənd ˈbæləntsɪz] Sicherungssystem gegenseitiger Kontrolle **III E**, 134
bald [bɔːld] kahl, glatzköpfig **II**
ball [bɔːl] Ball **I**; Kugel **III 4**, 71
⟨**bam!**⟩ [bæm] Bumm! **III 3**, 50
to **ban** [bæn] verbieten, auf den Index setzen **III 4**, 72
banana [bəˈnɑːnə] Banane **I**
band [bænd] Musikgruppe, Band **I**
  ⟨brass band⟩ [ˌbrɑːs ˈbænd] Blaskapelle **III 4**, 73
  marching band [ˈmɑːtʃɪŋ ˌbænd] Marschkapelle **II**
bandleader [ˈbændˌliːdə] Leiter(in) einer Musikgruppe **I**
⟨**bang**⟩ [bæŋ] Knall **III 1**, 13
banjo [ˈbændʒəʊ] Banjo **II**
bank [bæŋk] Bank, Geldinstitut **I**
  bank robber [ˈbæŋk ˌrɒbə] Bankräuber(in) **I**
  bottle bank [ˈbɒtl ˌbæŋk] Altglascontainer **II**
bank holiday [ˌbæŋk ˈhɒlədeɪ] Feiertag (im Mai und August) **II**
bar [bɑː] Bar, Kneipe **II**
  coffee bar [ˈkɒfi ˌbɑː] (kleines) Café **I**
+**barbecue** [ˈbɑːbɪkjuː] Grill (*im Freien*) **II**
bare [beə] nackt, bloß **II**
bargain [ˈbɑːgɪn] Handel; günstiges Angebot, Schnäppchen **III 1**, 9
to **bark** [bɑːk] bellen **I**
barrack [ˈbærək] Kaserne, Baracke **II**
barrier [ˈbæriə] Schranke, Sperre, Barriere **II**
baseball [ˈbeɪsbɔːl] Baseball **I**

to be **based in** ['beɪst ɪn] in ... seinen/ihren Sitz haben **III 6**, 117
basic ['beɪsɪk] grundlegend, Grund-, Basis- **II**
basket ['bɑ:skɪt] Korb **I**
basketball ['bɑ:skɪtbɔ:l] Basketball **I**
°**bass** [beɪs] Bass **I**
+**bat** [bæt] Schlagholz **II**
bathroom ['bɑ:θrʊm] Bad, Badezimmer **I**
+**batter** ['bætə] Schlagmann **II**
+spare **battery** [ˌspeə 'bætri] Ersatzbatterie **I**
battery-powered ['bætriˌpaʊəd] batteriebetrieben **II**
⟨**battle**⟩ ['bætl] Schlacht **III E**, 142
bay [beɪ] Bucht, Bai **I**
BBC [ˌbi:bi:'si:] *(Rundfunkanstalt)* **III 4**, 72
BC (= **before Christ**) [ˌbi:'si:] vor Christus **II**
to **be*** [bi:] sein **I**
beach [bi:tʃ] Strand **I**
beachgoer ['bi:tʃˌgəʊə] Strandurlauber(in) **I**
beachwatch ['bi:tʃwɒtʃ] Strandaufsicht, Strandwärter(in) **I**
laser **beam** ['leɪzə ˌbi:m] Laserstrahl **II**
⟨**bean-row**⟩ ['bi:n rəʊ] Bohnenreihe **III E**, 140
⟨jelly bean⟩ ['dʒeli bi:n] Geleebonbon **III E**, 131
teddy **bear** ['tedi ˌbeə] Teddybär **I**
to **bear*** [beə] ertragen, aushalten **II**
to **beat*** [bi:t] schlagen, besiegen **II**
⟨to beat time⟩ [bi:t 'taɪm] den Takt schlagen **III 1**, 13
beautiful ['bju:tɪfl] schön **I**
because [bɪ'kɒz] weil, da **I**
because of [bɪ'kɒz‿əv] wegen **II**
to **become*** [bɪ'kʌm] werden **II**
bed [bed] Bett **I**
bed and breakfast *(B&B)* [ˌbed‿n‿'brekfəst] Frühstückspension **I**
bedroom ['bedrʊm] Schlafzimmer **I**
beep [bi:p] Piepsen **II**
beer [bɪə] Bier **III 5**, 97
before [bɪ'fɔ:] vor **I**
BC (= *before Christ*) [ˌbi:'si:] vor Christus **II**
beggar ['begə] Bettler(in) **II**
to **begin*** [bɪ'gɪn] beginnen, anfangen **II**
+**beginner** [bɪ'gɪnə] Anfänger(in) **I**
beginning [bɪ'gɪnɪŋ] Anfang, Beginn **I**
to **behave** [bɪ'heɪv] sich benehmen, sich verhalten **III 6**, 113
behind [bɪ'haɪnd] hinter **I**
behind the scenes [bɪˌhaɪnd ðə 'si:nz] hinter den Kulissen **III 4**, 66
being ['bi:ɪŋ] (Lebe-)Wesen, Geschöpf **II**
to **believe** [bɪ'li:v] glauben **I**
bell [bel] Glocke **I**
⟨**bellows**⟩ ['beləʊz] Blasebalg **III E**, 141
to **belong to** [bɪ'lɒŋ tʊ] gehören (zu) **II**
below [bɪ'ləʊ] unterhalb, unten **I**
⟨**belt**⟩ [belt] Gürtel **III 3**, 52
bend [bend] Biegung, Kurve **II**
to **bend*** [bend] biegen, beugen, knicken **II**
bending ['bendɪŋ] Beugen **II**
benefit ['benɪfɪt] Vorteil, Nutzen **II**
to **benefit** ['benɪfɪt] profitieren, gut tun, nützen **III 6**, 112
beside [bɪ'saɪd] neben **II**
besides [bɪ'saɪdz] außerdem **II**
best [best] beste(r/s), der/die Beste **I**
bet [bet] Wette **II**
to **bet*** [bet] wetten **I**
better ['betə] besser **I**
better to be safe than sorry lieber auf Nummer sicher gehen **II**
between [bɪ'twi:n] zwischen **I**
beyond [bɪ'ɒnd] jenseits, über ... hinaus **III 3**, 53
bhangra ['bæŋgrə] *Musikrichtung aus Indien* **I**
bicycle ['baɪsɪkl] Fahrrad **II**
big [bɪg] groß **I**
bike [baɪk] (Fahr-)Rad **I**
exercise bike ['eksəsaɪz ˌbaɪk] Hometrainer **II**
mountain bike ['maʊntɪn ˌbaɪk] Geländefahrrad, Mountainbike **I**
bill [bɪl] ⟨Gesetzesvorlage⟩ **III E**, 135; Rechnung **I**
billion ['bɪliən] Billion, Milliarde *(AE)* **II**
Biology [baɪ'ɒlədʒi] Biologie **I**
biotechnology [ˌbaɪəʊtek'nɒlədʒi] Biotechnologie **III 6**, 115
bird [bɜ:d] Vogel **I**
+to **birdwatch** ['bɜ:dwɒtʃ] Vögel beobachten **I**
birdwatching ['bɜ:dˌwɒtʃɪŋ] Vögel beobachten **II**
biro ['baɪərəʊ] Kuli, Kugelschreiber **I**
birthday ['bɜ:θdeɪ] Geburtstag **I**
⟨**birthplace**⟩ ['bɜ:θpleɪs] Geburtsort **III 2**, 32
bit [bɪt] Stück(chen), Teil **I**
a bit [ə 'bɪt] ein wenig, ein bisschen **I**
to **bite*** [baɪt] beißen **II**
black [blæk] schwarz **I**
blackboard ['blækbɔ:d] Tafel **I**
blackout ['blækaʊt] Verdunkelung, Stromausfall **II**
to **blame** [bleɪm] beschuldigen, die Schuld zuschreiben **III 4**, 70
blank [blæŋk] leer **III 4**, 81
blanket ['blæŋkɪt] (Woll-)Decke **II**
potato **blight** [pə'teɪtəʊ ˌblaɪt] Kartoffelfäule **III 5**, 91
blind ['blaɪnd] blind **II**
+colour-blind ['kʌləblaɪnd] farbenblind **I**
blinding ['blaɪndɪŋ] blendend **II**
block [blɒk] (Häuser-)Block **III 2**, 33
bloke *(coll.)* [bləʊk] Kerl, Typ **II**
bloody ['blʌdi] verdammt **III 6**, 120
to **blow*** [bləʊ] wehen, blasen **III 2**, 37
⟨to blow one's mind out *(sl.)*⟩ [ˌbləʊ wʌnz 'maɪnd‿aʊt] umwerfen; high machen, sich berauschen **III 4**, 72
to blow up [ˌbləʊ‿'ʌp] aufblasen, aufpumpen **II**
blue [blu:] blau **I**
blues [blu:z] Blues *(Musikrichtung)* **II**
⟨slightly **bluish**⟩ [ˌslaɪtli 'blu:ɪʃ] leicht bläulich **III E**, 139
⟨to **bluster**⟩ ['blʌstə] toben **III E**, 144
board [bɔ:d] Brett, Tafel **I**
notice board ['nəʊtɪs ˌbɔ:d] schwarzes Brett, Anschlagtafel **I**
on board [ɒn 'bɔ:d] an Bord **II**
+to **board up** [ˌbɔ:d‿'ʌp] verschalen, mit Brettern vernageln **I**
boat [bəʊt] Boot **I**
boating ['bəʊtɪŋ] Bootfahren **III 3**, 52
body ['bɒdi] Körper **II**
⟨body count⟩ ['bɒdi kaʊnt] Anzahl der Menschen, Anzahl der Leichen **III 4**, 69
bodyguard ['bɒdigɑ:d] Leibwache **II**
boiler ['bɔɪlə] Boiler, Warmwasserbereiter **III 6**, 120
bone [bəʊn] Knochen **II**
to **boo** [bu:] auspfeifen, ausbuhen **II**
book [bʊk] Buch **I**
exercise book ['eksəsaɪz ˌbʊk] Übungsheft, Heft **I**
guide book ['gaɪd bʊk] Reiseführer *(Buch)* **I**
bookie ['bʊki] Buchmacher(in) **II**
bookshop ['bʊkʃɒp] Buchhandlung **I**
to **boom** [bu:m] boomen, florieren, einen Aufschwung nehmen **III 6**, 111
⟨**boost**⟩ [bu:st] Auftrieb, Verstärkung **III 4**, 68
boot [bu:t] Stiefel **I**
booth [bu:θ] Bude, Stand, Kabine, Zahlstelle **III 2**, 34
border ['bɔ:də] Grenze **II**
bore [bɔ:] Langweiler(in), langweilig(e Sache) **III 5**, 98
to get **bored** [bɔ:d] sich langweilen **II**
boring ['bɔ:rɪŋ] langweilig **I**
to be **born** [bɔ:n] geboren sein **II**
to **borrow** ['bɒrəʊ] (aus)leihen **I**
boss [bɒs] Chef(in), Boss, Vorgesetzte(r) **III 2**, 42
both [bəʊθ] beide **I**
to **bother** ['bɒðə] belästigen, plagen **I**
to bother about ['bɒðə‿əˌbaʊt] sich kümmern um **II**
bottle ['bɒtl] Flasche **I**
bottle bank ['bɒtl ˌbæŋk] Altglascontainer **II**
bottled ['bɒtld] in Flaschen (abgefüllt) **II**
bottom ['bɒtəm] Po **II**; unteres Ende, Fuß **I**
bouncy castle [ˌbaʊntsi 'kɑ:sl] (aufblasbare) Hüpfburg **I**
+**bowler** ['bəʊlə] *(Kricket)* Werfer(in) **II**
box [bɒks] Kiste, Schachtel **I**
cash box ['kæʃbɒks] Geldkassette **III 1**, 14
boxers *(pl.)* ['bɒksəz] Boxershorts **II**
boy [bɔɪ] Junge **I**
boyfriend ['bɔɪfrend] Freund **I**
bps (= **bits per second**) ['bi:'pi:'es] *Übertragungsgeschwindigkeit eines Modems* **I**
brain [breɪn] Gehirn **II**
brake [breɪk] Bremse **II**
⟨**branch**⟩ [brɑ:ntʃ] Zweig, Teil **III E**, 134
⟨**brand new**⟩ [ˌbrænd 'nju:] brandneu **III 2**, 30
⟨**brass band**⟩ [ˌbrɑ:s 'bænd] Blaskapelle **III 4**, 73
brave [breɪv] tapfer, mutig **II**
bread [bred] Brot **I**
⟨stick of French bread⟩ [ˌstɪk‿əv ˌfrentʃ 'bred] Stange Baguette **III E**, 139
break [breɪk] Pause **I**
to **break*** [breɪk] (zer)brechen, knacken **II**
⟨to break away⟩ [ˌbreɪk‿ə'weɪ] sich lossagen **III E**, 132
to break down [breɪk 'daʊn] eine Panne haben; zusammenbrechen **III 1**, 17
⟨to break up⟩ [breɪk‿'ʌp] sich trennen **III E**, 138
breakdown ['breɪkdaʊn] Panne; Zusammenbruch **III 1**, 13
breakfast ['brekfəst] Frühstück **I**
bed and breakfast *(B&B)* [ˌbed‿n‿'brekfəst] Frühstückspension **I**
breakneck speed [ˌbreɪknek 'spi:d] halsbrecherische Geschwindigkeit **III 4**, 70
⟨**breast**⟩ [brest] Brust **III E**, 130
Breton ['bretn] bretonisch; Bretone **II**
brewery ['bru:ri] Brauerei **III 5**, 98
bridge [brɪdʒ] Brücke **I**
watching **brief** ['wɒtʃɪŋ ˌbri:f] Beobachtungsauftrag **II**
⟨to **brief**⟩ [bri:f] instruieren **III 5**, 92
⟨**brief**⟩ [bri:f] kurz **III 1**, 13
bright [braɪt] hell, leuchtend **III 4**, 73
brightly ['braɪtli] hell, leuchtend **II**
⟨**brights** *(AE)*⟩ [braɪts] Fernlicht **III 2**, 34
to **bring*** [brɪŋ] bringen **I**
British ['brɪtɪʃ] britisch **I**
Briton ['brɪtn] Brite/Britin **II**
to **broadcast*** ['brɔ:dkɑ:st] senden, ausstrahlen, übertragen **III 4**, 66
broadsheet ['brɔ:dʃi:t] großformatige Zeitung **III 4**, 66
brochure ['brəʊʃə] Broschüre, Prospekt **I**
(exchange) **broker** [ɪks'tʃeɪndʒ ˌbrəʊkə] Börsenmakler(in), Devisenhändler(in) **III 2**, 30
brother ['brʌðə] Bruder **I**
brotherhood ['brʌðəhʊd] Bruderschaft, Bund **III 5**, 91
brown [braʊn] braun **I**
to **brush** [brʌʃ] bürsten, putzen **III 3**, 51; ⟨streifen⟩ **III E**, 130
⟨**bubble gum**⟩ ['bʌblgʌm] Blasenkaugummi **III 1**, 13
speech bubble ['spi:tʃ ˌbʌbl] Sprechblase **II**
buck *(AE)* *(coll.)* [bʌk] Dollar **II**
⟨**buddy** *(AE)*⟩ ['bʌdi] Kumpel **III 2**, 34
to **build*** [bɪld] (er)bauen **II**
builder ['bɪldə] ⟨Bauarbeiter⟩ **III E**, 138; +Erbauer(in), Begründer(in) **II**
building ['bɪldɪŋ] Gebäude **I**
bulimia [bʊ'lɪmiə] Bulimie, Ess-/Brechsucht **III 4**, 71
⟨**bull**⟩ [bʊl] Stier **III E**, 136
⟨**bullfight**⟩ ['bʊlfaɪt] Stierkampf **III E**, 136
bully, *(pl.)* -ies ['bʊli] Schlägertyp, Angeber(in) **I**

⟨to **bump into so.**⟩ [bʌmp] jmdn anstoßen **III E**, 130
bumper ['bʌmpə] Stoßstange **III 4**, 70
bungalow ['bʌŋgləʊ] Bungalow **II**
to **burn* up** [ˌbɜːn_'ʌp] verbrennen, verbrauchen **II**
to **bury** ['beri] begraben, beerdigen **III 5**, 90
bus [bʌs] Bus **I**
bus stop ['bʌs stɒp] Bushaltestelle **I**
double decker bus [ˌdʌbl dekə 'bʌs] Doppeldeckerbus **I**
bush [bʊʃ] Busch **II**
business ['bɪznɪs] Angelegenheit, Sache **II**; Geschäft **II**
businesslike ['bɪznɪslaɪk] geschäftstüchtig; nüchtern **II**
businessman ['bɪznɪsmæn] Geschäftsmann **II**
⟨to **busk**⟩ [bʌsk] Straßenmusik machen **III 1**, 23
busker ['bʌskə] Straßenmusikant(in) **III 5**, 97
to be **busy** ['bɪzi] beschäftigt sein **I**
but [bʌt] außer, bis auf, als **III 6**, 113
but [bʌt] aber **I**
butter ['bʌtə] Butter **II**
button ['bʌtn] Knopf, Schalter **II**
to **buy*** [baɪ] kaufen **I**
buzz [bʌz] ⟨euphorisches Hochgefühl⟩ **III 4**, 68; ⟨Reiz⟩ **III E**, 144
buzz-game ['bʌzˌgeɪm] *Name eines Spiels* **I**
by [baɪ] an, neben, bis **I**; von, durch **II**
by (+ *gerund*) [baɪ] durch, indem **III 2**, 32
by chance [ˌbaɪ 'tʃɑːnts] zufällig **III 5**, 95
⟨by now⟩ [baɪ 'naʊ] inzwischen **III E**, 143
to learn by heart [ˌlɜːn baɪ 'hɑːt] auswendig lernen **II**

C

cab [kæb] Taxi **III 2**, 30
⁺tossing the **caber** [ˌtɒsɪŋ ðə 'keɪbə] Baumstammwerfen *(schottische Sportart)* **II**
⟨**cabin**⟩ ['kæbɪn] Hütte **III E**, 140
cable ['keɪbl] Kabel **III 4**, 66
café ['kæfeɪ] Café **I**
motorway café ['məʊtəweɪ ˌkæfeɪ] Cafeteria auf der Autobahn **I**
cafeteria [ˌkæfə'tɪəriə] Cafeteria **I**
⁺**cage** [keɪdʒ] Käfig **I**
cake [keɪk] Kuchen **II**
calendar ['kæləndə] Kalender **I**
(phone) **call** [('fəʊn) kɔːl] Anruf **I**
to **call** [kɔːl] nennen, (an)rufen **I**
to be called [kɔːld] genannt werden; heißen **II**
⟨to call sth. off⟩ [kɔːl_'ɒf] abblasen, absagen **III 4**, 79
to **calm down** [kɑːm 'daʊn] sich beruhigen **III 2**, 34
calorie ['kælri] Kalorie **II**
camera ['kæmrə] Kamera, Fotoapparat **I**
cameraman ['kæmrəmæn] Kameramann **II**
camp [kæmp] (Ferien-)Lager **I**
to **camp** [kæmp] zelten **I**
campervan ['kæmpəˌvæn] Wohnwagen **I**
camping ['kæmpɪŋ] Zelten **I**
campsite ['kæmpsaɪt] Campingplatz **I**
can opener ['kæn ˌəʊpnə] Dosenöffner **II**
can [kæn] kann **I**
canal [kə'næl] Kanal **I**
canvas ['kænvəs] Segeltuch **II**
canyon *(AE)* ['kænjən] Schlucht **III 3**, 53
cap [kæp] Kappe, (Schirm-)Mütze **I**
capital ['kæpɪtl] Hauptstadt **I**
capital letter [ˌkæpɪtl 'letə] Großbuchstabe **I**
⟨space **capsule**⟩ ['speɪs ˌkæpsjuːl] Raumkapsel **III E**, 135
captain ['kæptɪn] Kapitän **I**
caption ['kæpʃn] Bildunterschrift, -überschrift **III 6**, 110
car [kɑː] Auto **I**
car crash ['kɑː ˌkræʃ] Autounfall **III 4**, 70
car park ['kɑː pɑːk] Parkplatz **I**
car rental ['kɑː ˌrentl] Autovermietung **I**
flash **card** ['flæʃ ˌkɑːd] Illustrationstafel, Flashcard **II**
credit card ['kredɪt ˌkɑːd] Kreditkarte **II**
to **care** [keə] sich kümmern, Interesse haben **III 1**, 8
she didn't care [keə] es war ihr egal **II**
to care *(about)* [keə] sich Sorgen machen (um) **II**
would you care to? [ˌwʊd juː 'keə] hätten Sie Lust (zu)? **II**
⟨**career**⟩ [kə'rɪə] Karriere **III E**, 138
careful ['keəfʊl] vorsichtig **I**
Caribbean [ˌkærɪ'biːən] karibisch; Karibik **II**
carnival ['kɑːnɪvl] Karneval **II**
carriage ['kærɪdʒ] Kutsche **III 6**, 114
carrot juice ['kærət ˌdʒuːs] Karottensaft **II**
to **carry** ['kæri] tragen **I**
⟨to carry a tune⟩ [ˌkæri_ə 'tjuːn] eine Melodie richtig singen **III 1**, 13
cartoon [kɑː'tuːn] Witzzeichnung **I**
cartoonist [kɑː'tuːnɪst] Karikaturenzeichner(in) **II**
⟨ivory **carving**⟩ ['aɪvrɪ ˌkɑːvɪŋ] Elfenbeinschnitzerei **III E**, 136
case [keɪs] Fall, Sache **II**
in case [keɪs] falls **II**
pencil case ['pentsl ˌkeɪs] Federmäppchen **I**
cash [kæʃ] Bargeld, Kleingeld **III 1**, 14
cash box ['kæʃbɒks] Geldkassette **III 1**, 14
extra cash [ˌekstrə 'kæʃ] Zuschlag, Sonderzahlung **II**
⟨**to cash it in**⟩ [ˌkæʃ_ɪt_'ɪn] einlösen, hinschmeißen, Schluss machen **III 1**, 8
cashier [kæ'ʃɪə] Kassierer(in) **III 6**, 111
casino [kə'siːnəʊ] Kasino **III 3**, 56
cassette [kə'set] Kassette **I**
cast [kɑːst] (Rollen-)Besetzung, Ensemble **II**
castle ['kɑːsl] Burg, Schloss **I**
bouncy castle [ˌbaʊntsi 'kɑːsl] (aufblasbare) Hüpfburg **I**
cat [kæt] Katze **I**
to rain cats and dogs ['reɪn ˌkæts_n_'dɒgz] heftig regnen, schütten, gießen **I**
catastrophic [ˌkætə'strɒfɪk] katastrophal **II**
to **catch*** [kætʃ] fangen; (einen Bus) erreichen **II**
category ['kætəgri] Kategorie, Klasse **II**
cause [kɔːz] Ursache, Grund **III 3**, 51
to **cause** [kɔːz] verursachen, hervorrufen, anrichten **I**
cave [keɪv] Höhle **I**
CD [ˌsiː'diː] CD *(Compact Disc)* **I**
to **cease** [siːs] enden, aufhören **III 6**, 120
celebrity [sə'lebrəti] Berühmtheit **II**
⟨celeb⟩ [səl'eb] *Abkürzung für* 'celebrity' **III 1**, 9
⁺**cellar** ['selə] Keller **I**
cello ['tʃeləʊ] Cello **I**
⁺**Celsius** ['selsiəs] Celsius **I**
Celt [kelt] Kelte/Keltin **II**
Celtic ['keltɪk] keltisch, Keltisch **II**
cent [sent] Cent, *Währungseinheit in den USA* **III 6**, 119
central ['sentrl] zentral **III 5**, 91
centre ['sentə] Zentrum **I**
sports centre ['spɔːts ˌsentə] Sportzentrum, Sportanlage **I**
century ['sentʃəri] Jahrhundert **III 2**, 32
ceremony ['serɪməni] Zeremonie, Feierlichkeit **II**
certain ['sɜːtn] bestimmt, gewiss **II**
certainly ['sɜːtnli] gewiss, sicherlich **II**
chain [tʃeɪn] Kette **III 1**, 12
chair ['tʃeə] Stuhl **I**
chairperson ['tʃeəˌpɜːsn] Vorsitzende(r) **III 3**, 58
chalk [tʃɔːk] Kreide **I**
chance [tʃɑːnts] Gelegenheit, Chance **II**
by chance [ˌbaɪ 'tʃɑːnts] zufällig **III 5**, 95
change ['tʃeɪndʒ] Wandel, Wechsel, Umschwung **II**
to **change** [tʃeɪndʒ] ändern; umsteigen **I**
⟨to change one's mind⟩ [ˌtʃeɪndʒ wʌnz 'maɪnd] seine Meinung ändern **III E**, 131
channel ['tʃænl] Kanal, Programm **III 4**, 66
character ['kærəktə] Charakter **I**
characteristic [ˌkærəktə'rɪstɪk] charakteristisch, kennzeichnend **II**
to be in **charge of sth.** [ɪn 'tʃɑːdʒ_əv] die Aufsicht haben über etw **II**
charity ['tʃærɪti] Wohltätigkeit **I**
charm [tʃɑːm] Charme **I**
⟨**Chartists**⟩ ['tʃɑːtɪsts] Chartisten **III E**, 147
⟨the **charts**⟩ [tʃɑːts] Hitparade **III 1**, 12
to **chase** [tʃeɪs] (herum)jagen **I**
chat [tʃæt] Unterhaltung, Plauderei (auch im Internet) **III 1**, 10
to **chat** [tʃæt] plaudern, chatten **III 1**, 10
chatroom ['tʃætrʊm] Chatroom *(Forum im Internet, wo man sich online unterhalten kann)* **III 1**, 10
cheap [tʃiːp] billig **I**
check [tʃek] ⟨Kontrolle⟩ **III E**, 147
check-in ['tʃekɪn] Abfertigungsschalter (am Flughafen), Einchecken **I**
check-out ['tʃekaʊt] Abschlusskontrolle, Auschecken **I**
⟨checks and balances⟩ [ˌtʃeks_ənd 'bæləntsɪz] Sicherungssystem gegenseitiger Kontrolle **III E**, 134
sound check ['saʊn(d) tʃek] Klang-, Tonkontrolle **I**
to **check** [tʃek] kontrollieren, überprüfen **I**
checklist ['tʃeklɪst] Kontrollliste, Checkliste **II**
cheek [tʃiːk] Wange, Backe **II**
cheer [tʃɪə] Jubel, Beifall **I**
to **cheer** [tʃɪə] jubeln, Beifall klatschen **II**
cheerful ['tʃɪəfl] fröhlich, vergnügt **III 5**, 90
cheese [tʃiːz] Käse **III 2**, 36
chemical ['kemɪkl] Chemikalie **I**
⟨**chemise**⟩ [ʃə'miːz] Unterkleid **III 6**, 113
chemist's ['kemɪsts] Apotheke, Drogerie **I**
cheque [tʃek] Scheck **II**
chest [tʃest] Brust **II**
chewing gum ['tʃuːɪŋ ˌgʌm] Kaugummi **II**
chicken ['tʃɪkɪn] Huhn, Hähnchen **II**
chieftain ['tʃiːftn] Häuptling, Anführer(in) **II**
child, *pl.*: **children** [tʃaɪld/'tʃɪldrn] Kind(er) **I**
an only child [ˌəʊnli 'tʃaɪld] Einzelkind **II**
childhood ['tʃaɪldhʊd] Kindheit **III 6**, 118
chimney sweeping ['tʃɪmni ˌswiːpɪŋ] Schornsteinreinigung **III 6**, 114
⟨**chin**⟩ [tʃɪn] Kinn **III E**, 138
⁺**Chinese** [tʃaɪ'niːz] chinesisch, Chinesisch **I**
chips *(pl.)* [tʃɪps] Pommes frites **I**
chocolate ['tʃɒklət] Schokolade **I**
⟨**choice**⟩ [tʃɔɪs] Wahl, Auswahl **III E**, 135
junior **choir** [ˌdʒuːniə 'kwaɪə] Chor der unteren Klassenstufen **I**
to **choose*** [tʃuːz] wählen, aussuchen **I**
chord [kɔːd] Akkord **III 1**, 12
chorus ['kɔːrəs] Refrain, Chor **II**
Christmas ['krɪstməs] Weihnachten **I**
⟨**chubby**⟩ ['tʃʌbɪ] pummelig **III E**, 138
church [tʃɜːtʃ] Kirche **I**
churchyard ['tʃɜːtʃˌjɑːd] Friedhof, Kirchhof **III 5**, 90
⁺to **churn** [tʃɜːn] sich heftig bewegen, aufwühlen **I**
cigar [sɪ'gɑː] Zigarre **III 4**, 73
cigarette [ˌsɪgr'et] Zigarette **I**
cinema ['sɪnəmə] Kino **I**
circle ['sɜːkl] Kreis **II**
⟨**citizen**⟩ ['sɪtɪzn] Staatsbürger(in) **III E**, 135
city ['sɪti] Großstadt, Innenstadt **I**
city shuttle ['sɪti ˌʃʌtl] Pendelverkehr zur Innenstadt **I**
⟨**civil war**⟩ [ˌsɪvl 'wɔː] Bürgerkrieg **III E**, 142
⟨civil rights movement⟩ [ˌsɪvl 'raɪts ˌmuːvmənt] Bürgerrechtsbewegung **III E**, 142

civilization [ˌsɪvlaɪ'zeɪʃn] Zivilisation **II**
civilized ['sɪvlaɪzd] zivilisiert **II**
to **clap** [klæp] klatschen, applaudieren **I**
clapping ['klæpɪŋ] Klatschen, Applaus **I**
class [klɑːs] Klasse **I**
classical music ['klæsɪkl 'mjuːzɪk] klassische Musik **I**
classroom ['klɑːsrʊm] Klassenzimmer **I**
⟨**clatter**⟩ ['klætə] Geklapper **III E**, 141
⟨to **clatter**⟩ ['klætə] klappern **III 1**, 13
clause [klɔːz] (Teil-)Satz **III 1**, 16
⟨**clay**⟩ [kleɪ] Lehm **III E**, 140
to **clean** [kliːn] reinigen, putzen **I**
clean [kliːn] sauber **I**
cleaning lady ['kliːnɪŋ ˌleɪdi] Zugehfrau, Putzfrau **I**
clear [klɪə] klar, hell, einleuchtend **I**
clever ['klevə] schlau, klug **I**
cliché ['kliːʃeɪ] Klischee **III 1**, 21
cliff [klɪf] Klippe **I**
    cliff-side ['klɪfsaɪd] Klippe(n) **I**
climb [klaɪm] Steigung, Aufstieg **II**
to **climb** [klaɪm] (hoch)klettern **I**
mountain **climber** ['maʊntɪn ˌklaɪmə] Bergsteiger(in) **II**
mountain **climbing** ['maʊntɪn ˌklaɪmɪŋ] Bergsteigen **II**
clinic ['klɪnɪk] Klinik **III 4**, 75
video **clip** ['vɪdiəʊ ˌklɪp] Videoclip **II**
⟨**clique**⟩ [kliːk] Clique **III 1**, 10
cloak [kləʊk] Umhang, (weiter) Mantel **II**
clock [klɒk] Uhr **I**
to **clock on** [ˌklɒk'ɒn] zu Arbeitsbeginn stempeln oder stechen **III 6**, 112
close [kləʊs] Straße, Hof **II**
to **close** [kləʊz] schließen **I**
close [kləʊs] genau **II**
close (*to*) [kləʊs] nah, dicht (bei) **I**
°**closing price** ['kləʊzɪŋ ˌpraɪs] Schlusskurs **II**
cloth [klɒθ] Tuch, Stoff **III 6**, 114
clothes ['kləʊðz] Kleidung, Kleider **I**
clothing ['kləʊðɪŋ] Kleidung **III 3**, 53
cloud [klaʊd] Wolke **II**
+**cloudy** ['klaʊdi] wolkig **I**
clown [klaʊn] Clown **III 2**, 34
club [klʌb] Klub, Verein **I**
    night club ['naɪt klʌb] Nachtclub **I**
clue [kluː] Ahnung **III 1**, 12; Anhaltspunkt, Hinweis **II**
clumsy ['klʌmzi] ungeschickt, tollpatschig **III 1**, 13
to **clutch** [klʌtʃ] greifen, packen, festhalten **II**
coach [kəʊtʃ] (Eisenbahn-)Wagen **II**
coal [kəʊl] Kohle **III 6**, 113
coast [kəʊst] Küste **I**
coastal ['kəʊstl] Küsten- **I**
coastguard ['kəʊstgɑːd] Küstenwache **I**
coat [kəʊt] Mantel **I**
    coat-hanger ['kəʊtˌhæŋə] Kleiderbügel **III 1**, 13
cobbled ['kɒbld] mit Kopfsteinpflaster gepflastert **III 5**, 94
cocaine [kəʊ'keɪn] Kokain **III 2**, 42
cocktail ['kɒkteɪl] Cocktail **III 4**, 70
code [kəʊd] Kode **I**
coffee ['kɒfi] Kaffee **I**
    coffee bar ['kɒfi ˌbɑː] (kleines) Café **I**
coin [kɔɪn] Münze **II**
coke [kəʊk] Cola **III 1**, 21
cold [kəʊld] Erkältung, Schnupfen **II**; Kälte **III 5**, 101
cold [kəʊld] kalt **I**
collage [kɒl'ɑːʒ] Collage **III 4**, 72
collar ['kɒlə] Hundehalsband **I**
colleague ['kɒliːg] Kollege/Kollegin **III 4**, 68
to **collect** [kə'lekt] sammeln **I**
collection ['kəlekʃn] Sammlung, Kollektion **II**
college ['kɒlɪdʒ] Hochschule, Universität, Institut **III 2**, 38
    college fees [ˌkɒlɪdʒ 'fiːz] Studiengebühren **III 2**, 38

⟨**colonist**⟩ ['kɒlənɪst] Kolonist(in), Siedler(in) **III E**, 133
colony ['kɒləni] Kolonie **III 6**, 114
color (*AE*) ['kʌlə] Farbe **III 1**, 15
colour ['kʌlə] Farbe **I**
    +colour-blind ['kʌləblaɪnd] farbenblind **I**
to **colour** ['kʌlə] kolorieren, färben **III 5**, 97
colourful ['kʌləfl] farbenprächtig, farbenfroh **II**
comb [kəʊm] Kamm **III 4**, 72
to **come*** [kʌm] kommen **I**
    Come along! ['kʌm‿əˌlɒŋ] Komm schon! **II**
    ⟨to come near so.'s toes⟩ jmdm ins Handwerk pfuschen **III E**, 138
    to come round [ˌkʌm 'raʊnd] vorbeikommen, herüberkommen **I**
    to come up [ˌkʌm‿'ʌp] hochkommen; aufkommen, passieren **III 3**, 50
comedian [kə'miːdiən] Komiker(in) **III 5**, 100
comedy ['kɒmədi] Komödie **II**
comfort ['kʌmpfət] Bequemlichkeit, Komfort **II**
comfortable ['kʌmpftəbl] bequem, komfortabel **I**
comfy (*coll.*) ['kʌmpfi] komfortabel, bequem **II**
comic ['kɒmɪk] Comic(heft) **I**
command [kə'mɑːnd] Befehl, Kommando **II**
commander [kə'mɑːndə] Befehlshaber(in), Kommandant(in) **II**
to **comment** (*on*) ['kɒmənt] kommentieren, sich äußern **III 1**, 21
commercial [kə'mɜːʃl] Werbespot **III 4**, 77
    commercial traveller [kəˌmɜːʃl 'trævlə] Handelsreisende(r) **II**
common ['kɒmən] allgemein **II**
    in common [ɪn 'kɒmən] gemeinsam **I**
communication [kəˌmjuːnɪ'keɪʃn] Übertragung, Kommunikation **II**
community [kə'mjuːnəti] Gemeinschaft, Gemeinde **II**
companion [kəm'pænjən] Begleiter(in), Kamerad(in) **II**
company ['kʌmpəni] Gesellschaft, Firma **II**
to **compare** [kəm'peə] vergleichen **I**
comparison [kəm'pærɪsn] Vergleich **I**
to **compensate** ['kɒmpənseɪt] **kompensieren, entschädigen III 6**, 120
competition [ˌkɒmpə'tɪʃn] Wettbewerb, Wettkampf **I**
competitive [kəm'petɪtɪv] konkurrierend, Wettkampf- **II**
competitor [kəm'petɪtə] Wettkämpfer(in), Mitbewerber(in) **II**
to **complain** [kəm'pleɪn] sich beschweren, sich beklagen, klagen **III 5**, 98
complaint [kəm'pleɪnt] Beschwerde, Klage **III 6**, 120
to **complete** [kəm'pliːt] vervollständigen **I**
complete [kəm'pliːt] vollständig, komplett **II**
compound (*word*) ['kɒmpaʊnd wɜːd] zusammengesetztes Wort **III 3**, 57
listening **comprehension** ['lɪsnɪŋ ˌkɒmprɪ'henʃn] Hörverstehen **I**
comprehensive school (*BE*) [ˌkɒmprɪ'hentsɪv ˌskuːl] Gesamtschule **III 1**, 15
computer [kəm'pjuːtə] Computer, Rechner **I**
    drum computer ['drʌm kəmˌpjuːtə] Rhythmusgerät **I**
the pros and **cons** [ˌprəʊz‿n‿'kɒnz] das Für und Wider, Pro und Contra **I**
to **concentrate** ['kɒntsntreɪt] (sich) konzentrieren **II**
concern [kən'sɜːn] Besorgnis **III 6**, 112
to be **concerned about** [kən'sɜːnd] sich interessieren für, sich Sorgen machen um **III 4**, 69
concert ['kɒnsət] Konzert **I**
conclusion [kən'kluːʒn] Abschluss, Schlussfolgerung, Schluss **III 4**, 67

concrete ['kɒŋkriːt] Beton **III 4**, 69
concussion [kən'kʌʃn] Gehirnerschütterung **II**
condition [kən'dɪʃn] Bedingung, Kondition **II**
confident ['kɒnfɪdnt] zuversichtlich; selbstbewusst, selbstsicher **III 5**, 94
to **confuse** [kən'fjuːz] verwirren, irritieren, verwechseln **III 1**, 11
congratulations [kənˌgrætʃʊ'leɪʃnz] Gratulation, Glückwunsch **II**
to **connect** [kə'nekt] verbinden, zusammenfügen **III 1**, 16
connection [kə'nekʃn] Verbindung, Zusammenhang, Anschluss **III 5**, 91
to **consider** [kən'sɪdə] betrachten, überlegen, in Erwägung ziehen **III 5**, 90
⟨to have no **consideration**⟩ [hæv ˌnəʊ kənsɪdə'reɪʃn] keine Rücksicht nehmen **III 2**, 34
⟨to **consist of**⟩ [kən'sɪst] bestehen aus **III E**, 147
constant ['kɒntstənt] konstant, ständig **III 3**, 50
⟨**constitution**⟩ [kɒntstɪ'tjuːʃn] Verfassung **III E**, 134
⟨**constitutional**⟩ [kɒntstɪ'tjuːʃnl] verfassungsmäßig **III E**, 135
to **construct** [kən'strʌkt] bauen, konstruieren **III 3**, 58
construction [kən'strʌkʃn] Bau, Konstruktion **III 3**, 52
to **consume** [kən'sjuːm] konsumieren, zu sich nehmen **III 6**, 120
contact ['kɒntækt] Kontakt, Verbindung **I**
    contact lens ['kɒntækt ˌlens] Kontaktlinse **III 4**, 73
to **contact** ['kɒntækt] Kontakt aufnehmen (mit) **I**
+**contactee** [kɒntæk'tiː] jmd, der mit einem UFO Kontakt hatte **II**
⟨to **contain**⟩ [kən'teɪn] (ent)halten **III E**, 137
container [kən'teɪnə] Behälter, Container **II**
content ['kɒntent] Inhalt **II**
    wax content ['wæks ˌkɒntent] Wachsgehalt **I**
context ['kɒntekst] Textzusammenhang, Kontext **I**
continent ['kɒntɪnənt] Festland, Kontinent **II**
⟨**continental shelf**⟩ [ˌkɒntɪnentl 'ʃelf] Kontinentalsockel **III E**, 144
to **continue** [kən'tɪnjuː] fortfahren, weitermachen; fortsetzen **II**
contrast ['kɒntrɑːst] Kontrast, Gegensatz **III 4**, 68
control [kən'trəʊl] Kontrolle **III 2**, 33
    remote control [rɪˌməʊt kən'trəʊl] Fernbedienung **III 4**, 74
    ⟨to take control⟩ [ˌteɪk kən'trəʊl] die Herrschaft übernehmen **III E**, 132
to **control** [kən'trəʊl] beherrschen, überwachen **II**
⟨**controller**⟩ [kən'trəʊlə] Leiter(in) **III 4**, 68
controversial [ˌkɒntrə'vɜːʃl] kontrovers, umstritten **III 4**, 69
+**controversy** [kən'trɒvəsi] Streitfrage, Kontroverse **II**
conversation [ˌkɒnvə'seɪʃn] Gespräch, Konversation **II**
cook [kʊk] Koch/Köchin **I**
to **cook** [kʊk] kochen **I**
cooking ['kʊkɪŋ] +Kochen, Essen **I**; Küche, Kochkünste **II**
cool [kuːl] kühl; locker, lässig **II**
coolness ['kuːlnəs] Lässigkeit **II**
to **cooperate** [kəʊ'ɒpreɪt] kooperieren **II**
cooperation [kəʊˌɒpə'reɪʃn] Zusammenarbeit, Kooperation **II**
coordination [kəʊˌɔːdɪ'neɪʃn] Koordination **II**
copy ['kɒpi] Kopie **I**
to **copy** ['kɒpi] kopieren, abschreiben **II**
copycat ['kɒpikæt] +Nachahmer(in) **II**; ⟨Nachahmungstäter(in)⟩ **III 4**, 69

⟨**coral**⟩ ['kɒrəl] Koralle **III E**, 136
⟨**core**⟩ [kɔ:] Kern **III E**, 140
+**corn** [kɔ:n] Getreide, Korn **II**
corner ['kɔ:nə] Ecke **I**
cornflakes ['kɔ:nfleɪks] Cornflakes **II**
Cornish ['kɔ:nɪʃ] kornisch, aus Cornwall **I**
to **correct** [kə'rekt] korrigieren, verbessern **I**
correct [kə'rekt] richtig, korrekt **I**
corrupt [kə'rʌpt] korrupt, verdorben, bestechlich **III 2**, 40
to **cost*** [kɒst] kosten **II**
costume ['kɒstju:m] Kostüm **I**
cottage ['kɒtɪdʒ] Cottage, Häuschen **I**
cotton ['kɒtn] Baumwolle **II**
couch potato ['kaʊtʃ pə,teɪtəʊ] jmd, der ständig vor dem Fernseher sitzt **II**
could [kʊd] konnte(n), könnte(n) **I**
⟨body **count**⟩ ['bɒdi kaʊnt] Anzahl der Menschen, Anzahl der Leichen **III 4**, 69
⟨to lose count⟩ [,lu:z 'kaʊnt] die Übersicht verlieren **III 4**, 70
to **count** [kaʊnt] zählen **II**
+**countdown** ['kaʊntdaʊn] Countdown **II**
counter ['kaʊntə] Theke **II**
country ['kʌntri] Land **I**
in the country ['kʌntri] auf dem Lande **II**
countryside ['kʌntrɪ,saɪd] Land, Landschaft **I**
county ['kaʊnti] Grafschaft, Verwaltungsbezirk **III 5**, 89
a **couple** *(of)* ['kʌpl‿əv] ein paar **II**
course [kɔ:s] Kurs(us), Lehrgang **II**
of course [əv 'kɔ:s] natürlich, selbstverständlich **I**
court [kɔ:t] (Tennis-)Platz, Spielfeld **II**
cousin ['kʌzn] Cousin(e) **I**
cover ['kʌvə] (Buch-)Umschlag **II**
to **cover** ['kʌvə] zudecken, abdecken **II**
cowboy ['kaʊbɔɪ] Cowboy; pfuschender Handwerker, Gauner **III 6**, 120
crack [kræk] Crack **III 2**, 42; Krach, Knall, Schlag **II**
to **crack** [kræk] knacken, aufbrechen **I**
⟨**craft**⟩ [krɑ:ft] Handwerk; Kunstgewerbe **III 1**, 9
⟨**crane**⟩ [kreɪn] Kran **III 5**, 92
crash [kræʃ] Krachen, Krach **II**
car crash ['kɑ: ,kræʃ] Autounfall **III 4**, 70
crash helmet ['kræʃ ,helmət] Sturzhelm **II**
to **crash** [kræʃ] zusammenbrechen, (zusammen)krachen **II**
crater ['kreɪtə] Krater **II**
crayon ['kreɪɒn] Farbstift **II**
craze [kreɪz] Fimmel **III 6**, 112
crazy ['kreɪzi] verrückt **I**
ice **cream** [aɪs 'kri:m] Eiskrem, (Speise-)Eis **I**
ice cream maker [aɪs 'kri:m ,meɪkə] Eismaschine **I**
to **create** [kri'eɪt] (er)schaffen, hervorbringen **III 3**, 58
creative [kri'eɪtɪv] kreativ **III 1**, 9
credit card ['kredɪt ,kɑ:d] Kreditkarte **II**
crew [kru:] +Besatzung **II**; Crew, Mannschaft **III 4**, 68
cricket ['krɪkɪt] ⟨Grille⟩ **III E**, 140; +Kricket *(Ballspiel mit Schläger und hartem Ball aus Kork)* **II**
crime [kraɪm] Verbrechen **III 2**, 42
crisp [krɪsp] Kartoffelchip **II**
crisp [krɪsp] knusprig **II**
to **criticize** ['krɪtɪsaɪz] kritisieren **III 1**, 13
crocodile ['krɒkədaɪl] Krokodil, Menschenschlange **II**
crop [krɒp] Getreide, Feldfrucht, Ernte **III 3**, 51
to **cross** [krɒs] überqueren, kreuzen **II**
crowd [kraʊd] (Menschen-)Menge **II**
to **crowd** [kraʊd] (sich) drängen **II**
crown jewels [,kraʊn 'dʒu:əlz] Kronjuwelen **I**
⟨**cruelty**⟩ ['kru:əlti] Grausamkeit **III E**, 136
⟨to **cruise**⟩ [kru:z] mit dem Auto in der Gegend herumfahren **III 1**, 9
to **cry** [kraɪ] rufen, schreien; weinen **I**
cuisine [kwɪz'ɪ:n] Küche **I**
cultural ['kʌltʃrəl] kulturell **III 1**, 21
culture ['kʌltʃə] Kultur **II**
cupboard ['kʌbəd] Schrank **I**
curriculum vitae *(CV)* [kə,rɪkjələm 'vi:taɪ] Lebenslauf **III 6**, 111
curry ['kʌri] Curry(gericht) **I**
curtain ['kɜ:tn] Vorhang **II**
customer ['kʌstəmə] Kunde/Kundin **II**
customs ['kʌstəmz] Zoll *(Verwaltung)* **I**
to **cut*** [kʌt] schneiden **II**
⟨to cut down⟩ [kʌt 'daʊn] fällen **III 3**, 49
⟨**cute**⟩ [kju:t] süß, niedlich **III E**, 138
CV *(curriculum vitae)* [kə,rɪkjələm 'vi:taɪ] Lebenslauf **III 6**, 111
to **cycle** ['saɪkl] Rad fahren, radeln **I**
cyclist ['saɪklɪst] Fahrradfahrer(in) **II**

D

dad [dæd] Papa, Vati **I**
daily ['deɪli] täglich, Tages- **III 4**, 66
dam [dæm] Staudamm **III 3**, 52
+**damage** ['dæmɪdʒ] Schaden **I**
to **damage** ['dæmɪdʒ] beschädigen **I**
⟨**damn**⟩ [dæm] verdammt **III 2**, 33
dampness ['dæmpnəs] Feuchtigkeit **III 5**, 90
dance [dɑ:nts] Tanz **II**
dancing ['dɑ:ntsɪŋ] Tanzen **II**
danger ['deɪndʒə] Gefahr **I**
dangerous ['deɪndʒrəs] gefährlich **I**
dare [deə] Mutprobe **III 1**, 8
⟨to **dare**⟩ [deə] wagen **III E**, 138
dark [dɑ:k] dunkel **I**
darkness ['dɑ:knəs] Dunkelheit **III 2**, 37
⟨**darling**⟩ ['dɑ:lɪŋ] Liebling **III 1**, 13
⟨**dart**⟩ [dɑ:t] Pfeil **III E**, 136
⟨**date**⟩ [deɪt] Verabredung **III E**, 130
up to date [,ʌp tə 'deɪt] modern, aktuell **I**
daughter ['dɔ:tə] Tochter **III 5**, 90
dawn [dɔ:n] Dämmerung, Tagesanbruch **II**
day [deɪ] Tag **I**
One Day Travelcard ['trævlkɑ:d] Tageskarte, Netzkarte *(London)* **II**
the other day [ði‿,ʌðə 'deɪ] neulich **III 2**, 41
daydream ['deɪdri:m] Tagtraum **II**
daylight ['deɪlaɪt] Tageslicht **I**
dead [ded] tot, verstorben **I**
deaf [def] taub **I**
deal [di:l] Handel, Abmachung **III 1**, 8
⟨the real deal *(AE)*⟩ [ðə 'rɪəl ,di:l] das Echte **III 1**, 8
to **deal*** ['di:l]
to deal in ['di:l‿ɪn] handeln mit **III 4**, 69
to deal with ['di:l wɪθ] sich befassen mit, umgehen mit, behandeln, erledigen **III 1**, 13
dealer ['di:lə] Händler(in), Dealer(in), Drogenhändler(in) **III 2**, 42
dear [dɪə] lieb, teuer **III 5**, 90
Oh, dear! [əʊ 'dɪə] Oh je! **I**
death [deθ] Tod **II**
debate [dɪ'beɪt] Debatte, Diskussion **III 4**, 68
December [dɪ'sembə] Dezember **I**
to **decide** [dɪ'saɪd] entscheiden **I**
decimal point [,desɪml 'pɔɪnt] Komma(stelle) **II**
decision [dɪ'sɪʒn] Entscheidung **III 4**, 72
declaration [,deklə'reɪʃn] Erklärung **II**
to **declare** [dɪ'kleə] angeben, deklarieren **I**
to **decline** [dɪ'klaɪn] ablehnen, ausschlagen **II**
to **decorate** ['dekəreɪt] dekorieren, verzieren **II**
deep [di:p] tief **II**
to **defeat** [dɪ'fi:t] besiegen, schlagen **II**
to **defend** [dɪ'fend] verteidigen **II**
to **define** [dɪ'faɪn] näher bestimmen, definieren **II**
definite ['defɪnət] ⟨bestimmt, eindeutig⟩ **III E**, 130; definitiv, ganz sicher **III 5**, 95
definition [,defɪ'nɪʃn] Definition, Festlegung **III 4**, 75
⟨to **defuse**⟩ [,di:'fju:z] entschärfen **III E**, 139
+**degree** [dɪ'gri:] Grad **I**
delay [dɪ'leɪ] Verzögerung, Verzug **III 6**, 120
deli *(AE)* ['deli] Delikatessen-, Feinkostgeschäft **III 2**, 39
+**delicatessen**, deli [,delikə'tesn, 'deli] Delikatessengeschäft, -lokal **I**
⟨**delight**⟩ [dɪ'laɪt] Freude, Entzücken **III 4**, 68
to **deliver** [dɪ'lɪvə] (aus)liefern, austragen **III 1**, 13
⟨**delivery work**⟩ [dɪ'lɪvri ,wɜ:k] Zustell-, Lieferantentätigkeit **III 6**, 112
demand [dɪ'mɑ:nd] Forderung, Verlangen, Nachfrage **III 6**, 112
to **demand** [dɪ'mɑ:nd] fordern, verlangen **II**
demo tape ['deməʊ ,teɪp] Demo(nstrations)band **I**
⟨**democracy**⟩ [dɪ'mɒkrəsi] Demokratie **III E**, 146
to **deny** [dɪ'naɪ] abstreiten, bestreiten, leugnen **III 5**, 95
deodorant [di'əʊdrnt] Deodorant **II**
department [dɪ'pɑ:tmənt] Abteilung **I**
department store [dɪ'pɑ:tmənt ,stɔ:] Kaufhaus **I**
departure [dɪ'pɑ:tʃə] Abflug, Abfahrt **I**
to **depend on** [dɪ'pend] abhängen von **II**; sich verlassen auf **III 6**,119
⟨to **depress**⟩ [dɪ'pres] deprimieren **III E**, 138
deputy head [,depjəti 'hed] stellvertretende(r) Schulleiter(in) **III 6**, 112
to **descend** [dɪ'send] absteigen, hinunterfahren **II**
to **describe** [dɪ'skraɪb] beschreiben **I**
description [dɪ'skrɪpʃn] Beschreibung **I**
design [dɪ'zaɪn] Design **I**
°Design and Technology [dɪ'zaɪn‿ən‿tek'nɒlədʒi] Gestalten und Technik **I**
to **design** [dɪ'zaɪn] entwerfen, konstruieren **II**
designer [dɪ'zaɪnə] Designer(in) **II**
desk [desk] Schreibtisch **I**
⟨**despite**⟩ [dɪ'spaɪt] trotz **III E**, 138
destination [destɪ'neɪʃn] Reiseziel, Bestimmungsort **III 2**, 32
to **destroy** [dɪ'strɔɪ] zerstören **I**
detail ['di:teɪl] Detail, Einzelheit **I**
detective [dɪ'tektɪv] Detektiv(in) **I**
smoke **detector** ['sməʊk dɪ,tektə] Rauchmelder **II**
to **develop** [dɪ'veləp] (sich) entwickeln **III 3**, 52
⟨**development**⟩ [dɪ'veləpmənt] Entwicklung **III E**, 143
⟨**devolution**⟩ [,di:və'lu:ʃn] Dezentralisierung **III E**, 146
diagnosis [,daɪəg'nəʊsɪs] Diagnose **II**
diagram ['daɪəgræm] Diagramm **III 2**, 43
to **dial** ['daɪəl] wählen **I**
dialogue ['daɪəlɒg] Dialog, Gespräch **I**
diary ['daɪəri] Tagebuch **I**
dictionary ['dɪkʃənəri] Wörterbuch **I**
didgeridoo [,dɪdʒəri'du:] Didgeridoo *(australisches Blasinstrument)* **II**
to **die** [daɪ] sterben **I**
diesel ['di:zl] Dieselöl, -motor **II**
diet ['daɪət] Diät **II**
difference ['dɪfrnts] Unterschied, Differenz **I**
different ['dɪfrnt] verschieden, anders(artig) **I**
difficult ['dɪfɪklt] schwierig **I**
difficulty ['dɪfɪklti] Schwierigkeit **III 4**, 69
to **dig*** [dɪg] graben **III 4**, 70
to **dim** [dɪm] dimmen, dämpfen, allmählich verdunkeln **III 4**, 68
diner *(AE)* ['daɪnə] Esslokal **III 1**, 17
+**dining room** ['daɪnɪŋ ,rʊm] Esszimmer **I**
dinner ['dɪnə] Abendessen **I**
dinnertime ['dɪnə,taɪm] Essenszeit **II**
dinosaur ['daɪnəsɔ:] Dinosaurier **II**

direct [dɪ'rekt] direkt **I**
direction [dɪ'rekʃn] Richtung, *Pl.:* Wegbeschreibung, Anweisungen, Hinweise **III 2**, 34
director [dɪ'rektə] Regisseur(in) **II**
⟨**dirt**⟩ [dɜ:t] Schmutz, Dreck **III 1**, 13
dirtiest ['dɜ:tiɪst] schmutzigste(r/s) **I**
dirty ['dɜ:ti] schmutzig **I**
disadvantage [ˌdɪsəd'vɑ:ntɪdʒ] Nachteil **III 1**, 11
to **disagree** [ˌdɪsə'gri:] ablehnen **I**
to **disappear** [ˌdɪsə'pɪə] verschwinden **III 4**, 68
to be **disappointed** [ˌdɪsə'pɔɪntɪd] enttäuscht sein **II**
disaster [dɪ'zɑ:stə] Katastrophe, Unglück **I**
disco ['dɪskəʊ] Disko(thek) **I**
to **discover** [dɪ'skʌvə] entdecken **II**
discovery [dɪ'skʌvri] Entdeckung **II**
⟨to **discriminate against**⟩ [dɪs'krɪmɪneɪt əˌgentst] diskriminieren, ungleich behandeln **III E**, 142
to **discuss** [dɪ'skʌs] diskutieren, besprechen **I**
discussion [dɪ'skʌʃn] Diskussion **III 3**, 58
disease [dɪ'zi:z] Krankheit **II**
⟨**disgrace**⟩ [dɪs'greɪs] Schande **III 1**, 8
dish [dɪʃ] Schale, Schüssel, flache, runde Form **III 6**, 117
to **disintegrate** [dɪ'sɪntɪgreɪt] (sich) auflösen, zersetzen **II**
⟨**dispatch** *(AE)* ⟩ [dɪ'spætʃ] Taxizentrale **III 2**, 34
to **dispose of** [dɪ'spəʊz‿ɒv] beseitigen, loswerden **I**
district ['dɪstrɪkt] Distrikt, Bezirk, (Stadt-) Viertel **III 2**, 30
divide [dɪ'vaɪd] Kluft, Wasserscheide **III 6**, 115
to **divide** [dɪ'vaɪd] aufteilen, dividieren **I**
⟨scuba **diving**⟩ ['sku:bə ˌdaɪvɪŋ] Sporttauchen **III E**, 139
to **do*** [du:] tun, machen **I**
How d'you do? [ˌhaʊ djʊ 'du:] Guten Tag! Sehr erfreut! **II**
to do well [du: 'wel] erfolgreich sein **II**
+to **dock** [dɒk] anlegen, andocken **II**
doctor ['dɒktə] Arzt/Ärztin, Doktor **II**
documentary [ˌdɒkjə'mentri] Dokumentarfilm **II**
dog [dɒg] Hund **I**
+guide dog ['gaɪd dɒg] Blindenhund **I**
hot dog ['hɒt dɒg] Hotdog *(langes weiches Brötchen mit Würstchen)* **I**
to rain cats and dogs ['reɪn ˌkæts‿n‿'dɒgz] heftig regnen, schütten, gießen **I**
⟨**doll**⟩ [dɒl] Puppe **III E**, 138
dollar ['dɒlə] *amerikanische Währung* **I**
donkey ['dɒŋki] Esel **III 1**, 10
door [dɔ:] Tür **I**
next door [ˌnekst 'dɔ:] nebenan **II**
⟨to **dot**⟩ [dɒt] übersäen, verstreuen **III 5**, 92
to **double** ['dʌbl] (sich) verdoppeln **II**
double ['dʌbl] doppelt(e/r) **I**
double decker bus [ˌdʌbl dekə 'bʌs] Doppeldeckerbus **I**
doubtful ['daʊtfl] zweifelhaft; zweifelnd, skeptisch **III 5**, 94
down [daʊn] +herunter, nieder **I**; nach unten **II**
to **download** [ˌdaʊn'ləʊd] herunterladen, downloaden **I**
downstairs [ˌdaʊn'steəz] unten; Erdgeschoss **I**
+**downstream** [ˌdaʊn'stri:m] stromabwärts **I**
+**downtown** *(AE)* [ˌdaʊn'taʊn] *südlicher Teil der Insel Manhattan in New York; sonst:* Stadtzentrum **I**
dozen ['dʌzn] Dutzend **II**
drab [dræb] trist, düster, grau **III 5**, 94
draft [drɑ:ft] Entwurf, Skizze **II**
to **drag** [dræg] schleppen, ziehen **III 4**, 72
⟨**dragon**⟩ ['drægn] Drachen **III E**, 145
to **drain** [dreɪn] leeren **II**
⟨**drake**⟩ [dreɪk] Erpel, Enterich **III 6**, 119
drama ['drɑ:mə] Drama, Theater **II**
Drama ['drɑ:mə] °Theaterspielen *(Fach)* **I**
dramatic [drə'mætɪk] dramatisch **III 3**, 49
to **draw*** [drɔ:] zeichnen **I**
to draw attention to [ˌdrɔ:‿ə'tentʃn] Aufmerksamkeit ziehen auf **II**
+**dreadful** ['dredfl] furchtbar, schrecklich **I**
dream [dri:m] Traum **II**
to **dream** [dri:m] träumen **II**
dress [dres] Kleid **I**
⟨to **dress up**⟩ [dres‿'ʌp] sich verkleiden **III E**, 133
to be **dressed** ['drest] gekleidet sein **III 5**, 94
dressing gown ['dresɪŋ ˌgaʊn] Morgenrock **II**
to **drift** [drɪft] (ab)treiben, (ab)driften **I**
drink [drɪŋk] Getränk **II**
to **drink*** [drɪŋk] trinken **I**
to **drive*** [draɪv] fahren **I**
to drive off [draɪv‿'ɒf] vertreiben **II**
to drive so. out [ˌdraɪv‿'aʊt] jmdn verjagen, hinausjagen **II**
driver ['draɪvə] Fahrer(in) **II**
long-distance truck driver [ˌlɒŋ'dɪstnts 'trʌk ˌdraɪvə] Fernfahrer(in) **II**
drop [drɒp] ⟨Sturz, Höhenunterschied⟩ **III 3**, 53; Tropfen **III 3**, 51
to **drop** [drɒp] fallen lassen, abwerfen **I**
⟨the penny has dropped⟩ [ðə ˌpeni həz 'drɒpt] Der Groschen ist gefallen. **III 6**, 119
to drop back [drɒp 'bæk] zurückfallen **II**
to drop in [drɒp‿ɪn] vorbeischauen **II**
⟨to drop so. off⟩ [drɒp] absetzen **III E**, 144
drowning ['draʊnɪŋ] Ertrinken **II**
drowsy ['draʊzi] schläfrig **II**
drug [drʌg] Droge **I**
Druid ['dru:ɪd] Druide **II**
drum [drʌm] Trommel **I**
drum computer ['drʌm kəmˌpju:tə] Rhythmusgerät **I**
°drum kit ['drʌm kɪt] Schlagzeugausrüstung **I**
to **dry up** [draɪ‿'ʌp] austrocknen **III 3**, 51
to **dub** [dʌb] synchron aufnehmen, synchronisieren **III 4**, 73
duck [dʌk] Ente **III 1**, 18
⟨**duckling**⟩ ['dʌklɪŋ] Entenküken, Entlein **III 6**, 119
⟨**dude**⟩ [du:d] Typ, Kerl **III E**, 130
⟨**due to**⟩ ['dju: tʊ] auf Grund, wegen **III 5**, 92
+due *(to)* [dju:] zurückzuführen (auf) **I**
⟨**duke**⟩ [dju:k] Herzog **III E**, 132
to **dump** [dʌmp] auskippen, hinwerfen **I**
during ['djʊərɪŋ] während **II**
dust [dʌst] Staub **II**
Dutch [dʌtʃ] holländisch, niederländisch **II**
⟨**dutiful**⟩ ['dju:tifl] pflichtbewusst, gehorsam **III 1**, 14
duty ['dju:ti] Zoll *(Gebühr)* **I**
to be on duty ['dju:ti] im Dienst sein, Aufsicht haben **II**
⟨to be **dyslexic**⟩ [dɪ'sleksɪk] Legastheniker(in) sein **III 6**, 115

E

each [i:tʃ] jede(r/s) Einzelne **I**
each other [ˌi:tʃ‿'ʌðə] einander **II**
ear [ɪə] Ohr **II**
early ['ɜ:li] früh **I**
to **earn** [ɜ:n] verdienen **III 6**, 111
earth [ɜ:θ] Erde **II**
earthquake ['ɜ:θkweɪk] Erdbeben **II**
to **ease** [i:z] lindern, erleichtern **III 5**, 95
+**east** [i:st] östlich, Osten **I**
eastern ['i:stən] östlich **III 3**, 50
easy ['i:zi] leicht, einfach **I**
to **eat*** [i:t] essen **I**
⟨**economy**⟩ [ɪ'kɒnəmi] Wirtschaft, Konjunktur **III 5**, 92
edge [edʒ] Ufer, Rand (eines Sees) **I**
to **edit** ['edɪt] herausgeben, redigieren **III 4**, 71
editor ['edɪtə] Herausgeber(in), Redakteur(in) **III 4**, 66
to **educate** ['edʒukeɪt] bilden, ausbilden **III 6**, 112
education [ˌedʒʊ'keɪʃn] Erziehung, Bildung, Ausbildung **III 4**, 66
effective [ɪ'fektɪv] effektiv, wirksam, wirkungsvoll **III 3**, 51
visual **effects** [ˌvɪʒuəl‿ɪ'fekts] (optische) Tricks **II**
efficient [ɪ'fɪʃnt] effizient, fähig, tüchtig **III 6**, 111
e.g. [ˌi: 'dʒi:] (= exempli gratia) zum Beispiel **III 1**, 19
egg [eg] Ei **I**
scrambled eggs [ˌskræmbld‿'egz] Rührei **II**
either ['aɪðə] eine(r, s) von beiden; beide **III 5**, 100
either ... or ['aɪðə ... 'ɔ:] entweder ... oder **II**
not ... either [nɒt 'aɪðə] auch nicht **III 1**, 8
elbow ['elbəʊ] Ellbogen **II**
+**elderly** ['eldəli] älter(e/r/s) **I**
⟨**eldest**⟩ ['eldɪst] der/die Älteste **III E**, 143
⟨to **elect**⟩ [ɪ'lekt] wählen **III E**, 147
⟨**election**⟩ [ɪ'lekʃn] Wahl, Abstimmung **III E**, 134
electric [ɪ'lektrɪk] elektrisch **I**
electrician [ˌelɪk'trɪʃn] Elektriker(in) **II**
electricity [ˌelɪk'trɪsəti] Elektrizität, Strom **I**
electronic [ˌelek'trɒnɪk] elektronisch **II**
+**elevator** *(AE)* ['elɪveɪtə] Aufzug, Fahrstuhl **I**
else [els] (sonst) noch, außerdem **I**
e-mail ['i:meɪl] elektronische Post, E-Mail **I**
embarrassing [ɪm'bærəsɪŋ] peinlich **III 6**, 113
emergency [ɪ'mɜ:dʒnsi] Notfall **II**; +Notfall-, Dringlichkeits- **I**
to **emigrate** ['emɪgreɪt] emigrieren, auswandern **III 5**, 90
⟨**emigration**⟩ [ˌemɪ'greɪʃn] Emigration, Auswanderung **III 5**, 93
emotion [ɪ'məʊʃn] Gefühl, Emotion **II**
emperor ['emprə] Kaiser **II**
⟨to **emphasise**⟩ ['empfəsaɪz] betonen, hervorheben **III 6**, 117
⟨**emphatic**⟩ [ɪm'fætɪk] emphatisch, nachdrücklich, verstärkend **III 6**, 118
to **employ** [ɪm'plɔɪ] beschäftigen **III 6**, 114
employee [ɪm'plɔɪi:] Arbeitsnehmer(in), Angestellte(r) **II**
employer [ɪm'plɔɪə] Arbeitgeber(in) **III 6**, 111
⟨**employment**⟩ [ɪm'plɔɪmənt] Beschäftigung **III 5**, 93
empty ['emti] leer **II**
to **encourage** [ɪn'kʌrɪdʒ] ermutigen, anregen, fördern, verleiten **III 6**, 112
+**encyclopedia** [ɪnˌsaɪklə'pi:diə] Enzyklopädie, Nachschlagewerk **II**
end [end] Ende, Schluss **I**
to put an end to sth. [ˌpʊt‿ən‿'end] einer Sache ein Ende setzen **II**
to **end** [end] (be)enden **I**
to end up [end‿'ʌp] enden, landen **III 1**, 8
to **endanger** [ɪn'deɪndʒə] ⟨gefährden⟩ **III 5**, 92
ending ['endɪŋ] Schluss, Ausgang, Ende **III 2**, 41
energy ['enədʒi] Energie **II**
⟨to **enforce**⟩ [ɪn'fɔ:s] durchsetzen **III E**, 133
engine ['endʒɪn] Motor **II**
fire engine ['faɪə‿ˌendʒɪn] Feuerwehrauto **II**
steam engine ['sti:m‿ˌendʒɪn] Dampfmaschine **III 6**, 114
engineer [ˌendʒɪ'nɪə] Ingenieur(in), Techniker(in) **III 6**, 111
engineering [ˌendʒɪ'nɪərɪŋ] Technik, Maschinenbau, Ingenieurwesen **III 3**, 58

English ['ɪŋglɪʃ] englisch, Englisch (*Fach*) I
to **enjoy** [ɪn'dʒɔɪ] genießen, mögen II
enjoyment [ɪn'dʒɔɪmənt] Freude, Spaß II
enough [ɪ'nʌf] genug, ausreichend I
⟨to **ensure**⟩ [ɪn'ʃɔː] sicher stellen III E, 142
to **enter** ['entə] einschreiben, auf die Liste setzen II; melden, sich beteiligen an II
entertainer [ˌentə'teɪnə] Unterhaltungskünstler(in) II
entertainment [ˌentə'teɪnmənt] Unterhaltung, Animation I
entrance ['entrənts] Eingang III 2, 32
entrepreneur [ˌɒntrəprə'nɜː] Unternehmer(in) III 6, 115
entry ['entri] Eintrag II
envelope ['envələʊp] (Brief-)Umschlag II
environment [ɪn'vaɪərnmənt] Umwelt I
environmental [ɪnˌvaɪərn'mentl] Umwelt- III 3, 48
environmentalist [ɪnˌvaɪərn'mentlɪst] Umweltschützer(in) III 3, 58
episode ['epɪsəʊd] Episode, Folge III 4, 76
⟨**equal**⟩ ['iːkwəl] gleich III E, 133
⟨**equally**⟩ ['iːkwəli] gleichermaßen III E, 142
equipment [ɪ'kwɪpmənt] Ausrüstung, Ausstattung II
+to **erase** [ɪ'reɪz] entfernen, löschen II
escape [ɪ'skeɪp] Flucht II
to **escape** [ɪ'skeɪp] entkommen, entfliehen II
especially [ɪ'speʃli] besonders, vor allem II
⟨to **establish**⟩ [ɪ'stæblɪʃ] gründen, einrichten III 5, 93
working-class **estate** [ˌwɜːkɪŋ 'klɑːs ɪˌsteɪt] Arbeitersiedlung III 5, 95
to **estimate** ['estɪmeɪt] schätzen III 6, 112
ethnic ['eθnɪk] ethnisch, einer bestimmten Volksgruppe zugehörig III 2, 30
+**euro** ['jʊərəʊ] Euro (*europäische Währung*) II
European [ˌjʊərə'piːən] europäisch II
to **evacuate** [ɪ'vækjueɪt] evakuieren, räumen III 3, 50
evacuation [ɪˌvækju'eɪʃn] Evakuierung, Räumung III 3, 50
⟨to **evaporate**⟩ [ɪ'væpreɪt] verdampfen, sich in Luft auflösen III 1, 8
even ['iːvn] sogar I
⟨**not even**⟩ [nɒt‿'iːvn] nicht einmal III E, 133
evening ['iːvnɪŋ] Abend I
event [ɪ'vent] Ereignis II
eventually [ɪ'ventʃuəli] schließlich, endlich III 5, 94
ever ['evə] je(mals), immer I
every ['evri] jede(r/s) I
everybody ['evriˌbɒdi] jeder, alle (zusammen) I
everyone ['evriwʌn] jeder I
everything ['evriθɪŋ] alles I
everywhere ['evriweə] überall I
exact [ɪg'zækt] exakt, genau I
exam [ɪg'zæm] Prüfung III 2, 40
  ⟨mock exam⟩ [ˌmɒk‿ɪg'zæm] Probeprüfung unter realistischen Bedingungen III E, 144
to **examine** [ɪg'zæmɪn] untersuchen II
example [ɪg'zɑːmpl] Beispiel I
excellent ['ekslnt] ausgezeichnet, exzellent I
except [ɪk'sept] außer II
excerpt ['eksɜːpt] Auszug III 5, 103
exchange [ɪks'tʃeɪndʒ] Austausch II
  (exchange) broker [ɪks'tʃeɪndʒ ˌbrəʊkə] Börsenmakler(in), Devisenhändler(in) III 2, 30
to **exchange** [ɪks'tʃeɪndʒ] aus-/umtauschen III 1, 11
to be **excited** [ɪk'saɪtɪd] aufgeregt sein II
excitement [ɪk'saɪtmənt] Aufregung II
exciting [ɪk'saɪtɪŋ] aufregend, spannend I
excuse [ɪk'skjuːs] Entschuldigung II
excuse me [ɪk'skjuːz miː] entschuldigen Sie I
⟨**executive**⟩ [ɪg'zekjətɪv] leitende(r) Angestellte(r) III E, 138
exercise bike ['eksəsaɪz ˌbaɪk] Hometrainer II
  exercise book ['eksəsaɪz ˌbʊk] Übungsheft, Heft I
to **exercise** ['eksəsaɪz] üben, trainieren II
⟨**exhaustion**⟩ [ɪg'zɔːstʃn] Erschöpfung III E, 136
exhibition [ˌeksɪ'bɪʃn] Ausstellung I
to **exist** [ɪg'zɪst] existieren, bestehen III 3, 49
to **exit** ['eksɪt] hinausgehen, von der Bühne abgehen II
⟨**exodus**⟩ ['eksədəs] Auszug, Abwanderung, Völkerwanderung III 5, 92
to **expect** [ɪk'spekt] erwarten II
expectation [ˌekspek'teɪʃn] Erwartung, Aussicht II
⟨to **expend**⟩ [ɪk'spend] aufwenden, verbrauchen III E, 141
expensive [ɪk'spentsɪv] teuer I
experience [ɪk'spɪəriənts] Erfahrung I
to **experience** [ɪk'spɪəriənts] erfahren, erleben, durchmachen III 6, 111
experiment [ɪk'sperɪmənt] Versuch, Experiment I
expert ['ekspɜːt] Experte/Expertin II
to **explain** [ɪk'spleɪn] erklären I
to **explode** [ɪk'spləʊd] explodieren III 6, 120
to **exploit** [ɪk'splɔɪt] ausbeuten, ausnutzen III 6, 112
exploitation [ˌeksplɔɪ'teɪʃn] Ausbeutung III 6, 113
to **express** [ɪk'spres] ausdrücken III 3, 59
expression [ɪk'spreʃn] Ausdruck II
to **extend** [ɪk'stend] ausstrecken, ausdehnen, verlängern III 5, 91
extra ['ekstrə] zusätzlich, extra I
  extra cash [ˌekstrə 'kæʃ] Zuschlag, Sonderzahlung II
  extra tuition [ˌekstrə tju'ɪʃn] Nachhilfe-, Förderunterricht III 6, 112
extraterrestrial [ˌekstrətə'restriəl] außerirdisch, Außerirdische(r) II
extreme [ɪk'striːm] Extrem, das Äußerste III 4, 70
extreme [ɪk'striːm] extrem, äußerste(r,s) III 6, 121
eye [aɪ] Auge II

F

fabled ['feɪbld] sagenhaft, fabelhaft II
face [feɪs] Gesicht I
  to make a face [feɪs] ein Gesicht ziehen II
⟨to be **faced with**⟩ ['feɪst wɪθ] konfrontiert sein mit III 5, 93
fact [fækt] Tatsache, Fakt I
  in fact [ɪn 'fækt] eigentlich I; tatsächlich II
factory ['fæktri] Fabrik, Werk II
to **fade** [feɪd] schwächer werden, ausblenden, ausbleichen III 1, 8
failure ['feɪljə] Misserfolg, Scheitern II
faint [feɪnt] schwach, matt II
fair [feə] Fest, Jahrmarkt II
fair [feə] gerecht III 1, 8
  fair (*old*) [feə] schön III 5, 98
Yours **faithfully**, ['feɪθfli] mit freundlichen Grüßen, hochachtungsvoll (*Briefschluss*) I
fake [feɪk] falsch, unecht III 4, 73
+**fall** (*AE*) [fɔːl] Herbst I
  ⟨fall (*AE*)⟩ [fɔːl] Herbst III E, 135
to **fall*** [fɔːl] fallen, stürzen I
  to fall asleep [ˌfɔːl‿ə'sliːp] einschlafen II
false [fɔːls] falsch II
fame [feɪm] Ruhm III 4, 71
family, (*pl.*) -ies ['fæməli] Familie I
famine ['fæmɪn] Hungersnot III 5, 91
famous ['feɪməs] berühmt I
fan [fæn] Anhänger(in), Fan II
fancy ['fæntsi] ausgefallen II; +Stell' dir vor! I
  Do you fancy ...? [dju: 'fæntsi] Hättest du Lust ...? II
⟨**fantail**⟩ ['fænteɪl] Pfauenrad III E, 141
fantastic [fæn'tæstɪk] fantastisch I
fantasy ['fæntəsi] Fantasie I
far [fɑː] weit I
fare [feə] Fahrpreis, Fahrgast III 2, 34
farm [fɑːm] Bauernhaus, Farm I
  farm hand ['fɑːm hænd] Landarbeiter(in) III 2, 32
farmer ['fɑːmə] Landwirt(in), Bauer/Bäuerin II
fascination [ˌfæsɪ'neɪʃn] Faszination, Reiz III 4, 70
fashion ['fæʃn] Mode I
fashionable ['fæʃnəbl] modisch, schick II
fast [fɑːst] schnell, rasch I
  to fast forward [ˌfɑːst 'fɔːwəd] vorspulen III 4, 74
to **fasten** ['fɑːsn] befestigen, anschnallen II
fat [fæt] fett, dick II
father ['fɑːðə] Vater I
fault [fɔːlt] Fehler, Schuld II
favorite (*AE*) ['feɪvrɪt] bevorzugt, Lieblings- I
favourite ['feɪvrɪt] bevorzugt, Lieblings- I
+**fax** [fæks] (Tele-)Fax II
fear [fɪə] Angst, Furcht III 5, 91
+**feast** [fiːst] Festmahl, Bankett II
feather ['feðə] Feder, Gefieder I
February ['februri] Februar I
⟨**federal**⟩ ['fedrəl] Bundes-, föderal III E, 134
college **fees** [ˌkɒlɪdʒ 'fiːz] Studiengebühren III 2, 38
to **feed*** [fiːd] füttern I
to **feel*** [fiːl] fühlen II
  to feel sorry for [fiːl 'sɒri] bemitleiden II
feeling ['fiːlɪŋ] Gefühl II
feet (*pl.*) [fiːt] Fuß (*englische Maßeinheit (3 ft. = 0,9144 m)*); sonst: Füße II
⟨**feisty**⟩ ['faɪsti] lebensfroh III 5, 90
fellow ['feləʊ] Typ, Mann, Kerl III 5, 94
female ['fiːmeɪl] weiblich; Frau III 4, 68
+**female** ['fiːmeɪl] weiblich II
fence [fents] Zaun II
⟨**Fenian**⟩ ['fiːniən] *irischer Freiheitskämpfer* III E, 142
ferry ['feri] Fähre II
fertilizer ['fɜːtɪlaɪzə] Dünger III 3, 51
festival ['festɪvl] Festival I
to **fetch** [fetʃ] (ab)holen I
(a) **few** [fjuː] wenige, ein paar I
⟨**fiancée**⟩ [fi'ɑ̃ːnseɪ] Verlobte III E, 138
⟨**fiction**⟩ ['fɪkʃn] Fiktion, Erzählliteratur III E, 149
  science fiction [ˌsaɪənts 'fɪkʃn] Science-fiction II
field [fiːld] Feld I
⟨**fiesta**⟩ [fi'estə] Fiesta (*span.*), Fest III E, 136
to **fight*** [faɪt] streiten, kämpfen I
figure ['fɪgə] Figur, Gestalt II
to **fill** [fɪl] einfügen, auffüllen I
film [fɪlm] Film I
  film-maker ['fɪlm ˌmeɪkə] Filmemacher(in) II
final ['faɪnl] (aller)letzte/r/s II
finally ['faɪnli] schließlich, endlich II
financial [faɪ'næntʃl] finanziell, Finanz- II
to **find*** [faɪnd] finden I
fine [faɪn] gut, prima I
finger ['fɪŋgə] Finger I
to **finish** ['fɪnɪʃ] beenden I
fire ['faɪə] Feuer I
  fire engine ['faɪə‿endʒɪn] Feuerwehrauto II
fireman ['faɪəmən] Feuerwehrmann II
fireplace ['faɪəpleɪs] (offener) Kamin I
⟨**fireworks**⟩ ['faɪəwɜːks] Feuerwerk III E, 136
first ['fɜːst] erste(r/s), der/die Erste I
  first aid [ˌfɜːst‿'eɪd] Erste Hilfe II
first ['fɜːst] zuerst II
  at first [ət 'fɜːst] zunächst II

fish [fɪʃ] Fisch **I**
to **fish** [fɪʃ] angeln **I**
fishing line ['fɪʃɪŋ ˌlaɪn] Angelschnur **I**
⟨nuclear **fission**⟩ [ˌnju:kliə 'fɪʃn] Kernspaltung **III E**, 139
⟨**fist**⟩ [fɪst] Faust **III E**, 138
to **fit** [fɪt] passen **I**
to fit in [fɪt‿'ɪn] hineinpassen, sich in die Gruppe einfügen **III 1**, 8
fit [fɪt] gesund, in Form **I**
to get fit [ˌget 'fɪt] fit werden **II**
all-round **fitness** [ˌɔ:lraʊnd 'fɪtnəs] Rundum-Fitness **II**
to **fix** [fɪks] befestigen, reparieren **I**
flame [fleɪm] Flamme **III 2**, 37
flash card ['flæʃ ˌkɑ:d] Illustrationstafel, Flashcard **II**
in a flash [flæʃ] blitzschnell **I**
to **flash** [flæʃ] aufblitzen, aufleuchten **II**
flashlight (*AE*) ['flæʃlaɪt] Taschenlampe **II**
flat [flæt] (Etagen-)Wohnung **I**
flat tyre [ˌflæt 'taɪə] platter Reifen, Plattfuß **I**
(*time* +) **flat** [flæt] sage und schreibe (nur) **III 4**, 72
flexible ['fleksɪbl] flexibel, flexible time = Gleitzeit **III 6**, 111
⟨with a slam and a **flick**⟩ [wɪð‿ə ˌslæm‿ənd‿ə 'flɪk] mit einer schnellen Handbewegung Tür oder Fenster zuschlagend **III E**, 141
flight [flaɪt] Flug **I**
to **fling* on** [ˌflɪŋ‿'ɒn] *(Kleidung)* schnell überwerfen, anziehen **II**
float [fləʊt] Festzugswagen, Umzugswagen **II**
flood [flʌd] Hochwasser, Überschwemmung **II**
to **flood** [flʌd] überfluten, überschwemmen **III 3**, 50
floor [flɔ:] Stockwerk, Etage; Fußboden **III 2**, 30
⟨floor manager⟩ ['flɔ: ˌmænɪdʒə] Aufnahmeleiter(in) **III 4**, 68
⟨ground floor⟩ [ˌgraʊnd 'flɔ:] Erdgeschoss **III E**, 135
+**flow** [fləʊ] Strömung, Fließen **I**
to **flow** [fləʊ] fließen **III 3**, 52
flower ['flaʊə] Blume **I**
flu [flu:] Grippe **II**
to **flush** [flʌʃ] spülen, die Wasserspülung betätigen **III 3**, 51
⟨**flute**⟩ [flu:t] Flöte **III E**, 143
to **fly*** [flaɪ] fliegen **I**
focus ['fəʊkəs] Brennpunkt, Blickpunkt, Blickrichtung **III 4**, 69
+focus group ['fəʊkəs ˌgru:p] Gruppengespräch, Gesprächsgruppe **II**
⟨to **focus**⟩ ['fəʊkəs] sich konzentrieren auf **III E**, 144
fog [fɒg] Nebel **I**
+**foggy** ['fɒgi] neb(e)lig **I**
folder ['fəʊldə] Mappe, Ordner **I**
folk [fəʊk] Volksmusik, Folk(-) **I**
Irish folk [ˌaɪərɪʃ 'fəʊk] *Musikrichtung aus Irland* **I**
⟨**folks**⟩ [fəʊks] Leute **III 1**, 14
to **follow** ['fɒləʊ] folgen **I**
⟨to follow through with sth.⟩ [ˌfɒləʊ 'θru:] etwas durchziehen **III 1**, 8
food [fu:d] Essen, Nahrung **I**
⟨processed food⟩ [ˌprəʊsest 'fu:d] konservierte Nahrung **III 1**, 20
fool [fu:l] Narr, Dummkopf **III 1**, 8
to **fool** [fu:l] zum Narren halten, hereinlegen **II**
foot, *pl.*: **feet** [fʊt] Fuß **I**; Fuß (*engl. Längenmaß, ca. 30 cm*) **II**
+on foot [ɒn 'fʊt] zu Fuß **II**
to step on so.'s foot [step] jmdm auf den Fuß treten **II**
football ['fʊtbɔ:l] Fußball **I**
footpath ['fʊtpɑ:θ] Fußweg, Pfad **I**
footprint ['fʊtprɪnt] Fußstapfen **I**
footwear ['fʊtweə] Schuhe **I**
for [fɔ:] für **I**; seit **II**; … lang **II**
⟨for good⟩ [fə 'gʊd] für immer **III E**, 138
⟨for sure⟩ [fə 'ʃʊə] ganz sicher **III E**, 144
for [fɔ:] denn **III 2**, 32
to **force** [fɔ:s] zwingen **III 1**, 10
forecast ['fɔ:kɑ:st] Vorhersage **III 4**, 76
forecaster ['fɔ:kɑ:stə] Meteorologe, Meteorologin **III 3**, 50
⟨**forehead**⟩ ['fɒrɪd] Stirn **III E**, 130
foreign ['fɒrɪn] ausländisch **III 2**, 32
foreigner ['fɒrɪnə] Ausländer(in) **III 5**, 94
forest ['fɒrɪst] Wald **III 3**, 55
forever [fə'revə] für immer **I**
⟨**forge**⟩ [fɔ:dʒ] Schmiede **III E**, 141
to **forget*** [fə'get] vergessen **I**
fork [fɔ:k] Gabel **III 1**, 20
form [fɔ:m] Form, Art **I**
to **form** [fɔ:m] formen, bilden **III 1**, 15
formal ['fɔ:ml] förmlich, formell, offiziell **I**
⟨**former**⟩ ['fɔ:mə] frühere(r), ehemalige(r) **III E**, 138
to fast **forward** [ˌfɑ:st 'fɔ:wəd] vorspulen **III 4**, 74
+**forward** ['fɔ:wəd] vorwärts **I**
⟨to lean forward⟩ [ˌli:n 'fɔ:wəd] sich vorlehnen **III E**, 130
to look forward (*to*) [ˌlʊk 'fɔ:wəd] sich freuen (auf) **I**
to **found** [faʊnd] gründen **III 5**, 98
⟨**founder**⟩ ['faʊndə] Gründer **III E**, 132
frail [freɪl] zart, zerbrechlich **II**
frame [freɪm] (Bilder-)Rahmen **I**
freak [fri:k] Fan, Anhänger(in) **I**
freckle ['frekl] Sommersprosse **III 5**, 95
free-time ['fri:taim] Freizeit, Freizeit- **III 1**, 9
free-climbing ['fri:ˌklaɪmɪŋ] Klettern ohne Ausrüstung **II**
free [fri:] frei, kostenlos **I**
free period [ˌfri: 'pɪəriəd] Hohlstunde, die zum selbstständigen Lernen gedacht ist **III 6**, 112
free trade [ˌfri: 'treɪd] Freihandel **III 6**, 114
freedom ['fri:dəm] Freiheit **I**
to **freeze*** [fri:z] frieren, gefrieren, einfrieren **III 6**, 120
°**French** [frentʃ] französisch, Französisch (*Fach*) **I**
⟨stick of French bread⟩ [ˌstɪk‿əv ˌfrentʃ 'bred] Stange Baguette **III E**, 139
frequency ['fri:kwəntsi] Frequenz, Häufigkeit **III 4**, 73
frequent ['fri:kwənt] häufig **II**
fresh [freʃ] frisch **II**
fresh water ['freʃ ˌwɔ:tə] Süßwasser **III 3**, 51
Friday ['fraɪdeɪ] Freitag **I**
fridge [frɪdʒ] Kühlschrank **I**
friend [frend] Freund(in) **I**
friendly ['frendli] freundlich, angenehm **I**
friendly match [ˌfrendli 'mætʃ] Freundschaftsspiel **I**
friendship ['frendʃɪp] Freundschaft **III 1**, 10
⟨**fries**⟩ [fraɪz] Pommes frites **III E**, 130
to **frighten** ['fraɪtn] erschrecken, Angst machen **II**
fringe [frɪndʒ] Franse, Rand- **II**
from [frɒm] von **I**
from … on [frəm … 'ɒn] ab … (*zeitl.*) **II**
⟨**front**⟩ [frʌnt] vorderer Teil **III 1**, 20
(*at*) the front [frʌnt] vorne **II**
in front (*of*) [ɪn 'frʌnt] davor, vor **I**
front [frʌnt] Vor-, Vorder- **I**
fruit [fru:t] Obst, Früchte **II**
to **fry** [fraɪ] frittieren, braten **I**
to **fuel** ['fju:əl] antreiben, anheizen, mit Brennstoff versorgen **III 6**, 112
full [fʊl] voll **I**
fun [fʌn] Spaß **I**
to make fun of [meɪk 'fʌn‿əv] sich lustig machen über **III 4**, 79
function ['fʌŋkʃn] Funktion, Aufgabe **II**
to **function** ['fʌŋkʃn] arbeiten, funktionieren **II**
⟨**fund**⟩ [fʌnd] Fonds, Fördermittel **III 5**, 93
⟨to **fund**⟩ [fʌnd] finanziell fördern **III E**, 136
funny ['fʌni] komisch, witzig, spaßig **I**
further ['fɜ:ðə] weiter **I**
furthermore [ˌfɜ:ðə'mɔ:] überdies, außerdem **III 6**, 120
future ['fju:tʃə] Zukunft **II**
future ['fju:tʃə] zukünftig **III 6**, 111
+**fuzzy** ['fʌzi] unscharf, verschwommen **II**

G

Gaelic ['geɪlɪk] gälisch, Gälisch **II**
⟨**gaggle**⟩ ['gægl] Herde, Schar (Gänse) **III 6**, 119
+**gallery** ['gæləri] Galerie **I**
to **gamble** ['gæmbl] (um Geld) spielen **II**
gambling ['gæmblɪŋ] (Glücks-)Spiel **II**
game [geɪm] Spiel **I**
°**Games** [geɪmz] Sport (*Fach*) **I**
gammon ['gæmən] geräucherter Schinken **II**
⟨**gander**⟩ ['gændə] Ganter, Gänserich **III 6**, 119
gang [gæŋ] Gang, Bande **III 2**, 37
gap [gæp] Lücke, Abstand **I**
garage ['gærɑ:ʒ] Garage **I**
garden ['gɑ:dn] Garten **I**
gardener ['gɑ:dnə] Gärtner(in) **III 2**, 32
gas [gæs] Gas **III 6**, 114
gas (*AE*) [gæs] Benzin **II**
gas station (*AE*) ['gæs ˌsteɪʃn] Tankstelle **II**
gate [geɪt] Tor **II**
gateway ['geɪtweɪ] Tor **III 2**, 32
GCSE [ˌdʒi:si:es'i:] *britischer Schulabschluss, der mit der mittleren Reife vergleichbar ist* **III 6**, 112
gear [gɪə] Ausrüstung **I**
geek [gi:k] Langweiler(in), Spießer(in) **II**
general ['dʒenrl] allgemein, generell **II**
to **generate** ['dʒenəreɪt] generieren, erzeugen **III 3**, 52
generation [ˌdʒenə'reɪʃn] Generation **II**
ladies and gentlemen [ˌleɪdiz‿n‿'dʒentlmən] meine Damen und Herren **III 1**, 14
gently ['dʒentli] sanft, mild **II**
geography [dʒi'ɒgrəfi] Erdkunde, Geografie **II**
°**Geography** [dʒi'ɒgrəfi] Erdkunde, Geografie (*Fach*) **I**
German ['dʒɜ:mən] deutsch, Deutsch (*Fach*) **I**
⟨**Germanic**⟩ [dʒə'mænɪk] germanisch **III 6**, 121
to **get*** [get] bekommen; werden **I**; etw holen **II**
to get back [get 'bæk] zurückkommen, ankommen **II**
to get behind [get bɪ'haɪnd] in Rückstand geraten **II**
to get bored [bɔ:d] sich langweilen **II**
to get into (*sth.*) [ˌget‿'ɪntə] einsteigen (in …) **I**
to get into trouble ['trʌbl] in Schwierigkeiten geraten **II**
to get off [ˌget‿'ɒf] aussteigen, absteigen (*Zug, Bus, Fahrrad*) **I**
to get on (*well with so.*) [ˌget‿ɒn 'wel] (gut mit jmdm) zurechtkommen **I**
to get out [ˌget‿'aʊt] aussteigen (*Auto, Wagen, Waggon*) **I**
to get so. to do sth. [get] jmdn dazu bringen, etwas zu tun **III 1**, 9
to get talking [get 'tɔ:kiŋ] ins Gespräch kommen **II**
+to get through ['get θru:] verschleißen **II**
to get up [get‿'ʌp] aufstehen (*vom Bett*) **II**
to get used to [get 'ju:zd] sich gewöhnen an **III 1**, 13
ghost [gəʊst] Geist, Gespenst **I**
+**giant** ['dʒaɪənt] Riese, Gigant **I**

⟨**giddying**⟩ ['gɪdiɪŋ] schwindelerregend **III 3**, 53
+**gift** [gɪft] Geschenk **II**
⟨**gig**⟩ [gɪg] Gig, Konzert **III E**, 138
gigantic [dʒaɪ'gæntɪk] gigantisch, riesig **II**
girl [gɜ:l] Mädchen **I**
girlfriend ['gɜ:lfrend] Freundin **I**
gist [dʒɪst] Kernpunkt, (das) Wesentliche **II**
to **give*** [gɪv] geben **I**
to give a talk ['tɔ:k] ein (Kurz-)Referat halten **I**
⟨to give off⟩ [gɪv‿'ɒf] verströmen **III 1**, 13
to give up [gɪv‿'ʌp] aufgeben **II**
glad [glæd] froh **III 4**, 69
⟨**glade**⟩ [gleɪd] Lichtung **III E**, 140
⟨to **glamorise**⟩ ['glæməraɪz] glorifizieren, idealisieren **III 4**, 71
glass [glɑ:s] Glas **I**
⟨**Glaswegian**⟩ [ˌglæz'wi:dʒn] Bewohner(in) Glasgows **III E**, 145
glen [glen] (enges) Tal **II**
global warming [ˌgləʊbl 'wɔ:mɪŋ] Erderwärmung durch den Treibhauseffekt **III 3**, 60
glove [glʌv] Handschuh **I**
glow [gləʊ] Glut, grelles Licht **II**
glum [glʌm] niedergeschlagen, bedrückt **III 5**, 94
to **go*** [gəʊ] gehen **I**; sagen **III 4**, 69
to go at so. ['gəʊ ət] auf jmdn losgehen **II**
to go for sth. ['gəʊ fɔ:] etw. anpacken, ausprobieren **II**
to go in for [gəʊ‿'ɪn fɔ:] sich beteiligen an (*Wettbewerb*) **II**
to go on [ˌgəʊ‿'ɒn] vorgehen **II**; weitermachen, fortsetzen **I**
⟨to go overboard on⟩ [gəʊ‿'əʊvəbɔ:d] es übertreiben mit **III 1**, 20
to go with ['gəʊ wɪð] passen zu **II**
goal [gəʊl] +Tor **II**; ⟨Ziel⟩ **III 5**, 92
⟨**goat**⟩ [gəʊt] Ziege **III E**, 136
God [gɒd] Gott **III 4**, 70
goddess ['gɒdes] Göttin **II**
goggles ['gɒglz] Schutzbrille **II**
gold [gəʊld] Gold **II**
golden ['gəʊldn] golden **I**
golf [gɒlf] Golf **I**
gone [gɒn] ausgegangen, zu Ende gegangen **I**
⟨for **good**⟩ [fə 'gʊd] für immer **III E**, 138
⟨good lookin'⟩ [ˌgʊd 'lʊkɪn] gut aussehend **III 1**, 8
good value [ˌgʊd 'vælju:] preisgünstig **III 5**, 94
to be good at (+ *gerund*) [gʊd] gut können **III 1**, 18
to be so good as to (+ *infinitive*) [səʊ 'gʊd‿əz] so gut sein zu (*Infinitiv*) **III 5**, 90
good [gʊd] gut **I**
goodbye, bye [(ˌgʊd)'baɪ] (auf) Wiedersehen, tschüs, servus (*regional*) **I**
goodie-goodie ['gʊdiˌgʊdi] Streber(in), Brave(r) **II**
goods [gʊdz] Güter, Waren **III 6**, 114
goose, *pl.*: **geese** [gu:s, gi:s] Gans **III 6**, 119
+**gorgeous** ['gɔ:dʒəs] prächtig, prachtvoll **I**
+**gorilla** [gə'rɪlə] Gorilla **I**
⟨**gosling**⟩ ['gɒzlɪŋ] junge Gans, Gänschen **III 6**, 119
⟨**gospel**⟩ ['gɒspl] Gospel; Evangelium **III 1**, 13
gossip ['gosɪp] Klatsch, Tratsch **II**
to **gossip** ['gɒsɪp] tratschen **III 1**, 10
to have* **got** [ˌhæv 'gɒt] haben **I**
⟨I gotta (*coll.*)⟩ [aɪ 'gɑtə] Ich muss **III 1**, 8
⟨**gotten** (*AE*)⟩ ['gɒtn] Partizip Perfekt von *'to get'* **III 1**, 13
government ['gʌvnmənt] Regierung **II**
⟨**governor**⟩ ['gʌvnə] Gouverneur **III E**, 132
dressing **gown** ['dresɪŋ ˌgaʊn] Morgenrock **II**
to **grab** [græb] packen, schnappen **II**
grade (*AE*) [greɪd] (Schul-)Note **III 1**, 8
⟨to make the grade⟩ [ˌmeɪk ðə 'greɪd] es zu etwas bringen **III 1**, 8
graffiti [grə'fi:ti] Graffiti **I**
grandchild ['grændtʃaɪld] Enkel(in) **III 5**, 90
grandfather ['grændˌfɑ:ðə] Großvater **II**
grandma ['grændmɑ:] Großmutter, Oma **I**
grandmother ['grændˌmʌðə] Großmutter **II**
grandparent ['grændˌpeərnt] Großelternteil **II**
grass [grɑ:s] Gras **II**
to be **grateful** ['greɪtfl] dankbar sein **I**
gray (*AE*) [greɪ] grau **III 1**, 15
graze [greɪz] Schürfwunde **II**
grease [gri:s] Fett, Schmiere, Pomade **III 4**, 69
great-grandmother [ˌgreɪt'grændˌmʌðə] Urgroßmutter **II**
great [greɪt] großartig, spitze **I**
⟨the great outdoors⟩ [greɪt‿ˌaʊt'dɔ:z] die freie Natur **III 1**, 11
greedy ['gri:di] gierig, gefräßig **II**
green [gri:n] grün **I**
greeting [gri:tɪŋ] Begrüßung, Gruß **II**
grey [greɪ] grau **I**
grid [grɪd] Netz, Gitter **II**
to **grin** [grɪn] grinsen **II**
ground [graʊnd] Boden, Grund, Gelände **III 3**, 50
⟨ground floor⟩ [ˌgraʊnd 'flɔ:] Erdgeschoss **III E**, 135
group [gru:p] Gruppe **I**
+focus group ['fəʊkəs ˌgru:p] Gruppengespräch, Gesprächsgruppe **II**
vocal group ['vəʊkl ˌgru:p] Musikgruppe mit Gesang **II**
to **grow*** [grəʊ] +anbauen **II**; wachsen **I**
to grow up [grəʊ‿'ʌp] aufwachsen **II**
grown-up ['grəʊnˌʌp] Erwachsene(r) **I**
growth [grəʊθ] Wachstum **III 6**, 112
⟨to **grunt**⟩ [grʌnt] brummen **III E**, 141
guess [ges] Vermutung, Schätzung **III 4**, 77
to **guess** [ges] raten, vermuten **I**
guest [gest] Gast **I**
guide [gaɪd] Fremdenführer(in) **II**
guide book ['gaɪd bʊk] Reiseführer (*Buch*) **I**
+guide dog ['gaɪd dɒg] Blindenhund **I**
guitar [gɪ'tɑ:] Gitarre **I**
⟨bubble **gum**⟩ ['bʌbl gʌm] Blasenkaugummi **III 1**, 13
chewing gum ['tʃu:ɪŋ ˌgʌm] Kaugummi **II**
gun [gʌn] Schusswaffe **III 2**, 42
guy [gaɪ] +Freund, Kumpel **I**; Junge, Kerl **II**; Typ **III 1**, 8
gym(*nasium*) [dʒɪm('neɪziəm)] Sporthalle **I**
gymnast ['dʒɪmnæst] Turner(in) **II**
gymnastics [dʒɪm'næstɪks] Turnen **II**

H

habit ['hæbɪt] Gewohnheit **III 4**, 67
habitat ['hæbɪtæt] Habitat, Lebensraum **III 3**, 49
hair [heə] Haar **I**
⟨pudding-bowl hair⟩ [ˌpʊdɪŋ bəʊl 'heə] Topfschnitt **III E**, 138
hairdresser ['heəˌdresə] Friseur(in) **III 6**, 111
half [hɑ:f] Hälfte **II**
half [hɑ:f] halb **I**
hall [hɔ:l] Diele, (Eingangs-) Halle **I**
assembly hall [ə'sembli ˌhɔ:l] Aula, Versammlungssaal **I**
village hall [ˌvɪlɪdʒ 'hɔ:l] Gemeindehaus **I**
hand [hænd] Hand **I**
farm hand ['fɑ:m hænd] Landarbeiter(in) **III 2**, 32
on the one hand ... on the other hand [ɒn ðə‿'wʌn hænd ... ɒn ðɪ‿'ʌðə hænd] einerseits ... andererseits **III 1**, 10
handbag ['hændbæg] Handtasche **I**
to **handle** ['hændl] umgehen mit **III 4**, 70
handlebar ['hændlbɑ:] Lenkstange, Lenker **II**
⟨**handloom**⟩ ['hændlu:m] Handwebstuhl **III 6**, 114
handout ['hændaʊt] Handout, ausgeteiltes Papier **III 3**, 61
handstand ['hændstænd] Handstand **II**
to **hang* out** [ˌhæŋ‿'aʊt] herumlungern **II**
hangout ['hæŋaʊt] Stammplatz, Stammlokal **II**
to **happen** ['hæpn] geschehen, passieren **I**
happy ['hæpi] froh, glücklich **I**
+**harbor** (*AE*) ['hɑ:bə] Hafen **I**
harbour ['hɑ:bə] Hafen **I**
hard [hɑ:d] hart **I**; schwer **III 5**, 90
hardly ['hɑ:dli] kaum **II**
to mean so. **harm** [ˌmi:n 'hɑ:m] jmdm. weh tun wollen **II**
⟨to **harm**⟩ [hɑ:m] verletzen **III E**, 136
harmless ['hɑ:mləs] ungefährlich, harmlos **II**
harmonica [hɑ:'mɒnɪkə] Mundharmonika **II**
+leather **harness** [ˌleðə 'hɑ:nɪs] Ledergeschirr, -gurtwerk **I**
+**harvest** ['hɑ:vɪst] Ernte **II**
hat [hæt] Hut **I**
hate [heɪt] Hass **III 3**, 54
to **hate** [heɪt] nicht mögen, hassen **I**
⟨**haunted house**⟩ [ˌhɔ:ntɪd 'haʊs] Spukhaus **III E**, 139
to **have*** [hæv] haben **I**
to have a look (*at*) [ˌhæv‿ə 'lʊk] (an)schauen, (an)gucken **II**
⟨to have a smoke⟩ [hæv‿ə 'sməʊk] (eine) rauchen **III 4**, 72
to have got [ˌhæv 'gɒt] haben **I**
⟨to have no consideration⟩ [hæv ˌnəʊ kənsɪdə'reɪʃn] keine Rücksicht nehmen **III 2**, 34
to have to do sth. [ˌhæv tə 'du:] etw tun müssen **II**
to have to do with [ˌhæv tə 'du:] mit etw zu tun haben **II**
he [hi:] er **I**
head [hed] Kopf **I**
deputy head [ˌdepjəti 'hed] stellvertretende(r) Schulleiter(in) **III 6**, 112
head word ['hed wɜ:d] Stichwort im Wörterbuch **III 5**, 101
to **head for** [hed] zugehen auf **II**
to head to/for [hed] zusteuern auf **III 2**, 33
headache ['hedeɪk] Kopfschmerz, Kopfweh **II**
heading ['hedɪŋ] ⟨Schacht⟩ **III 6**, 113; Überschrift **I**
headline ['hedlaɪn] Schlagzeile **II**
headphones ['hedfəʊnz] Kopfhörer **II**
+**headstone** ['hedstəʊn] Grabstein **II**
headteacher [ˌhed'ti:tʃə] Schulleiter(in) **I**
health [helθ] Gesundheit **II**
Health [helθ] °Gesundheitslehre (*Fach*) **I**
healthy ['helθi] gesund **I**
⟨top of the **heap**⟩ [ˌtɒp‿əv ðə 'hi:p] der/die Beste **III 2**, 30
to **hear*** [hɪə] hören **I**
heart [hɑ:t] Herz **II**
heart attack ['hɑ:t‿əˌtæk] Herzinfarkt **I**
⟨the very heart⟩ [ˌveri 'hɑ:t] Kern **III 2**, 30
to learn by heart [ˌlɜ:n baɪ 'hɑ:t] auswendig lernen **II**
heated ['hi:tɪd] geheizt **I**
heating ['hi:tɪŋ] Heizung **I**
heavy ['hevi] schwer **I**
hell [hel] Hölle **II**
hello [hə'ləʊ] hallo **I**
crash **helmet** ['kræʃ ˌhelmət] Sturzhelm **II**
help [help] Hilfe **I**
to **help** [help] helfen **I**
helpless ['helpləs] hilflos **I**
her [hɜ:] ihr/ihre **I**; sie (*Akk.*); ihr (*Dat.*) **I**
here ['hɪə] hier **I**
+**heritage** ['herɪtɪdʒ] Erbe **II**
hero ['hɪərəʊ] Held **III 6**, 119
hers [hɜ:z] ihre(r/s), der/die/das ihre **II**
hertz [hɜ:ts] Hertz (*Maßeinheit der Frequenz*) **III 4**, 73

hey! [heɪ] He! I
hi [haɪ] hallo I
to be **hidden** ['hɪdn] versteckt sein I
⟨**hide-out**⟩ ['haɪdaʊt] Versteck III 2, 33
to **hide*** [haɪd] (sich) verstecken, verbergen I
high-jump ['haɪˌdʒʌmp] Hochsprung II
high [haɪ] hoch I
high school (*AE*) ['haisku:l] Oberschule, Gesamtschule III 1, 9
highway ['haɪweɪ] Landstraße III 1, 13
to **hike** [haɪk] wandern III 3, 53
hiker ['haɪkə] Wanderer III 3, 53
hill [hɪl] Hügel I
him [hɪm] ihn, ihm I
himself [hɪm'self] sich (selbst) I
hint [hɪnt] Hinweis, Andeutung II
+to **hint** [hɪnt] andeuten, anspielen (auf) II
hip [hɪp] Hüfte III 1, 14
hip hop ['hɪpˌhɒp] Hip-Hop *(Musikrichtung)* II
his [hɪz] sein/seine I
⟨**hiss**⟩ [hɪs] Zischen III E, 141
to **hiss** [hɪs] zischen, fauchen II
historical [hɪ'stɒrɪkl] historisch, geschichtlich III 5, 91
history ['hɪstri] Geschichte II
History ['hɪstri] °Geschichte (*Fach*) I
hit [hɪt] Hit, Schlager II
to **hit*** [hɪt] +(auf)treffen (auf), erreichen I; schlagen, stoßen II
⟨to hit (*coll.*)⟩ [hɪt] reingehen in III E, 130
+**hitchhiker** ['hɪtʃhaɪkə] Anhalter(in), Tramper(in) II
⟨**hive**⟩ [haɪv] Bienenkorb III E, 140
hobby, (*pl.*) -ies ['hɒbi] Hobby I
hockey ['hɒki] Hockey I
to **hold*** [həʊld] halten II
+**holder** ['həʊldə] Inhaber(in), Pächter(in), Halter(in) II
record-holder ['rekɔ:d ˌhəʊldə] Rekordhalter(in) II
hole [həʊl] Loch I
holiday ['hɒlədeɪ] +Feiertag II; Ferien, Urlaub I
bank holiday [ˌbæŋk 'hɒlədeɪ] Feiertag (im Mai und August) II
holidaymaker ['hɒlədiˌmeɪkə] Urlauber(in) I
hols (= **holidays**) [hɒlz] Ferien I
home [həʊm] Heimat, Zuhause II
at home [ət‿'həʊm] zu Hause, daheim I
⟨home rule⟩ [ˌhəʊm 'ru:l] Selbstbestimmung III E, 142
make yourself at home [ˌmeɪk jɔ:self‿ət 'həʊm] machen Sie es sich gemütlich II
+mobile home [ˌməʊbaɪl 'həʊm] Wohnmobil I
homeless ['həʊmləs] heimatlos II
homepage ['həʊmpeɪdʒ] Homepage I
homework (*sing.*) ['həʊmwɜ:k] Hausaufgaben I
honest ['ɒnɪst] ehrlich, redlich III 5, 94
⟨**honey-bee**⟩ [ˌhʌni 'bi:] Honigbiene III E, 140
⟨**hoof**⟩ [hu:f] Huf III E, 141
⟨to **hook up**⟩ [hʊk‿'ʌp] einhaken III E, 130
⟨**hoop**⟩ [hu:p] Reifen III E, 141
hope [həʊp] Hoffnung II
to **hope** [həʊp] hoffen I
hopeful ['həʊpfl] hoffnungsvoll III 5, 94
horrible ['hɒrəbl] schrecklich, entsetzlich II
horror ['hɒrə] Entsetzen, Horror II
horse [hɔ:s] Pferd I
horse-riding ['hɔ:sˌraɪdɪŋ] Reiten II
⟨(*horse*)**shoe**⟩ [ʃu:] Hufeisen III E, 141
hospital ['hɒspɪtl] Krankenhaus, Klinik II
host [həʊst] Gastgeber(in) II
hostel ['hɒstl] Herberge I
youth hostel ['ju:θ ˌhɒstl] Jugendherberge I
youth **hostelling** ['ju:θ ˌhɒstlɪŋ] in Jugendherbergen übernachten I
hot [hɒt] heiß; scharf (gewürzt) I
hot dog ['hɒt dɒg] Hotdog *(langes weiches Brötchen mit Würstchen)* I
hotel [həʊ'tel] Hotel I
hour ['aʊə] Stunde I
house [haʊs] Haus I
⟨haunted house⟩ [ˌhɔ:ntɪd 'haʊs] Spukhaus III E, 139
House of Lords [ˌhaʊs‿əv 'lɔ:dz] britisches Oberhaus III 4, 72
⟨Upper House⟩ [ˌʌpə 'haʊs] Oberhaus III E, 147
⟨**housing**⟩ ['haʊzɪŋ] Wohnungsbeschaffung III 5, 93
to **hover** ['hɒvə] schweben II
how [haʊ] wie I
How are you? [ˌhaʊ‿'ɑ: ju:] Wie geht's (dir/euch/Ihnen)? I
How d'you do? [ˌhaʊ djʊ 'du:] Guten Tag! Sehr erfreut! II
how long ago? [ˌhaʊ lɒŋ‿ə'gəʊ] wie lange her? II
how many? ['haʊ ˌmeni] wie viele? I
how much? ['haʊ ˌmʌtʃ] wie viel? I
however [ˌhaʊ'evə] jedoch III 1, 13
huge [hju:dʒ] riesig, gewaltig II
huh? (*coll.*) [hʌ/hə] was? III 5, 98
hum [hʌm] Summen III 4, 73
human ['hju:mən] menschlich; Mensch III 3, 49
humour ['hju:mə] Humor II
hunger ['hʌŋgə] Hunger III 3, 54
hungry ['hʌŋgri] hungrig I
hurricane ['hʌrɪkən] Wirbelsturm, Orkan II
in a **hurry** ['hʌri] in Eile, eilig I
to **hurry** (*up*) [ˌhʌri‿'ʌp] (sich) beeilen I
to **hurt*** [hɜ:t] wehtun, schmerzen I
⟨**hurtful**⟩ ['hɜ:tfl] verletzend III E, 138
hydroelectric power [ˌhaɪdrəʊɪlektrɪk 'paʊə] Energie aus Wasserkraft III 3, 52
hygiene ['haɪdʒi:n] Gesundheitspflege, Hygiene II
+**hypnosis** [hɪp'nəʊsɪs] Hypnose II

I

I [aɪ] ich I
I'd (= *I would*) like [aɪd‿'laɪk] ich hätte gerne I
I'm (*I am*) [aɪm] ich bin I
ice [aɪs] Eis I
ice cream [aɪs 'kri:m] Eiskrem, (Speise-) Eis I
ice cream maker [aɪs 'kri:m ˌmeɪkə] Eismaschine I
ice skate ['aɪs ˌskeɪt] Schlittschuh II
ice-skating ['aɪsˌskeɪtɪŋ] Schlittschuhlaufen II
icon ['aɪkɒn] Ikone, Idol III 4, 70
+**icy** ['aɪsi] eisig I
idea [aɪ'dɪə] Eindruck, Vorstellung II; Idee, Einfall I
ideal [aɪ'dɪəl] ideal, hervorragend I
to **identify** [aɪ'dentɪfaɪ] identifizieren III 3, 53
idiot ['ɪdiət] Idiot I
if [ɪf] +ob II; wenn, falls I
to **ignore** [ɪg'nɔ:] hinwegsehen, ignorieren II
ill [ɪl] krank II
illegal [ɪ'li:gl] ungesetzlich, illegal I
illness ['ɪlnəs] Krankheit II
+**image** ['ɪmɪdʒ] Bild, Image II
to **imagine** [ɪ'mædʒɪn] sich vorstellen, annehmen I
immigrant ['ɪmɪgrənt] Einwanderer / Einwanderin II
⟨**immigration**⟩ [ˌɪmɪ'greɪʃn] Immigration, Einwanderung III 5, 92
⟨**immovable**⟩ [ɪ'mu:vəbl] unbeweglich III E, 141
⟨**impact**⟩ ['ɪmpækt] Auswirkung; Aufprall III 3, 49
important [ɪm'pɔ:tnt] wichtig II
impossible [ɪm'pɒsəbl] unmöglich III 5, 100
to **impress** [ɪm'pres] beeindrucken III 1, 11
impression [ɪm'preʃn] Eindruck III 2, 36
to **improve** [ɪm'pru:v] verbessern II
improvement [ɪm'pru:vmənt] Verbesserung III 6, 114
to **improvise** ['ɪmprəvaɪz] improvisieren II
in [ɪn] in/im I
in a flash [flæʃ] blitzschnell I
in a hurry ['hʌri] in Eile, eilig I
in case [keɪs] falls II
in common [ɪn 'kɒmən] gemeinsam I
in fact [ɪn 'fækt] eigentlich I
in front [ɪn 'frʌnt] vorne I
in order to (+ *infinitive*) [ɪn‿'ɔ:də tʊ] um ... zu ... *(Infinitiv)* III 6, 113
in public ['pʌblɪk] in der Öffentlichkeit II
+in return [ɪn rɪ'tɜ:n] dafür I
⟨in search of⟩ [ɪn 'sɜ:tʃ‿əv] auf der Suche nach III 5, 92
in the meantime [ɪn ðə 'mi:ntaɪm] in der Zwischenzeit III 1, 14
⟨in time⟩ [ɪn 'taɪm] mit der Zeit; rechtzeitig III 1, 10
in total [ɪn 'təʊtl] insgesamt, total II
inch [ɪntʃ] Zoll (*Längenmaß, ca. 2,54 cm*) III 3, 50
to **include** [ɪn'klu:d] einschließen, einbeziehen II
income ['ɪŋkʌm] Einkommen III 5, 95
⟨**incontinence**⟩ [ɪn'kɒntɪnents] Inkontinenz III 4, 69
to **increase** [ɪn'kri:s] (an)steigen, zunehmen II
⟨**independence**⟩ [ˌɪndɪ'pendənts] Unabhängigkeit III E, 133
independent [ˌɪndɪ'pendənt] unabhängig I
⟨**index**⟩ ['ɪndeks] Index, Hinweis, Anzeichen III 5, 92
Indian ['ɪndiən] Inder(in) I; +Indianer(in) II
+Seminole Indian ['semɪnəʊl‿ɪndiən] *Angehörige(r) eines indianischen Stamms* I
indirect [ˌɪndɪ'rekt] indirekt, mittelbar III 4, 78
⟨**individual**⟩ [ˌɪndɪ'vɪdʒuəl] einzeln III E, 134
+**individualist** [ˌɪndɪ'vɪdʒuəlɪst] Individualist(in) II
indoor [ˌɪn'dɔ:] Innen-, Hallen- I
indoors [ɪn'dɔ:z] drinnen, zu Hause II
industrial [ɪn'dʌstriəl] industriell III 6, 114
industry ['ɪndəstri] Industrie II
to **infect** [ɪn'fekt] infizieren, anstecken, verseuchen III 5, 90
influence ['ɪnfluənts] Einfluss II
to **influence** ['ɪnfluents] beeinflussen III 4, 69
to **inform** [ɪn'fɔ:m] informieren, benachrichtigen II
informal [ɪn'fɔ:ml] informell, nicht förmlich III 6, 120
information [ˌɪnfə'meɪʃn] Information I
⟨to **inherit**⟩ [ɪn'herɪt] erben III E, 147
to **inject** [ɪn'dʒekt] (ein)spritzen II
injection [ɪn'dʒekʃn] Spritze, Injektion II
to **injure** ['ɪndʒə] verletzen II
injury ['ɪndʒəri] Verletzung III 3, 53
inside [ˌɪn'saɪd] im Innern (von) I
insider [ˌɪn'saɪdə] Eingeweihte(r), Insider(in) II
⟨**insight**⟩ ['ɪnsaɪt] Einblick, Verständnis III 1, 10
inspiration [ˌɪntspr'eɪʃn] Eingebung, Inspiration II
to **install** [ɪn'stɔ:l] installieren, einbauen II
instead of [ɪn'sted‿əv] anstelle von, statt II
institution [ˌɪnstɪ'tju:ʃn] Institution, Einrichtung II
+to **instruct** [ɪn'strʌkt] anweisen, instruieren II
instruction [ɪn'strʌkʃn] Anweisung, Anleitung II
+**instructions** [ɪn'strʌkʃnz] Anweisungen, Instruktionen I
instrument ['ɪnstrəmənt] Instrument I
to **insult** [ɪn'sʌlt] beleidigen, beschimpfen III 5, 100

insurance [ɪn'ʃʊərns] Versicherung **II**
intelligence [ɪn'telɪdʒnts] Intelligenz **II**
intelligent [ɪn'telɪdʒnt] intelligent **II**
to **intend** [ɪn'tend] beabsichtigen **III 3**, 50
intention [ɪn'tenʃn] Absicht, Intention **I**
interest ['ɪntrəst] Interesse **II**
to be **interested** *(in)* ['ɪntrəstɪd‿ɪn] interessiert sein (an) **II**
interesting ['ɪntrəstɪŋ] interessant **I**
⟨**intermission**⟩ [ˌɪntə'mɪʃn] Pause **III 1**, 13
international [ˌɪntə'næʃnl] international **I**
Internet ['ɪntənet] Internet **I**
to **interrupt** [ˌɪntə'rʌpt] unterbrechen, jmdm ins Wort fallen **III 3**, 59
interruption [ˌɪntə'rʌpʃn] Unterbrechung **III 3**, 59
intersection *(AE)* [ɪntə'sekʃn] Kreuzung **III 1**, 13
interview ['ɪntəvjuː] Interview **I**
to **interview** ['ɪntəvjuː] interviewen, befragen **I**
interviewer ['ɪntəvjuːə] Interviewer(in) **II**
into ['ɪntə] in ... hinein **I**
I'm into ... ['ɪntə] ich stehe auf .../ ich bin begeistert von ... **I**
to **introduce** [ˌɪntrə'djuːs] einleiten **III 3**, 56; vorstellen, bekannt machen **II**
to **invade** [ɪn'veɪd] einmarschieren **II**
to **invent** [ɪn'vent] erfinden **II**
invention [ɪn'ventʃn] Erfindung **II**
inventor [ɪn'ventə] Erfinder(in) **II**
⟨to **invest**⟩ [ɪn'vest] investieren **III 5**, 93
to **investigate** [ɪn'vestɪgeɪt] untersuchen, nachforschen, ermitteln **III 6**, 120
invitation [ˌɪnvɪ'teɪʃn] Einladung **II**
to **invite** [ɪn'vaɪt] einladen **I**
to **involve** [ɪn'vɒlv] einbeziehen, verwickeln **II**
Irish ['aɪərɪʃ] irisch, Irisch **II**
Irish folk [ˌaɪərɪʃ 'fəʊk] *Musikrichtung aus Irland* **I**
Irishman/woman ['aɪərɪʃmən/ˌwʊmən] Ire/Irin **III 2**, 38
iron age ['aɪən‿eɪdʒ] Eisenzeit **II**
iron ore [ˌaɪən‿'ɔː] Eisenerz **III 6**, 114
⟨**ironically**⟩ [aɪ'rɒnɪkli] ironischerweise **III E**, 142
irony ['aɪrəni] Ironie **III 4**, 68
irregular [ɪ'regjələ] unregelmäßig **II**
irrigation [ˌɪrɪ'geɪʃn] Bewässerung **III 3**, 52
is [ɪz] ist **I**
's *(is)* [ɪz] ist **I**
isn't *(is not)* ['ɪznt] ist nicht **I**
island ['aɪlənd] Insel **II**
⟨**isle**⟩ [aɪl] Insel **III E**, 140
issue ['ɪʃuː] Frage, Angelegenheit **III 3**, 52
⟨to **issue money**⟩ [ˌɪʃuː 'mʌni] Geld drucken **III E**, 134
°**IT** *(Information Technology)* [ˌaɪ'tiː: (ˌɪnfə'meɪʃn tek'nɒlədʒi)] Informatik **I**
it [ɪt] es **I**
+**Italian** [ɪ'tæliən] italienisch, Italienisch **I**
item ['aɪtəm] ⟨Ding⟩ **III E**, 137; +Gegenstand, Artikel **I**
itself [ɪt'self] (es) selbst, sich **II**
⟨**ivory carving**⟩ ['aɪvri ˌkɑːvɪŋ] Elfenbeinschnitzerei **III E**, 136

J

jacket ['dʒækɪt] Jacke, Jackett **I**
jail [dʒeɪl] Gefängnis **III 2**, 42
traffic **jam** ['træfɪk ˌdʒæm] Verkehrsstau **II**
⟨**jamb**⟩ [dʒæmb] Tür- oder Fensterpfosten **III E**, 141
January ['dʒænjuri] Januar **I**
jazz [dʒæz] Jazz *(Musikrichtung)* **I**
jealous ['dʒeləs] eifersüchtig **III 1**, 8
+**jeans** [dʒiːnz] Jeans **I**
⟨**jelly bean**⟩ ['dʒeli biːn] Geleebonbon **III E**, 131
crown **jewels** [ˌkraʊn 'dʒuːəlz] Kronjuwelen **I**
jewellery ['dʒuːəlri] Juwelen, Schmuck **II**
+**jewelry** *(AE)* ['dʒuːəlri] Schmuck **I**
+**Jewish** ['dʒuːɪʃ] jüdisch **I**
⟨to **jingle**⟩ ['dʒɪŋgl] klimpern **III 1**, 12
job [dʒɒb] Job, Arbeit, Stelle **I**
to **jog** [dʒɒg] anstoßen, antippen **II**; ⟨joggen, laufen⟩ **III 1**, 23
to **join** [dʒɔɪn] beitreten, Mitglied werden **II**
to join in *(with)* [ˌdʒɔɪn‿'ɪn] teilnehmen (an) **II**
+to join so. [dʒɔɪn] sich jmdm. anschließen **II**
joke [dʒəʊk] Witz **III 1**, 19
journalist ['dʒɜːnlɪst] Journalist(in) **III 4**, 66
journey ['dʒɜːni] Reise **II**
joy [dʒɔɪ] Freude, Vergnügen **II**
to **judge** [dʒʌdʒ] beurteilen, einschätzen **III 3**, 50
jug [dʒʌg] Krug, Kanne **II**
to **juggle** ['dʒʌgl] jonglieren **I**
carrot **juice** ['kærət ˌdʒuːs] Karottensaft **II**
orange juice ['ɒrɪndʒ ˌdʒuːs] Orangensaft **II**
July [dʒʊ'laɪ] Juli **I**
to **jump** [dʒʌmp] springen **I**
jumper ['dʒʌmpə] Strickjacke **I**
June [dʒuːn] Juni **I**
junior choir [ˌdʒuːniə 'kwaɪə] Chor der unteren Klassenstufen **I**
just [dʒʌst] +genau **II**; gerade, eben **I**; nur, bloß **II**
⟨**justice**⟩ ['dʒʌstɪs] Richter(in); Gerechtigkeit **III E**, 134

K

to **keep*** [kiːp] (be)halten **I**
to keep *(warm)* [kiːp] (warm) bleiben **II**
to keep doing sth. [ˌkiːp 'duːɪŋ] etw. immer wieder, ununterbrochen tun **II**
⟨to keep out⟩ [kiːp‿'aʊt] sich heraushalten **III E**, 143
to keep sth. up [kiːp‿'ʌp] etw. (durch)halten **II**
to keep up *(with so.)* [ˌkiːp‿'ʌp] Schritt halten (mit jmdm) **II**
kerb [kɜːb] Bordsteinkante **II**
⟨**kettle**⟩ ['ketl] Kessel **III E**, 132
key [kiː] Schlüssel(-) **II**
key word ['kiː wɜːd] Schlüsselbegriff **I**
keyboard ['kiːbɔːd] elektronische Orgel, Keyboard **I**
keyboarder ['kiːbɔːdə] Keyboardspieler(in) **I**
kick [kɪk] (Fuß-)Tritt, Stoß **II**
to **kick** [kɪk] treten, (mit dem Fuß) stoßen **II**
kid [kɪd] Kind **I**; ⟨**Kitz, Zicklein**⟩ **III 6**, 119
to **kill** [kɪl] töten, umbringen **II**
⟨serial **killer**⟩ [ˌsiːrɪəl 'kɪlə] Serienkiller, Massenmörder **III 4**, 68
kilo ['kiːləʊ] Kilo(gramm) **III 6**, 119
kilometre [kɪ'lɒmɪtə] Kilometer **I**
kind [kaɪnd] Art, Sorte **I**
What kind *(of)* ...? [kaɪnd] Was für eine/welche Art ...? **I**
king [kɪŋ] König **I**
⟨**kiss**⟩ [kɪs] Kuss **III 1**, 10
kit [kɪt] Ausrüstung **II**
°drum kit ['drʌm kɪt] Schlagzeugausrüstung **I**
kitchen ['kɪtʃɪn] Küche **I**
knee-bend ['niːbend] Kniebeuge **II**
knife, *(pl.)* -ves [naɪf] Messer **I**
knight [naɪt] Ritter **I**
knob [nɒb] Knopf, Knauf **II**
knock [nɒk] Klopfen, Pochen **II**
°to **knock** [kɒk] klopfen **I**
to knock so. out [nɒk‿'aʊt] jmdn. bewusstlos schlagen/werden lassen **II**
to be **knocked down** [biː ˌnɒkt 'daʊn] umgefahren werden **II**
⟨**knot**⟩ [nɒt] Knoten **III 1**, 13
to **know*** [nəʊ] wissen, kennen **I**
knowledge ['nɒlɪdʒ] Wissen, Kenntnis **II**
Korean [kə'riːən] Koreaner(in) **III 2**, 38
kung fu film [ˌkʊŋ 'fuː fɪlm] Kung-Fu-Film **I**

L

label ['leɪbl] Etikett, Label **II**
laborer *(AE)* ['leɪbrə] ungelernte(r) Arbeiter(in), Hilfsarbeiter(in) **III 2**, 32
labour ['leɪbə] Arbeit, Arbeitskräfte **II**
⟨**lad**⟩ [læd] Junge **III E**, 144
ladder ['lædə] Leiter **II**
lady ['leɪdi] Dame, Frau **I**
cleaning lady ['kliːnɪŋ ˌleɪdi] Zugehfrau, Putzfrau **I**
ladies and gentlemen [ˌleɪdiz‿n‿'dʒentlmən] (meine) Damen und Herren **III 1**, 14
lake [leɪk] See **II**
lamb [læm] Lamm(fleisch) **II**
land [lænd] Land **I**
to **land** [lænd] landen, von Bord gehen **III 2**, 32
lander ['lændə] Landeeinheit **II**
landing ['lændɪŋ] Landung **II**
landmine ['lændmaɪn] Landmine **III 4**, 71
landscape ['lændskeɪp] Landschaft **I**
lane [leɪn] Gasse, Sträßchen **II**; Spur **III 2**, 33
language ['læŋgwɪdʒ] Sprache **II**
⟨to **lap**⟩ [læp] plätschern **III E**, 140
large [lɑːdʒ] groß, weitläufig **II**
laser beam ['leɪzə ˌbiːm] Laserstrahl **II**
to **last** [lɑːst] (an)dauern, (an)halten **III 1**, 10
last [lɑːst] letzte(r/s), der/die Letzte **I**
at last [ət 'lɑːst] endlich **III 1**, 13
the last word [ðə ˌlɑːst 'wɜːd] der letzte Schrei **III 5**, 94
late [leɪt] spät **I**
to be late *(for)* [leɪt] zu spät kommen (für), spät dran sein **II**
lately ['leɪtli] in letzter Zeit **III 1**, 13
later ['leɪtə] später **I**
latest ['leɪtɪst] neueste(r/s), zuletzt erschienene(r/s) **I**
Latin ['lætɪn] lateinisch, Latein **I**
⟨**latitude**⟩ ['lætɪtjuːd] Breitengrad **III 3**, 52
⟨**latte**⟩ ['lattə] Latte *(ital.)*, Milchkaffee **III E**, 130
to **laugh** [lɑːf] lachen **I**
laughter ['lɑːftə] Gelächter, Lachen **II**
+**launch** [lɔːntʃ] Abschuss **II**
to **launch** [lɔːntʃ] +abschießen **II**; ⟨einführen⟩ **III 5**, 93
laundry ['lɔːndri] Wäsche **III 3**, 51
law [lɔː] Gesetz **II**
⟨to pass a law⟩ [pɑːs] ein Gesetz verabschieden **III E**, 146
+**lawn** [lɔːn] Rasen **I**
lawyer ['lɔɪə] Rechtsanwalt, -anwältin **III 6**, 120
layer ['leɪə] Schicht, Lage **III 4**, 69
layout ['leɪaʊt] Gestaltung, Layout **I**
lazy ['leɪzi] faul **II**
lead singer [ˌliːd 'sɪŋə] Leadsänger(in) **II**
to **lead*** [liːd] führen **III 1**, 10
leader ['liːdə] Anführer(in) **II**
⟨to **lean forward**⟩ [ˌliːn 'fɔːwəd] sich vorlehnen **III E**, 130
to **learn*** [lɜːn] lernen **I**
to learn by heart [ˌlɜːn baɪ 'hɑːt] auswendig lernen **II**
learning tip ['lɜːnɪŋ ˌtɪp] Lerntipp **I**
at **least** [ət 'liːst] zumindest **II**
least said soonest mended [ˌliːst 'sed ˌsuːnəst 'mendɪd] je weniger geredet wird, desto schneller wird es wieder gut **II**
leather ['leðə] Leder **I**
+leather harness [ˌleðə 'hɑːnɪs] Ledergeschirr, -gurtwerk **I**
⟨**leather-aproned**⟩ [ˌleðə‿'eɪprənd] lederbeschürzt **III E**, 141
to **leave*** [liːv] weggehen, verlassen **I**

to leave behind [ˌliːv bɪ'haɪnd] zurück-, hinterlassen **II**
left out [left‿'aʊt] ausgeschlossen **III 1**, 10
left [left] links **I**
leg [leg] Bein **II**
legal ['liːgl] gesetzlich, legal **II**
legend ['ledʒənd] Legende **I**
to **lend*** [lend] (ver)leihen **I**
contact **lens** ['kɒntækt ˌlens] Kontaktlinse **III 4**, 73
leotard ['liːətɑːd] Trikot, Gymnastikanzug **II**
less [les] weniger **I**
lesson ['lesn] Unterrichtsstunde **I**
to **let*** [let] lassen, jmdm etw erlauben **III 3**, 51
let's (*let us*) [lets] lass(t) uns **I**
⟨to let go⟩ [let 'gəʊ] loslassen **III E**, 130
⟨to let oneself in for sth.⟩ [ˌlet wʌnself 'ɪn fɔː] sich auf etwas einlassen, sich etwas einbrocken **III 5**, 94
letter ['letə] Buchstabe; Brief **I**
capital letter [ˌkæpɪtl 'letə] Großbuchstabe **I**
level ['levl] Ebene, Niveau **II**
liar ['laɪə] Lügner(in) **II**
⟨**liberty**⟩ ['lɪbəti] Freiheit **III E**, 133
librarian [laɪ'breəriən] Bibliothekar(in) **II**
library ['laɪbri] Bibliothek, Bücherei **I**
⁺to **lie** [laɪ] lügen **II**
to **lie*** [laɪ] liegen **I**
life, (*pl.*) -ves [laɪf] Leben **I**
lifebelt ['laɪfbelt] Rettungsgurt, Rettungsring **I**
lifeboat ['laɪfbəʊt] Rettungsboot **I**
lifeguard ['laɪfgɑːd] Rettungsschwimmer(in) **I**
lifejacket ['laɪfˌdʒækɪt] Schwimmweste **I**
lifeline ['laɪflaɪn] Rettungsleine **I**
lifetime ['laɪftaɪm] Lebenszeit, Leben **I**
light [laɪt] Licht **I**
⟨to run a red light⟩ [ˌrʌn‿ə red 'laɪt] eine rote Ampel überfahren **III E**, 130
traffic light ['træfɪk ˌlaɪt] Ampel **I**
lighthouse ['laɪthaʊs] Leuchtturm **I**
to **light*** (*up*) [laɪt‿'ʌp] aufleuchten, (*sich*) erhellen, anzünden **III 4**, 69
to **like** [laɪk] mögen, gerne haben **I**
I'd (= *I would*) like [aɪd‿'laɪk] ich hätte gerne **I**
would you like to? [ˌwʊd ˌjuː 'laɪk tə] möchtest du?/möchtet ihr/möchten Sie? **I**
like [laɪk] (ebenso) wie **I**
⟨**like**⟩ [laɪk] als ob **III 1**, 8
likely ['laɪkli] wahrscheinlich **II**
to be **likely to** (+ *infinitive*) ['laɪkli] wahrscheinlich tun **III 4**, 77
⟨**limelight**⟩ ['laɪmlaɪt] Rampenlicht **III E**, 138
limit ['lɪmɪt] Grenze **III 1**, 12
to **limit** ['lɪmɪt] limitieren, begrenzen **III 4**, 67
line [laɪn] Leitung; Warteschlange **III 1**, 10; Linie **I**; Zeile **II**
fishing line ['fɪʃɪŋ ˌlaɪn] Angelschnur **I**
⁺supply line [sə'plaɪ ˌlaɪn] Versorgungsleitung **I**
to stand in line (*AE*) [ˌstænd‿ɪn 'laɪn] Schlange stehen **III 1**, 20
to **line up** [ˌlaɪn‿'ʌp] (sich) aufstellen **II**
link [lɪŋk] Verbindung **III 1**, 11
⟨to **link up**⟩ [lɪŋk‿'ʌp] miteinander verbunden sein **III E**, 148
⟨**linnet**⟩ ['lɪnɪt] Hänfling **III E**, 140
lip [lɪp] Lippe **III 4**, 69
⁺**lipstick** ['lɪpstɪk] Lippenstift **II**
list [lɪst] Liste **I**
to **listen** ['lɪsn] zuhören **I**
listening comprehension ['lɪsnɪŋ ˌkɒmprɪ'henʃn] Hörverstehen **I**
litre (*BE*) ['liːtə] Liter **III 3**, 51
to **litter** ['lɪtə] verstreuen, übersäen **II**
little ['lɪtl] klein **I**; wenig **II**
a little [ə 'lɪtl] ein wenig, ein bisschen **III 4**, 68

to **live** [lɪv] wohnen, leben **I**
live [laɪv] lebendig, direkt, live **I**
to **liven up** [ˌlaɪvn‿'ʌp] beleben, aufmuntern **II**
living ['lɪvɪŋ] Lebensunterhalt **III 6**, 113
living room ['lɪvɪŋ ˌrʊm] Wohnzimmer **I**
ll. (= **lines**) [laɪnz] Zeilen **I**
⟨**loads**⟩ [ləʊdz] jede Menge **III E**, 144
loaf, *pl.*: loaves [ləʊf, ləʊvz] Laib **III 6**, 119
⟨**loafer** (*AE*)⟩ ['ləʊfə] Halbschuh, Freizeitschuh **III E**, 130
local ['ləʊkl] lokal, örtlich, Orts- **I**
location [ləʊ'keɪʃn] Standort, (Dreh-)Ort **II**
loch [lɒk/lɒx] See *(schottisch)* **II**
logo ['ləʊgəʊ] Logo, Emblem **I**
⟨to **loll**⟩ [lɒl] hängen **III 1**, 13
Londoner ['lʌndənə] Londoner(in) **II**
lonely (*n or adj*) ['ləʊnli] einsam; einsame Person **III 4**, 69
to **long** (*for*) ['lɒŋ ˌfɔː] sich sehnen (nach) **II**
long [lɒŋ] lang **I**
how long ago? [ˌhaʊ lɒŋ‿ə'gəʊ] wie lange her? **II**
long-distance truck driver [ˌlɒŋ'dɪstnts 'trʌk ˌdraɪvə] Fernfahrer(in) **II**
long-jump ['lɒŋˌdʒʌmp] Weitsprung **II**
look [lʊk] Blick, Anblick **II**
to have a look (*at*) [ˌhæv‿ə 'lʊk] (an)schauen, (an)gucken **II**
to **look** [lʊk] aussehen **II**; schauen, betrachten **I**
to look after [ˌlʊk‿'ɑːftə] schauen nach, sorgen für **I**
to look for ['lʊk fɔː] suchen **II**
to look forward (*to*) [ˌlʊk 'fɔːwəd] sich freuen (auf) **I**
to look sth. up [ˌlʊk‿'ʌp] etw nachschlagen **I**
looks pl. [lʊks] Aussehen **III 1**, 9
loose [luːs] lose, locker **II**
to **lose*** [luːs] verlieren **I**
⟨to lose count⟩ [ˌluːz 'kaʊnt] die Übersicht verlieren **III 4**, 70
loser ['luːzə] Verlierer(in) **II**
lost [lɒst] verloren **I**
to be lost [lɒst] sich verlaufen haben **I**
a **lot** [ə 'lɒt] viel, eine Menge **I**
lots of ['lɒts‿əv] viele (von) **I**
loud [laʊd] laut **I**
⟨**louse**, *pl.*: **lice**⟩ [laʊs, laɪs] Laus **III 6**, 119
⟨**lousy**⟩ ['laʊzi] verlaust, lausig **III 6**, 119
love [lʌv] (in) Liebe; herzlichst **I**
to be in love [ɪn 'lʌv] verliebt sein **III 1**, 20
to **love** [lʌv] lieben, gern haben, mögen **I**
lovely ['lʌvli] hübsch, schön **I**
lover ['lʌvə] Liebhaber(in), Geliebte(r) **II**
low [ləʊ] niedergeschlagen, schwach **III 1**, 8; niedrig **I**
⟨**loyal**⟩ ['lɔɪəl] loyal, treu **III E**, 142
luck [lʌk] Glück **I**
lucky ['lʌki] Glücks- **III 3**, 54
to be lucky ['lʌki] Glück haben **II**
lunch [lʌntʃ] Mittagessen **I**
lung [lʌŋ] Lunge **II**

M

to **e-mail** ['iːmeɪl] jmdm eine E-Mail schreiben **III 1**, 8
machine [mə'ʃiːn] Apparat, Maschine **II**
mad [mæd] verrückt, wahnsinnig **I**
madam ['mædəm] gnädige Frau *(Anrede)* **I**
magazine [ˌmægə'ziːn] Zeitschrift **I**
magic ['mædʒɪk] magisch, zauberhaft **II**
mail [meɪl] Post **II**
main [meɪn] Haupt- **II**
⟨**majesty**⟩ ['mædʒəsti] Majestät **III E**, 146
major ['meɪdʒə] größter, Haupt- **I**
majority [mə'dʒɒrəti] Mehrheit **III 4**, 67
make-up ['meɪkʌp] Makeup, Maske **II**
to **make*** [meɪk] machen **I**; schaffen, erreichen **III 4**, 72
make yourself at home [ˌmeɪk jɔːself‿ət 'həʊm] machen Sie es sich gemütlich **II**
to make a face [feɪs] ein Gesicht ziehen **II**
to make fun of [meɪk 'fʌn‿əv] sich lustig machen über **III 4**, 79
⟨to make it⟩ ['meɪk‿ɪt] es schaffen **III 2**, 30
to make so. do sth. ['meɪk ˌsʌmwʌn 'duː ˌsʌmθɪŋ] jmdn veranlassen etw zu tun **I**
to make sure [ˌmeɪk 'ʃʊə] sicherstellen **I**
⟨to make the grade⟩ [ˌmeɪk ðə 'greɪd] es zu etwas bringen **III 1**, 8
to make the most of sth. [məʊst] das Beste aus etw machen **I**
⟨to make the team⟩ [ˌmeɪk ðə 'tiːm] ins Team aufgenommen werden **III 1**, 8
to make up [ˌmeɪk‿'ʌp] (sich) ausdenken, erfinden **I**
⟨to make up for sth.⟩ [ˌmeɪk‿'ʌp] etwas ausgleichen **III E**, 138
ice cream **maker** [aɪs 'kriːm ˌmeɪkə] Eismaschine **I**
male [meɪl] männlich; Mann **III 4**, 68
shopping **mall** (*AE*) ['ʃɒpɪŋ ˌmɔːl] Einkaufszentrum **I**
man, (*pl.*) men [mæn/men] Mann / Männer **I**
to **manage** ['mænɪdʒ] bewältigen, schaffen **II**
manager ['mænɪdʒə] Manager(in), Geschäftsführer(in), leitende(r) Angestellte(r), Direktor(in) **III 4**, 77
⟨floor manager⟩ ['flɔː ˌmænɪdʒə] Aufnahmeleiter(in) **III 4**, 68
⟨**mania**⟩ ['meɪniə] Manie **III 4**, 73
⟨**manipulative**⟩ [mə'nɪpjələtɪv] manipulierend **III 4**, 70
manned [mænd] bemannt **II**
manner ['mænə] Art und Weise **III 4**, 68
⟨**mansion**⟩ ['mæntʃn] Herrenhaus, Villa **III 4**, 68
⁺**manufacturer** [ˌmænjə'fæktʃərə] Hersteller(in), Produzent(in), Fabrikant(in) **II**
how **many?** ['haʊ ˌmeni] wie viele? **I**
map [mæp] Stadtplan, Landkarte **I**
mind map ['maɪnd mæp] *etwa:* Gedankennetz **I**
Marathon ['mærəθn] Marathon **I**
March [mɑːtʃ] März **I**
to **march** [mɑːtʃ] marschieren **III 2**, 37
marching band ['mɑːtʃɪŋ ˌbænd] Marschkapelle **II**
mark (*BE*) [mɑːk] (Schul-)Note **III 1**, 15
to **mark** [mɑːk] markieren **I**
marked [mɑːkt] markiert **I**
market ['mɑːkɪt] Markt **I**
⁺**marketing** ['mɑːkɪtɪŋ] Vertrieb, Absatz, Marketing **II**
marriage ['mærɪdʒ] Ehe, Heirat **III 4**, 71
to **marry** ['mæri] heiraten **II**
to be married ['mærid] verheiratet sein **II**
to get married [ˌget 'mærɪd] heiraten **II**
marsh [mɑːʃ] Marschland, Sumpf **I**
⟨**mask**⟩ [mɑːsk] Maske **III 6**, 117
mass [mæs] Menge, Masse **II**
match [mætʃ] Streichholz; Spiel (*Sport*) **I**
friendly match [ˌfrendli 'mætʃ] Freundschaftsspiel **I**
to **match** [mætʃ] zuordnen **I**
mate [meɪt] Freund(in), Kumpel **II**
raw **material** [ˌrɔː mə'tɪəriəl] Rohstoff **III 6**, 114
°**Maths** [mæθs] Mathe(matik) *(Fach)* **I**
matter ['mætə] Sache, Angelegenheit **II**
maximum (*n. or adj.*) ['mæksɪməm] Maximum; maximal **III 6**, 112
May [meɪ] Mai **I**
may [meɪ] dürfen, können **I**
maybe ['meɪbi] vielleicht **I**
mayor [meə] Bürgermeister(in) **II**
me [miː] mich **I**
⟨on me⟩ [ɒn 'miː] auf meine Kosten/Rechnung **III 2**, 33
meal [miːl] Mahlzeit, Essen **I**
to **mean*** [miːn] bedeuten; meinen **I**
⟨to be meant to be sth.⟩ [ment] etw sein sollen **III 1**, 13

to mean (+ *to* + *infinitive*) [mi:n] beabsichtigen, vorhaben **III 3**, 56
to mean so. harm [ˌmi:n 'hɑ:m] jmdm weh tun wollen **II**
meaning ['mi:nɪŋ] Bedeutung, Sinn **II**
meaningless ['mi:nɪŋləs] sinnlos, bedeutungslos **II**
means [mi:nz] Mittel **II**
in the **meantime** [ɪn ðə 'mi:ntaɪm] in der Zwischenzeit **III 1**, 14
⟨**measure**⟩ ['meʒə] Maßstab **III 5**, 92
mechanic [mɪ'kænɪk] Mechaniker(in) **II**
media ['mi:diə] Medien **II**
medicine ['medsn] Medizin **II**
to **meet*** [mi:t] treffen, begegnen **I**
Pleased to meet you. [pli:zd] Angenehm. Sehr erfreut. **II**
⟨to meet with⟩ ['mi:t wɪθ] stoßen auf **III E**, 142
meeting ['mi:tɪŋ] Treffen, Begegnung **I**
to **melt** (*away*) [melt] schmelzen **III 2**, 30
member ['membə] Mitglied **I**
membership ['membəʃɪp] Mitgliedschaft **III 4**, 70
memory ['memri] Erinnerung **I**; Gedächtnis **I**
⟨to **menace**⟩ ['menəs] bedrohen **III 3**, 50
to **mend** [mend] ausbessern, reparieren **I**
least said soonest mended [ˌli:st 'sed ˌsu:nəst 'mendɪd] je weniger geredet wird, desto schneller wird es wieder gut **II**
to **mention** ['menʃn] erwähnen **II**
menu ['menju:] Speisekarte **III 2**, 36
merit ['merɪt] Verdienst, Leistung **II**
mess [mes] Unordnung, Durcheinander **II**
message ['mesɪdʒ] Mitteilung, Nachricht, Botschaft **III 3**, 53
metal ['metl] Metall **II**
meter ['mi:tə] Zähler, Taxameter **III 2**, 34
to **miaow** [ˌmi:'aʊ] miauen **II**
mice (*pl.*) [maɪs] Mäuse **II**
⁺**microphone** ['maɪkrəfəʊn] Mikrofon **I**
microwave oven [ˌmaɪkrəʊweɪv‿'ʌvn] Mikrowellenherd **II**
⁺**mid-town** ['mɪdtaʊn] *mittlerer Teil der Insel Manhattan in New York* **I**
⟨mid-Atlantic states⟩ [mɪdətˌlæntɪk 'steɪts] Staaten an der Ostküste der USA **III 2**, 33
⁺**middle** ['mɪdl] Mitte **I**
middle (*n. or adj.*) ['mɪdl] Mitte; mittler(e/r/s) **III 4**, 72
midnight ['mɪdnaɪt] Mitternacht **II**
might [maɪt] könnte(n), dürfte(n) **II**
mile [maɪl] Meile *(Längenmaß = 1,61 km)* **I**
military ['mɪlɪtri] militärisch, Militär- **II**
mill [mɪl] Mühle, Fabrik **III 6**, 114
millennium [mɪ'leniəm] Jahrtausend **III 4**, 72
million ['mɪljən] Million **I**
mind map ['maɪnd mæp] *etwa:* Gedankennetz **I**
⟨to blow one's mind out (*sl.*)⟩ [ˌbləʊ wʌnz 'maɪnd‿aʊt] umwerfen; high machen, sich berauschen **III 4**, 72
⟨to change one's mind⟩ [ˌtʃeɪndʒ wʌnz 'maɪnd] seine Meinung ändern **III E**, 131
to **mind** [maɪnd] etw dagegen haben **II**
mine [maɪn] Mine, Bergwerk **III 6**, 113
miner ['maɪnə] Bergarbeiter(in) **III 2**, 32
mineral ['mɪnərəl] Mineral, Mineral- **III 1**, 20
⟨to **mingle**⟩ ['mɪŋgl] sich unter die Leute mischen **III 1**, 12
minibus ['mɪnɪbʌs] Kleinbus **I**
minimal ['mɪnɪml] gering, minimal **II**
minimum ['mɪnɪməm] Minimum **II**
Prime **Minister** [ˌpraɪm 'mɪnɪstə] Premierminister(in) **II**
minority [maɪ'nɒrəti] Minderheit **III 4**, 67
⁺**minus** ['maɪnəs] minus **I**
minute ['mɪnɪt] Minute **I**
⟨**mirror**⟩ ['mɪrə] Spiegel **III E**, 138
miserable ['mɪzrəbl] unglücklich, miserabel **II**
misery ['mɪzri] Qual, Misere **II**
to **misread*** [mɪs'ri:d] falsch lesen **III 2**, 33
Miss [mɪs] Fräulein (*Anrede*) **I**
to **miss** [mɪs] ⟨aussetzen⟩ **III 1**, 13; nicht treffen, verfehlen **II**; verpassen, versäumen **I**
to be missing ['mɪsɪŋ] fehlen **II**
mission ['mɪʃn] Auftrag, Mission **II**
mistake [mɪ'steɪk] Fehler **I**
⟨to **mistreat**⟩ [mɪs'tri:t] misshandeln **III E**, 136
misunderstanding [ˌmɪsʌndə'stændɪŋ] Missverständnis **III 5**, 95
mixed bag [ˌmɪkst 'bæg] bunte Mischung, Allerlei **III 5**, 96
⁺**mobile home** [ˌməʊbaɪl 'həʊm] Wohnmobil **I**
mobile phone [ˌməʊbaɪl 'fəʊn] Mobiltelefon, Handy **I**
⟨**mock exam**⟩ [ˌmɒk‿ɪg'zæm] Probeprüfung unter realistischen Bedingungen **III E**, 144
model ['mɒdl] Modell **I**
modem ['məʊdem] Modem **I**
modern ['mɒdn] modern, zeitgemäß **II**
mom (*AE*) [mɒm] Mama, Mutti **II**
at the **moment** ['məʊmənt] im Moment, zur Zeit **I**
monarchy ['mɒnəki] Monarchie, Königshaus **III 4**, 71
monastery ['mɒnəstri] Kloster (für Mönche) **III 5**, 98
Monday ['mʌndeɪ] Montag **I**
money ['mʌni] Geld **I**
pocket money ['pɒkɪt ˌmʌni] Taschengeld **I**
⟨to issue money⟩ [ˌɪʃu: 'mʌni] Geld drucken **III E**, 134
monitor ['mɒnɪtə] Monitor, Kontrollbildschirm **III 4**, 68
to **monitor** ['mɒnɪtə] überwachen **III 1**, 10
monkey ['mʌŋki] Affe **III 1**, 13
⟨**monopoly**⟩ [mə'nɒpli] Monopol **III E**, 133
⁺**monorail** ['mɒnəreɪl] Einschienenbahn **II**
⁺**monotone** ['mɒnətəʊn] monotoner Klang **II**
monster ['mɒnstə] Ungeheuer, Monster **II**
month [mʌntθ] Monat **II**
⁺**monument** ['mɒnjəmənt] Baudenkmal, Monument **II**
⁺**moon** [mu:n] Mond **I**
moonlight ['mu:nlaɪt] Mondlicht **II**
⟨**moose** (*sg. and pl.*)⟩ [mu:s] Elch(e) **III 6**, 119
⁺**moped** ['məʊped] Moped, Kleinkraftrad **I**
more [mɔ:] mehr **I**
not ... any more [ˌnɒt ... ˌeni 'mɔ:] (überhaupt) nicht mehr, keine ... mehr **II**
morning ['mɔ:nɪŋ] Morgen, Vormittag **I**
most (*of*) ['məʊst‿əv] meiste(r/s) **I**
to make the most of sth. [məʊst] das Beste aus etw machen **I**
mostly ['məʊstli] meistens, hauptsächlich **II**
mother ['mʌðə] Mutter **I**
motion picture ['məʊʃn ˌpɪktʃə] Film (*wörtl.:* Bewegungsbild) **II**
motorbike ['məʊtəˌbaɪk] Motorrad **I**
motorcycle ['məʊtəˌsaɪkl] Motorrad **II**
motorcyclist ['məʊtəˌsaɪklɪst] Motorradfahrer(in) **II**
motorhome ['məʊtəˌhəʊm] Wohnmobil **I**
motorway café ['məʊtəweɪ ˌkæfeɪ] Cafeteria auf der Autobahn **I**
⁺**motto** ['mɒtəʊ] Motto, Leitsatz **I**
mountain ['maʊntɪn] Berg **II**
mountain bike ['maʊntɪn ˌbaɪk] Geländefahrrad, Mountainbike **I**
mountain climber ['maʊntɪn ˌklaɪmə] Bergsteiger(in) **II**
mountain climbing ['maʊntɪn ˌklaɪmɪŋ] Bergsteigen **II**
mouse, *pl.*: **mice** [maʊs, maɪs] Maus **I**
moustache [mə'stɑ:ʃ] Schnurrbart **III 4**, 73
°**mouth** [maʊθ] Mund **I**
move [mu:v] Bewegung, Schritt, Zug, Umzug **III 4**, 70
to **move** [mu:v] (sich) bewegen; umziehen **I**
movement ['mu:vmənt] Bewegung **III 2**, 37
⟨civil rights movement⟩ [ˌsɪvl 'raɪts ˌmu:vmənt] Bürgerrechtsbewegung **III E**, 142
movie (*AE*) ['mu:vi] Film **I**
moving ['mu:vɪŋ] beweglich **II**
mph [ˌempi:'eɪtʃ] Meilen pro Stunde **III 4**, 71
Mr ['mɪstə] Herr (*Anrede*) **I**
Mrs ['mɪsɪz] Frau (*Anrede für verheiratete Frauen*) **I**
Ms [mɪz/məz] Frau (*Anrede*) **I**
much [mʌtʃ] viel **I**
how much? ['haʊ ˌmʌtʃ] wie viel? **I**
mud [mʌd] Schlamm, Matsch **II**
muddy ['mʌdi] schmutzig, schlammig **II**
muesli ['mju:zli] Müsli **II**
muffin ['mʌfɪn] weiches Brötchen, kleiner Kuchen **II**
⟨**mug**⟩ [mʌg] Trottel **III 6**, 115
⟨**mule**⟩ [mju:l] Maultier, Maulesel **III 1**, 13
to **multiply** ['mʌltɪplaɪ] multiplizieren, (sich) vervielfachen **III 6**, 119
mum [mʌm] Mama, Mutti **I**
mummy ['mʌmi] Mami, Mutti **II**
murmur ['mɜ:mə] Gemurmel **II**
muscle ['mʌsl] Muskel **II**
museum [mju:'zi:əm] Museum **I**
music ['mju:zɪk] Musik **I**
Music ['mju:zɪk] Musik (*Fach*) **I**
classical music ['klæsɪkl 'mju:zɪk] klassische Musik **I**
pop music ['pɒp ˌmju:zɪk] Popmusik **I**
rock music ['rɒk ˌmju:zɪk] Rockmusik **I**
musical ['mju:zɪkl] Musical **I**
musician [mju:'zɪʃn] Musiker(in) **I**
Muslim ['mʊzlɪm] moslemisch, mohammedanisch **II**
must [mʌst] müssen **I**
to **mutter** ['mʌtə] murmeln **II**
my [maɪ] mein/meine **I**
mysteriously [mɪ'stɪəriəsli] geheimnisvoll, mysteriös **II**
mystery ['mɪstri] Geheimnis, Mysterium **I**
myth [mɪθ] Mythos **II**

N

nah (*coll.*) [næ:] nö **III 5**, 98
nail [neɪl] Nagel **I**
naked ['neɪkɪd] nackt **III 6**, 113
name [neɪm] Name **I**
to **name** [neɪm] nennen **II**
to name after (*BE*)/for (*AE*) ['neɪm‿ɑ:ftə] benennen nach **III 3**, 52
⟨**named**⟩ [neɪmd] namens **III 1**, 12
nanny ['næni] Kindermädchen **III 4**, 79
⟨**nappy** (*BE*)⟩ ['næpi] Windel **III 4**, 69
narrator [nə'reɪtə] Erzähler(in) **II**
narrow ['nærəʊ] eng, schmal **II**
nasty ['nɑ:sti] scheußlich, abscheulich **II**
nation ['neɪʃn] Nation, Volk **II**
national park [ˌnæʃnl 'pɑ:k] Nationalpark **II**
national ['næʃnl] staatlich, national **II**
nationality [ˌnæʃn'æləti] Nationalität **I**
⁺**native** ['neɪtɪv] Eingeborene(r), Ureinwohner(in) **I**
⟨**native**⟩ ['neɪtɪv] Heimat- **III E**, 143
Native American [ˌneɪtɪv‿ə'merɪkən] amerikanische(r) Ureinwohner(in) **II**
natural ['nætʃrl] natürlich **I**
nature ['neɪtʃə] Natur **II**
navigation [ˌnævɪ'geɪʃn] Navigation, Schiffsverkehr **I**
near [nɪə] in der Nähe, nah **I**
⁺**nearer** ['nɪərə] näher **I**
nearly ['nɪəli] fast, beinahe **I**
necessary ['nesəsri] nötig, notwendig **I**
neck [nek] Hals, Genick **II**
to **need** [ni:d] brauchen **I**
to need to [ni:d] müssen **II**

needn't ['ni:dnt] nicht brauchen **I**
negative ['negətɪv] negativ, verneinend **I**
neighbor (*AE*) ['neɪbə] Nachbar(in) **III 1**, 15
neighbour ['neɪbə] Nachbar(in) **II**
neighbourhood ['neɪbəhʊd] Nachbarschaft **II**
neighbouring ['neɪbrɪŋ] benachbart, angrenzend **III 5**, 100
neither ['naɪðə] keine(r) (von beiden); auch nicht **I**
neither … nor ['naɪðə…'nɔ:] weder … noch **I**
neon ['ni:ɒn] Neon **III 3**, 56
nervous ['nɜ:vəs] **III 2**, 41
net [net] Netz **I**
⟨**netspeak**⟩ ['netspi:k] Internet-Zeichensprache **III 1**, 10
never ['nevə] nie(mals) **I**
new [nju:] neu **I**
⟨brand new⟩ [ˌbrænd 'nju:] brandneu **III 2**, 30
newcomer ['nju:kʌmə] Neuling, Neuankömmling **III 2**, 32
news (*sing.*) [nju:z] Nachrichten, Neuigkeit(en) **I**
newspaper ['nju:speɪpə] Zeitung **I**
next [nekst] nächste(r/s), der/die Nächste **I**
next door [ˌnekst 'dɔ:] nebenan **II**
⁺next to ['nekst tu:] neben, in der Nähe von **I**
nice [naɪs] hübsch, nett **I**
nickname ['nɪkneɪm] Spitzname **II**
night [naɪt] Nacht **I**
night club ['naɪt klʌb] Nachtclub **I**
no [nəʊ] nein; kein/keine **I**
no one ['nəʊwʌn] niemand **I**
no way (*coll.*) [ˌnəʊ 'weɪ] auf keinen Fall, keineswegs **I**
nobody ['nəʊbədi] niemand **I**
to **nod** [nɒd] nicken **II**
noise [nɔɪz] Geräusch, Lärm **II**
noisy [nɔɪzi] laut, geräuschvoll **I**
nomad ['nəʊmæd] Nomade/Nomadin **II**
to **nominate** ['nɒmɪneɪt] ernennen, nominieren **II**
nomination [ˌnɒmɪ'neɪʃn] Nominierung, Ernennung **II**
⟨**non-fiction**⟩ ['nɒnfɪkʃn] Sachtexte **III E**, 149
non-stop [ˌnɒn'stɒp] pausenlos, ununterbrochen **I**
non-verbal [nɒn'vɜ:bl] nonverbal, ohne Worte **III 4**, 80
none [nʌn] keine(r/s) **II**
nonsense ['nɒnsəns] Unsinn, Quatsch **II**
noon [nu:n] Mittag **II**
nor [nɔ:] noch, (und) auch nicht **I**
neither … nor ['naɪðə…'nɔ:] weder … noch **I**
normal ['nɔ:ml] normal **I**
Norman ['nɔ:mən] Normanne/Normannin **II**
north [nɔ:θ] Norden, nördlich **I**
⟨North Carolinian⟩ [ˌnɔ:θ kærə'lɪnjən] Bewohner(in) North Carolinas **III 3**, 50
⟨**northerner**⟩ ['nɔ:ðənə] Person aus dem Norden **III 6**, 115
nose [nəʊz] Nase **I**
not [nɒt] nicht **I**
(*not*) after all [ˌɑ:ftə‿'ɑ:l] doch (nicht) **I**
not … any more [ˌnɒt … ˌeni 'mɔ:] (überhaupt) nicht mehr, keine … mehr **II**
⟨not even⟩ [nɒt‿'i:vn] nicht einmal **III E**, 133
not … at all [ˌnɒt‿ə'tɔ:l] überhaupt nicht **I**
not … either [nɒt‿'aɪðə] auch nicht **III 1**, 8
not … yet [jet] noch nicht **I**
note [nəʊt] Banknote **II**; Note, Ton **III 4**, 73; Notiz, (kurzer) Brief, Mitteilung **II**
to **note** (*down*) [ˌnəʊt 'daʊn] notieren, (auf)schreiben **I**
vocabulary **notebook** [vəʊˌkæbjəlri 'nəʊtbʊk] Vokabelheft **I**
nothing ['nʌθɪŋ] nichts **I**
notice board ['nəʊtɪs ˌbɔ:d] Schwarzes Brett, Anschlagtafel **I**
to take notice (*of*) [ˌteɪk 'nəʊtɪs] beachten, Notiz nehmen (von) **I**
to **notice** ['nəʊtɪs] bemerken, wahrnehmen **II**
novel ['nɒvl] Roman **III 4**, 68
November [nəʊ'vembə] November **I**
now [naʊ] nun, jetzt **I**
⟨by now⟩ [baɪ 'naʊ] inzwischen **III E**, 143
now and then [ˌnaʊ‿n‿'ðen] ab und zu **I**
nowhere ['nəʊweə] nirgends, nirgendwo **I**
⟨**nuclear fission**⟩ [ˌnju:kliə 'fɪʃn] Kernspaltung **III E**, 139
numb [nʌm] taub, gefühllos **II**
number (*no.*) ['nʌmbə] Zahl, Nummer (Nr.) **I**
nurse [nɜ:s] Krankenschwester, -pfleger **II**
nut [nʌt] Nuss **III 5**, 89

O

10 **o'clock** [ə'klɒk] 10 Uhr **I**
to **obey** [əʊ'beɪ] gehorchen, befolgen **III 2**, 32
object ['ɒbdʒɪkt] Gegenstand, Objekt **II**
observer [əb'zɜ:və] Beobachter(in) **II**
to be **obsessed** (*by*) [əb'sest] besessen sein (von) **II**
⟨**obsession**⟩ [əb'seʃn] fixe Idee, Besessenheit **III 4**, 71
ocean ['əʊʃn] Ozean, Meer **III 3**, 51
October [ɒk'təʊbə] Oktober **I**
odd [ɒd] ungewöhnlich, merkwürdig, eigenartig **III 6**, 119
odd one out [ˌɒd wʌn‿'aʊt] das Nichtdazupassende scheidet aus **I**
⟨**odor** (*AE*)⟩ ['əʊdə] Geruch **III 1**, 13
of [ɒv/əv] von/vom **I**
of course [əv 'kɔ:s] natürlich, selbstverständlich **I**
⟨of its own⟩ [əv‿ɪts‿'əʊn] eigen **III 1**, 13
off [ɒf] weg, fort **I**
offer ['ɒfə] Angebot **II**
to **offer** (*to do sth.*) ['ɒfə] anbieten (etw. zu tun) **II**
office ['ɒfɪs] ⟨Amt⟩ **III E**, 134; Arbeitszimmer, Büro **I**
post office ['pəʊst‿ˌɒfɪs] Postamt **II**
official [ə'fɪʃl] Beamter, Beamtin, Funktionär(in) **III 3**, 50
official [ə'fɪʃl] offiziell **I**
⟨**offspring** (*sg. and pl.*)⟩ ['ɒfsprɪŋ] Sprössling, Nachkommen, Nachwuchs **III 6**, 119
often ['ɒfn] oft, öfters **I**
Oh, dear! [əʊ 'dɪə] Oh je! **I**
oil [ɔɪl] Öl **I**
oil slick ['ɔɪl slɪk] Ölteppich **I**
OK [əʊ'keɪ] in Ordnung, okay **I**
old [əʊld] alt **I**
old-fashioned [ˌəʊld'fæʃnd] altmodisch **III 4**, 73
omelette ['ɒmlet] Omelett **III 2**, 36
on [ɒn] auf, an/am **I**; über, zu **III 4**, 69
on air [ɒn‿'eə] auf Sendung **III 4**, 66
on board [ɒn 'bɔ:d] an Bord **II**
⟨on me⟩ [ɒn 'mi:] auf meine Kosten/Rechnung **III 2**, 33
on purpose ['pɜ:pəs] absichtlich **II**
⟨on record⟩ [ˌɒn 'rekɔ:d] schriftlich festgehalten, verzeichnet **III 5**, 92
on the one hand … on the other hand [ɒn ðə‿'wʌn hænd … ɒn ðɪ‿'ʌðə hænd] einerseits … andererseits **III 1**, 10
on time [ɒn 'taɪm] pünktlich **II**
once [wʌnts] einmal **II**
one [wʌn] eins **I**
⟨one way⟩ ['wʌnweɪ] Einbahn- **III 2**, 33
the only ones [wʌnz] die Einzigen **I**
One Day Travelcard ['trævlkɑ:d] Tageskarte, Netzkarte *(London)* **II**
onion ['ʌnjən] Zwiebel **III 2**, 32
online [ˌɒn'laɪn] online **III 1**, 8
only ['əʊnli] einzig(e) **III 4**, 70
an only child [ˌəʊnli 'tʃaɪld] Einzelkind **II**
only ['əʊnli] erst **III 5**, 95; nur **I**
to **open** ['əʊpn] öffnen, aufmachen **I**
open ['əʊpn] offen **I**
open-air [ˌəʊpn'eə] im Freien, Freiluft- **II**
can **opener** ['kæn ˌəʊpnə] Dosenöffner **II**
opening ['əʊpnɪŋ] Eröffnung, Beginn **I**
°**opening price** ['əʊpnɪŋ ˌpraɪs] Eröffnungskurs **II**
soap **opera** ['səʊp‿ˌɒprə] Seifenoper **III 4**, 66
operating theatre ['ɒpəreɪtɪŋ ˌθɪətə] Operationssaal **II**
operation [ˌɒpr'eɪʃn] Operation **II**
⟨tour **operator**⟩ [ˌtʊə‿'ɒpreɪtə] Reiseveranstalter **III E**, 136
opinion [ə'pɪnjən] Meinung, Ansicht **II**
⁺**opponent** [ə'pəʊnənt] Gegenspieler(in), Gegner(in) **II**
⟨**opportunity**⟩ [ˌɒpə'tju:nəti] Gelegenheit, Chance, Möglichkeit **III 5**, 92
opposite ['ɒpəzɪt] Gegenteil; gegenüber **I**
optimistic [ˌɒptɪ'mɪstɪk] optimistisch **II**
⟨**option**⟩ ['ɒpʃn] Wahl, Option **III E**, 130
or [ɔ:] oder **I**
either … or ['aɪðə … 'ɔ:] entweder … oder **II**
orange juice ['ɒrɪndʒ ˌdʒu:s] Orangensaft **II**
⁺**orbit** ['ɔ:bɪt] Erdumlaufbahn **II**
senior **orchestra** [ˌsi:niə‿'ɔ:kɪstrə] Orchester der oberen Klassenstufen **I**
order ['ɔ:də] Auftrag, Bestellung **III 6**, 121; Reihenfolge **II**
in order to (*+ infinitive*) [ɪn‿'ɔ:də tʊ] um … zu … *(Infinitiv)* **III 6**, 113
postal order ['pəʊstl‿ˌɔ:də] Postanweisung **II**
to **order** ['ɔ:də] befehlen, anordnen; bestellen **III 5**, 97
ordinary ['ɔ:dnəri] gewöhnlich, normal **III 5**, 95
iron **ore** [ˌaɪən‿'ɔ:] Eisenerz **III 6**, 114
organization [ˌɔ:gnaɪ'zeɪʃn] Organisation, Veranstalter **I**
to **organize** ['ɔ:gnaɪz] organisieren, durchführen **I**
organizer ['ɔ:gnaɪzə] Organisator(in) **II**
⟨**origin**⟩ ['ɒrɪdʒɪn] Ursprung **III E**, 132
original [ə'rɪdʒnl] original, ursprünglich **II**
originally [ə'rɪdʒnli] ursprünglich, anfänglich **II**
other ['ʌðə] andere(r/s) **I**
each other [ˌi:tʃ‿'ʌðə] einander **II**
the other day [ði‿ˌʌðə 'deɪ] neulich **III 2**, 41
otherwise ['ʌðəwaɪz] sonst, ansonsten **II**
ouch! [aʊtʃ] au!, autsch! **I**
our ['aʊə] unser **I**
ours ['aʊəz] der/die/das Unsere **I**
⁺**ourselves** [ˌaʊə'selvz] wir (selbst) **II**
out (*of*) [aʊt] hinaus, heraus **I**
out loud [ˌaʊt 'laʊd] laut (vorlesen, sprechen) **II**
out of shape [ˌaʊt‿əv 'ʃeɪp] außer Form **II**
to drive so. out [ˌdraɪv‿'aʊt] jmdn verjagen, hinausjagen **II**
to get out [ˌget‿'aʊt] aussteigen *(Auto, Wagen, Waggon)* **I**
to hang out [ˌhæŋ‿'aʊt] herumlungern **II**
to set out to do sth. [ˌset‿'aʊt] etw fest vorhaben **II**
to stick out ['stɪk‿aʊt] herausstrecken **II**
to work out [wɜ:k‿'aʊt] ausarbeiten, herausfinden **II**
outdoor [ˌaʊt'dɔ:] Freiluft-, Außen-, (für) draußen, im Freien **III 5**, 94
⟨the great **outdoors**⟩ [greɪt‿ˌaʊt'dɔ:z] die freie Natur **III 1**, 11
⁺**outdoors** [ˌaʊt'dɔ:z] im Freien, draußen **II**
outer space [ˌaʊtə 'speɪs] der äußere Weltraum **II**
outfit ['aʊtfɪt] Kleidung, Ausstattung **II**
outnumbered [ˌaʊt'nʌmbəd] zahlenmäßig unterlegen **II**

output ['aʊtpʊt] Ertrag, Ausstoß, Produktion, Leistung **III 6**, 114
outside [aʊt'saɪd] draußen **I**
outsider [ˌaʊt'saɪdə] Außenseiter(in) **II**
outstanding [ˌaʊt'stændɪŋ] hervorragend, überragend **II**
⁺**oval** ['əʊvl] oval **II**
microwave **oven** [ˌmaɪkrəʊweɪv‿'ʌvn] Mikrowellenherd **II**
over ['əʊvə] hinüber **I**
all over [ˌɔ:l‿əʊvə] überall (in) **II**
over and over again [ˌəʊvə‿ənd‿ˌəʊvə‿ə'gen] immer wieder, wieder und wieder **III 5**, 97
over there [ˌəʊvə 'ðeə] da drüben **I**
to push so. over [ˌpʊʃ‿'əʊvə] jmdn umstoßen **I**
overall [ˌəʊvr'ɔ:l] insgesamt, allgemein **II**
overboard ['əʊvəbɔ:d] über Bord **I**
⟨to go overboard on⟩ [gəʊ‿'əʊvəbɔ:d] es übertreiben mit **III 1**, 20
to **overlook** [ˌəʊvə'lʊk] überschauen; mit Blick über/auf **I**
overseas [ˌəʊvə'si:z] in/im Übersee **II**
⟨to **oversleep***⟩ [ˌəʊvə'sli:p] verschlafen **III E**, 130
overtime ['əʊvətaɪm] Überstunden **II**
overuse [ˌəʊvə'ju:s] übermäßiger Gebrauch **III 3**, 51
to **own** [əʊn] besitzen **II**
⟨of its **own**⟩ [əv‿ɪts‿'əʊn] eigen **III 1**, 13
own [əʊn] eigene(r/s) **I**
on one's own [ˌɒn wʌnz‿'əʊn] allein, ohne Hilfe **II**
owner ['əʊnə] Eigentümer(in), Besitzer(in) **I**

P

p (*pence, pl. of penny*) [pents] *britische Währung (100 pence = £1)* **I**
to **pack** [pæk] packen **I**
package ['pækɪdʒ] Paket **III 2**, 33
page [peɪdʒ] Seite **I**
pain [peɪn] Schmerz, Leid(en) **II**
paint [peɪnt] Farbe **I**
to **paint** [peɪnt] anmalen, streichen **I**
painter ['peɪntə] (Kunst-)Maler(in) **II**
⁺**painting** ['peɪntɪŋ] Gemälde, Bild **I**
pair [peə] Paar **I**
⟨**pal**⟩ [pæl] Kumpel, Freund(in) **III 1**, 11
palace ['pælɪs] Palast **II**
pale [peɪl] bleich, blass **II**
pan [pæn] Pfanne **III 2**, 37
pancake ['pænkeɪk] Pfannkuchen **II**
⟨**pane**⟩ [peɪn] Scheibe **III E**, 139
panel ['pænl] Podium **III 3**, 58
to **panic** ['pænɪk] in Panik geraten **II**
pants (*AE*) [pænts] Hose **II**
paparazzi [ˌpæpər'ætsi] Paparazzi, aufdringliche Skandalreporter(innen) **III 4**, 70
paper ['peɪpə] Papier **II**; Zeitung **II**
parade [pə'reɪd] Parade, Aufmarsch **II**
paragraph ['pærəgrɑ:f] Absatz, Abschnitt **III 6**, 114
paramedic [ˌpærə'medɪk] Sanitäter(in) **II**
parcel ['pɑ:sl] Paket, Päckchen **II**
parents ['peərnts] Eltern **I**
park ['θi:m ˌpɑ:k] Park **I**
car park ['kɑ: ˌpɑ:k] Parkplatz **I**
national park [ˌnæʃnl 'pɑ:k] Nationalpark **II**
theme park ['θi:m ˌpɑ:k] Erlebnispark **I**
to **park** [pɑ:k] parken **III 2**, 33
part [pɑ:t] Rolle **II**; Teil **I**
to take part (*in*) [ˌteɪk 'pɑ:t] teilnehmen (an) **I**
to **part** [pɑ:t] sich trennen, auseinandergehen **II**
particular [pə'tɪkjələ] besondere(r/s), bestimmte(r/s) **III 4**, 70
partly ['pɑ:tli] teilweise, zum Teil **II**
partner ['pɑ:tnə] Partner(in) **I**
parts (*pl.*) [pɑ:ts] Gegend, Region **II**
party ['pɑ:ti] ⟨Partei⟩ **III E**, 134; Party, Fest **I**
⟨to **party**⟩ ['pɑ:ti] feiern **III 1**, 12
to **pass** [pɑ:s] +(einen Ball) passen **II**; ⟨verabschieden⟩ **III E**, 133; vorbeifahren, vorbeikommen **II**; weitergeben **III 3**, 53
⟨to pass a law⟩ [pɑ:s] ein Gesetz verabschieden **III E**, 146
to pass on [pɑ:s‿'ɒn] entschlafen, verscheiden **III 5**, 90
passenger ['pæsndʒə] Reisende(r), Fahrgast, Passagier **II**
passport ['pɑ:spɔ:t] (Reise-)Pass **III 2**, 32
past [pɑ:st] Vergangenheit **III 5**, 95
past [pɑ:st] nach **I**; vorbei (an) **II**
pasta ['pæstə] Nudeln, Teigwaren **II**
pastrami [pəs'trɑ:mi] Pastrami *(eine jüdische Rauchfleischspezialität)* **III 2**, 39
pasty ['pæsti] (Fleisch-)Pastete **II**
⟨to **patent**⟩ ['peɪtənt] patentieren (lassen) **III 6**, 117
path [pɑ:θ] Weg, Pfad **I**
patient ['peɪʃnt] Patient(in) **II**
to **pause** [pɔ:z] innehalten, stoppen, stehen bleiben **III 5**, 95
pavement ['peɪvmənt] Bürgersteig, Gehweg **II**
paw [pɔ:] Pfote **II**
pay [peɪ] Bezahlung, Vergütung **II**
to **pay*** [peɪ] (be)zahlen **I**
⁺to pay attention [ˌpeɪ‿ə'tenʃn] aufmerksam sein, achtsam sein **I**
payment ['peɪmənt] Zahlung **II**
°**PE** (*Physical Education*) [ˌpi:'i: ('fɪzɪkl ˌedʒʊ'keɪʃn)] Sport, Turnen **I**
peace [pi:s] Frieden **II**
peaceful ['pi:sfl] friedlich **II**
peanut ['pi:nʌt] Erdnuss **III 1**, 13
⟨**pedestal**⟩ ['pedɪstl] Podest, Sockel **III 4**, 70
pedestrian [pɪ'destriən] Fußgänger(in) **II**
pen [pen] Füller, Füllfederhalter **I**
pencil ['pentsl] Bleistift **I**
pencil case ['pentsl ˌkeɪs] Federmäppchen **I**
pencil sharpener ['pentsl ˌʃɑ:pnə] Bleistiftspitzer **I**
penfriend ['penfrend] Brieffreund(in) **I**
⟨the **penny has dropped**⟩ [ðə ˌpeni həz 'drɒpt] Der Groschen ist gefallen. **III 6**, 119
⟨penny pl.: pennies or pence⟩ ['peni] Penny **III 6**, 119
penthouse ['penthaʊs] Penthouse, Dachterrassenwohnung **III 5**, 94
people ['pi:pl] Leute, Menschen **I**
⟨**pep talk**⟩ ['pep ˌtɔ:k] aufmunternde Worte **III E**, 130
per [pɜ:] pro **III 4**, 72
percent [pə'sent] Prozent **I**
perception [pə'sepʃn] Wahrnehmung **III 2**, 37
perfect ['pɜ:fɪkt] perfekt, vollkommen **I**
to **perform** [pə'fɔ:m] aufführen, vorführen **II**; durchführen **II**
perhaps [pə'hæps] vielleicht **I**
period ['pɪəriəd] Periode, Zeitspanne, Zeitalter; Unterrichtsstunde **III 6**, 112
free period [ˌfri: 'pɪəriəd] Hohlstunde, die zum selbstständigen Lernen gedacht ist **III 6**, 112
permanent ['pɜ:mənənt] permanent, ständig **III 4**, 76
⟨**permission**⟩ [pə'mɪʃn] Erlaubnis **III E**, 146
work **permit** ['wɜ:k ˌpɜ:mɪt] Arbeitserlaubnis **III 6**, 112
to **permit** [pə'mɪt] erlauben **III 3**, 53
person ['pɜ:sn] Person **I**
personal ['pɜ:snəl] persönlich **III 1**, 10
personality [ˌpɜ:sə'næləti] Persönlichkeit **III 1**, 11
to **persuade** [pə'sweɪd] überreden, überzeugen **III 3**, 59
pet [pet] Haustier, Liebling **II**
petrol station ['petrl ˌsteɪʃn] Tankstelle **I**
phenomenon [fɪ'nɒmɪnən] Phänomen **III 4**, 71
phew! [fju:] puh! **I**
phone [fəʊn] Telefon **I**
(*phone*) call [('fəʊn) kɔ:l] Anruf **I**
mobile phone [ˌməʊbaɪl 'fəʊn] Mobiltelefon, Handy **I**
to **phone** [fəʊn] telefonieren, anrufen **I**
photo ['fəʊtəʊ] Foto **I**
to take a photo [ˌteɪk‿ə 'fəʊtəʊ] ein Foto machen **II**
photographer [fə'tɒgrəfə] Fotograf(in) **III 4**, 66
photography [fə'tɒgrəfi] Fotografie (*nicht:* Foto, Bild!); Aufnahmen **III 4**, 71
phrasal verb [ˌfreɪzl 'vɜ:b] Verb mit Präposition oder kurzem Adverb **III 6**, 120
phrase [freɪz] Phrase, kurzer Satz **I**
piano [pi'ænəʊ] Klavier, Piano **II**
piccolo ['pɪkələʊ] Piccolo(-flöte) **I**
to **pick up** [pɪk‿'ʌp] abholen **II**; +aufheben, -lesen **II**; hochheben, übernehmen **III 2**, 33
to pick (*out*) [ˌpɪk‿'aʊt] (heraus)picken, (heraus)suchen **I**
picnic ['pɪknɪk] Picknick **I**
picture ['pɪktʃə] Bild **I**
motion picture ['məʊʃn ˌpɪktʃə] Film (*wörtl.:* Bewegungsbild) **II**
pie [paɪ] Pastete, gedeckter Kuchen **III 6**, 117
piece [pi:s] Stück, Teil **I**
pile [paɪl] Haufen, Stapel **II**
pilot ['paɪlət] Pilot(in) **I**
pin [pɪn] Nadel **II**
⟨to **pin**⟩ [pɪn] festhalten **III E**, 137
pink [pɪŋk] pink **I**
pioneer [ˌpaɪə'nɪə] Pionier **I**
pirate ['paɪərət] Pirat(in) **I**
pit [pɪt] Grube, Zeche **III 6**, 113
pitch [pɪtʃ] (Fußball-)Feld, (Sport-)Platz **II**; ⟨Anreiz⟩ **III 5**, 93
place [pleɪs] Ort, Platz **I**
to take place [ˌteɪk 'pleɪs] stattfinden **II**
to **place** [pleɪs] setzen, platzieren **II**
plain [pleɪn] schlicht, einfach **I**
plan [plæn] Plan **I**
to **plan** [plæn] planen, vorhaben **I**
plane [pleɪn] Flugzeug **I**
planet ['plænɪt] Planet **II**
plant [plɑ:nt] Pflanze; Werk, Fabrik **III 3**, 48
plastic ['plæstɪk] Plastik **I**
plate [pleɪt] Teller **I**
play [pleɪ] Theaterstück **I**
role play ['rəʊl pleɪ] Rollenspiel **I**
to **play** [pleɪ] spielen **I**
player ['pleɪə] Spieler(in) **I**
record player ['rekɔ:d ˌpleɪə] (Schall-)Plattenspieler **II**
playground ['pleɪgraʊnd] (Schul-)Hof **II**
playtime ['pleɪtaɪm] *(Schule)* Pause **II**
plaza ['plɑ:zə] Piazza, Gebäudekomplex **III 2**, 34
⟨to **plead**⟩ [pli:d] bitten **III 1**, 13
(un)pleasant [(ʌn)'pleznt] (un)angenehm **III 6**, 121
please [pli:z] bitte **I**
as you please [ˌaz ju: 'pli:z] wie es dir/euch/Ihnen beliebt **I**
Pleased to meet you. [pli:zd] Angenehm. Sehr erfreut. **II**
plenty ['plenti] reichlich, im Überfluss **II**
plot [plɒt] Handlung (eines Romans, Theaterstücks) **III 2**, 40
⟨**plug**⟩ [plʌg] Stecker **III 6**, 115
plus [plʌs] plus, extra **II**
pm [ˌpi:'em] nachmittags *(12-24 Uhr)* **I**
⟨to **poach**⟩ [pəʊtʃ] wildern **III E**, 136
pocket ['pɒkət] (Hosen-/Jacken-)Tasche **I**
pocket money ['pɒkɪt ˌmʌni] Taschengeld **I**
poem ['pəʊɪm] Gedicht **I**
poet ['pəʊɪt] Dichter(in), Poet(in) **II**
point [pɔɪnt] Punkt **I**
decimal point [ˌdesɪml 'pɔɪnt] Komma(stelle) **II**
point of view [ˌpɔɪnt‿əv'vju:] Standpunkt, Sicht, Perspektive **III 2**, 41
to get so.'s point (*coll.*) [pɔɪnt] jmdn verstehen **II**

to see no point in sth. [ˌsiː nəʊ ˈpɒɪnt‿ɪn] etw für sinnlos halten **II**
to **point out** [pɔɪnt‿ˈaʊt] zeigen auf, hinweisen **III 2**, 37
poisonous [ˈpɔɪznəs] giftig **II**
⟨red-hot **poker**⟩ [ˌred hɒt ˈpəʊkə] rotglühender Schürhaken **III E**, 137
pole [pəʊl] Pol **III 3**, 51
police [pəˈliːs] Polizei **I**
policeman [pəˈliːsmən] Polizist **II**
Polish [ˈpəʊlɪʃ] polnisch **III 1**, 16
polite [pəˈlaɪt] höflich **I**
political [pəˈlɪtɪkl] politisch **III 6**, 114
⟨**politician**⟩ [ˌpɒlɪˈtɪʃn] Politiker(in) **III E**, 135
⟨**politics**⟩ [ˈpɒlətɪks] Politik **III E**, 135
to **pollute** [pəˈluːt] verschmutzen **III 3**, 49
pollution [pəˈluːʃn] Verschmutzung **III 3**, 49
polo shirt [ˈpəʊləʊ ˌʃɜːt] Polohemd **I**
swimming **pool** [ˈswɪmɪŋ ˌpuːl] Swimmingpool **I**
poor [pɔː] arm **II**; schlecht, gering, schwach **III 6**, 112
pop music [ˈpɒp ˌmjuːzɪk] Popmusik **I**
popular [ˈpɒpjələ] beliebt, populär **I**
popularity [ˌpɒpjəˈlærəti] Beliebtheit, Popularität **II**
population [ˌpɒpjəˈleɪʃn] Bevölkerung **III 3**, 49
trading **port** [ˈtreɪdɪŋ ˌpɔːt] Handelshafen **III 6**, 114
position [pəˈzɪʃn] Position **I**
to **position** [pəˈzɪʃn] aufstellen, in Position bringen **II**
positive [ˈpɒzətɪv] positiv, bejahend **I**
possibility [ˌpɒsəˈbɪləti] Gelegenheit, Möglichkeit **II**
possible [ˈpɒsəbl] möglich **I**
post [pəʊst] Post **II**
post office [ˈpəʊst‿ˌɒfɪs] Postamt **II**
to **post** [pəʊst] abschicken, zur Post geben **II**
postal order [ˈpəʊstl‿ˌɔːdə] Postanweisung **II**
postcard [ˈpəʊstkɑːd] Postkarte **I**
poster [ˈpəʊstə] Poster, Plakat **I**
postman [ˈpəʊstmən] Briefträger(in), Postbote/-botin **II**
posture [ˈpɒstʃə] (Körper-)Haltung **II**
potato, *pl.* -oes [pəˈteɪtəʊ] Kartoffel **II**
couch potato [ˈkaʊtʃ pəˌteɪtəʊ] jmd, der ständig vor dem Fernseher sitzt **II**
potato blight [pəˈteɪtəʊ ˌblaɪt] Kartoffelfäule **III 5**, 91
£ (**pound sterling**) [paʊnd] Pfund *(britische Währung)* **I**
poverty [ˈpɒvəti] Armut **II**
power [ˈpaʊə] Kraft, Stärke, Macht **II**
hydroelectric power [ˌhaɪdrəʊɪlektrɪk ˈpaʊə] Energie aus Wasserkraft **III 3**, 52
power station [ˈpaʊə ˌsteɪʃn] Kraftwerk **III 3**, 58
battery-**powered** [ˈbætriˌpaʊəd] batteriebetrieben **II**
powerful [ˈpaʊəfl] ⟨leistungsstark⟩ **III E**, 139; ⟨mächtig⟩ **III E**, 134
practical [ˈpræktɪkl] praktisch **I**
to **practise** [ˈpræktɪs] +ausüben, praktizieren **II**; üben, proben **I**
+to **pray** [preɪ] beten **II**
prayer [preə] Gebet **III 5**, 90
+to **predict** [prɪˈdɪkt] vorhersagen, prophezeien **II**
to **prefer** [prɪˈfɜː] vorziehen, lieber mögen **III 3**, 55
prefix [ˈpriːfɪks] Präfix, Vorsilbe **III 5**, 102
prehistoric [ˌpriːhɪˈstɒrɪk] vorgeschichtlich, prähistorisch **II**
to **prepare** [prɪˈpeə] vorbereiten **II**
to be **prepared** [prɪˈpeəd] vorbereitet sein **II**
⟨**preposterous**⟩ [prɪˈpɒstrəs] grotesk, absurd **III E**, 144
⟨**Presbyterian**⟩ [ˌprezbɪˈtɪəriən] Presbyterianer(in) *(Anhänger(in) einer protestantischen Kirche)* **III E**, 143

prescription [prɪˈskrɪpʃn] Verordnung, Rezept **II**
present [ˈpreznt] Gegenwart **III 5**, 95; Geschenk **I**
to **present** [prɪˈzent] präsentieren **III 3**, 59
present [ˈpreznt] gegenwärtig, momentan; anwesend **III 5**, 98
presentation [ˌpreznˈteɪʃn] Präsentation, Darbietung, Moderation **III 4**, 73
presenter [prɪˈzentə] Moderator(in) **III 4**, 66
president [ˈprezɪdnt] Präsident/in **III 3**, 52
the **press** [pres] die Presse **III 4**, 70
press-up [ˈpresʌp] Liegestütz **II**
to **press** [pres] drücken **II**
pressure [ˈpreʃə] Druck **III 1**, 8
to **pretend** *(to)* [prɪˈtend] vorgeben (zu), vortäuschen **I**
pretty [ˈprɪti] hübsch, nett **II**
pretty [ˈprɪti] ziemlich **III 2**, 34
to **prevent** [prɪˈvent] verhindern, vermeiden **II**
price [praɪs] Preis **I**
°closing price [ˈkləʊzɪŋ ˌpraɪs] Schlusskurs **II**
°opening price [ˈəʊpnɪŋ ˌpraɪs] Eröffnungskurs **II**
⟨price range⟩ [ˈpraɪs ˌreɪndʒ] Preisklasse **III E**, 139
+price shopper [ˈpraɪs ˌʃɒpə] Schnäppchenjäger(in) **II**
to **pride oneself on sth** [ˈpraɪd wʌnself ɒn] sich einer Sache rühmen **III 5**, 100
Prime Minister [ˌpraɪm ˈmɪnɪstə] Premierminister(in) **II**
princess [ˈprɪnses] Prinzessin **III 4**, 70
to **print** *(out)* [prɪnt] (aus)drucken **I**
printer [ˈprɪntə] Drucker **I**
⟨**prison**⟩ [ˈprɪzn] Gefängnis **III E**, 147
prisoner [ˈprɪznə] Gefangene(r), Häftling **III 5**, 91
private [ˈpraɪvət] privat **III 1**, 18
prize [praɪz] Preis, Gewinn **I**
the **pros and cons** [ˌprəʊz‿n‿ˈkɒnz] das Für und Wider, Pro und Contra **I**
probably [ˈprɒbəbli] wahrscheinlich **II**
problem [ˈprɒbləm] Problem **I**
⟨**processed food**⟩ [ˌprəʊsest ˈfuːd] konservierte Nahrung **III 1**, 20
to **produce** [prəˈdjuːs] produzieren, herstellen **I**
producer [prəˈdjuːsə] Produzent(in), Hersteller(in) **II**
production [prəˈdʌkʃn] Herstellung, Produktion **II**
professional [prɒˈfeʃnl] professionell **III 2**, 34
profile [ˈprəʊfaɪl] Porträt; Profil **III 4**, 73
profit [ˈprɒfɪt] Gewinn, Profit **II**
+**program** *(AE)* [ˈprəʊgræm] (Computer-)Programm **I**
programme *(BE)* [ˈprəʊgræm] Sendung **II**
progress [ˈprəʊgres] Fortschritt(e), Verlauf **III 6**, 114
project [ˈprɒdʒekt] Projekt **I**
promise [ˈprɒmɪs] Versprechen, Zusicherung **II**
to **promise** [ˈprɒmɪs] versprechen **II**
to **promote** [prəˈməʊt] fördern, werben für; befördern **III 4**, 70
promotion [prəˈməʊʃn] Förderung, Unterstützung **II**
prompt [prɒmpt] prompt, unverzüglich **III 6**, 120
pronunciation [prəˌnʌntsiˈeɪʃn] Aussprache **III 4**, 79
proof [pruːf] Beweis **III 5**, 94
proper [ˈprɒpə] passend, geeignet **II**
properly [ˈprɒpli] ordentlich, pünktlich **II**
⟨**prosperity**⟩ [prɒsˈperəti] Wohlstand **III 5**, 92
to **protect** [prəˈtekt] (be)schützen **II**
⟨**protection**⟩ [prəˈtekʃn] Schutz **III E**, 136
to **protest** [prəˈtest] protestieren **III 2**, 41
proud *(of)* [praʊd] stolz (auf) **II**
to **prove** [pruːv] beweisen **III 4**, 68

to **provide** [prəˈvaɪd] zur Verfügung stellen, versorgen mit, sorgen für **III 3**, 51
+**psychic** [ˈsaɪkɪk] telepathisch **II**
pub [pʌb] Kneipe, Pub, Lokal **I**
in **public** [ˈpʌblɪk] in der Öffentlichkeit **II**
public [ˈpʌblɪk] öffentlich **II**
publicity [pʌbˈlɪsɪti] Publicity, öffentliche Aufmerksamkeit **III 6**, 113
to **publish** [ˈpʌblɪʃ] veröffentlichen, verlegen **III 2**, 32
⟨**pudding-bowl hair**⟩ [ˌpʊdɪŋ bəʊl ˈheə] Topfschnitt **III E**, 138
⟨**puff**⟩ [pʌf] Zug an der Zigarette **III 1**, 14
to **pull** [pʊl] ziehen **I**
punctuation [ˌpʌŋktʃuˈeɪʃn] Zeichensetzung, Interpunktion **I**
to **punish** [ˈpʌnɪʃ] bestrafen **III 2**, 43
pupil [ˈpjuːpl] Schüler(in) **I**
puppet [ˈpʌpɪt] (Hand-)Puppe, Marionette **II**
⟨**purchase**⟩ [ˈpɜːtʃəs] Kauf **III 1**, 14
to **purchase** [ˈpɜːtʃəs] kaufen, erwerben **III 6**, 120
purple [ˈpɜːpl] ⟨lila⟩ **III E**, 144; ⟨violett⟩ **III E**, 140
purse [pɜːs] Portmonee, Geldbörse **I**
to **push** [pʊʃ] stoßen, schieben **II**
to push so. over [ˌpʊʃ‿ˈəʊvə] jmdn umstoßen **I**
to **put*** [pʊt] setzen, stellen, legen **I**
to put an end to sth. [ˌpʊt‿ən‿ˈend] einer Sache ein Ende setzen **II**
to put on [ˌpʊt‿ˈɒn] herausbringen, auf die Bühne bringen **I**
to put up [ˌpʊt‿ˈʌp] aufgeben, aufhängen **I**

Q

qualification [ˌkwɒlɪfɪˈkeɪʃn] Qualifikation **III 6**, 111
quality [ˈkwɒləti] Qualität **II**
quarter *(to/past)* [ˈkwɔːtə] Viertel (vor/nach) **I**
queen [kwiːn] Königin **I**
question [ˈkwestʃən] Frage **I**
queue [kjuː] (Menschen-)Schlange **II**
quick [kwɪk] schnell, rasch **I**
quiet [ˈkwaɪət] Stille, Ruhe **II**
quiet [ˈkwaɪət] ruhig **I**
quite [kwaɪt] ziemlich **I**
quiz [kwɪz] Fragespiel, Quiz **I**

R

⟨**rabbit**⟩ [ˈræbɪt] Kaninchen **III E**, 136
race [reɪs] (Wett-)Rennen **II**
to **race** [reɪs] um die Wette rennen, rasen **II**
racist [ˈreɪsɪst] Rassist(in); rassistisch **III 5**, 100
racket [ˈrækɪt] (Tennis-)Schläger **II**
radio [ˈreɪdiəʊ] Radio **I**
+whitewater **rafting** [ˌwaɪtwɔːtə ˈrɑːftɪŋ] Wildwasserfahren **I**
⟨to **raid**⟩ [reɪd] plündern, überfallen **III 1**, 20
⟨**railings**⟩ [ˈreɪlɪŋz] Geländer **III E**, 147
railroad *(AE)* [ˈreɪlrəʊd] Eisenbahn **III 5**, 90
railway [ˈreɪlweɪ] Eisenbahn **I**
rain [reɪn] Regen **II**
to **rain** [reɪn] regnen **I**
to rain cats and dogs [ˈreɪn ˌkæts‿n‿ˈdɒgz] heftig regnen, schütten, gießen **I**
rainy [ˈreɪni] regnerisch **II**
⟨price **range**⟩ [ˈpraɪs ˌreɪndʒ] Preisklasse **III E**, 139
ranger *(AE)* [ˈreɪndʒə] Ranger, Aufseher im Nationalpark **III 3**, 53
rap [ræp] Rap *(Musikrichtung)* **II**
+**rapids** [ˈræpɪdz] Stromschnellen **I**
rat [ræt] Ratte **II**
rat-bag [ˈrætbæg] Miststück **II**

rate [reɪt] Rate, Kurs **III 2**, 32
rather ['rɑːðə] eher, lieber, ziemlich **II**
⟨**ratings**⟩ ['reɪtɪŋz] Einschaltquoten, Zuschauerzahlen **III 4**, 68
⟨to **rattle**⟩ ['rætl] klappern **III 1**, 13
raw material [ˌrɔː mə'tɪəriəl] Rohstoff **III 6**, 114
to X-**ray** ['eksreɪ] durchleuchten, röntgen **II**
to **reach** [riːtʃ] erreichen, gelangen **I**
to **react** [ri'ækt] reagieren **I**
reaction [ri'ækʃn] Reaktion **III 5**, 100
to **read*** [riːd] lesen **I**
ready ['redi] fertig, bereit (sein) **I**
real [rɪəl] echt, wirklich **I**
⟨the real deal *(AE)* ⟩ [ðə 'rɪəl ˌdiːl] das Echte **III 1**, 8
realism ['rɪəlɪzm] Realismus **III 4**, 69
reality [ri'æləti] Wirklichkeit, Realität **II**
+virtual reality [ˌvɜːtʃuəl ri'æləti] virtuelle Realität **II**
to **realize** ['rɪəlaɪz] bemerken, erkennen, realisieren **II**
really ['rɪəli] in Wirklichkeit, eigentlich **II**; wirklich **I**
reason ['riːzn] Grund, Ursache **II**
⟨**reasonable**⟩ ['riːznəbl] vernünftig, angemessen **III 5**, 93
rebel ['rebl] Rebell(in) **III 1**, 12
⟨to **recall**⟩ [rɪ'kɔːl] erinnern **III E**, 141
to **receive** [rɪ'siːv] erhalten, empfangen **II**
recent ['riːsnt] kürzlich, jüngste(r/s), neueste(r/s) **III 6**, 112
in recent years [ɪn ˌriːsnt 'jɪəz] in den letzten Jahren **III 6**, 112
receptionist [rɪ'sepʃnɪst] Dame/Herr am Empfang **III 5**, 98
+**recipe** ['resɪpi] (Koch-)Rezept **II**
⟨to **recite**⟩ [rɪ'saɪt] rezitieren **III E**, 138
reconstruction [ˌriːkən'strʌkʃn] Wiederherstellung, Rekonstruktion **II**
record ['rekɔːd] Rekord **II**; Schallplatte **I**
⟨on record⟩ [ˌɒn 'rekɔːd] schriftlich festgehalten, verzeichnet **III 5**, 92
record player ['rekɔːd ˌpleɪə] (Schall-)Plattenspieler **II**
record-holder ['rekɔːd ˌhəʊldə] Rekordhalter(in) **II**
to **record** [rɪ'kɔːd] aufzeichnen, aufnehmen **I**
recorder [rɪ'kɔːdə] (Video-/Kassetten-) Rekorder **I**
recording [rɪ'kɔːdɪŋ] Aufzeichnung, (Ton-) Aufnahme **I**
to **recover** [rɪ'kʌvə] sich erholen **III 6**, 120
recovery [rɪ'kʌvri] Genesung, Erholung **II**
recreation [ˌrekri'eɪʃn] Erholung **III 3**, 52
to **recycle** [ˌriː'saɪkl] recyceln, wiederaufbereiten, wiederverwerten **III 3**, 61
red [red] rot **I**
⟨red-hot poker⟩ [ˌred hɒt 'pəʊkə] rotglühender Schürhaken **III E**, 137
to **reduce** [rɪ'djuːs] verringern, reduzieren **II**
to **refer to** [rɪ'fɜː] sich beziehen auf **III 6**, 120
reference ['refrənts] Bezug, Erwähnung; Referenz **III 4**, 72
to **reflect** [rɪ'flekt] reflektieren, widerspiegeln **III 4**, 69
⟨**refrigerator**⟩ [rɪ'frɪdʒəreɪtə] Kühlschrank **III 1**, 20
refuge ['refjuːdʒ] Zuflucht **III 3**, 52
to **refuse** [rɪ'fjuːz] ablehnen, verweigern **II**
regard [rɪ'gɑːd] (Hoch-)Achtung, Wertschätzung **II**
regional ['riːdʒnl] regional **III 4**, 66
to **register** ['redʒɪstə] sich eintragen, sich einschreiben **II**
to **regret** [rɪ'gret] bedauern, bereuen **III 6**, 120
regular ['regjələ] regelmäßig **II**
to **rehearse** [rɪ'hɜːs] proben, üben **I**
to be **related** *(to)* [rɪ'leɪtɪd] mit etw zusammenhängen, mit jmdm verwandt sein **II**
relation [rɪ'leɪʃn] Relation, Beziehung, Verhältnis **III 4**, 70; Verwandte(r) **II**
relationship [ˌrɪ'leɪʃnʃɪp] Beziehung, Verhältnis **II**
relative ['relətɪv] Verwandte(r) **I**
to **relax** [rɪ'læks] ausruhen, sich erholen **I**
reliable [rɪ'laɪəbl] zuverlässig **III 6**, 111
religion [rɪ'lɪdʒn] Religion **II**
+**religious** [rɪ'lɪdʒəs] religiös **II**
to **remain** [rɪ'meɪn] zurückbleiben **II**
to **remember** [rɪ'membə] sich erinnern (an), denken (an) **I**
to **remind so. of sth.** [rɪ'maɪnd] jmdn an etwas erinnern **III 4**, 69
remote control [rɪˌməʊt kən'trəʊl] Fernbedienung **III 4**, 74
⟨to **remove**⟩ [rɪ'muːv] wegnehmen **III E**, 130
rent [rent] Miete **II**
to **rent** [rent] mieten **III 5**, 94
rental ['rentl] Miet- **I**
car rental ['kɑː ˌrentl] Autovermietung **I**
to **repair** [rɪ'peə] reparieren **II**
to **repeat** [rɪ'piːt] wiederholen **I**
repetition [ˌrepɪ'tɪʃn] Wiederholung **II**
to **replace** [rɪ'pleɪs] ersetzen, austauschen **II**
replica ['replɪkə] Nachbildung **II**
report [rɪ'pɔːt] (Schul-)Zeugnis **II**; Bericht **I**
to **report** [rɪ'pɔːt] berichten **I**
to report back [rɪˌpɔːt 'bæk] sich zurückmelden **II**
reporter [rɪ'pɔːtə] Reporter(in), Journalist(in) **I**
⟨to **represent**⟩ [ˌreprɪ'zent] vertreten **III E**, 142
⟨**representation**⟩ [ˌreprɪzen'teɪʃn] Vertretung **III E**, 133
⟨**representative**⟩ [ˌreprɪ'zentətɪv] Volksvertreter(in) **III E**, 134
republic [rɪ'pʌblɪk] Republik **III 5**, 89
⟨**reputation**⟩ [ˌrepjə'teɪʃn] Ruf **III 5**, 93
to **require** [rɪ'kwaɪə] brauchen, benötigen, erfordern **III 6**, 111
rescue ['reskjuː] Rettung **I**
to **rescue** ['reskjuː] retten **I**
research [rɪ'sɜːtʃ] **Forschung III 6**, 111
⟨to **research**⟩ [rɪ'sɜːtʃ] erforschen **III 5**, 93
+**reservation** [ˌrezə'veɪʃn] Reservat **I**
⟨**reserve**⟩ [rɪ'zɜːv] Reservat **III E**, 136
reservoir ['rezəvwɑː] Stausee, Reservoir **III 3**, 52
resident ['rezɪdnt] Bewohner(in), Einwohner(in), Anwohner(in) **III 3**, 50
to **resolve** [rɪ'zɒlv] lösen (z. B. einen Konflikt) **III 6**, 120
resources [rɪ'zɔːsɪz] Ressourcen, Reserven, Bodenschätze **III 3**, 48
respectable [rɪ'spektəbl] anständig, ehrbar, ansehnlich **III 5**, 95
response [rɪ'spɒnts] Antwort, Erwiderung, Reaktion **III 6**, 120
responsibility [rɪˌspɒntsə'bɪləti] Verantwortung **II**
to be **responsible** [rɪ'spɒntsəbl] verantwortlich sein **I**
rest [rest] Rast, Pause **I**; Rest **II**
to **rest** [rest] rasten, ausruhen **III 3**, 50
restaurant ['restrɔːŋ] Restaurant **I**
⟨**restless**⟩ ['restləs] rastlos, unruhig **III 1**, 13
to **restore** [rɪ'stɔː] wiederherstellen, restaurieren **II**; zurückgeben **III 3**, 51
⟨**restroom** *(AE)*⟩ ['restruːm] öffentliche Toilette **III 1**, 20
⟨restroom attendant⟩ ['restruːm‿ətendənt] Toilettenmann/-frau **III 1**, 20
result [rɪ'zʌlt] Ergebnis **I**
to **retire** [rɪ'taɪə] in den Ruhestand gehen, sich zurückziehen **III 6**, 111
return [rɪ'tɜːn] Rückkehr **III 5**, 91
+in return [ɪn rɪ'tɜːn] dafür **I**
to **return** [rɪ'tɜːn] zurückkehren **II**
to **revise** [rɪ'vaɪz] wiederholen **II**
revision [rɪ'vɪʒn] Wiederholung (des Stoffs) zur Prüfungsvorbereitung **III 6**, 112
revolution [ˌrevl'uːʃn] Revolution **III 6**, 114
revolutionary [ˌrevl'uːʃnri] revolutionär, nie da gewesen **III 4**, 73
to **reward** [rɪ'wɔːd] belohnen, auszeichnen **II**
to **rewind*** [ˌriː'waɪnd] zurückspulen **III 4**, 74
to **rewrite*** [ˌriː'raɪt] neu schreiben **II**
rhyme [raɪm] Reim **II**
+to **rhyme** [raɪm] (sich) reimen **II**
rhythm ['rɪðm] Rhythmus **II**
rice [raɪs] Reis **II**
rich [rɪtʃ] reich **II**
ride [raɪd] Fahrt, Ritt **III 2**, 33
+to thumb a ride [ˌθʌm‿ə 'raɪd] per Anhalter fahren, trampen **II**
to **ride*** [raɪd] fahren, reiten **I**
rider ['raɪdə] Fahrer(in) **II**
+**rigging** ['rɪgɪŋ] Tauwerk, Takelage **II**
⟨civil **rights movement**⟩ [ˌsɪvl 'raɪts ˌmuːvmənt] Bürgerrechtsbewegung **III E**, 142
right [raɪt] rechts; richtig **I**
all right [ɔːl 'raɪt] in Ordnung **I**
right away [ˌraɪt‿ə'weɪ] sofort **II**
right down to the end [ˌraɪt daʊn tə ði‿'end] bis zum Schluss **III 5**, 90
to be right [biː 'raɪt] Recht haben **III 4**, 70
⟨to be **right back**⟩ [biː 'raɪt ˌbæk] gleich zurück sein **III 1**, 10
⟨**rim**⟩ [rɪm] Rand **III 3**, 53
ring [rɪŋ] Ring **I**
⟨short-pitched ring⟩ [ˌʃɔːtpɪtʃt 'rɪŋ] kurzes, helles Klingeln **III E**, 141
to **ring* so. up** [ˌrɪŋ‿'ʌp] jmdn anrufen **I**
rip-off ['rɪpɒf] Wucher, Nepp **II**
to **rip so. off** *(sl.)* [rɪp 'ɒf] ausnehmen, schröpfen **III 2**, 33
risk [rɪsk] Gefahr, Risiko **II**
risky ['rɪski] gefährlich, riskant **II**
river ['rɪvə] Fluss **I**
road [rəʊd] Straße **I**
⟨**roadie**⟩ ['rəʊdi] Tour-/ Bühnenhelfer(in) **III 1**, 12
bank **robber** ['bæŋk ˌrɒbə] Bankräuber(in) **I**
robot ['rəʊbɒt] Roboter **II**
rock [rɒk] Fels **I**
rock music [ˌrɒk 'mjuːzɪk] Rockmusik **I**
soft rock ['sɒft ˌrɒk] Softrock *(Musikrichtung)* **II**
rock'n'roll [ˌrɒkn'rəʊl] Rock'n'Roll *(Musikrichtung)* **II**
rocky ['rɒki] felsig, steinig **I**
role [rəʊl] Rolle **I**
role play ['rəʊl pleɪ] Rollenspiel **I**
Roman ['rəʊmən] Römer(in) **II**
⟨**Romance**⟩ [rəʊ'mænts] romanisch **III 6**, 121
roof [ruːf] Dach **I**
room [ruːm] Zimmer **I**
+dining room ['daɪnɪŋ ˌrʊm] Esszimmer **I**
living room ['lɪvɪŋ ˌrʊm] Wohnzimmer **I**
rope [rəʊp] Seil, Tau **I**
rose [rəʊz] Rose **III 1**, 10
to **rot** [rɒt] verrotten, (ver)faulen **I**
rough [rʌf] rau, schwierig, hart **III 3**, 50
⟨**round**⟩ [raʊnd] Runde **III E**, 142
round [raʊnd] rund **II**
round [raʊnd] um … herum **I**
all the year round [raʊnd] das ganze Jahr über **II**
all-round fitness [ˌɔːlraʊnd 'fɪtnəs] Rundum-Fitness **II**
to come round [ˌkʌm 'raʊnd] vorbeikommen, herüberkommen **I**
rounders ['raʊndəz] Schlagball **II**
route [ruːt] Route, Strecke **I**
rover ['rəʊvə] Vagabund; Erkundungsfahrzeug **II**
row [rəʊ] Reihe **I**
to **rub** [rʌb] reiben **I**
⟨to rub off⟩ [rʌb‿'ɒf] (sich) abwischen, abgehen **III E**, 139
rubber ['rʌbə] Radiergummi **I**
rubbish ['rʌbɪʃ] Abfall, Müll **I**
rude [ruːd] unhöflich **III 1**, 21
+**rugby** ['rʌgbi] Rugby *(Ballspiel mit eiförmigem Ball aus Leder)* **II**

⟨**ruin**⟩ ['ru:ɪn] Ruine **III 5**, 93
rule [ru:l] Herrschaft **II**; Regel **I**
⟨home rule⟩ [ˌhəʊm 'ru:l] Selbstbestimmung **III E**, 142
to **rule** [ru:l] herrschen, regieren; entscheiden; angesagt sein **III 1**, 9
ruler ['ru:lə] Herrscher(in) **II**; Lineal **I**
⟨to **rumble**⟩ ['rʌmbl] donnern **III 1**, 13
to **run*** [rʌn] führen, leiten **II**; rennen, laufen **I**
⟨to run a red light⟩ [ˌrʌn‿ə red 'laɪt] eine rote Ampel überfahren **III E**, 130
to run away [ˌrʌn‿ə'weɪ] weglaufen **II**
to run over [rʌn‿'əʊvə] überfahren **III 4**, 70
running-track ['rʌnɪŋˌtræk] Aschenbahn **II**
rupee [ru:'pi:] *indische Währung* **II**
to **rush** [rʌʃ] eilen, stürzen **III 4**, 68
Russian ['rʌʃn] russisch, Russisch **II**
⟨to **rust**⟩ [rʌst] rosten **III E**, 141
rye [raɪ] Roggen **III 2**, 39

S

to **sack** (*coll.*) [sæk] entlassen **II**
sad [sæd] traurig **I**
safe [seɪf] sicher **I**
better to be safe than sorry lieber auf Nummer sicher gehen **II**
safety ['seɪfti] Sicherheit **I**
to **sail** [seɪl] segeln **I**
+**sailing trip** ['seɪlɪŋ ˌtrɪp] Segeltörn **I**
sailor ['seɪlə] Matrose, Seemann **II**
salary ['sæləri] Gehalt **III 6**, 111
sale [seɪl] +Ausverkauf, Schlussverkauf **II**; Verkauf **I**
salt [sɔ:lt] Salz **I**
salt water ['sɔ:lt ˌwɔ:tə] Salzwasser **III 3**, 51
same [seɪm] gleich, dasselbe **I**
⟨**sanctuary**⟩ ['sæŋktʃʊəri] Zuflucht, Schutzgebiet **III E**, 137
sand [sænd] Sand **I**
sandwich ['sændwɪtʃ] Sandwich, belegtes Brot **III 1**, 13
sandy ['sændi] rötlich, rotblond *(Haarfarbe)* **II**
sarcastic [sɑ:'kæstɪk] sarkastisch **II**
satellite ['sætlaɪt] Satellit **I**
Saturday ['sætədeɪ] Samstag **I**
sauce [sɔ:s] Sauce (Soße) **III 4**, 68
sausage ['sɒsɪdʒ] Würstchen **I**
to **save** [seɪv] +retten **I**; sichern, abspeichern **I**; sparen **III 2**, 33
saw [sɔ:] Säge **II**
sawmill ['sɔ:mɪl] Sägemühle, Sägewerk **III 6**, 112
Saxons ['sæksnz] (die) Sachsen **II**
saxophone ['sæksəfəʊn] Saxophon **I**
to **say*** [seɪ] sagen, reden **I**
⟨**scale**⟩ [skeɪl] Ausmaß, Maßstab **III 3**, 53
scalpel ['skælpl] Skalpell **II**
⟨to **scan**⟩ [skæn] (einen Text) nach etwas Bestimmtem absuchen **III E**, 148
scandal ['skændl] Skandal **III 4**, 66
Scandinavian [ˌskændɪ'neɪviən] Skandinavier **III 2**, 32
to be **scared** ['skeəd] Angst haben, verschreckt sein **II**
scarf, (*pl.*) -ves [skɑ:f] Schal, Halstuch **I**
scene [si:n] Szene **I**
behind the scenes [bɪˌhaɪnd ðə 'si:nz] hinter den Kulissen **III 4**, 66
scenery ['si:nəri] Bühnenbild, Kulisse **I**
school [sku:l] Schule **I**
comprehensive school (*BE*) [ˌkɒmprɪ'hentsɪv ˌsku:l] Gesamtschule **III 1**, 15
high school (*AE*) ['haisku:l] Oberschule, Gesamtschule **III 1**, 9
schoolboy ['sku:lbɔɪ] Schuljunge **II**
schoolfriend ['sku:lfrend] Schulfreund(in) **I**
schoolmaster ['sku:lˌmɑ:stə] Schulmeister, Lehrer **III 5**, 90
schoolwatch ['sku:lwɒtʃ] Schulaufsicht, Schulwärter(in) **I**
Science ['saɪənts] °(Natur-)Wissenschaften (*Fach*) **I**
science ['saɪənts] Wissenschaft **II**
science fiction [ˌsaɪənts 'fɪkʃn] Science-fiction **II**
scientist ['saɪəntɪst] Wissenschaftler(in) **I**
scissors ['sɪzəz] Schere **I**
+**score** [skɔ:] Punkte, Spielstand **II**
+to **score** [skɔ:] Punkte erzielen **II**
Scottish ['skɒtɪʃ] schottisch **I**
scrambled eggs [ˌskræmbld‿'egz] Rührei **II**
scrapbook ['skræpbʊk] Sammelalbum **I**
scratch [skrætʃ] Kratzer **II**
scream [skri:m] Schrei, Heulen **II**
⟨to **scream**⟩ [skri:m] schreien, brüllen **III E**, 137
screen [skri:n] Leinwand **II**
script [skrɪpt] Drehbuch, Textbuch **I**
⟨**scruffy**⟩ ['skrʌfi] vergammelt, verlottert **III E**, 130
⟨**scuba diving**⟩ ['sku:bə ˌdaɪvɪŋ] Sporttauchen **III E**, 139
sculpture ['skʌlptʃə] Skulptur **II**
sea [si:] Meer, (die) See **I**
seabird ['si:bɜ:d] Seevogel **I**
⟨in **search of**⟩ [ɪn 'sɜ:tʃ‿əv] auf der Suche nach **III 5**, 92
season ['si:zn] Jahreszeit **I**
seat [si:t] Sitz(platz) **II**
⟨to **seat**⟩ [si:t] einen Sitzplatz zuweisen **III E**, 130
seatbelt ['si:tbelt] Sicherheitsgurt **II**
to be **seated** ['si:tɪd] sitzen, sich setzen **III 2**, 37
second ['seknd] Sekunde; zweite(r/s) **II**
+**second-hand** ['sekndˌhænd] gebraucht, aus zweiter Hand **I**
+**secret** ['si:krət] Geheimnis **II**
secret ['si:krət] geheim, verborgen **I**
⟨secret society⟩ [ˌsi:krɪt sə'saɪəti] Geheimbund **III E**, 133
secretary ['sekrətri] Sekretär(in) **III 1**, 16
section ['sekʃn] Absatz, Abschnitt **II**
to **see*** [si:] sehen, erblicken **I**; verstehen **III 1**, 8
see you ['si: ˌju] bis bald **III 1**, 10
to see no point in sth. [ˌsi: nəʊ 'pɒɪnt‿ɪn] etw für sinnlos halten **II**
to **seem** [si:m] (er)scheinen **I**
self-catering [ˌself'keɪtrɪŋ] Selbstversorgung **I**
⟨**self-evident**⟩ [ˌself'evɪdnt] selbstverständlich **III E**, 133
sell-out ['selaʊt] Ausverkauf **II**
to **sell*** [sel] verkaufen **I**
+**Seminole Indian** ['semɪnəʊl‿ɪndiən] *Angehörige(r) eines indianischen Stamms* **I**
to **send*** [send] schicken, senden **I**
sender ['sendə] Absender(in) **II**
senior orchestra [ˌsi:niə‿'ɔ:kɪstrə] Orchester der oberen Klassenstufen **I**
sensational [sen'seɪʃnl] sensationell **III 4**, 70
sense [sens] Sinn **II**
sensible ['sensɪbl] vernünftig **II**
sensitive ['sentsɪtɪv] sensibel, empfindlich, einfühlsam **III 4**, 69
sensitivity [ˌsentsɪ'tɪvəti] Sensibilität, Einfühlsamkeit, Empfindlichkeit **III 5**, 100
sentence ['sentns] Satz **I**
separate ['seprət] getrennt, separat **I**
September [sep'tembə] September **I**
⟨**serial killer**⟩ [ˌsi:rɪəl 'kɪlə] Serienkiller, Massenmörder **III 4**, 68
serious ['sɪəriəs] ernsthaft, seriös **II**
to take seriously [ˌteɪk 'sɪəriəsli] ernst nehmen **III 1**, 12
servant ['sɜ:vnt] Diener(in) **I**
to **serve** [sɜ:v] servieren; (be)dienen **III 5**, 94
service ['sɜ:rvɪs] Dienst(leistung), Service **I**
session ['seʃn] +Sitzung, Treffen **II**
set [set] Satz, Garnitur **II**
to **set*** (*up*) [ˌset‿'ʌp] (auf)stellen, (auf)bauen **I**
to set off [ˌset‿'ɒf] losziehen, (eine Reise) antreten **II**
to be set in ['set‿ɪn] in ... spielen **II**
to set aside [ˌset‿ə'saɪd] einplanen, beiseite legen **III 6**, 112
to set out to do sth. [ˌset‿'aʊt] etw fest vorhaben **II**
setting ['setɪŋ] Schauplatz, Umgebung **II**
to **settle** ['setl] (be)siedeln **II**
to settle into [ˌsetl‿'ɪntu] sich einleben **III 3**, 50
+**settler** ['setlə] Siedler(in) **II**
several ['sevrl] einige, mehrere **II**
sewage ['su:ɪdʒ] Abwasser **I**
sex [seks] Geschlecht **III 2**, 35
sexist ['seksɪst] sexistisch **III 2**, 35
Sgt., sergeant ['sɑ:dʒnt] Feldwebel **III 4**, 72
⟨**shade**⟩ [ʃeɪd] Jalousie, Rollo **III 1**, 20
shadow ['ʃædəʊ] Schatten **II**
to **shake** [ʃeɪk] schütteln **II**
shall (*old*) [ʃæl] werde(n) **II**
⟨**shameful**⟩ ['ʃeɪmfl] schändlich **III 2**, 32
shamrock ['ʃæmrɒk] Klee(blatt) **III 5**, 97
shape [ʃeɪp] Gestalt, (äußere) Form **I**
out of shape [ˌaʊt‿əv 'ʃeɪp] außer Form **II**
to **share** [ʃeə] teilen **III 2**, 32
sharp [ʃɑ:p] scharf, hart **II**
pencil **sharpener** ['pentsl ˌʃɑ:pnə] Bleistiftspitzer **I**
to **shave** [ʃeɪv] (sich) rasieren **III 1**, 20
she [ʃi:] sie (*sing.*) **I**
⟨**shed**⟩ [ʃed] Schuppen **III E**, 144
sheep, *pl.*: **sheep** [ʃi:p] Schaf(e) **I**
sheepdog ['ʃi:pdɒg] Schäferhund, Hirtenhund **I**
⟨**sheer**⟩ [ʃɪə] steil, jäh **III 3**, 53
shelf, *pl.*: **shelves** [ʃelf, ʃelvz] Regal, Regalbrett **III 6**, 113
⟨continental shelf⟩ [ˌkɒntɪnentl 'ʃelf] Kontinentalsockel **III E**, 144
shelter ['ʃeltə] Schutz, Obdach, Unterstand **III 3**, 50
+**shepherd** ['ʃepəd] Schäferhund; Schäfer **I**
to work **shift** [ˌwɜ:k 'ʃɪft] Schicht arbeiten, Schichtdienst machen **I**
⟨to **shift**⟩ [ʃɪft] (sich) bewegen **III 1**, 13
to **shine*** [ʃaɪn] scheinen **II**
ship [ʃɪp] Schiff **I**
⟨**shipload**⟩ ['ʃɪpləʊd] Schiffsladung **III E**, 133
shipyard ['ʃɪpjɑ:d] Werft **III 6**, 114
polo **shirt** ['pəʊləʊ ˌʃɜ:t] Polohemd **I**
to feel **shivery** ['ʃɪvri] frösteln **II**
shock [ʃɒk] Schreck, Schock **I**
to **shock** [ʃɒk] schockieren **III 6**, 113
shoe [ʃu:] Schuh **I**
to **shoot*** [ʃu:t] schießen, erschießen **III 4**, 68
shop [ʃɒp] Geschäft, Laden **I**
video shop ['vɪdiəʊ ˌʃɒp] Videothek, Videoladen **I**
+**shoplifter** ['ʃɒpˌlɪftə] Ladendieb(in) **I**
+price **shopper** ['praɪs ˌʃɒpə] Schnäppchenjäger(in) **II**
shopping ['ʃɒpɪŋ] Einkaufen **I**
shopping mall (*AE*) ['ʃɒpɪŋ ˌmɔ:l] Einkaufszentrum **I**
to go shopping [ˌgəʊ 'ʃɒpɪŋ] Einkaufen gehen **I**
⟨**shore**⟩ [ʃɔ:] Ufer, Strand **III E**, 140
short-cut ['ʃɔ:tkʌt] Abkürzung **I**
short [ʃɔ:t] kurz **I**
⟨short-pitched ring⟩ [ˌʃɔ:tpɪtʃt 'rɪŋ] kurzes, helles Klingeln **III E**, 141
⟨to stop short⟩ [stɒp 'ʃɔ:t] plötzlich stehen bleiben **III 1**, 13
to **shorten** ['ʃɔ:tn] verkürzen, kürzen **III 6**, 116
shorts [ʃɔ:ts] kurze Hose, Shorts **I**
should [ʃʊd/ʃəd] sollen **I**
shoulder ['ʃəʊldə] Schulter **I**
to **shout** [ʃaʊt] rufen **I**
to **shovel** ['ʃʌvl] schaufeln, schippen **II**
show [ʃəʊ] Show **I**
talk show ['tɔ:k ˌʃəʊ] Talkshow, Gesprächsrunde **II**

to **show*** [ʃəʊ] zeigen I
to show off [ˌʃəʊ‿ˈɒf] angeben I
shower [ˈʃaʊə] Dusche; Schauer III 1, 20
⟨to **shuffle**⟩ [ˈʃʌfl] mischen, durchwühlen III 4, 69
to **shut*** [ʃʌt] schließen I
to shut up [ˌʃʌt‿ˈʌp] den Mund halten II
+**shuttle** [ˈʃʌtl] Transporter II
city shuttle [ˈsɪti ˌʃʌtl] Pendelverkehr zur Innenstadt I
shy [ʃaɪ] schüchtern II
sick [sɪk] krank, übel I
⟨to be sick of doing sth.⟩ [sɪk] etwas satt haben III E, 144
side [saɪd] Seite I
sidewalk *(AE)* [ˈsaɪdwɔːk] Gehsteig III 2, 32
to **sigh** [saɪ] seufzen III 1, 13
sight [saɪt] Sehenswürdigkeit I
sightseeing [ˈsaɪtˌsiːɪŋ] Besichtigung von Sehenswürdigkeiten I
sign [saɪn] Schild, Zeichen II
to **sign** [saɪn] unterzeichnen, unterschreiben I
signal [ˈsɪgnl] Signal I
signpost [ˈsaɪnpəʊst] Wegweiser I
silence [ˈsaɪlents] Stille III 3, 53
⟨to **silence**⟩ [ˈsaɪlents] zum Schweigen bringen III 3, 53
silent [ˈsaɪlənt] still, stumm II
silly [ˈsɪli] Dumme(r), Dummkopf I
silly [ˈsɪli] dumm, kindisch I
silver [ˈsɪlvə] Silber I
similar [ˈsɪmɪlə] ähnlich, gleichartig II
similarity [ˌsɪmɪˈlærəti] Ähnlichkeit III 5, 95
simple [ˈsɪmpl] einfach, gewöhnlich I
⟨**simplicity**⟩ [sɪmˈplɪsəti] Einfachheit III 6, 115
since [sɪnts] seit I
since [sɪnts] da III 1, 16
sincere [sɪnˈsɪə] aufrichtig III 4, 68
Yours **sincerely**, [jɔːz sɪnˈsɪəli] Mit freundlichen Grüßen *(Briefschluss)* II
to **sing** [sɪŋ] singen I
singer [ˈsɪŋə] Sänger(in) I
lead singer [ˌliːd ˈsɪŋə] Leadsänger(in) II
singing [ˈsɪŋɪŋ] Singen II
single *(n. or adj.)* [ˈsɪŋgl] Single; einzeln, einzig III 1, 12
to **sink*** [sɪŋk] sinken, (ab)fallen II
sir [sɜː] mein Herr *(Anrede)* I
siren [ˈsaɪərən] Sirene II
sister [ˈsɪstə] Schwester I
baby sister [ˌbeɪbi ˈsɪstə] (ganz) kleine Schwester I
sit-up [ˈsɪtʌp] Klappmesser II
to **sit*** [sɪt] sitzen I
to sit down [sɪt ˈdaʊn] sich setzen II
site [saɪt] Gelände, Platz II
situation [ˌsɪtjuˈeɪʃn] Situation, Arbeitsstelle II
size [saɪz] Größe I
skate [skeɪt] Rollschuh, Schlittschuh II
ice skate [ˈaɪs ˌskeɪt] Schlittschuh II
skateboard [ˈskeɪtbɔːd] Skateboard II
+**skating** [ˈskeɪtɪŋ] Schlittschuhlaufen, Rollschuhlaufen II
ice-skating [ˈaɪsˌskeɪtɪŋ] Schlittschuhlaufen II
sketch [sketʃ] Sketch, Szene II
ski-jumping [ˈskiːdʒʌmpɪŋ] Skispringen II
skill [skɪl] Fähigkeit, Fertigkeit II
skilled worker [ˌskɪld ˈwɜːkə] Facharbeiter(in) III 6, 114
to **skim** [skɪm] flüchtig lesen, überfliegen II
skin [skɪn] Haut, Fell III 4, 70
skinny [ˈskɪni] mager, dürr II
skirt [skɜːt] Rock I
skull [skʌl] Schädel II
sky [skaɪ] Himmel II
sky-diving [ˈskaɪˌdaɪvɪŋ] Fallschirmspringen II
skyline [ˈskaɪlaɪn] +(Stadt-) Silhouette, Skyline I
skyscraper [ˈskaɪskreɪpə] Wolkenkratzer III 2, 30

⟨with a **slam and a flick**⟩ [wɪð‿ə ˌslæm‿ənd‿ə ˈflɪk] mit einer schnellen Handbewegung Tür oder Fenster zuschlagend III E, 141
slang [slæŋ] Slang, Jargon III 6, 121
⟨**slaughter**⟩ [ˈslɔːtə] Abschlachten, Gemetzel III E, 136
slave [sleɪv] Sklave/Sklavin II
sleep [sliːp] Schlaf II
to **sleep*** [sliːp] schlafen I
sleeping bag [ˈsliːpɪŋ ˌbæg] Schlafsack I
oil **slick** [ˈɔɪl slɪk] Ölteppich I
⟨**slick**⟩ [slɪk] glatt III 1, 13
slide [slaɪd] Dia(positiv) I
to **slide*** [slaɪd] rutschen III 1, 13
⟨**slightly bluish**⟩ [ˌslaɪtli ˈbluːɪʃ] leicht bläulich III E, 139
to **slip** [slɪp] (aus)rutschen, (aus)gleiten II
°**slogan** [ˈsləʊgən] Slogan, Wahl-/Werbespruch I
slow [sləʊ] langsam II
to **slumber** [ˈslʌmbə] schlummern, schlafen II
⟨to **slump**⟩ [slʌmp] plumpsen III E, 144
⟨**slut**⟩ [slʌt] Schlampe III 5, 95
small [smɔːl] klein I
smart [smɑːt] schick, flott; schlau III 5, 94
to **smash** [smæʃ] zerschlagen, zerschmettern II
smell [smel] Geruch, Duft II
to **smell** [smel] riechen II
smile [smaɪl] Lächeln I
to **smile** [smaɪl] lächeln I
smoke detector [ˈsməʊk dɪˌtektə] Rauchmelder II
⟨to have a smoke⟩ [hæv‿ə ˈsməʊk] (eine) rauchen III 4, 72
to **smoke** [sməʊk] rauchen I
smoking [ˈsməʊkɪŋ] (das) Rauchen I
to **smuggle** [ˈsmʌgl] schmuggeln I
smuggler [ˈsmʌglə] Schmuggler(in) I
snack [snæk] Imbiss I
+**snail-mail** [ˈsneɪlmeɪl] Schneckenpost II
⟨**sneaker**⟩ [ˈsniːkə] Freizeitschuh mit leiser Sohle III 1, 13
to **snort** [snɔːt] schnauben II
snow [snəʊ] Schnee I
to **snow** [snəʊ] schneien I
so [səʊ] so (sehr); so, also I
so that [səʊ ˈðæt] so dass, damit III 1, 16
soap opera [ˈsəʊp‿ˌɒprə] Seifenoper III 4, 66
⟨**sob**⟩ [sɒb] schluchz! III 2, 34
social [ˈsəʊʃl] sozial; gesellschaftlich III 1, 20
society [səˈsaɪəti] Gesellschaft III 6, 114
⟨secret society⟩ [ˌsiːkrɪt səˈsaɪəti] Geheimbund III E, 133
sock [sɒk] Socke I
soda *(AE)* [ˈsəʊdə] Limonade, süßes Erfrischungsgetränk III 4, 68
sofa [ˈsəʊfə] Sofa, Couch I
soft [sɒft] weich, zart III 4, 77
soft-drink [ˌsɒft ˈdrɪŋk] alkoholfreies Getränk III 4, 77
soft rock [ˈsɒft ˌrɒk] Softrock *(Musikrichtung)* II
software [ˈsɒftweə] Software I
soldier [ˈsəʊldʒə] Soldat(in) II
⟨**solution**⟩ [səˈluːʃn] Lösung III E, 143
⟨to **solve**⟩ [sɒlv] lösen III E, 139
some [sʌm] einige I
some [sʌm] irgend ein III 5, 94
somebody [ˈsʌmbədi] jemand I
somehow [ˈsʌmhaʊ] irgend wie II
someone [ˈsʌmwʌn] jemand I
+**something** [ˈsʌmθɪŋ] etwas I
sometime [ˈsʌmtaɪm] irgendwann III 1, 16
sometimes [ˈsʌmtaɪmz] manchmal I
somewhere [ˈsʌmweə] irgendwo I
son [sʌn] Sohn III 5, 90
⟨theme **song**⟩ [ˈθiːm sɒŋ] Titelsong III 1, 14
songwriter [ˈsɒŋraɪtə] Texter(in)/Komponist(in), Liedermacher(in) III 5, 90
soon [suːn] bald, rasch I

least said soonest mended [ˌliːst ˈsed ˌsuːnəst ˈmendɪd] je weniger geredet wird, desto schneller wird es wieder gut II
as **soon as** [əzˈsuːn‿əz] sobald III 1, 16
sore throat [ˌsɔː ˈθrəʊt] Halsschmerzen, Halsweh II
⟨**sorely**⟩ [ˈsɔːli] schlimm, arg, sehr III 5, 90
sorry [ˈsɒri] (es) tut mir Leid I
better to be safe than sorry lieber auf Nummer sicher gehen II
to feel sorry for [fiːl ˈsɒri] bemitleiden II
sort [sɔːt] Sorte, Art II
to **sort** [sɔːt] sortieren III 1, 15
sound [saʊnd] Klang, Ton I
sound check [ˈsaʊn(d) tʃek] Klang-, Tonkontrolle I
to **sound** [saʊnd] klingen I
source [sɔːs] Quelle, Ursprung II
south [saʊθ] südlich, Süden I
southern [ˈsʌðən] südlich, Süd- II
+**southernmost** [ˈsʌðənməʊst] südlichste(r/s) I
souvenir [ˌsuːvnˈɪə] Souvenir, Andenken I
+**Soviet** [ˈsəʊviət] sowjetisch II
space [speɪs] Raum II
outer space [ˌaʊtə ˈspeɪs] der äußere Weltraum II
⟨space capsule⟩ [ˈspeɪs ˌkæpsjuːl] Raumkapsel III E, 135
space travel [ˈspeɪs ˌtrævl] Raumfahrt II
+**spacecraft** [ˈspeɪskrɑːft] Raumfahrzeug II
spaceship [ˈspeɪsʃɪp] Raumschiff II
spacious [ˈspeɪʃəs] geräumig, weitläufig II
+**spare battery** [ˌspeə ˈbætri] Ersatzbatterie I
⟨**spark**⟩ [spɑːk] Funke III E, 141
to **speak*** [spiːk] sprechen I
to speak up [spiːk‿ˈʌp] laut und deutlich sprechen III 4, 80
speaker [ˈspiːkə] °Lautsprecher I; Sprecher(in) II
special [ˈspeʃl] Sonderangebot, Angebot des Tages III 2, 36
special [ˈspeʃl] besondere(r/s) I
⟨**species**⟩ [ˈspiːʃiːz] Spezies, Art III E, 137
spectacular [spekˈtækjələ] spektakulär III 5, 97
⟨**speech**⟩ [spiːtʃ] Rede III E, 134
speech bubble [ˈspiːtʃ ˌbʌbl] Sprechblase II
+**speed** [spiːd] Geschwindigkeit I
breakneck speed [ˌbreɪknek ˈspiːd] halsbrecherische Geschwindigkeit III 4, 70
to **spell*** [spel] buchstabieren I
spelling [ˈspelɪŋ] Rechtschreibung II
to **spend*** [spend] verbrauchen, ausgeben; verbringen I
spider [ˈspaɪdə] Spinne II
to **spill*** [spɪl] auslaufen, verschütten I
to **spin*** [spɪn] spinnen III 6, 113
to **splash** [splæʃ] plantschen, spritzen II
⟨to **split**⟩ [splɪt] (ab)spalten III E, 147
to split* up [ˌsplɪt‿ˈʌp] sich (voneinander) trennen I
⟨to **splutter**⟩ [ˈsplʌtə] prusten III E, 144
spokesman/spokeswoman [ˈspəʊksmən/ˌwʊmən] Sprecher(in) III 3, 50
sponge [spʌndʒ] Schwamm I
sponsor [ˈspɒntsə] Sponsor(in) II
sport [spɔːt] Sport I
sports centre [ˈspɔːts ˌsentə] Sportzentrum, Sportanlage I
sportsfield [ˈspɔːtsfiːld] Sportplatz I
sporty [ˈspɔːti] sportlich II
to **spot** [spɒt] entdecken I
to **spread*** *(over)* [spred] sich ausdehnen, (sich) verbreiten (über) II
spring [sprɪŋ] Frühling I
to **spurt** [spɜːt] sprinten, spurten II
°**spy**, *(pl.)* spies [spaɪ] Spion(in), Spitzel I
square [skweə] Platz II
⟨**square**⟩ [skweə] eckig III E, 141
⟨to **stab**⟩ [stæb] (er)stechen III E, 136
stable [ˈsteɪbl] stabil III 6, 114
stack [stæk] Stapel III 1, 14
to **stack up** [stæk‿ˈʌp] aufstapeln III 4, 68

staff [stɑ:f] Personal **III 6**, 111
staffroom ['stɑ:frum] Lehrerzimmer **I**
stage [steɪdʒ] Bühne **I**
+**stairs** (*pl.*) [steəz] Treppe **I**
⟨**stale**⟩ [steɪl] muffig, schal, abgestanden **III 1**, 13
stall [stɔ:l] (Verkauf-)Stand **I**
stamina ['stæmɪnə] Durchhaltevermögen, Ausdauer **II**
stamp [stæmp] Briefmarke **II**
⟨to **stamp**⟩ [stæmp] stempeln **III E**, 133
to **stand*** [stænd] stehen **I**
I can't stand (*it*) [ˌkɑ:nt 'stænd] ich halte (es) nicht aus, ich ertrage (es) nicht **II**
⟨to stand for⟩ ['stænd fɔ:] stehen für **III 3**, 49
to stand in line (*AE*) [ˌstænd‿ɪn 'laɪn] Schlange stehen **III 1**, 20
to stand out [stænd‿'aʊt] herausragen **III 1**, 8
to stand up [stænd‿'ʌp] aufstehen (vom Stuhl) **II**
standard ['stændəd] Standard, Norm **III 4**, 79
star [stɑ:] Star **II**; Stern **I**
⟨**stardom**⟩ ['stɑ:dəm] Berühmtheit, Status eines Stars **III 4**, 70
to **stare** [steə] starren **II**
⟨**starfish**⟩ ['stɑ:fɪʃ] Seestern **III E**, 136
⟨**start**⟩ [stɑ:t] Anfang, Start **III 2**, 30
to **start** [stɑ:t] anfangen, beginnen **I**
to **startle** ['stɑ:tl] erschrecken, aufschrecken **II**
state [steɪt] Staat **I**; Zustand, Status **II**
⟨mid-Atlantic states⟩ [mɪdətˌlæntɪk 'steɪts] Staaten an der Ostküste der USA **III 2**, 33
statement ['steɪtmənt] Feststellung, Behauptung, Aussage **II**
station ['steɪʃn] Haltestelle, Station **I**
gas station (*AE*) ['gæs ˌsteɪʃn] Tankstelle **II**
petrol station ['petrl ˌsteɪʃn] Tankstelle **I**
power station ['paʊə ˌsteɪʃn] Kraftwerk **III 3**, 58
statistics (*sg. or pl.*) [stə'tɪstɪks] Statistik **III 6**, 116
statue ['stætju:] Statue, Standbild **II**
statuette [ˌstætju'et] Statuette **II**
to **stay** [steɪ] bleiben **I**
to stay tuned [ˌsteɪ 'tju:nd] dranbleiben, den Sender beibehalten **III 4**, 66
steady ['stedi] ständig, ununterbrochen **II**
to **steal*** [sti:l] stehlen **II**
steam [sti:m] Dampf **II**
steam engine ['sti:m‿endʒɪn] Dampfmaschine **III 6**, 114
⟨**steamer**⟩ ['sti:mə] Dampfer **III 2**, 32
⟨**steel**⟩ [sti:l] Stahl **III 6**, 117
steep [sti:p] steil **II**
to **steer** [stɪə] steuern, lenken **III 1**, 13
step [step] Schritt, Stufe, Abschnitt **I**
to **step in** [step‿'ɪn] eintreten, einsteigen **III 2**, 34
+to step off [step‿'ɒf] aussteigen **II**
to step on so.'s foot [step] jmdm auf den Fuß treten **II**
stepfather ['stepfɑ:ðə] Stiefvater **I**
stick [stɪk] Stock **I**
⟨stick of French bread⟩ [ˌstɪk‿əv ˌfrentʃ 'bred] Stange Baguette **III E**, 139
walking stick ['wɔ:kɪŋ ˌstɪk] Gehstock, Spazierstock **II**
to **stick*** [stɪk] kleben **I**
to stick out [stɪk‿'aʊt] herausstrecken **II**
+to stick to sth. ['stɪk] etw treu bleiben, bleiben (bei) **II**
sticker ['stɪkə] Sticker, Aufkleber **I**
⟨**still**⟩ [stɪl] still; reglos **III 1**, 13
still [stɪl] noch **I**
stocking ['stɒkɪŋ] Strumpf **III 6**, 113
stomach ['stʌmək] Magen, Bauch **II**
stomach ache ['stʌmək‿eɪk] Magenschmerzen **II**
stone [stəʊn] Stein **I**
⟨to **stone**⟩ [stəʊn] steinigen **III E**, 136
stop [stɒp] Halt, Stopp **I**
bus stop ['bʌs stɒp] Bushaltestelle **I**
to **stop** [stɒp] anhalten, stoppen **I**
⟨to stop short⟩ [stɒp 'ʃɔ:t] plötzlich stehen bleiben **III 1**, 13
store ['stɔ:] (großes) Geschäft, Laden **I**
department store [dɪ'pɑ:tmənt ˌstɔ:] Kaufhaus **I**
storm [stɔ:m] Sturm **I**
+**stormy** ['stɔ:mi] stürmisch **I**
story ['stɔ:ri] Geschichte **I**
storyteller ['stɔ:riˌtelə] Geschichtenerzähler(in) **II**
straight away [ˌstreɪt‿ə'weɪ] sofort **III 1**, 10
straight ['streɪt] geradeaus **I**
to **straighten** ['streɪtn] gerade richten **III 1**, 14
strange [streɪndʒ] merkwürdig, sonderbar **I**
stranger ['streɪndʒə] Fremde(r) **III 1**, 16
straw [strɔ:] Stroh **I**
to **stray** [streɪ] herumschweifen, herumstreunen **I**
stream [stri:m] Bach, Flüsschen, Strom **III 3**, 51
street [stri:t] Straße **I**
⟨**street-wise**⟩ ['stri:tˌwaɪz] erfahren im Leben auf der Straße **III 4**, 69
stress [stres] Betonung **I**; +Stress, Anspannung **II**
to **stress** [stres] betonen **I**
stressful ['stresfʊl] stressig **II**
to **stretch** [stretʃ] (sich) strecken, dehnen **III 1**, 13
stretching ['stretʃɪŋ] Strecken, Dehnen **II**
strict [strɪkt] strikt, streng **III 6**, 119
string [strɪŋ] Faden; Saite **I**
⟨to **string* along**⟩ [strɪŋ‿ə'lɒŋ] hinhalten **III E**, 130
strip [strɪp] Streifen **I**
to **stroke** [strəʊk] streicheln **II**
strong [strɒŋ] stark, streng, rau **II**
structure ['strʌktʃə] Struktur, Aufbau **II**
⟨**stubborn**⟩ ['stʌbən] stur, störrisch, hartnäckig **III 1**, 14
student ['stju:dnt] Student(in) **II**
student (*AE*) ['stju:dnt] Schüler(in) **III 1**, 9
studio ['stju:diəʊ] Studio **II**
to **study** ['stʌdi] für die Schule lernen **III 6**, 112; studieren **II**
stuff [stʌf] Zeug, Sachen **II**
to **stuff** [stʌf] füllen, stopfen **II**
stunt [stʌnt] Kunststück **II**
stuntman ['stʌntmən] Stuntman, Double **II**
stupid ['stju:pɪd] Dummkopf, Blödmann **II**
stupid ['stju:pɪd] dumm, dämlich **I**
style [staɪl] Stil **I**
subject ['sʌbdʒɪkt] (Unterrichts-)Fach; Thema **I**
⟨to be subject to⟩ ['sʌbdʒɪkt] Untertan(in) sein **III E**, 133
suburb ['sʌbɜ:b] Vorort **III 5**, 94
subway (*AE*) ['sʌbweɪ] U-Bahn **III 2**, 30
+**success** [sək'ses] Erfolg **II**
successful [sək'sesfl] erfolgreich **II**
such [sʌtʃ] solch(e/r/s) **I**
such as ['sʌtʃ‿əz] wie zum Beispiel **II**
to **suck** [sʌk] saugen, lutschen **III 4**, 68
sucker ['sʌkə] Idiot(in) **II**
sudden ['sʌdn] plötzlich, unerwartet **II**
suddenly ['sʌdnli] plötzlich **I**
⟨**suffrage**⟩ ['sʌfrɪdʒ] Wahlrecht **III E**, 146
to **suggest** [sə'dʒest] andeuten, suggerieren, vorschlagen **III 2**, 32
suggestion [sə'dʒestʃn] Vorschlag **I**
suit [su:t] +Anzug **II**; Kostüm **III 4**, 73
⟨**suitable**⟩ ['su:təbl] passend, angemessen **III E**, 148
suitcase ['su:tkeɪs] Koffer **I**
to **sum up** [sʌm‿'ʌp] zusammenfassen **III 4**, 71
summary ['sʌmri] Zusammenfassung **II**
summer ['sʌmə] Sommer **I**
sun [sʌn] Sonne **II**
Sunday ['sʌndeɪ] Sonntag **I**
sunglasses ['sʌnglɑ:sɪz] Sonnenbrille **II**
sunny ['sʌni] sonnig **I**
sunshine ['sʌnʃaɪn] Sonnenschein **II**
⟨**suntan**⟩ ['sʌntæn] Sonnenbräune **III E**, 136
super ['su:pə] super, spitze **I**
suppleness ['sʌplnəs] Elastizität, Flexibilität **II**
supply [sə'plaɪ] Versorgung; Vorrat **III 3**, 51
+supply line [sə'plaɪ ˌlaɪn] Versorgungsleitung **I**
support [sə'pɔ:t] Unterstützung **III 4**, 71
to **support** [sə'pɔ:t] unterstützen **II**
⟨**supporter**⟩ [sə'pɔ:tə] Anhänger(in) **III E**, 134
supporting actor [səˌpɔ:tɪŋ‿'æktə] Schauspieler in einer Nebenrolle **II**
to **suppose** [sə'pəʊz] denken, meinen, annehmen, vermuten **II**
to be supposed to do sth. [sə'pəʊzd] etw tun sollen **III 1**, 13
sure [ʃʊə] sicher, klar **I**
⟨for sure⟩ [fə 'ʃʊə] ganz sicher **III E**, 144
to make sure [ˌmeɪk 'ʃʊə] sicherstellen **I**
surface ['sɜ:fɪs] Oberfläche **II**
surfing ['sɜ:fɪŋ] Surfen **I**
surgeon ['sɜ:dʒn] Chirurg **II**
surprise [sə'praɪz] Überraschung **II**
to be **surprised** (*at*) [sə'praɪzd] überrascht sein (über) **II**
to **surround** [sə'raʊnd] umgeben, umstellen **III 3**, 49
survey ['sɜ:veɪ] Untersuchung, Umfrage **III 4**, 67
surveyor [sə'veɪə] Gutachter(in) **II**
to **survive** [sə'vaɪv] überleben **II**
⟨to **suspect**⟩ [sə'spekt] verdächtigen, einen Verdacht hegen, misstrauen **III E**, 136
⟨to **sustain**⟩ [sə'steɪn] unterhalten **III 5**, 93
⟨to **sway**⟩ [sweɪ] sich wiegen, schaukeln **III 1**, 13
to **swear*** [sweə] fluchen **II**
sweat [swet] Schweiß **III 1**, 13
sweater ['swetə] Pullover **II**
sweatshirt ['swetʃɜ:t] Sweatshirt **I**
sweatshop ['swetʃɒp] Ausbeuterbetrieb **II**
⟨**sweaty**⟩ ['sweti] verschwitzt **III E**, 130
Swede [swi:d] Schwede/Schwedin **III 2**, 32
chimney **sweeping** ['tʃɪmni ˌswi:pɪŋ] Schornsteinreinigung **III 6**, 114
sweet [swi:t] Bonbon, (*pl.*) Süßigkeiten **I**
sweet [swi:t] süß, niedlich **I**
⟨to **swell***⟩ [swel] anschwellen **III 1**, 14
to **swerve** [swɜ:v] ausschwenken **III 1**, 13
to **swim*** [swɪm] schwimmen **I**
swimming ['swɪmɪŋ] Schwimmen **II**
swimming pool ['swɪmɪŋ ˌpu:l] Swimmingpool **I**
swimsuit ['swɪmsu:t] Badeanzug **II**
⟨to **swindle**⟩ ['swɪndl] betrügen, beschummeln **III 2**, 32
to **switch on** [ˌswɪtʃ‿'ɒn] einschalten **II**
sword [sɔ:d] Schwert **II**
⟨to **swot up**⟩ [swɒt‿'ʌp] pauken **III E**, 144
syllable ['sɪləbl] Silbe **I**
symbol ['sɪmbl] Symbol **III 1**, 10
symptom ['sɪmptəm] Anzeichen, Symptom **II**
synonym ['sɪnənɪm] Synonym **III 4**, 75
system ['sɪstəm] System **II**

T

tabby ['tæbi] getigert; getigerte Katze **II**
table [teɪbl] Tisch **I**
tabloid ['tæblɔɪd] kleinformatige, bebilderte Zeitung **III 4**, 66
to **take*** [teɪk] dauern, (Zeit) brauchen **III 2**, 30; nehmen, (hin)bringen **I**
I can't take (*it*) any more! [aɪ ˌkɑ:nt 'teɪk‿ɪt‿eni mɔ:] Ich halte das nicht mehr aus! **III 2**, 34
to take a photo [ˌteɪk‿ə 'fəʊtəʊ] ein Foto machen **II**
⟨to take control⟩ [ˌteɪk kən'trəʊl] die Herrschaft übernehmen **III E**, 132

to take notice (*of*) [ˌteɪk 'nəʊtɪs] beachten, Notiz nehmen (von) **I**
to take off [ˌteɪk‿'ɒf] starten, abheben **I**
to take part (*in*) [ˌteɪk 'pɑ:t] teilnehmen (an) **I**
to take place [ˌteɪk 'pleɪs] stattfinden **II**
to take seriously [ˌteɪk 'sɪəriəsli] ernst nehmen **III 1**, 12
to take to sth./so. [teɪk] auf Anhieb mögen, begeistert sein von **III 1**, 13
to take turns [tɜ:n] (sich) miteinander abwechseln **I**
takings (*pl.*) ['teɪkɪŋz] Einnahmen **II**
talent ['tælənt] Talent, Begabung **III 5**, 100
talented ['tæləntɪd] begabt, talentiert **II**
to tell **tales** [ˌtel 'teɪlz] petzen, klatschen **II**
talk [tɔ:k] Gespräch **I**
⟨pep talk⟩ ['pep ˌtɔ:k] aufmunternde Worte **III E**, 130
talk show ['tɔ:k ˌʃəʊ] Talkshow, Gesprächsrunde **II**
to give a talk [ˌgɪv‿ə 'tɔ:k] ein (Kurz-) Referat halten **I**
to **talk** (*about*) ['tɔ:k‿əˌbaʊt] sprechen, reden (über) **I**
tall [tɔ:l] hoch, groß, lang **II**; +hohe(r/s) **I**
tangled ['tæŋgld] verheddert **II**
tank [tæŋk] Tank **I**
tanker ['tæŋkə] Tanker, Tankschiff **I**
⟨to **tap**⟩ [tæp] klopfen **III 1**, 13
+**tape** [teɪp] (Ton-)Band **II**
demo tape ['deməʊ ˌteɪp] Demo(nstrations)band **I**
task [tɑ:sk] Aufgabe **III 1**, 14
⟨**tattoo**⟩ [tə'tu:] Tätowierung **III 1**, 12
tax [tæks] Steuer **III 5**, 95
⟨**taxation**⟩ [tæk'seɪʃn] Besteuerung **III E**, 133
taxi ['tæksi] Taxi **I**
tea [ti:] Tee **I**
to **teach*** [ti:tʃ] unterrichten, lehren **II**
teacher ['ti:tʃə] Lehrer(in) **I**
team [ti:m] ⟨Gespann⟩ **III 1**, 13; Mannschaft, Team **II**
⟨to make the team⟩ [ˌmeɪk ðə 'ti:m] ins Team aufgenommen werden **III 1**, 8
teapot ['ti:pɒt] Teekanne **I**
tear [tɪə] Träne **II**
to **tear*** (*off*) [teə] (ab)reißen **II**
to **tease** [ti:z] auf den Arm nehmen, necken **II**
technical ['teknɪkl] technisch **II**
techno ['teknəʊ] Techno *(Musikrichtung)* **II**
technological [ˌteknə'lɒdʒɪkl] technologisch, technisch **III 6**, 114
technology [tek'nɒlədʒi] Technologie, Technik **II**
°Design and Technology [dɪ'zaɪn‿ən‿tek'nɒlədʒi] Gestalten und Technik **I**
teddy bear ['tedi ˌbeə] Teddybär **I**
⟨**teen** ⟩ [ti:n] Teenager **III 1**, 9
⟨**teenage**⟩ ['ti:neɪdʒ] Jugend-/ Teenager- **III 1**, 10
teenager ['ti:neɪdʒə] Teenager, Jugendliche(r) **II**
telephone ['telɪfəʊn] Telefon **I**
telescope ['telɪskəʊp] Teleskop, Fernrohr **II**
television ['telɪvɪʒn] Fernsehen **II**
to **tell*** [tel] erzählen **I**
to tell so. to do sth. [tel] jmdm. sagen, dass er/sie etw. tun soll **II**
to tell tales [ˌtel 'teɪlz] petzen, klatschen **II**
telly ['teli] Fernseher **I**
temperature ['temprətʃə] Temperatur, Fieber **II**
temple ['templ] Tempel **II**
temporary ['tempərəri] vorübergehend, befristet, temporär **III 4**, 76
(ten) times [ˌten 'taɪmz] (zehn)mal **II**
+**tennis** ['tenɪs] Tennis **I**
⟨**tension**⟩ ['tenʃn] Spannung **III E**, 142
tent [tent] Zelt **I**
term [tɜ:m] (Schul-) Trimester, Semester **I**; ⟨Amtsperiode⟩ **III E**, 134; Ausdruck, Terminus **II**
terminal ['tɜ:mɪnl] Terminal **I**
terrible ['terəbl] schrecklich, furchtbar **I**
terrifying ['terəfaɪɪŋ] erschreckend, grauenvoll **II**
test [test] Test **I**
to **test** [test] prüfen, testen **II**; testen **I**
tetanus ['tetnəs] Wundstarrkrampf, Tetanus **II**
+**text** [tekst] Text **I**
textiles (*pl.*) ['tekstaɪlz] Textilien **III 6**, 116
than [ðæn/ðən] als **I**
°to **thank** [θæŋk] danken **I**
thank you ['θæŋk‿jʊ] danke **I**
⟨**thankful**⟩ ['θæŋkfl] dankbar **III E**, 130
thanks [θæŋks] danke **I**
that [ðæt] das; dass **I**
so that [səʊ 'ðæt] so dass, damit **III 1**, 16
the [ðə/ði] der/die/das **I**
the 60s ['sɪkstiz] die Sechziger (Jahre) **II**
the ... the [ðə ... ðə] je ... desto **II**
operating **theatre** ['ɒpəreɪtɪŋ ˌθɪətə] Operationssaal **II**
theatreland ['θɪətəˌlænd] Theaterviertel **I**
their [ðeə] ihr/ihre *(pl.)* **I**
theirs [ðeəz] ihre(r/s), der/die/das ihre **II**
them [ðem] sie *(Akk.)*; ihnen *(Dat.)* **I**
theme [θi:m] Thema **I**
theme park ['θi:m ˌpɑ:k] Erlebnispark **I**
⟨theme song⟩ ['θi:m sɒŋ] Titelsong **III 1**, 14
themselves [ðəm'selvz] sich, (sie) selbst **II**
then [ðen] dann, danach **I**
now and then [ˌnaʊ‿n‿'ðen] ab und zu **I**
theory ['θɪəri] Theorie **II**
there is / are [ðeə(r)‿'ɪz / 'ɑ:] es gibt, da ist/sind **I**
thermometer [θə'mɒmɪtə] Thermometer **II**
these [ði:z] dies (sind), das (sind); diese(r/s) (*pl.*) **I**
they [ðeɪ] sie (*pl.*) **I**
thick [θɪk] dick, dicht **I**
thief, *pl.*: **thieves** [θi:f, θi:vz] Dieb **III 6**, 119
thigh [θaɪ] Oberschenkel **II**
thin [θɪn] dünn **I**
thing [θɪŋ] Sache, Ding **I**
to **think*** [θɪŋk] denken, glauben, meinen **I**
third [θɜ:d] Drittel; *bis auf* 'half' *und* 'quarter' *entsprechen die Bruchzahlen den Ordinalzahlen* **III 4**, 67
to be **thirsty** ['θɜ:sti] Durst haben **II**
this [ðɪs] dies (ist), das (ist); diese(r/s) (*sing.*) **I**
those [ðəʊz] jene, diese (*pl.*) **I**
though [ðəʊ] jedoch, dennoch, trotzdem; obwohl **III 1**, 10
as though [əz 'ðəʊ] als ob **III 4**, 70
thought [θɔ:t] Gedanke, Denken **III 5**, 99
thoughtful ['θɔ:tfl] gedankenvoll, nachdenklich **III 4**, 69
thousand ['θaʊznd] tausend **I**
threat [θret] Bedrohung **III 3**, 50
to **threaten** ['θretn] drohen, bedrohen **II**
thriller ['θrɪlə] Thriller, spannender Film **II**
sore **throat** [ˌsɔ: 'θrəʊt] Halsschmerzen, Halsweh **II**
through [θru:] durch, über **I**
throughout [θru'aʊt] überall (in) **II**
to **throw*** (*away*) [θrəʊ] (weg)werfen **I**
to throw up (*coll.*) [θrəʊ‿'ʌp] kotzen **II**
+**thrower** ['θrəʊə] Werfer(in) **II**
+**thumb** [θʌm] Daumen **II**
+to **thumb a ride** [ˌθʌm‿ə 'raɪd] per Anhalter fahren, trampen **II**
thunderstorm ['θʌndəˌstɔ:m] Gewitter **II**
Thursday ['θɜ:zdeɪ] Donnerstag **I**
ticket ['tɪkət] Flugschein, Fahrkarte **I**
tie [taɪ] Krawatte **I**
⟨to **tie up**⟩ [taɪ‿'ʌp] fesseln **III E**, 136
⟨**tiger**⟩ ['taɪgə] Tiger **III 5**, 92
⟨**tight**⟩ [taɪt] eng **III E**, 130
tights [taɪts] Strumpfhose **I**
till [tɪl] bis **III 1**, 12
time [taɪm] (Uhr-)Zeit **I**
ahead of time [ə'hed‿əv 'taɪm] im Voraus **II**
all the time [ˌɔ:l ðə 'taɪm] die ganze Zeit **II**
any time [ˌeni 'taɪm] jederzeit **I**
⟨in time⟩ [ɪn 'taɪm] mit der Zeit; rechtzeitig **III 1**, 10
on time [ɒn 'taɪm] pünktlich **II**
time out [ˌtaɪm‿'aʊt] Auszeit; Zeitbedarf **II**
⟨time-shift⟩ ['taɪmʃɪft] Zeitverschiebung **III 5**, 99
⟨to beat time⟩ [bi:t 'taɪm] den Takt schlagen **III 1**, 13
(*time* +) **flat** [flæt] sage und schreibe (nur) **III 4**, 72
(ten) **times** [ˌten 'taɪmz] (zehn)mal **II**
timetable ['taɪmˌteɪbl] Stundenplan **I**
tiny ['taɪni] winzig **III 3**, 50
tip [tɪp] Hinweis, Tipp **II**; Trinkgeld **III 6**, 111
learning tip ['lɜ:nɪŋ ˌtɪp] Lerntipp **I**
⟨**tire** (*AE*)⟩ ['taɪə] Reifen **III 1**, 13
⟨to **tire**⟩ [taɪə] ermüden **III 6**, 115
to be **tired** ['taɪəd] müde (sein) **I**
title ['taɪtl] Titel, Überschrift **I**
to [tʊ/tu] in/im, zu **I**
toast [təʊst] Toast(brot) **II**
today [tə'deɪ] heute **I**
toe [təʊ] (Fuß-)Zehe **II**
⟨to come near so.'s toes⟩ jmdm ins Handwerk pfuschen **III E**, 138
together [tə'geðə] zusammen **I**
toilet ['tɔɪlɪt] Toilette **I**
to **tolerate** ['tɒləreɪt] tolerieren, dulden **III 6**, 120
toll [təʊl] Maut, Gebühr **III 2**, 33
tomato, (*pl.*) -oes [tə'mɑ:təʊ] Tomate **I**
tomorrow [tə'mɒrəʊ] morgen **I**
tone [təʊn] Ton **III 4**, 68
to **tone up** [ˌtəʊn‿'ʌp] stärken, festigen **II**
tongue [tʌŋ] Zunge **II**
tonight [tə'naɪt] heute Abend, heute Nacht **I**
too [tu:] auch, ebenfalls **I**; zu (sehr, viel) **I**
tooth, *pl.* **teeth** [tu:θ, ti:θ] Zahn, Zähne **II**
top [tɒp] Spitzen-, Spitze **III 1**, 9; Top, ärmelloses T-Shirt **I**
⟨top of the heap⟩ [ˌtɒp‿əv ðə 'hi:p] der/die Beste **III 2**, 30
top [tɒp] obere/r/s **II**
top [tɒp] oben **I**
topic ['tɒpɪk] Thema **I**
⟨to **topple**⟩ ['tɒpl] umfallen, umwerfen **III 3**, 50
torch [tɔ:tʃ] Taschenlampe **II**
tornado, pl. -o(*e*)s [tɔ:'neɪdəʊ] Wirbelsturm, Tornado **II**
⟨**tortoiseshell**⟩ ['tɔ:təʃʃel] Schildkrötenpanzer **III E**, 136
to **toss** [tɒs] werfen **II**
+**tossing the caber** [ˌtɒsɪŋ ðə 'keɪbə] Baumstammwerfen *(schottische Sportart)* **II**
in **total** [ɪn 'təʊtl] insgesamt, total **II**
total ['təʊtl] völlig, ganz **III 1**, 10
to **touch** [tʌtʃ] berühren, anfassen **II**
touchscreen ['tʌtʃˌskri:n] Kontaktbildschirm, Tastenbildschirm **II**
tough [tʌf] hart, zäh **III 1**, 8
⟨to **toughen**⟩ ['tʌfn] härten, aushärten **III E**, 141
tour [tʊə] Reise, Tour **II**
⟨tour operator⟩ [ˌtʊə‿'ɒpreɪtə] Reiseveranstalter **III E**, 136
to **tour** [tʊə] reisen, besichtigen **I**
tourism ['tʊərɪzm] Tourismus **I**
tourist ['tʊərɪst] Tourist(in) **I**
toward(*s*) [tə'wɔ:d(z)] auf ... zu, in Richtung auf, (ent)gegen **I**
towel ['taʊəl] Handtuch **II**
tower ['taʊə] Turm **I**
town [taʊn] (Klein-)Stadt **I**
trace [treɪs] Spur **II**
track [træk] Spur, Weg, Pfad **I**
⟨to **track**⟩ [træk] aufspüren **III 5**, 92
tracksuit ['træksu:t] Jogginganzug **II**
⟨**trade**⟩ [treɪd] Handel **III 5**, 93
free trade [ˌfri: 'treɪd] Freihandel **III 6**, 114

trading port ['treɪdɪŋ ˌpɔ:t] Handelshafen III 6, 114
trader ['treɪdə] Händler(in) II
traditional [trə'dɪʃnl] traditionell I
traffic ['træfɪk] Verkehr I
traffic jam ['træfɪk ˌdʒæm] Verkehrsstau II
traffic light ['træfɪk ˌlaɪt] Ampel I
tragedy ['trædʒədi] Tragödie I
trail [treɪl] Weg, Pfad, Spur III 3, 53
trailer ['treɪlə] Wohnwagen *(AE)*; Anhänger *(BE)* III 3, 50
train [treɪn] (U-Bahn-) Zug I
to **train** [treɪn] trainieren II
trainer ['treɪnə] Trainer(in) II; Turnschuh I
training ['treɪnɪŋ] Ausbildung, Schulung III 6, 110; Training I
to **translate** [træns'leɪt] übersetzen I
transplant ['trænsplɑ:nt] Transplantation II
transport ['trænspɔ:t] Transport, Beförderung I
travel ['trævl] ⟨(das) Reisen⟩ III 1, 10; Reise- I
space travel ['speɪs ˌtrævl] Raumfahrt II
travel agent ['trævl ˌeɪdʒnt] Reisebüroangestellte(r) II
to **travel** ['trævl] reisen I
One Day **Travelcard** ['trævlkɑ:d] Tageskarte, Netzkarte *(London)* II
commercial **traveller** [kəˌmɜ:ʃl 'trævlə] Handelsreisende(r) II
treasure ['treʒə] Schatz II
to **treat** [tri:t] behandeln, umgehen (mit) II
tree [tri:] Baum I
trend [trend] Trend, Tendenz, Richtung III 1, 9
⟨**trial**⟩ [traɪəl] Gerichtsverfahren III E, 146
tribe [traɪb] Stamm II
trick [trɪk] Trick III 3, 55
trickle ['trɪkl] Rinnsal, Tröpfeln III 3, 51
+**tricky** ['trɪki] kompliziert, schwierig II
trip [trɪp] Kurzreise, Trip I
+sailing trip ['seɪlɪŋ ˌtrɪp] Segeltörn I
tropical ['trɒpɪkl] tropisch III 3, 50
trouble ['trʌbl] Ärger, Schwierigkeiten II
to get into trouble ['trʌbl] in Schwierigkeiten geraten II
⟨**troublesome**⟩ ['trʌblsəm] schwierig, lästig III 2, 32
trousers ['traʊzəz] Hose(n) I
long-distance **truck driver** [ˌlɒŋ'dɪstnts 'trʌk ˌdraɪvə] Fernfahrer(in) II
true [tru:] wahr I
⟨yours truly⟩ [ˌjɔ:z 'tru:li] ich höchstpersönlich III 1, 14
trumpet ['trʌmpɪt] Trompete II
trunks [trʌŋks] Badehose(n) II
to **trust** [trʌst] vertrauen III 1, 10
truth [tru:θ] Wahrheit III 1, 8
to **try** [traɪ] versuchen, probieren I
T-shirt ['ti:ʃɜ:t] T-Shirt I
tube [tju:b] *Name der Londoner U-Bahn (wörtlich:* Röhre) I
Tuesday ['tju:zdeɪ] Dienstag I
extra **tuition** [ˌekstrə tju'ɪʃn] Nachhilfe-, Förderunterricht III 6, 112
tune [tju:n] Melodie III 5, 97
⟨to carry a tune⟩ [ˌkæri‿ə 'tju:n] eine Melodie richtig singen III 1, 13
to stay **tuned** [ˌsteɪ 'tju:nd] dranbleiben, den Sender beibehalten III 4, 66
tunnel ['tʌnl] Tunnel I
turf [tɜ:f] Torf; Rasen III 5, 90
+**turkey** ['tɜ:ki] Truthahn II
Turkish ['tɜ:kɪʃ] türkisch, Türkisch I
turn [tɜ:n] Abbiegen III 2, 33
it's his/her turn [tɜ:n] er/sie ist an der Reihe I
to take turns [tɜ:n] (sich) miteinander abwechseln I
to **turn** [tɜ:n] (um)drehen, wenden I; abbiegen III 2, 33
to turn down [ˌtɜ:n 'daʊn] herunterdrehen, leiser stellen I
to turn into ['tɜ:n‿ɪntʊ] (sich) verwandeln in II
to turn so. on [tɜ:n‿'ɒn] jmdn anmachen III 4, 72
TV [ˌti:'vi:] Fernseher I
twice [twaɪs] zweimal I
twin [twɪn] Zwilling III 1, 13
two [tu:] zwei I
type [taɪp] Typ, Art, Sorte III 4, 66
to **type** [taɪp] tippen, mit der Maschine schreiben II
typical ['tɪpɪkl] typisch I
flat **tyre** [ˌflæt 'taɪə] platter Reifen, Plattfuß I

U

U-turn ['ju:tɜ:n] Kehrtwende III 2, 33
UFO *(Unidentified Flying Object)* [ˌju:ef'əʊ] UFO (unbekanntes Flugobjekt) II
ugly ['ʌgli] hässlich I
umbrella [ʌm'brelə] (Regen-)Schirm II
⟨**unanimous**⟩ [ju:'nænɪməs] einstimmig, einmütig III E, 133
uncle ['ʌŋkl] Onkel I
unconscious [ʌn'kɒntʃəs] bewusstlos, unbewusst III 3, 53
uncooperative [ˌʌnkəʊ'ɒprətɪv] wenig entgegenkommend, wenig hilfsbereit III 4, 70
under ['ʌndə] unter I
to **underachieve** [ˌʌndərə'tʃi:v] hinter den Erwartungen zurückbleiben III 6, 112
Underground ['ʌndəgraʊnd] U-Bahn I
to **underline** [ˌʌndə'laɪn] unterstreichen I
underpants *(pl.)* ['ʌndəpænts] Unterhose II
to **understand*** [ˌʌndə'stænd] verstehen I
understatement [ˌʌndə'steɪtmənt] Untertreibung, Understatement III 6, 119
⟨**underwear**⟩ ['ʌndəweə] Unterwäsche III E, 139
unemployed [ˌʌnɪm'plɔɪd] arbeitslos III 6, 111
unemployment [ˌʌnɪm'plɔɪmənt] Arbeitslosigkeit III 6, 115
uneven [ʌn'i:vn] ungerade; uneben III 1, 20
unforgivable [ˌʌnfə'gɪvəbl] unverzeihlich III 4, 70
unfortunately [ʌn'fɔ:tʃnətli] unglücklicherweise, leider II
⟨**unicorn**⟩ ['ju:nɪkɔ:n] Einhorn III E, 141
unidentified [ˌʌnaɪ'dentɪfaɪd] unbekannt, nicht identifiziert II
uniform ['ju:nɪfɔ:m] Uniform I
unique [ju:'ni:k] einzigartig III 3, 52
unit ['ju:nɪt] Lektion, Einheit I
unknown [ʌn'nəʊn] unbekannt II
unless [ʌn'les] wenn nicht, es sei denn III 1, 8
to **unlock** [ʌn'lɒk] aufschließen, entriegeln III 1, 14
to be **unlucky** [ʌn'lʌki] Pech haben II
unmanned [ʌn'mænd] unbemannt II
+**unnatural** [ʌn'nætʃrl] unnatürlich II
(un)pleasant [(ʌn)'pleznt] (un)angenehm III 6, 121
⟨**unpredictable**⟩ [ˌʌnprɪ'dɪktəbl] unvorhersehbar III E, 141
unrest [ʌn'rest] Unruhen, Unzufriedenheit III 5, 91
unskilled worker [ˌʌnskɪld 'wɜ:kə] Hilfsarbeiter(in), ungelernte(r) Arbeiter(in) III 6, 114
until [ən'tɪl] bis I
unused [ˌʌn'ju:zd] unbenutzt, nicht mehr benutzt I
+**unusual** [ʌn'ju:ʒl] ungewöhnlich II
up [ʌp] oben (auf); hinauf I
it's up to you [ˌʌp tə 'ju:] es liegt an dir/Ihnen II
up to ['ʌp tʊ] bis zu III 3, 50
up to date [ˌʌp tə 'deɪt] modern, aktuell I
⟨**Upper House**⟩ [ˌʌpə 'haʊs] Oberhaus III E, 147
+to **uproot** [ʌp'ru:t] entwurzeln, herausreißen I
⟨**upset**⟩ [ʌp'set] bestürzt III E, 144
upstairs [ʌp'steəz] (nach) oben, im/ins obere(n) Stockwerk III 4, 72
+**upstairs** [ˌʌp'steəz] oben; Obergeschoss I
+to **upturn** [ʌp'tɜ:n] umdrehen, umwerfen I
urban ['ɜ:bən] städtisch III 1, 10
us [ʌs] uns I
use [ju:s] Gebrauch III 3, 51
to **use** [ju:z] benutzen, gebrauchen I
⟨to use up⟩ [ju:z‿'ʌp] aufbrauchen, verbrauchen III 3, 49
to get **used to** [get 'ju:zd] sich gewöhnen an III 1, 13
used to do sth. [ˌju:st tə 'du:] pflegte zu tun, machte früher II
useful ['ju:sfl] nützlich, brauchbar I
usual ['ju:ʒl] gewöhnlich, üblich II
usually ['ju:ʒli] gewöhnlich, normalerweise I
utterance ['ʌtrnts] Äußerung II

V

vacation *(AE)* [və'keɪʃn] Urlaub, Ferien I
vaccination [ˌvæksɪ'neɪʃn] Impfung II
⟨**vagabond**⟩ ['vægəbɒnd] Vagabund III 2, 30
value ['vælju:] Wert III 2, 32
good value [ˌgʊd 'vælju:] preisgünstig III 5, 94
van [væn] Kleinlaster, Lieferwagen I
vanilla [və'nɪlə] Vanille I
varied ['veərɪd] verschieden(artig), unterschiedlich II
various ['veəriəs] verschiedene I
vegetable ['vedʒtəbl] Gemüse II
⟨**veil**⟩ [veɪl] Schleier III E, 140
verandah [və'rændə] Veranda II
phrasal **verb** [ˌfreɪzl 'vɜ:b] Verb mit Präposition oder kurzem Adverb III 6, 120
⟨vice **versa**⟩ [ˌvaɪsi 'vɜ:sə] umgekehrt III E, 135
verse [vɜ:s] Strophe, Vers II
version ['vɜ:ʃn] Version II
⟨the **very heart**⟩ [ˌveri 'hɑ:t] Kern III 2, 30
very ['veri] sehr I
vet *(veterinarian)* [vet (ˌvetrɪ'neəriən)] Tierarzt/-ärztin I
via [vaɪə] über II
vibes *(vibrations)* [vaɪbz (vaɪ'breɪʃnz)] Vibrationen, Schwingungen I
⟨**vice versa**⟩ [ˌvaɪsi 'vɜ:sə] umgekehrt III E, 135
video ['vɪdiəʊ] Video I
video clip ['vɪdiəʊ ˌklɪp] Videoclip II
video shop ['vɪdiəʊ ˌʃɒp] Videothek, Videoladen I
view [vju:] Aussicht, Blick, Ansicht I
point of view [ˌpɔɪnt‿əv'vju:] Standpunkt, Sicht, Perspektive III 2, 41
viewer ['vju:ə] Fernsehzuschauer(in) III 4, 66
Viking ['vaɪkɪŋ] Wikinger(in) II
village ['vɪlɪdʒ] Dorf, Ortschaft I
village hall [ˌvɪlɪdʒ 'hɔ:l] Gemeindehaus I
vinegar ['vɪnɪgə] Essig I
violence ['vaɪələnts] Gewalt III 4, 66
violent ['vaɪələnt] brutal, gewalttätig, heftig III 4, 68; ⟨gewaltsam⟩ III E, 139
violet ['vaɪələt] violett II
violin [ˌvaɪə'lɪn] Geige, Violine II
VIP [ˌvi:ai'pi:] berühmte Persönlichkeit III 4, 81
⟨**virgin**⟩ ['vɜ:dʒɪn] Jungfrau III 1, 8
+**virtual reality** [ˌvɜ:tʃuəl ri'æləti] virtuelle Realität II
virtual ['vɜ:tʃuəl] virtuell II
⟨**visible**⟩ ['vɪzəbl] sichtbar III E, 139
visit ['vɪzɪt] Besuch III 5, 90
to **visit** ['vɪzɪt] besuchen I
visitor ['vɪzɪtə] Besucher(in) II
visual effects [ˌvɪʒuəl‿ɪ'fekts] (optische) Tricks II
vocabulary notebook [vəʊˌkæbjəlri 'nəʊtbʊk] Vokabelheft I

vocal group ['vəʊkl ˌgru:p] Musikgruppe mit Gesang **II**
vocals ['vəʊklz] Gesang **II**
voice [vɔɪs] Stimme **I**
volleyball ['vɒlibɔ:l] Volleyball **I**
volume ['vɒlju:m] Lautstärke **III 4**, 68
voluntary ['vɒləntri] freiwillig **III 6**, 110
volunteer [ˌvɒlən'tɪə] Freiwillige(r) **I**
vote [vəʊt] Abstimmung, Wahl; Stimme **III 3**, 58
to **vote** [vəʊt] wählen **II**
vowel ['vauəl] Vokal **III 4**, 79

W

wage [weɪdʒ] (Arbeits-)Lohn **II**
⟨**waist**⟩ [weɪst] Taille **III E**, 130
to **wait** [weɪt] warten **I**
to wait for ['weɪt fɔ:] warten auf **II**
waiter ['weɪtə] Kellner **II**
to **wake*** (*up*) [ˌweɪk‿'ʌp] (auf)wachen **I**
walk [wɔ:k] Spaziergang **I**
to **walk** [wɔ:k] spazierengehen **I**
walking stick ['wɔ:kɪŋ ˌstɪk] Gehstock, Spazierstock **II**
wall [wɔ:l] Wand **I**
wallet ['wɒlɪt] Brieftasche **II**
to **wander** ['wɒndə] herumwandern **II**
to **want** [wɒnt] wollen, wünschen **I**
⟨I wanna (*coll.*).⟩ [aɪ 'wɒnə] Ich will **III 1**, 8
war [wɔ:] Krieg **II**
⟨civil war⟩ [ˌsɪvl 'wɔ:] Bürgerkrieg **III E**, 142
to **warm up** [ˌwɔ:m‿'ʌp] aufwärmen **II**
warm [wɑ:m] warm **I**
global **warming** [ˌgləʊbl 'wɔ:mɪŋ] Erderwärmung durch den Treibhauseffekt **III 3**, 60
to **warn** [wɔ:n] warnen **I**
warning ['wɔ:nɪŋ] Warnung **II**
to **wash** [wɒʃ] waschen, putzen **I**
waste [weɪst] Abfall, Müll **I**
to **waste** [weɪst] verschwenden **III 1**, 20
watch [wɒtʃ] Armbanduhr **I**
to **watch** [wɒtʃ] anschauen, zuschauen **I**
to watch TV [ˌwɒtʃ ti:'vi:] fernsehen **I**
watching brief ['wɒtʃɪŋ ˌbri:f] Beobachtungsauftrag **II**
water ['wɔ:tə] Wasser **I**
fresh water ['freʃ ˌwɔ:tə] Süßwasser **III 3**, 51
salt water ['sɔ:lt ˌwɔ:tə] Salzwasser **III 3**, 51
water-skiing ['wɔ:təski:ɪŋ] Wasserskifahren **I**
to **water** ['wɔ:tə] gießen, bewässern **III 3**, 51
⟨**wattles**⟩ ['wɒtlz] Flechtwerk **III E**, 140
wave [weɪv] Welle **I**
to **wave** [weɪv] wehen, winken **III 1**, 13
wax content ['wæks ˌkɒntent] Wachsgehalt **I**
way [weɪ] Art und Weise; Weg **I**
in a bad way [ˌbæd 'weɪ] in einem schlechten Zustand **II**
no way (*coll.*) [ˌnəʊ 'weɪ] auf keinen Fall, keineswegs **I**
we [wi:] wir **I**
weak [wi:k] schwach **III 2**, 40
wealth [welθ] Reichtum **III 6**, 115
weapon ['wepən] Waffe **II**
to **wear*** [weə] anhaben, tragen **I**
⟨**weary**⟩ ['wɪəri] müde **III 3**, 50
weather ['weðə] Wetter **I**
to **weave*** [wi:v] weben **III 6**, 113
weaver ['wi:və] Weber(in) **III 6**, 114
⟨**wedding**⟩ ['wedɪŋ] Hochzeit **III E**, 144
Wednesday ['wenzdeɪ] Mittwoch **I**
wee (*regional*) [wi:] winzig, klein **III 5**, 90
week [wi:k] Woche **I**
weekday ['wi:kdeɪ] Wochentag, Arbeitstag **II**
weekend [ˌwi:k'end] Wochenende **I**
to **weigh** [weɪ] wiegen **II**
⟨**weight**⟩ [weɪt] Gewicht **III E**, 138
weirdo ['wɪədəʊ] verrückter Typ **III 1**, 10
to **welcome** ['welkəm] begrüßen, willkommen heißen **II**
welcome ['welkəm] willkommen **I**
you're welcome [ˌjɔ: 'welkəm] bitte sehr, nichts zu danken **II**
well [wel] (Öl-)Quelle, Bohrloch **II**
+**well-managed** [ˌwel'mænɪdʒd] gut organisiert, gut geführt **I**
well [wel] gut **II**; nun gut, na ja **I**
as well as [əz 'wel‿əz] sowie, sowohl als auch **II**
to do well [du: 'wel] erfolgreich sein **II**
Welsh [welʃ] walisisch, Walisisch **I**
west [west] westlich, Westen **I**
western ['westən] Western **II**
wet [wet] nass **I**
what [wɒt] was? **I**; welche(r/s), was für eine(r/s) **I**
What about ...? [ˌwɒt‿ə'baʊt] Was ist mit ...? **I**
What kind (*of*) ...? [kaɪnd] Was für eine/welche Art ...? **I**
whatever [wɒt'evə] was (auch immer), egal was **II**
wheel [wi:l] Rad **I**
wheelchair ['wi:ltʃeə] Rollstuhl **II**
when [wen] wenn, wann **I**
whenever [wen'evə] jedesmal wenn; wann auch immer **III 2**, 32
where [weə] wo, wohin, woher **I**
where (*from/to*) [weə] woher/wohin **I**
whether ['weðə] ob **I**
which [wɪtʃ] welche(r/s) **I**
while [waɪl] +(eine) Weile **I**
while [waɪl] während **II**
to **whine** [waɪn] jammern, wimmern, quengeln **II**
whisky ['wɪski] Whisky **II**
whistle ['wɪsl] (Triller-)Pfeife **II**
white [waɪt] weiß **I**
+the whites [waɪts] die Weißen **I**
white-faced ['waɪtfeɪst] mit weißem Gesicht **II**
+**whitewater rafting** [ˌwaɪtwɔ:tə 'rɑ:ftɪŋ] Wildwasserfahren **I**
who [hu:] wer, wem, wen **I**; der/die/das, welche(r/s) **I**
whole [həʊl] ganz, komplett **I**
whom [hu:m] ⟨dem, den, der, die *(Relativpronomen, Objektfall)*⟩ **III 3**, 53; wem, wen **II**
whose [hu:z] deren, dessen **II**
+**whose** [hu:z] wessen **I**
why [waɪ] warum **I**
+**wicket** ['wɪkɪt] Krickettor **II**
wide [waɪd] weit **II**
⟨**widow**⟩ [wɪdəʊ] Witwe **III E**, 144
wild [waɪld] wild **I**
wildlife ['waɪldlaɪf] Tierwelt **I**
⟨**will**⟩ [wɪl] Wille, Testament **III 1**, 13
+**will** [wɪl] werden **I**
⟨**willful** (*AE*)⟩ ['wɪlfl] eigenwillig **III 1**, 13
to be **willing** to (+ *infinitive*) ['wɪlɪŋ tʊ] bereit sein, gewillt sein zu (+ *Infinitiv*) **III 6**, 111
to **win*** [wɪn] gewinnen **I**
⟨to **wince**⟩ [wɪnts] zusammenzucken **III E**, 139
wind [wɪnd] Wind **III 3**, 50
window ['wɪndəʊ] Fenster **I**
+**windy** ['wɪndi] windig **I**
wine [waɪn] Wein **I**
⟨**wing**⟩ [wɪŋ] Flügel **III E**, 140
winner ['wɪnə] Gewinner(in) **II**
winter ['wɪntə] Winter **I**
⟨to **wipe**⟩ [waɪp] abwischen **III E**, 130
wire [waɪə] ⟨Draht, Kabel, Leitung⟩ **III E**, 139
wish [wɪʃ] Wunsch **III 3**, 54
to **wish** [wɪʃ] wünschen **II**
witch [wɪtʃ] Hexe **I**
with [wɪð] mit **I**
⟨with a slam and a flick⟩ [wɪð‿ə ˌslæm‿ənd‿ə 'flɪk] mit einer schnellen Handbewegung Tür oder Fenster zuschlagend **III E**, 141
within [wɪ'ðɪn] in, innerhalb **II**
without [wɪ'ðaʊt] ohne **I**
⟨to **wobble**⟩ ['wɒbl] wackeln, schwabbeln **III 1**, 13
woman, (*pl.*) **women** ['wʊmən/'wɪmɪn] Frau(en) **I**
⟨**wonder**⟩ ['wʌndə] Verwunderung **III 2**, 32
to **wonder** ['wʌndə] sich fragen, sich wundern **II**
wonderful ['wʌndəfl] wunderbar, wundervoll **II**
+**wood** [wʊd] Holz **II**
woods [wʊdz] Wald **I**
word [wɜ:d] Wort **I**
compound (*word*) ['kɒmpaʊnd wɜ:d] zusammengesetztes Wort **III 3**, 57
head word ['hed wɜ:d] Stichwort im Wörterbuch **III 5**, 101
key word ['ki: wɜ:d] Schlüsselbegriff **I**
the last word [ðə ˌlɑ:st 'wɜ:d] der letzte Schrei **III 5**, 94
work [wɜ:k] Arbeit **I**
⟨delivery work⟩ [dɪ'lɪvri ˌwɜ:k] Zustell-, Lieferantentätigkeit **III 6**, 112
work permit ['wɜ:k ˌpɜ:mɪt] Arbeitserlaubnis **III 6**, 112
to **work** [wɜ:k] arbeiten **I**
to work out [wɜ:k‿'aʊt] ausarbeiten, herausfinden **II**; ⟨funktionieren, aufgehen⟩ **III E**, 135
to work shift [ˌwɜ:k 'ʃɪft] Schicht arbeiten, Schichtdienst machen **I**
worker ['wɜ:kə] Arbeiter(in) **II**
skilled worker [ˌskɪld 'wɜ:kə] Facharbeiter(in) **III 6**, 114
unskilled worker [ˌʌnskɪld 'wɜ:kə] Hilfsarbeiter(in), ungelernte(r) Arbeiter(in) **III 6**, 114
workforce ['wɜ:kfɔ:s] Arbeiterschaft, Arbeitskräfte **III 6**, 112
working-class estate [ˌwɜ:kɪŋ 'klɑ:s‿ɪˌsteɪt] Arbeitersiedlung **III 5**, 95
workout ['wɜ:kaʊt] Training **II**
works (*sg. and pl.*) [wɜ:ks] Werk, Fabrik, Betrieb **III 6**, 114
workshop ['wɜ:kʃɒp] Werkstatt **II**
world [wɜ:ld] Welt **I**
⟨**worn**⟩ [wɔ:n] abgenutzt **III 1**, 13
to be **worried** ['wʌrid] besorgt sein **III 2**, 32
to **worry** ['wʌri] sich Sorgen machen **I**
worse [wɜ:s] schlechter **II**
worst [wɜ:st] schlechteste(r/s) **I**
worth [wɜ:θ] wert **III 4**, 71
would play [ˌwʊd/ˌwəd 'pleɪ] spielte gewöhnlich **II**
I'd (= *I would*) like [aɪd‿'laɪk] ich hätte gerne **I**
would (= *used to*) [wʊd] pflegte, -st, -t, -n zu tun, tat, -est, -et, -en früher **III 1**, 12
would you care to [ˌwʊd ju: 'keə] hätten Sie Lust (zu) **II**
would you like to? [ˌwʊd ju: 'laɪk tə] möchtest du?/möchtet ihr/möchten Sie? **I**
⟨**wound**⟩ [wu:nd] Wunde **III E**, 139
wow! [waʊ] *Ausruf der Bewunderung* **I**
to **wrap** [ræp] einwickeln, verpacken **II**
wrist [rɪst] Handgelenk **II**
to **write*** (*down*) [ˌraɪt 'daʊn] (auf)schreiben **I**
to write sth. off [ˌraɪt‿'ɒf] abschreiben **II**
writer ['raɪtə] Schriftsteller(in) **II**
wrong [rɒŋ] falsch **I**
to go wrong [ˌgəʊ 'rɒŋ] schief gehen **II**

X

X-ray ['eksreɪ] Röntgenaufnahme, -strahl **II**
to X-ray ['eksreɪ] durchleuchten, röntgen **II**

Y

yard [jɑ:d] *englisches Längenmaß (= 0,914 m)* **II**; Hof **III 2**, 32
⟨to **yawn**⟩ [jɔ:n] gähnen **III E**, 138
yeah [jeə] ja **I**
year [jɪə] (Schul-)Jahr; Jahrgang, Klasse **I**
all the year round [raʊnd] das ganze Jahr über **II**
yellow ['jeləʊ] gelb **I**
yep *(coll.)* [jep] ja **II**
yes [jes] ja **I**
+**yesterday** ['jestədeɪ] gestern **I**
yet [jet] doch **III 4**, 70
not ... yet [jet] noch nicht **I**
yo-yo ['jəʊjəʊ] Jojo **II**
yoga ['jəʊgə] Joga **I**
you [ju:] du, ihr, Sie **I**
it's up to you [ˌʌp tə 'ju:] es liegt an dir/Ihnen/euch **II**
young [jʌŋ] jung **I**
younger ['jʌŋgə] jünger(e/r/s) **I**
your [jɔ:] dein/deine, euer/eure, Ihr/Ihre **I**
you're welcome [ˌjɔ: 'welkəm] bitte sehr, nichts zu danken **II**
+**yours** [jɔ:z] deine(r/s), eure(r/s), Ihre(r/s) **I**
Yours faithfully, ['feɪθfli] mit freundlichen Grüßen, hochachtungsvoll *(Briefschluss)* **I**
Yours sincerely, [ˌjɔ:z sɪn'sɪəli] Mit freundlichen Grüßen *(Briefschluss)* **II**
⟨yours truly⟩ [ˌjɔ:z 'tru:li] ich höchstpersönlich **III 1**, 14
yourself [jɔ:'self] dich (selbst) **I**
+**yourselves** [jɔ:'selvz] euch (selbst) **II**
youth [ju:θ] Jugendliche(r) **II**
youth hostel ['ju:θ ˌhɒstl] Jugendherberge **I**
youth hostelling ['ju:θ ˌhɒstlɪŋ] in Jugendherbergen übernachten **I**
youthful ['ju:θfl] jugendlich **III 5**, 94

Z

zero ['zɪərəʊ] null **I**
Zulu ['zu:lu] *afrikanische Sprache* **II**

Boys' names

Alan ['ælən]
Alfie ['ælfi]
Alfred ['ælfrɪd]
Andrew ['ændru:]
Archie ['ɑ:tʃi]
Arthur ['ɑ:θə]
Barry ['bæri]
Bart [bɑ:t]
Ben [ben]
Benjamin ['bendʒəmɪn]
Bernie ['bɜ:ni]
Billy ['bɪli]
B.J. ['bi: 'dʒeɪ]
Bob [bɒb]
Bruce [bru:s]
Burt [bɜ:t]
Carlos ['kɑ:lɒs]
⟨**Christy**⟩ ['krɪsti]
Daniel ['dænjəl]
Dick [dɪk]
Dinsy ['dɪnzi]
Ed [ed]
Eddie ['edi]
Farrukh ['færuk]
Floyd [flɔɪd]
Gary ['gæri]
George [dʒɔ:dʒ]
Glen [glen]
+**Greg** [greg]
Harry ['hæri]
Hassan [hə'sɑ:n]
Henry ['henri]
Imran ['ɪmrən]
Jake [dʒeɪk]
James [dʒeɪmz]
Jasmit ['dʒæzmɪt]
+**Jason** ['dʒeɪsn]
Jeff [dʒef]
Jerry ['dʒeri]
Jim [dʒɪm]
Jimmy ['dʒɪmi]
Joe [dʒəʊ]
John [dʒɒn]
Jonathan ['dʒɒnəθən]
Jose [həʊ'zeɪ]
Joshua ['dʒɒʃjuə]
Julian ['dʒu:liən]
Karl [kɑ:l]
Kelvin ['kelvɪn]
Ken [ken]
Kevin ['kevɪn]
Khalid [kɑ:'li:d]
Lance [lɑ:nts]
Larry ['læri]
+**Lee** [li:]
Liam ['lɪəm]
Marc [mɑ:k]
Mark [mɑ:k]
Matt [mæt]
Matthew ['mæθju:]
Michael ['maɪkl]
Mike [maɪk]
Nathan ['neɪθən]
Nick [nɪk]
Oliver ['ɒlɪvə]
Pat [pæt]
Patrick ['pætrɪk]
Paul [pɔ:l]
Pete [pi:t]
Peter ['pi:tə]
Phil [fɪl]
Rizwan ['rɪzwən]
Ron ['rɒn]
Roy [rɔɪ]
Sam [sæm]
Sanjay ['sændʒeɪ]
Scout [skaʊt]
Stan [stæn]
Steve [sti:v]
Terry ['teri]
Tim [tɪm]
Timmy ['tɪmi]
Timothy ['tɪməθi]
Tony ['təʊni]
Trevor ['trevə]
Viktor ['vɪktə]
Wayne [weɪn]
William ['wɪljəm]

Girls' names

Abby ['æbi]
Alexis [ə'leksɪs]
Angel ['eɪndʒl]
Angela ['ændʒlə]
Anna ['ænə]
Ann*(e)* [æn]
+**Ashley** ['æʃli]
Brenda ['brendə]
Bridget ['brɪdʒɪt]
Brigid ['brɪdʒɪd]
Britney ['brɪtni]
Brooke [brʊk]
Carmen ['kɑ:men]
Charlotte ['ʃɑ:lət]
Claire [kleə]
Clara ['klɑ:rə]
Dale [deɪl]
Denise [də'ni:z]
Diana [daɪ'ænə]
Elizabeth [ɪ'lɪzəbəθ]
Emily ['emɪli]
Eva ['i:və]
Faith ['feɪθ]
Fanny ['fæni]
Farrah ['færə]
Georgina [dʒɔ:'dʒi:nə]
Gina ['dʒi:nə]
Hamida [hæ'mɪdə]
Hannah ['hænə]
Hilary ['hɪlri]
Irene ['aɪri:n]
Jean [dʒi:n]
Jessica ['dʒesɪkə]
Joan [dʒəʊn]
Joanna [dʒəʊ'ænə]
Joanne [dʒəʊ'æn]
Judy ['dʒu:di]
Julia ['dʒu:liə]
Karen ['kærən]
Kate [keɪt]
Kerstin ['kɜ:stɪn]
Lauren ['lɔ:rən]
Linda ['lɪndə]
Liz [lɪz]
Lucy ['lu:si]
Lynn [lɪn]
Maggie ['mægi]
Mandy ['mændi]
Margaret ['mɑ:grət]
Mary ['meəri]
Mary Ann [ˌmeəri_'æn]
Mary-Ellen [ˌmæri'_elən]
Maudine ['mɔ:di:n]
Maureen ['mɔ:ri:n]
Molly ['mɒli]
Nicola ['nɪkələ]
Nora ['nɔ:rə]
Pamela ['pæmlə]
Pramila [præ'mɪlə]
Rachel ['reɪtʃl]
Rhaune [rəʊn]
⟨**Rhoda**⟩ ['rəʊdə]
Rukshana ['rʌkʃɑ:nə]
Samantha [sə'mæntθə]
Sarah ['seərə]
Selima [sə'li:mə]
Shamira [ʃə'mi:rə]
+**Shannon** ['ʃænən]
Sharon ['ʃærən]
Signora [si:'njɔ:rə]
⟨**Sinead**⟩ [ʃɪ'neɪd]
Sissy ['sɪsi]
Stella ['stelə]
Stephanie ['stefəni]
Sue [su:]
Susan ['su:zn]
Susie ['su:zi]
⟨**Suzanne**⟩ [su:'zæn]
Tara ['tɑ:rə]
Tessa ['tesə]
Velvet ['velvɪt]
Wendy ['wendi]
Wilma ['wɪlmə]

Surnames

Allen ['ælən]
Anselmo [ænt'selməʊ]
Aziz [ə'zi:z]
Baldwin ['bɔ:ldwɪn]
Barling ['bɑ:lɪŋ]
Barrett ['bærət]
Bell ['bel]
Blake [bleɪk]
Blewitt ['blu:ɪt]
Block [blɒk]
Boocock ['bu:kɒk]
Braden ['breɪdn]
Bradley ['brædli]
Brady ['breɪdi]
Brandt [brænt]
Brezner ['breznə]
Brown [braʊn]
Browne ['braʊn]
Burns [bɜ:nz]
Clifford ['klɪfəd]
Clifton ['klɪftən]
Coleman ['kəʊlmən]
+**Cooper** ['ku:pə]
Copeland ['kəʊplənd]
Craig [kreɪg]
Cummings ['kʌmɪŋz]
Daly ['deɪli]
Davis ['deɪvɪs]
Dawson ['dɔ:sn]
Delamitri [ˌdelə'mi:tri]
Driver ['draɪvə]
Dunford ['dʌnfd]
Evans ['evnz]
Fitzgerald [fɪts'dʒerəld]
Fitzwarren ['fɪtsˌwɒrən]
Forth [fɔ:θ]
Glory ['glɔ:ri]
Gray [greɪ]
Grimsby ['grɪmzbi]
⟨**Harney**⟩ ['hɑ:ni]
Harrington ['hærɪŋtən]
Harrison ['hærɪsn]
Henrey ['henri]
Herrick ['herɪk]
+**Hopkins** ['hɒpkɪnz]
Howard ['haʊəd]
James [dʒeɪmz]
Jones [dʒəʊnz]
Kapadia [kə'pædɪə]
Kwang [kwæŋ]
Laslett-O'Brien [ˌlɑ:zlət_əʊ 'braɪən]
Lee [li:]
Lenoir [lə'nwɑ:]
+**Lucid** ['lu:sɪd]
Lynch [lɪntʃ]
Macintosh ['mækɪntɒʃ]
Manning ['mænɪŋ]
Martin ['mɑ:tɪn]
+**Maryn** ['mærɪn]
McBride [mək'braɪd]
McNamara [ˌmæknə'mɑ:rə]
Melrose ['melrəʊz]
Mills [mɪlz]
Modi ['məʊdi]
Moloney [mə'ləʊni]
Moore ['mɔ:]
Morton ['mɔ:tn]
Norris ['nɒrɪs]
Norton ['nɔ:tn]
O'Brien [əʊ'braɪən]
O'Donnell [əʊ'dɒnl]
O'Hare [əʊ'heə]
Osceola [ˌɒskɪ'əʊlə]
Patel [pə'tel]
Pell [pel]
Pitman ['pɪtmən]
Pollard ['pɒlɑ:d]
Quentin ['kwentɪn]
+**Reed** ['ri:d]
Roberts ['rɒbəts]
Roche [rəʊtʃ]
⟨**Rushworth**⟩ ['rʌʃwəθ]
Sampson ['sæmpsn]
Scott [skɒt]
Sherry ['ʃeri]
Smith [smɪθ]
Stewart ['stju:ət]
Storr [stɔ:]
Sullivan ['sʌlɪvn]
⟨**Sweetman**⟩ ['swi:tmən]
Todd [tɒd]
Trelawne [trɪ'lɔ:n]
Troublemaker ['trʌblˌmeɪkə]
Wilson ['wɪlsn]
Winter ['wɪntə]
Wong [wɒŋ]

Geographical names

Aberdeen [ˌæbəˈdiːn]
Africa [ˈæfrɪkə]
Alton Towers [ˌɔːltn ˈtaʊəz]
America [əˈmerɪkə]
⟨Amsterdam⟩ [ˌæmpstəˈdæm]
Arizona [ˌærɪˈzəʊnə]
Asia [ˈeɪʃə]
+Atlantic [ətˈlæntɪk]
Australia [ɒsˈtreɪliə]
+the Bahamas [bəˈhɑːməz]
⟨Balbriggan⟩ [bælˈbrɪgən]
Banbridge [ˈbænbrɪdʒ]
Bantry Bay [ˌbæntri ˈbeɪ]
Bath [bɑːθ]
⟨Battersea⟩ [ˈbætəsi]
Battery Park [ˌbætri ˈpɑːk]
Belfast [belˈfɑːst]
⟨Bellborough Court⟩ [ˌbelbrə ˈkɔːt]
Benidorm [ˈbenɪdɔːm]
⟨Birmingham⟩ [ˈbɜːmɪŋəm]
Black Velvet Cliffs [ˌblæk velvɪt ˈklɪfs]
Blackburn [ˈblækbɜːn]
⟨Bogside⟩ [bɒgsaɪd]
Boston [ˈbɒstn]
Bright Angel Trail [ˌbraɪt‿ˌeɪndʒl ˈtreɪl]
Bristol [ˈbrɪstl]
Britain [ˈbrɪtn]
the British Isles [ˌbrɪtɪʃ‿ˈaɪlz]
Broadway [ˈbrɔːdweɪ]
Bronx [brɒŋks]
Cairo [ˈkaɪrəʊ]
California [ˌkælɪˈfɔːniə]
Cambridge [ˈkeɪmbrɪdʒ]
+Canada [ˈkænədə]
⟨Canary Islands⟩ [kəˈneəri‿ˌaɪləndz]
Capel Street [ˈkeɪpl ˌstriːt]
Capitol [ˈkæpitl]
Cardiff [ˈkɑːdɪf]
Castle Garden [ˌkɑːsl ˈgɑːdn]
+Chicago [ʃɪˈkɑːgəʊ]
China [ˈtʃaɪnə]
Chinatown [ˈtʃaɪnətaʊn]
Clifford [ˈklɪfəd]
Colorado [ˌkɒlrˈɑːdəʊ]
Corbridge [ˈkɔːbrɪdʒ]
Cork [kɔːk]
Cornwall [ˈkɔːnwɔːl]
Creekville [ˈkriːkvɪl]
Cumbria [ˈkʌmbriə]
Deepdale Lane [ˈdiːpdeɪl ˌleɪn]
Denmark [ˈdenmɑːk]
Derbyshire [ˈdɑːbɪʃə]
Derry [ˈderi]
Dingle Bay [ˌdɪŋgl ˈbeɪ]
Down [daʊn]
Drumnadrochit [ˌdrɒmnəˈdrɒxɪt]
Dublin [ˈdʌblɪn]
East River [ˌiːst ˈrɪvə]
Easter Island [ˈiːstə‿ˌaɪlənd]
Edgecombe [ˈedʒkəm]
Edgecombe County [ˈedʒkəm ˌkaʊnti]
Edinburgh [ˈedɪnbrə]
Ellis Island [ˌelɪs‿ˈaɪlənd]
England [ˈɪŋglənd]
Essex [ˈesɪks]
Europe [ˈjʊərəp]
European Union [ˌjʊərəˈpiːən ˈjuːnjən]
Everglades [ˈevəgleɪdz]
Falmouth [ˈfælməθ]
+Florida [ˈflɒrɪdə]
France [frɑːnts]
Galway [ˈgɔːlweɪ]
Germany [ˈdʒɜːməni]
Glasgow [ˈglɑːzgəʊ]
Grand Canyon [ˌgræn ˈkænjən]
Great Britain [ˌgreɪt ˈbrɪtn]
+Gulf of Mexico [ˌgʌlf‿əv ˈmeksɪkəʊ]
Hadrian's Wall [ˌheɪdriənz ˈwɔːl]
Hampstead Heath [ˌhæmstəd ˈhiːθ]
Harlem [ˈhɑːləm]
Hawaii [həˈwaiː]
Hebrides [ˈhebrɪdiːz]
Helston [ˈhelstən]
Highlands [ˈhaɪləndz]
Holland [ˈhɒlənd]
Hollywood [ˈhɒliwʊd]
Hull [hʌl]
Illinois [ˌɪlɪˈnɔi]
India [ˈɪndiə]
⟨Innisfree⟩ [ˌɪnɪʃˈfriː]
Ireland [ˈaɪələnd]
+Islamorada [ˌɪzləməˈrɑːdə]
Isle of Skye [ˌaɪl‿əv ˈskaɪ]
Islington [ˈɪzlɪŋtən]
Italy [ˈɪtli]
Jamaica [dʒəˈmeɪkə]
⟨Jamestown⟩ [ˈdʒeɪmztaʊn]
Java [ˈdʒɑːvə]
Kansas [ˈkænzəs]
Kerry [ˈkeri]
+Key West [ˌkiː ˈwest]
+Keys [kiːz]
⟨Kildare Street⟩ [kɪlˈdeə ˌstriːt]
Kilkelly [kɪlˈkeli]
Korea [kəˈriːə]
Lake Mead [ˌleɪk ˈmiːd]
+Lake Michigan [ˌleɪk ˈmɪʃɪgən]
Lancashire [ˈlæŋkəʃə]
Land's End [ˌlændz‿ˈend]
Las Vegas [ˌlæs ˈveɪgəs]
Liffey [ˈlɪfi]
Little Ukraine [ˌlɪtl juːˈkreɪn]
Liverpool [ˈlɪvəpuːl]
Llanfair P.G. [ˈhlænfeə ˌpiːˈdʒiː]
Loch Lomond [ˌlɒk/lɒx ˈləʊmənd]
Loch Ness [ˌlɒk/lɒx ˈnes]
London [ˈlʌndən]
⟨Londonderry⟩ [ˈlʌndənˌderi]
Los Angeles [lɒs‿ˈændʒɪliːz]
Lowlands [ˈləʊləndz]
Machynlleth [məˈkʌnhleθ]
+Maine [meɪn]
Manchester [ˈmæntʃestə]
Manhattan [ˌmænˈhætn]
⟨Maryland⟩ [ˈmeərilænd]
Massachusetts [ˌmæsəˈtʃuːsɪts]
Mayo [ˈmeɪəʊ]
Mexico [ˈmeksɪkəʊ]
+Miami Beach [maɪˌæmi ˈbiːtʃ]
Milwaukee [ˈmɪlwɔːkiː]
Missouri [mɪˈzʊəri]
Montana [mɒnˈtænə]
Munich [ˈmjuːnɪk]
Nevada [nəˈvɑːdə]
+New England [ˌnjuː‿ˈɪŋglənd]
+New Jersey [ˌnjuːˈdʒɜːzi]
New Orleans [ˌnjuː‿ˈɔːlianz]
New York [ˌnjuː ˈjɔːk]
Newcastle upon Tyne [ˌnjuːkɑːsl‿əpɒn ˈtaɪn]
Norfolk [ˈnɔːfək]
Norfolk Broads [ˌnɔːfək ˈbrɔːdz]
+North Carolina [ˌnɔːθ kærəˈlaɪnə]
North Tyneside [ˌnɔːθ ˈtaɪnsaɪd]
⟨Northern Ireland⟩ [ˌnɔːðn‿ˈaɪələnd]
Notting Hill [ˌnɒtɪŋ ˈhɪl]
O'Connell Bridge [əʊˈkɒnl ˌbrɪdʒ]
Ontario [ɒnˈteəriəʊ]
+Overseas Highway [ˌəʊvəsiːz ˈhaɪweɪ]
Oxford [ˈɒksfəd]
Pall Mall [pæl ˈmæl]
Paris [ˈpærɪs]
Pennsylvania [ˌpentsɪlˈveɪniə]
Penzance [penˈzænts]
Philadelphia [ˌfɪləˈdelfiə]
⟨Philly ⟩ [ˈfɪli]
Phoenix [ˈfiːnɪks]
Plymouth [ˈplɪməθ]
Princeville [ˈprɪntsvɪl]
Red Rock Canyon [ˌred rɒk ˈkænjən]
the Republic of Ireland [rɪˌpʌblɪk‿əv‿ˈaɪələnd]
Riviera [ˌrɪviˈeərə]
Rocky Mount [ˌrɒki ˈmaʊnt]
Rome [rəʊm]
San Diego [ˌsæn diˈeɪgəʊ]
Scilly Isles [ˈsɪli‿aɪlz]
Scotland [ˈskɒtlənd]
Sennen Cove [ˌsenən ˈkəʊv]
Sicily [ˈsɪsɪli]
Slough [slaʊ]
Snowdonia [snəʊˈdəʊniə]
Spain [speɪn]
St Columba [ˌsnt kəˈlʌmbə]
St Ives [snt‿ˈaɪvz]
Staffordshire [ˈstæfədʃə]
Staten Island [ˌstætn‿ˈaɪlənd]
Stonehenge [ˌstəʊnˈhendʒ]
⟨Sun Belt⟩ [ˈsʌn belt]
Surrey [ˈsʌri]
Swansea [ˈswɒnzi]
Temple Bar [ˌtempl ˈbɑː]
+the Netherlands [ˈneðələndz]
the West Indies [ˌwest‿ˈɪndiz]
Times Square [ˌtaimz ˈskweə]
Tokyo [ˈtəʊkiəʊ]
Toronto [təˈrɒntəʊ]
Trinidad [ˈtrɪnɪdæd]
Tucson [ˈtuːsɒn]
Turkey [ˈtɜːki]
Ulster [ˈʌlstə]
the United Kingdom [juːˌnaɪtɪd ˈkɪŋdəm]
the United States (*US*) [juːˌnaɪtɪd ˈsteɪts]
⟨Virginia⟩ [vəˈdʒɪnjə]
Wales [weɪlz]
Wall Street [ˈwɔːl ˌstriːt]
⟨the Wash⟩ [wɒʃ]
Washington DC [ˌwɒʃɪŋtən ˌdiːˈsiː]
Westbury [ˈwestbri]
Windsor [ˈwɪndzə]
Yorkshire [jɔːkʃə]
Yorkshire Dales [ˌjɔːkʃə ˈdeɪlz]
Yosemite [jəʊˈsemɪti]

Other names

+American Airlines [əˈmerɪkən‿ˈeəˌlaɪnz]
Anthony Burgess [ˌæntəni ˈbɜːdʒəs]
⟨Apollo⟩ [əˈpɒləʊ]
Barbie [ˈbɑːbi]
+Barnes and Noble [ˈbɑːnz‿ən ˈnəʊbl]
⟨Battle of the Boyne⟩ [ˌbætl‿əv ðə ˈbɔɪn]
Bayeux Tapestry [baɪˌjɜː ˈtæpɪstri]
BBC [ˌbiːbiːˈsiː]
Beano [ˈbiːnəʊ]
Ben Elton [ˌben‿ˈeltn]
Betsy Byars [ˌbetsi ˈbaɪəz]
Big Ben [bɪg ˈben]
+Blacky [ˈblæki]
the Book of Kells [ˌbʊk‿əv ˈkels]
Boudicca [ˈbuːdɪkə]
⟨Boy George⟩ [ˌbɔɪ ˈdʒɔːdʒ]
Boyzone [ˈbɔɪzəʊn]
Britrail Pass [ˈbrɪtreɪl ˌpɑːs]
Brixton [ˈbrɪkstn]
+Calvin Klein [ˌkælvɪn ˈklaɪn]
Camden Lock [ˌkæmdən ˈlɒk]
Camden Passage [ˌkæmdən ˈpæsɪdʒ]
Celtica [ˈkeltɪkə]
Central Park [ˈsentrl ˌpɑːk]
⟨Charles I⟩ [ˌtʃɑːlz]
Chicago Cub [ʃɪˌkɑːgəʊ ˈkʌb]
+Chinatown [ˈtʃaɪnətaʊn]
Chris de Burgh [ˌkrɪs də ˈbɜːg]
Christian Barnard [ˌkrɪstʃən bɑːˈnɑːd]
Chrysler Building [ˈkraɪzlə ˌbɪldɪŋ]
Circle Line [ˈsɜːkl ˌlaɪn]
CNN [ˌsiːenˈen]
Congress [ˈkɒŋgres]
⟨Conservative Party⟩ [kənˈsɜːvətɪv]
Covent Garden [ˌkɒvnt ˈgɑːdn]
Red Cross [ˌred ˈkrɒs]
Daniel Boone [ˌdænjəl ˈbuːn]
Democrat [ˈdeməkræt]
Dick Whittington [ˌdɪk ˈwɪtɪŋtən]
Disney World [ˈdɪzni ˌwɜːld]
Doc Martens [ˌdɒk ˈmɑːtɪnz]
⟨Duke of York⟩ [djuːk‿əv jɔːk]
⟨East India Company⟩ [ˌiːst‿ˌɪndiə ˈkʌmpəni]
Edvard Munch [ˌedvəd ˈmʊŋk]
⟨Elizabeth I⟩ [ɪˈlɪzəbəθ ðə ˈfɜːst]
Elton John [ˌeltn ˈdʒɒn]
⟨Emmeline Pankhurst⟩ [ˌemɪliːn ˈpæŋkhɜːst]
Empire State Building [ˌempaɪə ˈsteɪt ˌbɪldɪŋ]
Enid Blyton [ˌiːnɪd ˈblaɪtn]
Equitable Building [ˈekwɪtəbl ˌbɪldɪŋ]
Evita [evˈiːtə]
⟨Farrukh Dhondy⟩ [ˌfærʊk ˈdɒndi]
Fred Astaire [ˌfred‿əsˈteə]
⟨Fred Flintstone⟩ [ˌfred ˈflɪntstəʊn]
Friends of the Earth [ˈfrendz‿əv ði‿ˈɜːθ]
Gagarin [gəˈgɑːrɪn]
Galahad [ˈgæləhæd]
Garret A. Morgan [ˌgærɪt‿eɪ ˈmɔːgn]
⟨Gary Barlow⟩ [ˌgæri ˈbɑːləʊ]
Gary Trudeau [ˌgæri ˈtruːdəʊ]
George H. Reavis [ˌdʒɔːdʒ‿eɪtʃ ˈriːvɪs]
+George Mikes [ˌdʒɔːdʒ ˈmiːkeʃ]
George Thorogood [ˌdʒɔːdʒ ˈθʌrəgʊd]
⟨George Washington ⟩ [ˌdʒɔːdʒ ˈwɒʃɪŋtən]
Ginger Rogers [ˌdʒɪndʒə ˈrɒdʒəz]
Giovanni Schiaparelli [ˌdʒiːəʊˈvɑːni ˌskæpəˈreli]
Girlzone [ˈgɜːlzəʊn]
⟨Glorious and Bloodless Revolution⟩ [ˌglɔːrɪəs‿ənd ˌblʌdles revˈluːʃn]
Gosforth & Sons [ˈgɒsfɔːθ‿ən ˌsʌnz]
⟨Granville Wilson⟩ [ˌgrænvɪl ˈwɪlsn]
Guinness [ˈgɪnɪs]
Hadrian [ˈheɪdriən]
Harold [ˈhærəld]
Harrods [ˈhærədz]
Hea Sukh Lee [heə ˌsʊk ˈliː]
Heathrow [ˌhiːθˈrəʊ]
Henry Hudson [ˌhenri ˈhʌdzn]
⟨Henry VIII⟩ [ˌhenri ði‿ˈeɪtθ]
Herbert Hoover [ˌhɜːbət ˈhuːvə]
High Street [ˈhaɪ striːt]
Hoover Dam [ˌhuːvə ˈdæm]
House of Commons [ˌhaʊs‿əv ˈkɒmənz]
House of Representatives [ˌhaʊs‿əv reprɪˈzentətɪvz]
⟨Howard Donald⟩ [ˌhaʊəd ˈdɒnəld]
Hubble [ˈhʌbl]
⟨'I Spy'⟩ [aɪ ˈspaɪ]

Ian Jack [ˌi:ən ˈdʒæk]
⟨**IRA**⟩ [ˌaɪɑ:‿ˈeɪ]
⟨**Irish Republican Army**⟩ [ˌaɪrɪʃ rɪˌpʌblɪkən‿ˈɑ:mi]
Islington Green [ˌɪslɪŋtən ˈgri:n]
Jack the Ripper [ˌdʒæk ðə ˈrɪpə]
James Cook [ˌdʒeɪmz ˈkʊk]
⟨**James II**⟩ [ˌdʒeɪmz ðə ˈseknd]
James Watt [ˌdʒeɪmz ˈwɒt]
⟨**Jason Orange**⟩ [dʒeɪsn‿ˈɒrɪndʒ]
Jennifer Kolby [ˌdʒenɪfə ˈkɒlbi]
Jesus [ˈdʒi:zəs]
John Lennon [ˌdʒɒn ˈlenən]
Joseph Shabalala [ˌdʒəʊzɪf ˈʃɑ:bəlɑ:lə]
Katherine Anne Porter [ˌkæθri:n‿ˌæn ˈpɔ:tə]
Kennedy Movie Theater [ˌkenədi ˈmu:vi ˌθɪətə]
King Arthur [ˌkɪŋ‿ˈɑ:θə]
King Kong [ˌkɪŋ ˈkɒŋ]
Kirrin Cottage [ˌkɪrɪn ˈkɒtɪdʒ]
Labour [ˈleɪbə]
Ladysmith Black Mambazo [ˈleɪdismɪθ ˌblæk məmˈbɑ:zəʊ]
Lancelot [ˈlɑ:ntsəlɒt]
⟨**Lee Hill**⟩ [ˌli: ˈhɪl]
Leonardo da Vinci [ˌli:əˈnɑ:dəʊ də ˈvɪntʃi]
Leonardo di Caprio [ˌli:əˈnɑ:dəʊ‿dɪ‿ˈkæpriəʊ]
Levi Strauss [ˌli:vaɪ ˈstraʊs]
Liberal Democrats [ˌlɪbrl ˈdeməkræts]
+**Little Italy** [ˌlɪtl‿ˈɪtli]
London Dungeon [ˌlʌndən ˈdʌndʒn]
Lord Kitchener [ˌlɔ:d ˈkɪtʃɪnə]
+**Lower East Side** [ˌləʊə‿ˈi:st saɪd]
+**Macy's** [ˈmeɪsiz]
Madonna [məˈdɒnə]
Maeve Binchy [ˌmeɪv ˈbɪntʃi]
Magna Carta [ˌmægnə ˈkɑ:tə]
Marilyn Monroe [ˈmærɪlɪn mənˈrəʊ]
Mariner [ˈmærɪnə]
⟨**Mark Owen**⟩ [ˌmɑ:k‿ˈəʊɪn]
Marks and Spencer [ˌmɑ:ks nd ˈspentsə]
Mars [mɑ:z]
Mayflower [ˈmeɪflaʊə]
Megan [ˈmegən]
Mercury [ˈmɜ:kjri]
Merlin the Magician [ˌmɜ:lɪn ðə məˈdʒɪʃn]
Metropolitan [ˌmetrəˈpɒlɪtn]
Michael Jackson [ˌmaɪkl ˈdʒæksn]
⟨**Michael Rosen**⟩ [ˌmaɪkl ˈrəʊzn]
Midas [ˈmaɪdəs]
Milly [ˈmɪli]
+**Mir crew** [ˈmɪə ˌkru:]
Mona Lisa [ˌməunə ˈli:sə]
Monty [ˈmɒnti]
the **Monument** [ˈmɒnjəmənt]
Moon and Stars [ˌmu:n‿ən ˈstɑ:z]
Morgan le Fay [ˌmɔ:gn lə ˈfeɪ]
Mumbles View [ˌmʌmblz ˈvju:]
NASA [ˈnæsə]
Nessie [ˈnesi]
New Globe Theatre [ˌnju: ˈgləʊb ˈθɪətə]
New York Philharmonic [ˌnju: ˈjɔ:k ˌfɪlhɑ:ˈmɒnɪk]
New Zealand [ˌnju: ˈzi:lənd]
⟨**Newcomen**⟩ [ˈnju:kʌmən]
North Sea [ˌnɔ:θ ˈsi:]
Odeon [ˈəʊdiən]
+**O'Hare** [əʊˈheə]
Orbiter [ˈɔ:bɪtə]
+**Orchard Street** [ˈɔ:tʃəd ˌstri:t]
Orion [əˈraɪən]
Oscar [ˈɒskə]
Oscar Wilde [ˌɒskə ˈwaɪld]
⟨**Oval Office**⟩ [ˈəʊvl‿ˌɒfɪs]
Oxford Street [ˈɒksfəd ˌstri:t]
Pathfinder [ˈpɑ:θˌfaɪndə]
Paul McCartney [ˌpɔ:l məˈkɑ:tni]
Paul Simon [ˌpɔ:l ˈsaɪmən]
Penryn College [penˌrɪn ˈkɒlɪdʒ]
Percival Lowell [ˌpɜ:sɪvl ˈləʊəl]
⟨**Peter Minuit**⟩ [ˌpi:tə ˈmɪnjuɪt]
Petticoat Lane [ˌpetɪkəʊt ˈleɪn]
+**Pilgrim** [ˈpɪlgrɪm]
the **Plush** [plʌʃ]
Princess Elaine [prɪnˈses ɪˈleɪn]
+**Puritan** [ˈpjʊərɪtn]
Queen Elizabeth [ˌkwi:n‿ɪˈlɪzəbəθ]
⟨Queen's University⟩ [ˌkwi:nz ju:nɪˈvɜ:səti]
Queensway [ˈkwi:nzweɪ]
Red Cross [ˌred ˈkrɒs]
Red Nose Day [ˌred ˈnəʊz ˌdeɪ]
Republican [rɪˈpʌblɪkən]
Right Guard [ˈraɪt gɑ:d]
⟨**Riverdance**⟩ [ˈrɪvədɑ:nts]
⟨**Robbie Williams**⟩ [ˌrɒbi ˈwɪljəmz]
Robert Frost [ˌrɒbət ˈfrɒst]
Rolling Stones [ˌrəʊlɪŋ ˈstəʊnz]
Ronan Keating [ˌrəʊnən ˈki:tɪŋ]
Ros Chast [ˌrɒz ˈtʃɑ:st]
⟨**Rosie Rushton**⟩ [ˌrəʊzi ˈrʌʃtən]
⟨**Royal Ulster Constabulary**⟩ [ˌrɔɪəl‿ˌʌlstə kənˈstæbjʊlri]
⟨**RUC**⟩ [ˌɑ:ju:ˈsi:]
+**Saks Fifth Avenue** [ˈsæks ˌfɪfθ ˈævənju:]
San Juan [sæn ˈhwɑ:n]
⟨**Seamus Heaney**⟩ [ˌʃeɪməs ˈhi:ni]
+**Sears Tower** [ˌsɪəz ˈtaʊə]
Sgt. Pepper [ˌsɑ:dʒnt ˈpepə]
Shelly Merkes [ˌʃeli ˈmɜ:ks]
Slattery's [ˈslætriz]
Sloane Square [ˌsləʊn ˈskweə]
+**SoHo** [ˈsəʊhəʊ]
Sojourner [sɒˈdʒɜ:nə]
+**Speedwell** [ˈspi:dwel]
Sputnik [ˈspʌtnɪk]
St. Anthony [snt‿ˈæntəni]
St. Patrick [sntˈpætrɪk]
Starlight Express [ˌstɑ:laɪt‿ɪkˈspres]
Statue of Liberty [ˌstætʃu:‿əv ˈlɪbəti]
Stuart Lodge [ˌstjʊət ˈlɒdʒ]
Superman [ˈsu:pəmæn]
⟨**Supreme Court**⟩ [su:ˌpri:m ˈkɔ:t]
Suzi Quatro [ˌsu:zi ˈkwætrəʊ]
⟨**Take That**⟩ [ˌteɪk ˈðæt]
Temple [ˈtempl]
Thanksgiving [ˌθæŋksˈgɪvɪŋ]
The Windrush [ˈwɪndrʌʃ]
Third World [ˌθɜ:d ˈwɜ:ld]
⟨**Thomas Jefferson**⟩ [ˌtɒməs ˈdʒefəsn]
+**Tiffany's** [ˈtɪfniz]
Tinto [ˈtɪntəʊ]
Tom Petty & The Heartbreakers [ˌtɒm ˈpeti‿ənd ðə ˌhɑ:tbreɪkəz]
Toni Morrison [ˌtəʊni ˈmɒrɪsn]
Top Girls [ˈtɒp ˌgɜ:lz]
Tottenham Court Road [ˌtɒtnəm kɔ:t ˈrəʊd]
Tower Hill station [ˈtaʊə ˌhɪl ˈsteɪʃn]
Tower of London [ˌtaʊə‿əv ˈlʌndən]
Trafalgar Square [trəˌfælgə ˈskweə]
Trinity Church [ˈtrɪnɪti ˌtʃɜ:tʃ]
Trinity College [ˌtrɪnɪti ˈkɒlɪdʒ]
United Nations (*UN*) [ju:ˌnaɪtɪd ˈneɪʃnz]
Victoria Line [vɪkˈtɔ:riə ˌlaɪn]
Walter Frederick [ˌwɔ:ltə ˈfredrɪk]
⟨**Watson**⟩ [ˈwɒtsn]
⟨**West India Company**⟩ [ˌwest‿ɪndiə ˈkʌmpəni]
the West End [ˌwest‿ˈend]
Westminster Bridge [ˌwestmɪnstə ˈbrɪdʒ]
Whitney Houston [ˌwɪtni ˈhju:stn]
Wild West [ˌwaɪld ˈwest]
⟨**William Butler Yeats**⟩ [ˌwɪljəm ˌbʌtlə ˈjeɪts]
William Frisbie [ˌwɪljəm ˈfrɪzbi]
⟨**William of Orange**⟩ [ˌwɪljəm‿əv‿ˈɒrɪndʒ]
⟨**William Penn**⟩ [ˌwɪljəm pen]
William Shakespeare [ˌwɪljəm ˈʃeɪkspɪə]
William the Conqueror [ˌwɪljəm ðə ˈkɒŋkrə]
Wonky Towers [ˌwɒŋki ˈtaʊəz]
World Trade Center [ˌwɜ:ld ˈtreɪd ˌsentə]
⟨**Wright Brothers**⟩ [ˈraɪt ˌbrʌðez]
Yankee Stadium [ˌjæŋki ˈsteɪdiəm]
YHA (*Youth Hostelling Association*) [ˌju:θ ˌhɒstlɪŋ əˌsəʊʃiˈeɪʃn]

Classroom phrases

Talking about stories, poems, songs …

I liked / didn't like the story.	Diese Geschichte hat mir (nicht) gefallen.
I thought it was brilliant / interesting / funny / sad / exciting / terrible / boring.	Ich fand sie toll / interessant / lustig / traurig / spannend / schrecklich / langweilig.
It was OK, but I liked … better.	Sie war OK, aber … hat mir besser gefallen.
The main / minor characters …	Die Haupt-/Nebenfiguren …
The plot / setting / theme …	Die Handlung / der Schauplatz / das Thema …
The suspense …	Die Spannung …
It was told from an interesting point of view.	Die Erzählperspektive war interessant.
The plot was hard to follow.	Die Handlung war schwer verständlich.
There wasn't much action in the story.	Es passierte nicht viel in der Geschichte.
The ending was unexpected / predictable.	Der Schluss war unerwartet / vorauszusagen.
What is the writer trying to tell us?	Was will uns der/die Autor/in damit sagen?
I like the music, but not the words.	Die Musik finde ich gut, aber nicht den Text.

Having a discussion …

What do you think?	Was meinst du?
Sorry, but I disagree entirely.	Tut mir leid, ich bin ganz anderer Meinung.
In my opinion …	Meiner Meinung nach … / Meines Erachtens …
I can see your point, but …	Ich verstehe dein Argument, aber …
I think you're right / wrong.	Ich denke, du hast Recht / Unrecht.
The point I'm trying to make is …	Was ich sagen will, ist …
That's one way of looking at it, but …	So kann man's auch sehen, aber …
I don't follow you.	Ich verstehe nicht, was du meinst.
On the one hand …, on the other hand …	Einerseits …, andererseits …
One of the main (dis)advantages is …	Einer der Hauptvor-/nachteile ist …
I don't think that's relevant.	Das finde ich nicht wichtig.
Can I interrupt you there for a second?	Darf ich dich ganz kurz unterbrechen?
There's another aspect to this, though …	Da gibt es aber einen weiteren Aspekt …

Giving a presentation …

My presentation is about …	Das Thema meines Vortrags/Referats ist …
If you have any questions, …	Wenn ihr irgendwelche Fragen habt, …
… I'd be happy to answer them at the end.	… beantworte ich sie gerne zum Schluss.
I'd like to begin with … Then/after that …	Beginnen möchte ich mit … Anschließend …
I think it's important to point out that …	Ein wichtiger Punkt ist, dass …
Another interesting aspect is …	Ein weiterer interessanter Aspekt ist …
Finally, to sum up, …	Zum Schluss, zusammenfassend, …
Thank you for listening.	Vielen Dank für eure Aufmerksamkeit.

Working at a computer …

My computer has crashed.	Mein Rechner ist abgestürzt.
What does this message mean?	Was bedeutet diese Meldung?
It won't accept my passwort.	Mein Kennwort wird nicht angenommen.
What's the address of the website?	Was ist die Adresse von der Website?
Have they got an e-mail address?	Haben sie eine E-mail-Adresse?
I've saved it on disk.	Ich habe es auf Diskette gespeichert.

Irregular verbs

infinitive	simple past	past participle	German
be [bi:]	was, were [wɒz, wɜ:]	been [bi:n]	sein
beat [bi:t]	beat [bi:t]	beaten ['bi:tn]	schlagen
become [bɪ'kʌm]	became [bɪ'keɪm]	become [bɪ'kʌm]	werden
begin [bə'gɪn]	began [bə'gæn]	begun [bə'gʌn]	beginnen
bend [bend	bent [bent]	bent [bent]	beugen, biegen
bet [bet]	bet [bet]	bet [bet]	wetten
bite [baɪt]	bit [bɪt]	bitten ['bɪtn]	beißen
blow [bləʊ]	blew [blu:]	blown [bləʊn]	blasen
break [breɪk]	broke [brəʊk]	broken ['brəʊkn]	brechen
bring [brɪŋ]	brought [brɔ:t]	brought [brɔ:t]	bringen
broadcast ['brɔ:dkɑ:st]	broadcast ['brɔ:dkɑ:st]	broadcast ['brɔ:dkɑ:st]	senden
build [bɪld]	built [bɪlt]	built [bɪlt]	bauen
buy [baɪ]	bought [bɔ:t]	bought [bɔ:t]	kaufen
catch [kætʃ]	caught [kɔ:t]	caught [kɔ:t]	fangen
choose [tʃu:z]	chose [tʃəʊz]	chosen ['tʃəʊzn]	(aus)wählen
come [kʌm]	came [keɪm]	come [kʌm]	kommen
cost [kɒst]	cost [kɒst]	cost [kɒst]	kosten
cut [kʌt]	cut [kʌt]	cut [kʌt]	schneiden
deal (with) [di:l]	dealt [delt]	dealt [delt]	(be)handeln
dig [dɪg]	dug [dʌg]	dug [dʌg]	graben
do [du:]	did [dɪd]	done [dʌn]	machen, tun
draw [drɔ:]	drew [dru:]	drawn [drɔ:n]	zeichnen
drink [drɪŋk]	drank [dræŋk]	drunk [drʌŋk]	trinken
drive [draɪv]	drove [drəʊv]	driven ['drɪvn]	fahren
eat [i:t]	ate [et]	eaten ['i:tn]	essen
fall [fɔ:l]	fell [fel]	fallen ['fɔ:ln]	fallen
feed [fi:d]	fed [fed]	fed [fed]	füttern
feel [fi:l]	felt [felt]	felt [felt]	(sich) fühlen
fight [faɪt]	fought [fɔ:t]	fought [fɔ:t]	kämpfen
find [faɪnd]	found [faʊnd]	found [faʊnd]	finden
fling [flɪŋ]	flung [flʌŋ]	flung [flʌŋ]	werfen, schleudern
fly [flaɪ]	flew [flu:]	flown [fləʊn]	fliegen
forget [fə'get]	forgot [fə'gɒt]	forgotten [fə'gɒtn]	vergessen
freeze [fri:z]	froze [frəʊz]	frozen ['frəʊzn]	gefrieren
get [get]	got [gɒt]	got [gɒt]	holen, bekommen
give [gɪv]	gave [geɪv]	given ['gɪvn]	geben
go [gəʊ]	went [went]	gone [gɒn]	gehen
grow [grəʊ]	grew [gru:]	grown [grəʊn]	wachsen, (an)bauen
hang [hæŋ]	hung [hʌŋ] hanged [hæŋgd]	hung [hʌŋ] hanged [hæŋgd]	hängen
have [hæv]	had [hæd]	had [hæd]	haben
hear [hɪə]	heard [hɜ:d]	heard [hɜ:d]	hören
hide [haɪd]	hid [hɪd]	hidden ['hɪdn]	(sich) verstecken
hit [hɪt]	hit [hɪt]	hit [hɪt]	schlagen
hold [həʊld]	held [held]	held [held]	halten
hurt [hɜ:t]	hurt [hɜ:t]	hurt [hɜ:t]	verletzen, wehtun
keep [ki:p]	kept [kept]	kept [kept]	(be)halten
know [nəʊ]	knew [nju:]	known [nəʊn]	wissen, kennen
lead [li:d]	led [led]	led [led]	führen
learn [lɜ:n]	learned [lɜ:nt], learnt [lɜ:nt]	learned [lɜ:nt], learnt [lɜ:nt]	lernen
leave [li:v]	left [left]	left [left]	(ver)lassen

infinitive	simple past	past participle	German
lend [lend]	lent [lent]	lent [lent]	(ver)leihen
let [let]	let [let]	let [let]	lassen
lie [laɪ]	lay [leɪ]	lain [leɪn]	liegen
light [laɪt]	lit [lɪt]	lit [lɪt]	beleuchten, anzünden
lose [lu:z]	lost [lɒst]	lost [lɒst]	verlieren
make [meɪk]	made [meɪd]	made [meɪd]	machen
mean [mi:n]	meant [ment]	meant [ment]	bedeuten
meet [mi:t]	met [met]	met [met]	treffen, begegnen
pay [peɪ]	paid [peɪd]	paid [peɪd]	zahlen, bezahlen
put [pʊt]	put [pʊt]	put [pʊt]	setzen, stellen, legen
read [ri:d]	read [red]	read [red]	lesen
rewind [ˌri:ˈwaɪnd]	rewound [ˌri:ˈwaʊnd]	rewound [ˌri:ˈwaʊnd]	zurückspulen
rid [rɪd]	rid [rɪd]	rid [rɪd]	befreien (von)
ride [raɪd]	rode [rəʊd]	ridden [ˈrɪdn]	reiten, fahren
ring [rɪŋ]	rang [ræŋ]	rung [rʌŋ]	klingeln, anrufen
run [rʌn]	ran [ræn]	run [rʌn]	laufen, rennen
say [seɪ]	said [sed]	said [sed]	sagen
see [si:]	saw [sɔ:]	seen [si:n]	sehen
sell [sel]	sold [səʊld]	sold [səʊld]	verkaufen
send [send]	sent [sent]	sent [sent]	schicken, senden
set [set]	set [set]	set [set]	setzen, stellen, legen
shine [ʃaɪn]	shone [ʃɒn]	shone [ʃɒn]	scheinen
show [ʃəʊ]	showed [ʃəʊd]	shown [ʃəʊn]	zeigen
shoot [ʃu:t]	shot [ʃɒt]	shot [ʃɒt]	schießen
shut [ʃʌt]	shut [ʃʌt]	shut [ʃʌt]	schließen
sing [sɪŋ]	sang [sæŋ]	sung [sʌŋ]	singen
sink [sɪŋk]	sank [sæŋk]	sunk [sʌŋk]	sinken
sit [sɪt]	sat [sæt]	sat [sæt]	sitzen
sleep [sli:p]	slept [slept]	slept [slept]	schlafen
slide [slaɪd]	slid [slɪd]	slid [slɪd]	rutschen
speak [spi:k]	spoke [spəʊk]	spoken [ˈspəʊkn]	sprechen
spell [spel]	spelled [spelt], spelt [spelt]	spelled [spelt], spelt [spelt]	buchstabieren
spend [spend]	spent [spent]	spent [spent]	ausgeben (*Geld*), verbringen (*Zeit*)
spill [spɪl]	spilled [spɪlt], spilt [spɪlt]	spilled [spɪlt], spilt [spɪlt]	ausschütten, vergießen
spin [spɪn]	spun [spʌn]	spun [spʌn]	drehen, spinnen
split [splɪt]	split [splɪt]	split [splɪt]	aufsplitten, trennen
stand [stænd]	stood [stʊd]	stood [stʊd]	stehen
steal [sti:l]	stole [stəʊl]	stolen [stəʊln]	stehlen
stick [stɪk]	stuck [stʌk]	stuck [stʌk]	kleben, stecken
swear [sweə]	swore [swɔ:]	sworn [swɔ:n]	schwören; fluchen
swell [swel]	swelled [sweld]	swollen [ˈswəʊlən]	anschwellen
swim [swɪm]	swam [swæm]	swum [swʌm]	schwimmen
take [teɪk]	took [tʊk]	taken [ˈteɪkn]	nehmen, (hin)bringen
tell [tel]	told [təʊld]	told [təʊld]	erzählen, sagen
think [θɪŋk]	thought [θɔ:t]	thought [θɔ:t]	denken
throw [θrəʊ]	threw [θru:]	thrown [θrəʊn]	werfen
understand [ˌʌndəˈstænd]	understood [ˌʌndəˈstʊd]	understood [ˌʌndəˈstʊd]	verstehen
wake [weɪk]	woke [wəʊk]	woken [ˈwəʊkn]	wecken, aufwachen
wear [weə]	wore [wɔ:]	worn [wɔ:n]	tragen (*Kleidung*)
weave [wi:v]	wove [wəʊv]	woven [wəʊvn]	weben
win [wɪn]	won [wʌn]	won [wʌn]	gewinnen
write [raɪt]	wrote [rəʊt]	written [ˈrɪtn]	schreiben

Quellenverzeichnis

Bildquellen

Aufschlag: Superstock (pitcher); The Slide File (cross); Paul Williams/Superbild (taxi); S. 8: Mauritius/SST (football team); S. 9: TEEN Magazine, Petersen Publishing Co., Los Angeles, CA (cover); Ray Jeannotte, Auburn, WA (dance); Photodisc (cruising); S. 10: Erich Bach/Superbild (boy); Bernd Ducke/Superbild (Manchester); S. 11: F. Bouillot-MP/Superbild (girl); Superstock (Montana); S. 12: PP/Bavaria; S.14: Puffin Books; S. 15: Reso/Superbild (girl); Mauritius/Dr. Johannes (boy); S. 19: Cartoon: © Bill Stott from *The Crazy World of School*, Exley Publications Ltd; S. 23: Cartoon: *Punch*; S. 30: Wolfgang Volz/Bilderberg (Stock Exchange); Mauritius/ Nakamura (Manhattan skyline); Frieder Blickle (Chrysler Building); Mauritius/Macia (Central Park); S. 31 Mauritius/Dr. Müller (Broadway); Superstock (UN Building); Corbis/Picture Press/James Marshall (man); Aurora/ Bilderberg/Jose Azel (police car); Bernd Ducke/Superbild (Chinatown); S. 32: Bettman/ Corbis/Picture Press; S. 33 Cartoon: © Ros Chast, *The New Yorker*; S. 33-34: *Doonesbury* by Gary Trudeau © UPS; S. 37: Mauritius/J. Müller; S. 38: BSIP/ Superbild (Clara); Mauritius/Grafica (Hea); Frieder Blickle/Bilderberg (Jim); S. 39: Corbis/ Picture Press/ Robert Holmes; S. 41: Cartoon: from *Doonesbury* by Gary Trudeau © UPS; S. 43: Peter Ginter/Bilderberg (policewoman); Eugene Richards, Brooklyn (Harlem scene); S. 48: action press/Wolf Winter (smoking chimneys); Mauritius (Planet Earth); Kennan Ward/Corbis/Picture Press (Denali N.P.); dpa (Greenpeace); AKG (bear hunt); dpa/Waltraud Grubitzsch (Leuna 2000 refinery); S. 49: Mauritius/Wendler (tiger); Mauritius/Kugler (scene in India); S. 50: dpa/Roberto Schmidt; S. 52: Marc Garanger/ Corbis/Picture Press (Hoover Dam); Rick Doyle/ Corbis/Picture Press (Lake Mead); S. 53: Owen Franken/Corbis/Picture Press; S. 54: Mauritius/Benelux Press (woman); Mauritius/age fotostock (man); S. 56: Jonathan Blair/Corbis/Picture Press (highway); Dilip Mehta/ Contact Press Images/PNI (Las Vegas); S. 61: Cartoons from Chicken Soup for the Teenage Soul II, Health Communications Inc., Deerfield Beach, FL: 1. © Dave Carpenter; 2.-3. © Randy Glasbergen; S.66: action press (film scene, Diana); dpa/Waltraud Grubitzsch (radio presenter); action press/O. Taubert (poster sticker); S. 67: Gabe Palacio/Aurora/PNI (newspaper); action press/Siglo (interview); dpa/Wolfgang Thieme (editorial staff); S. 70: dpa (Diana); action press (Marilyn Monroe); action press/Zenpress (Michael Jackson); S. 71: action press (Madonna, William); S. 72: AKG; S. 73: AKG (screaming fans); action press (Beatles in Hamburg); action press/Farabola (Ringo); action press/Rex/David Magnus (John); action press/O. Elsner (Paul); dpa/Marcel Noecker (George); S. 76: AKG (Mona Lisa); AKG/©The Munch-Ellingsen Group/VG Bild-Kunst 2001 (The Cry); S. 78: AKG; S. 79: AKG; S. 80: Cartoon: Sipress, *The Spectator*; S. 88: dpa/Fotoreport (Cranberries); dpa (U2); Roger Ressmeyer/Corbis/Picture Press (Clannad); dpa/ Xamax (Boyzone); Outlet Records, Belfast (Dubliners); dpa/Fotoreport (Enya); dpa/Ralf Hirschberger (Van Morrison); S. 89: The Slide File; S. 90-91: The Slide File; S. 92: The Slide File; S. 93: The Slide File (Dublin skyline, ruined cottages); J. Allan Cash (computer factory); non-copyright material (Sweetman); dpa/Bildarchiv/Mori (Mary Harney); S. 94: The Slide File; S. 95: The Slide File; S. 97: The Slide File; S. 102: The Slide File; S. 103: The Slide File; S. 109: Cartoon: © Sidney Harris, New Haven CT; S. 110: Bilderberg/ Thomas Ernsting (mine); Richard Greenhill (mechanic); Erica Macmillan, Sutton Coldfield (Save the Children); Topham Picturepoint/IPA (Job Centre); Sally Greenhill (medical training); S. 111: Sally Greenhill (paper boys); Richard Greenhill (vacuum cleaner); S. 112: Paula Solloway/UNP; S. 113/114: Mary Evans Picture Library; S. 115: Cartoons: *The Spectator* (1. Robert Thompson; 2. Nick Downes); S. 118: Richard Greenhill; S. 119: Cartoon: *The Spectator* (M.T.); S. 123 Cartoon: *The Spectator* (Hunter); S. 132: Mary Evans Picture Library; S. 133: Mary Evans Picture Library (Boston Tea Party); James P. Blair/Corbis/Picture Press (Jefferson); S. 134: Mary Evans Picture Library (G. Washington); Bettmann/ Corbis/Picture Press (voting machine); Corbis (President); Arthur Grace/Stock, Boston/PNI (Supreme Court justices); Mauritius-Vidler (Congress); S. 135: Mauritius (Capitol; Supreme Court); Superstock (Oval Office); S. 136: WSPA Welttierschutzgesellschaft e.V. (bullfight, donkey); Shaen Adey; Gallo Images/Corbis (gift shop); S. 137: Earl & Nazima Kowall/Corbis/Picture Press (elephant); WSPA Welttierschutzgesellschaft e.V. (dancing bear); World Wildlife Fund (Chinese medicines); S. 138: Jimmy Gaston/© The Telegraph Group Ltd 2000; S. 139: Bettmann/Corbis/Picture Press; S. 140: The Slide File; S. 142: David Lomax/Camera Press/Picture Life Press; S. 143: The Slide File; S. 145: Cartoons: aus Helmut Reisener, *Motivationstechniken im Fremdsprachenunterricht*, Max Hueber Verlag 1989; S. 147: Cartoon: Geoff Thompson, *The Spectator*; Mary Evans Picture Library (Mrs Pankhurst); S. 156: Bowman-Scope/Superbild; S. 158: dpa/Fotoreport; S. 159: Okapia; S. 161: By courtesy of the National Portrait Gallery, London.

Textquellen

S. 8: *It's tough to be a teenager* by Tony Overman from *Chicken Soup for the Teenage Soul* II, Health Communications, Deerfield Beach, FL; S. 10/11: *E-mates* © The Daily Telegraph; S. 12: *Into the great wide open* by Tom Petty/Jeff Lynne, Neue Welt Musikverlag GmbH, München und EMI Songs Musikverlag GmbH, Hamburg; S. 13/14: from *The Glory Girl* by Betsy Byars, Penguin Putnam; S. 22: *The dare rap* by Shelley Merkes from *Chicken Soup for the Kid's Soul*, Health Communications, Deerfield Beach, FL; S. 44: *Why is crime down?* Copyright, May 25, 1998 *U.S.News & World Report*; S. 49: *The environment …* reprinted with permission from The World Almanac for Kids 1998. Copyright © 1997 World Almanac Education Group. All rights reserved; S. 50: *Irene tests evacuation-weary residents* from *USA Today*; S. 51: *A waterpoem* by Gina Douthwaite from *Picture a Poem*, Random House, London; *Facts about water/Major threats to water* reprinted with permission from The World Almanac for Kids 1998. Copyright © 1997 World Almanac Education Group. All rights reserved; S. 52: Hoover Dam brochure from the U.S. Bureau of Reclamation, Lower Colorado Region; S. 53: *The fog parted* from *The Lost Continent* by Bill Bryson, Transworld Publishers, London; S. 54: *If I could change the world* by Kofi Ansuhenne/David Jost, © 1995 by Edition Live Songs/Edition Shark Media Songs; S. 68/69: from *Popcorn* by Ben Elton, Simon & Shuster, London; S. 70/71: *We all have blood on our hands* from *The Times*, 3 September 1997; S. 71: *A call from the editor* by Ian Jack, Granta, London; S. 72: *A day in the life* by John Lennon/Paul McCartney, Sony/ATV Music Publishing LLC; für D/A/ CH/Osteuropa: Sony/ATV Music Publishing Germany GmbH; *The holes in our roads* from *The Daily Mail*, January 1967; S. 90: *Kilkelly* by Peter L. Jones/Steve Jones, Edition Copyright Management International und Musik-Edition Discoton GmbH (BMG UFA Musikverlage), München; S. 92/93: Extracts from the Radio National program *Background Briefing* reproduced by kind permission of the Australian Broadcasting Corporation; S. 94/95: From *Evening Class* by Maeve Binchy, copyright © 1997 by Maeve Binchy. Used by permission of Dell Publishing, a division of Random House; S. 112: *Asleep in class?* by David Harrison from *The Observer*, July 19, 1998; S. 115: *Simplicity of electricity* Reprinted by permission of PDF on behalf of Michael Rosen © Michael Rosen: as printed in the original volume; S. 130: *Diary of a date* by Colin Beavan from YM Magazine; S. 131: *Going to jump?* by Jennifer Long from *English Power*, The Jacaranda Press, Milton, Queensland; S. 136/137: *Suntan and slaughter* by Emily Hayes © Bliss Magazine; S. 138: *In many ways I'm a terrible pop star* by Jan Moir © *The Daily Telegraph*, 1999; S. 140: *The Lake Isle of Innisfree* by W. B. Yeats from *The Rose* (1893), Macmillan, London; S. 141: *The forge* by Seamus Heaney from *Door into the Dark*, Faber & Faber, London; S. 144: © Rosie Rushton, from *Just don't make a scene, Mum*, Piccadilly Press, London; S. 158: *Long and winding road leaads Sir Paul back to The Cavern* © *The Daily Telegraph*, 1999.

THE UNITED STATES OF AMERICA
CT = Connecticut
DE = Delaware
MA= Massachusetts
MD = Maryland
NH = New Hampshire
NJ = New Jersey
RI = Rhode Island
VT = Vermont
NE= New England
major highways
time zones, compared with Central European Time 12⁰⁰ (noon)
Nationalpark
New England
0 500 1000 km
0 300 500 Miles
CANADA
USA
MEXICO
RUSSIA
PACIFIC OCEAN
ATLANTIC OCEAN
Gulf of Mexico
THE BAHAMAS
Brit.Columbia
Alberta
Saskatchewan
Manitoba
Ontario
Québec
New Bruns-wick
Washington
Oregon
California
Idaho
Nevada
Utah
Arizona
Montana
Wyoming
Colorado
New Mexico
North Dakota
South Dakota
Nebraska
Kansas
Oklahoma
Texas
Minnesota
Iowa
Missouri
Arkansas
Louisiana
Wisconsin
Illinois
Michigan
Indiana
Ohio
Kentucky
Tennessee
Mississippi
Alabama
Georgia
Florida
South Carolina
North Carolina
Virginia
West Virginia
Pennsylvania
New York
Maine
Rocky Mountains
Sierra Nevada
Appalachians
Lake Superior
Lake Huron
L. Michigan
Lake Erie
L. Ontario
Mississippi R.
Missouri R.
Ohio R.
Arkansas R.
Rio Grande
Columbia R.
Pacific Time
Mountain Time
Central Time
Eastern Time
Hawaii 3600 km
Alaska
Yukon R.
Bering Strait
Bering Sea
Aleutian Islands
St. Lawrence I.
Alaska Time
0 500 1000 km
0 200 400 600 Miles
Hawaii-Aleutian Time
Hawaii
Kauai
Honolulu
Maui
0 200 Miles

Manhattan
Lincoln Square
Central Park West
The Lake
West 65th Street
Central Park
Lincoln Center
West 60th St
East 75th St
Avenue
East 70th Street
Columbus Circle
Fifth Avenue
East 65th Street
Broadway
Madison
Plaza Hotel
East 60th Street
Henry Hudson Parkway
151st Street
Harlem River
Harlem
The Bronx
Broadway
Riverside Park
Hudson River
Columbia University
110th Street
East Harlem
Wards Island
Upper West Side
Central Park
Reservoir
96th Street
Upper East Side
Fifth Ave
F.D. Roosevelt Drive
Lincoln Center
Broadway
Tenth Avenue
Ninth Avenue
Lincoln Tunnel
United Nations
Roosevelt Island
Queens
Museum of Modern Art
East 57th Street
West 42nd Street
Times Square
Rockefeller Center
Railway
West 34th Street
Midtown
Second Ave
First Avenue
Queensboro Bridge
Lower West Side
Madison Square Garden
Empire State Building
Queens Midtown Tunnel
Hudson River
Broadway
West 14th Street
East 23rd Street
West Village
Greenwich Village
Highway
East 14th Street
Lower East Side
Holland Tunnel
Westside
Soho
Little Ukraine
East River
Tribeca
Little Italy
Broadway
Battery Park City
World Trade Center
China town
Downtown
South St
Williamsburg Bridge
Wall Street
Manhattan Bridge
Brooklyn Bridge
Ellis Island
Battery Park
Ferry
Brooklyn Battery Tunnel
Brooklyn
Liberty Island
Statue of Liberty
Statue of Liberty